The Neolithic of Britain and Ireland

The Neolithic of Britain and Ireland provides a comprehensive overview of this exciting period, covering the last few hundred years of the Mesolithic and the arrival and spread of the Neolithic up to the start of the early Beaker period: roughly 2000 years of prehistory.

Drawing on the latest excavations and the results of new scientific techniques, this book considers what life was like for people in the Neolithic and how they were treated when they died. It explores in detail the monuments constructed from stone and wood, the most famous of which is Stonehenge, but also includes many other sites such as chambered tombs and causewayed enclosures. It considers some of the key ways we interpret evidence from the Neolithic to offer insights into social organisation and belief systems at this time. The new edition contains the results of the latest ancient DNA evidence, which has seen this period of prehistory undergoing considerable revision in the last few years. Exciting new finds and excavations are also included.

This is an accessible introduction for students new to the study of the Neolithic and also acts as a reference for students and scholars already researching this area.

Vicki Cummings is Professor of Neolithic Archaeology at Cardiff University. Her research has focused on the start and spread of the Neolithic in Britain, Ireland and north-west Europe. She has a particular research interest in Early Neolithic monumentality, especially chambered tombs, and has excavated sites in Wales, Scotland and Ireland. More recently her work has focused on the Early Neolithic of Orkney as well as Early Neolithic kinship. She is the author of *Monuments in the Making: Raising the Great Dolmens in Early Neolithic Northern Europe* (with Colin Richards).

Routledge Archaeology of Northern Europe

The British Palaeolithic
Human Societies at the Edge of the Pleistocene World
Paul Pettitt, Mark White

The Neolithic of Britain and Ireland
Vicki Cummings

Iron Age Lives
The Archaeology of Britain and Ireland 800 BC – AD 400
Ian Armit

The Mesolithic in Britain
Landscape and Society in Times of Change
Chantal Conneller

Formative Britain
The Archaeology if Britain AD 400 – 1100
Martin Carver

For more information about this series, please visit: https://www.routledge.com/Routledge-Archaeology-of-Northern-Europe/book-series/ARCHNEUR

The Neolithic of Britain and Ireland

Second Edition

Vicki Cummings

LONDON AND NEW YORK

Designed cover image: Getty Images

Second edition published 2025
by Routledge
4 Park Square, Milton Park, Abingdon, Oxon OX14 4RN

and by Routledge
605 Third Avenue, New York, NY 10158

Routledge is an imprint of the Taylor & Francis Group, an informa business

© 2025 Vicki Cummings

The right of Vicki Cummings to be identified as author of this work has been asserted in accordance with sections 77 and 78 of the Copyright, Designs and Patents Act 1988.

All rights reserved. No part of this book may be reprinted or reproduced or utilised in any form or by any electronic, mechanical, or other means, now known or hereafter invented, including photocopying and recording, or in any information storage or retrieval system, without permission in writing from the publishers.

Trademark notice: Product or corporate names may be trademarks or registered trademarks, and are used only for identification and explanation without intent to infringe.

First edition published by Routledge 2017

British Library Cataloguing-in-Publication Data
A catalogue record for this book is available from the British Library

ISBN: 978-1-032-43793-4 (hbk)
ISBN: 978-1-032-43790-3 (pbk)
ISBN: 978-1-003-38732-9 (ebk)

DOI: 10.4324/9781003387329

Typeset in Helvetica Neue
by Apex CoVantage, LLC

Contents

Acknowledgements	vii
List of figures	ix
1 Introducing the Neolithic of Britain and Ireland	1
2 Britain and Ireland in the fifth millennium cal BC: the calm before the storm	15
3 All change: the transition to the Neolithic in Britain and Ireland	36
4 A brave new world: life in the early Neolithic of Britain and Ireland	55
5 Of earth, bone, timber and stone: mortuary practice and monumentality in the early Neolithic of Britain and Ireland	100
6 Circles and lines: the middle Neolithic of Britain and Ireland	152
7 Lines and landscapes of descent: life in the late Neolithic of Britain and Ireland	181
8 Ritual and religion in the round: mortuary practice and monumentality in the late Neolithic of Britain and Ireland	206

9 Beakers, copper and bronze: the start of a new era in Britain and Ireland — 253

10 The Neolithic of Britain and Ireland: overview and future directions — 282

Bibliography — 289
Index — 319

Acknowledgements

The first edition of this book was published in 2017 with the explicit aim of presenting the evidence from across Neolithic Britain and Ireland in equal measure. In writing that edition, it was clear why Wessex, the Boyne Valley and Orkney dominate so many previous accounts of the Neolithic. I worked hard to shift the focus to, or at least try to include, all other parts of Britain and Ireland in that account. Within 12 months of the publication of the book, however, a significant change occurred in Neolithic studies: the publication of ancient DNA studies on individuals from the Mesolithic, Neolithic and Bronze Age. These studies had a profound effect on the study of this period of time. As a result the last five or so years have been some of most exciting and intellectually challenging in all the time I have been studying this fascinating period. This has meant that some of the chapters in this second edition are completely different from the first edition – notably the transition to the Neolithic chapter and the chapter on the Beaker period. There are other changes throughout too.

The change in Neolithic studies has coincided with a change in my own circumstances. Most of the new edition was written while I was at the University of Central Lancashire, and I would like to thank colleagues there for being so supportive over the years. The remainder of the new edition was written in my new role at Cardiff University, and I would like to thank colleagues at Cardiff for welcoming me (back). A particular note of thanks to David Clarke, Dylan Foster Evans, Urfan Khaliq, Nick Jones, Mark Llewellyn and Jacqui Mulville for all their help in settling in. I have reproduced a number of images provided by colleagues: many thanks to Hugo Anderson-Whymark, Dot Boughton, Fraser Brown, Nick Card, Andrew Cochrane, Bryony Coles, Dan Lee, Mark Lewis at Tenby Museum, Kathleen McLeod at the Tomb of the Eagles, Donald Murphy of Archaeological Consulting Services, Mike Parker Pearson, Adam Parsons, Rick Peterson, the late Alan Saville, Antonia Thomas, Mike Seager Thomas, Adam Stanford, Peter Style and Mick Wysocki. At Routledge I would like to thank Manas Roy and Matthew Gibbons.

Over the years I have discussed various aspects of the Neolithic with colleagues, and I would like to offer thanks to: Hugo Anderson-Whymark, Richard Bradley, Kenny Brophy, Jane Downes, Chris Fowler, Chris Gee, Ollie Harris, Robert Hensey, Andy Jones, Sam Moore, Jim Morris, Mike Parker Pearson, Josh Pollard, Rick Peterson, Guillaume Robin, David Robinson, Gary Robinson, Julian Thomas, Graeme Warren and Mick Wysocki. Rick Peterson has suffered endless questions on different aspects of the Neolithic as well as lending me virtually all of his books. I have also discussed many ideas with Colin Richards, who deserves a special mention not only for these discussions but also for some top-notch trips to various Neolithic sites the length and breadth of Britain, Ireland and beyond as we contemplated dolmens, stone circles and the quality of fish and chip establishments. I must also extend my gratitude to Richard Holmes for all his support throughout the writing of this book.

My greatest thanks are to Alasdair Whittle, who first introduced me to the Neolithic and who has been enormously supportive ever since. Alasdair taught me both the Neolithic and theory as an undergraduate at Cardiff, nurtured me through my master's degree, then took me on as a research student. After that I worked with Alasdair first as a research assistant and then as a research associate at Cardiff, and together we wrote *Places of Special Virtue* and edited *Going Over*, along with penning various other papers along the way. Even after I left his employ, Alasdair continued to provide endless support, references and advice. In relation to this book he offered comments on the overall structure of the book, which was invaluable at the design stage, and then read and commented on all the chapters subsequently. This second edition, like the first, is dedicated to him with thanks for all his help over the years.

Figures

1.1	Plan of the chambered tomb of Hazleton North, Gloucestershire (after Saville 1990)	2
1.2	Excavations of the two chambers at Hazleton North produced well-preserved skeletal remains in both chambers (after Saville 1990)	3
1.3	The biological relationships between people deposited at Hazleton North as demonstrated by the aDNA study at Hazleton North	4
1.4	Plan of the main mound at Knowth, showing the large central passage tomb surrounded by smaller tombs (after Eogan 1986)	5
1.5	One of the intricately carved designs on the kerbstones encircling the mound at Knowth	6
1.6	The Knowth macehead recovered from the eastern chamber (after Eogan and Richardson 1982)	7
1.7	Structure Eight at the Ness of Brodgar, courtesy of Ness of Brodgar Trust/Scott Pike	9
1.8	The dramatic mountain of Benbulbin, Co. Sligo, Ireland	11
1.9	The rock outcrops around Garn Turne in Pembrokeshire, Wales	12
2.1	The five main late Mesolithic midden sites on Oronsay in relation to the present coastline (solid line) and the coastline at the time of occupation (dotted line: after Mellars 1987)	17
2.2	The shell midden of Caisteal nan Gillean I, Oronsay, with the hills of Jura visible in the distance	18
2.3	The excavation plan of the midden of Cnoc Coig, showing the location of the hearths, the huts and the midden in relation to the outcrops on the shore (after Mellars 1987)	19
2.4	The location of sites from the fifth millennium cal BC mentioned in the text	21
2.5	The late Mesolithic Lydstep boar covered by a tree trunk (after Chatterton 2006)	22

2.6	One of the baskets from Clowanstown, Co. Meath	24
2.7	Antler mattock (T-axe) from Meiklewood, Stirling	27
2.8	The movement of stone tools in northern Britain as evidenced from the excavations at Stainton West	30
3.1	The estimated locations and dates of different domestic animal species in the Fertile Crescent in western Asia (after Zeder 2008)	39
3.2	Northern France at the start of the fifth millennium BC, showing the location of farming groups (Villeneuve-Saint-Germain and Cardial) and hunter-gatherers, and sites named in the text (after Scarre 2011). Plan of the house at Le Haut Mée (top left, after Cassen *et al.* 1998) and Grave K at Höedic (after Péquart and Péquart 1954)	42
3.3	Breton monuments from the fifth millennium BC. Top: Barnenez; bottom: Le Grand Menhir Brisé	43
3.4	Distinctive fifth-millennium BC hunter-gatherer pottery from northern Germany (left) and Belgium (right) (after Hartz *et al.* 2007 and Crombé and Vanmortfort 2007)	45
3.5	North-west Europe towards the end of the fifth millennium BC, indicating the main cultural groups discussed in the text	47
3.6	Suggested dates for the first appearance of Neolithic things in Britain and Ireland (after Whittle *et al.* 2011, figure 15.8)	50
3.7	Diagram indicating the appearance of elements of the Neolithic package in parts of Britain and Ireland	51
3.8	Diagram indicating the appearance of elements of the Neolithic package in south-east and south-central England (after Whittle *et al.* 2011, figure 14.179)	52
4.1	Location of sites named in this chapter, excluding houses, middens and pits	57
4.2	The Langdale Pikes, Cumbria, source of Group VI axes (mountains to the right). The picture is taken from the Copt Howe rock art site in the Langdale valley	58
4.3	A polished stone axe from near Hayscastle, Pembrokeshire	59
4.4	The known extraction sites for stone axes in Britain and Ireland (after Clough and Cummins 1988). The size of the dot and text relates to the quantities of axes known to have come from these sources: the larger the dot, the more axes produced	60
4.5	Jadeitite axes on display at the recent World of Stonehenge exhibit at the British Museum	61
4.6	Tievebulliagh mountain, Co. Antrim, one of the sources of Group IX axes	62
4.7	The Shulishader axe, Lewis, was found hafted	64
4.8	A selection of early Neolithic stone tools	65
4.9	Plan of the features of the flint mines at Cissbury. The edge of the flint extraction area is obscured by a later Iron Age rampart (after Russell 2000)	67
4.10	Plan of some of the galleries of the flint mines at Cissbury (after Russell 2000). S marks a vertical shaft from the surface	68
4.11	Early Neolithic bowl pottery from Windmill Hill, Wiltshire (after Keiller 1965)	70
4.12	Carinated bowls from Ballintaggart, Co. Armagh and Cairnholy I, Dumfries and Galloway (after Thompson *et al.* 2015)	71

4.13	Early Neolithic bowl found in the chambered tomb of Blasthill, Kintyre. It has been flattened by material subsequently placed on top of it. Residue on the pot was radiocarbon dated to 3630–3360 cal BC	72
4.14	Beacharra bowls from Beacharra, Argyll and Bute (after Scott 1969)	73
4.15	A fragment of Neolithic basketry from Twyford, Co. Westmeath	75
4.16	The Coneybury Anomaly showing the mass of animal bones and stone tools deposited	77
4.17	A portion of the Céide Fields, Co. Mayo, exposed by removing the overlying peat	82
4.18	Reconstruction drawing of the pottery found alongside the Sweet Track, one of which contained hazelnuts	84
4.19	The timber hall at Claish	88
4.20	The timber halls at Warren Field and Balbridie, Aberdeenshire (after Brophy 2007 and Murray *et al.* 2009)	89
4.21	The location of houses, middens and pit sites discussed in Chapter 4	90
4.22	The house at Ballyglass, Co. Mayo (after Smyth 2020)	91
4.23	Examples of early Neolithic houses from Ireland (after Smyth 2014)	92
4.24	Eilean Dhomnuil, North Uist. This islet was occupied in the early Neolithic	94
4.25	Timber house 4 at Ha'Breck, Wyre, Orkney	95
4.26	The Sweet Track, Somerset, under excavation	96
5.1	The location of sites discussed in this chapter, except chambered tombs (see Figure 5.4) and causewayed enclosures (see Figure 5.27) *= Norton Bevant, Beckhampton Road and South Street	101
5.2	The flat graves at Barrow Hills, Oxfordshire (after Barclay and Halpin 1997)	102
5.3	Excavations at George Rock Shelter which produced the disarticulated remains of two early Neolithic individuals	103
5.4	The distribution of early Neolithic chambered tombs and dolmens	106
5.5	Plans of a selection of Cotswold-Severn chambered tombs. Top from left to right: Ty Isaf, Powys; Penywyrlod, Powys; Parc le Breos Cwm, Glamorgan. Bottom: West Kennet, Wiltshire (after Corcoran 1969a)	107
5.6	West Kennett Cotswold-Severn monument	108
5.7	View looking into the chambers at West Kennet	109
5.8	Plans of a selection of Clyde (western Scottish) chambered tombs. Top: Gort na h'Ulaidhe, Kintyre, middle: Monamore, Arran and bottom: East Bennan, Arran (after Henshall 1972)	109
5.9	Blasthill chambered tomb, Kintyre, looking at the façade	110
5.10	Plans of a selection of stalled (northern Scottish) chambered tombs. Top left: Warehouse North, Caithness; top right: Blackhammer, Rousay; bottom left: Knowe of Yarso, Rousay; bottom right: Kierfea Hill, Rousay (after Henshall 1963)	110
5.11	Midhowe stalled cairn, Rousay, Orkney, showing the stalls which divide up the chamber	111
5.12	Plans of a selection of court cairns (Irish chambered tombs) Top left: Ballymarlagh, Co. Antrim, top right: Audleystown, Co. Down (dual court cairn), bottom left: Browndod, Co. Antrim, and bottom right: Deerpark, Co. Sligo (central court cairn) after de Valera 1960	111

5.13	The court cairn at Ballymacdermot, Co. Armagh	112
5.14	The distinctive façade at Cairnholy I, creating a forecourt at the front of the chambered tomb	114
5.15	The sequence of construction at Mid Gleniron I, Dumfries and Galloway (after Corcoran 1969b)	115
5.16	Creevykeel, Co. Sligo, looking into the enclosed court	116
5.17	The complete burial at Hazleton North of the 'flint knapper' (Photo Alan Saville)	118
5.18	The position of skulls at the Knowe of Yarso, Rousay, Orkney (after Richards 1988). The grey indicates patches of human bone. As found in some caves, this may represent a particular interest in skulls	119
5.19	Rib fragment with embedded leaf-shaped arrowhead tip from Penywyrlod. Photo Michael Wysocki	120
5.20	The key dates in the construction and use of five Cotswold-Severn chambered tombs	123
5.21	Excavations at Garn Turne, Pembrokeshire. The enormous capstone was quarried from a pit in front of where the monument now lies	127
5.22	The dolmen at Brownshill, Co. Carlow, where the capstone weighs approximately 160 tonnes	128
5.23	Pentre Ifan, Pembrokeshire, where the capstone can be seen balancing on three supporting stones	130
5.24	The timber mortuary structure at Street House, North Yorkshire (after Vyner 1984). The three large posts of the timber mortuary structure are marked in black: note postholes are also present in the forecourt. The façade consists of a bedding trench which had timbers set upright in it. The grey indicates the presence of a clay and earth mound, and the rest are contemporary, or later, stone elements	131
5.25	The excavation plan of Giants Hills 1, Skendleby, Lincolnshire (after Field 2006)	134
5.26	The monumental complex at Hambledon Hill, Dorset. The earliest monument is the main causewayed enclosure in the centre – further earthworks were added later on	138
5.27	The distribution of definite and probable causewayed enclosures in Britain and Ireland (after Oswald *et al*. 2001 and Whittle *et al*. 2011). Circles are causewayed enclosures, squares are tor enclosures	139
5.28	The plans of selected causewayed enclosures in Britain and Ireland. Left Donegore Hill, Co. Antrim; centre Freston, Suffolk; right Haddenham, Cambridgeshire (after Oswald *et al*. 2001)	140
5.29	The internal features (pits) at Etton, Cambridgeshire (after Pryor 1999)	145
5.30	Reconstruction of Whitehawk causewayed enclosure	146
5.31	Plans of pit and post-defined cursus monuments. Left Douglasmuir, centre Holywood North, right Bannockburn (after Thomas 2007a)	148
6.1	Location of sites mentioned in this chapter, except passage tombs (see Figure 6.4)	154
6.2	Impressed wares from Westbourne, Sussex	155
6.3	The stone house at Smerquoy, Orkney	157
6.4	The distribution of passage tombs in Britain and Ireland, with sites named in the text	160

6.5	Looking down the passage at Knowth, Co. Meath	161
6.6	A selection of chamber plans from Irish passage tombs (after Powell 2016). Top left Carrowkeel F, Co. Sligo; top row middle Loughcrew L, Co. Meath; top right Newgrange, Co. Meath; bottom left Dowth South, Co. Meath; bottom centre Seefin, Co. Wicklow	162
6.7	A selection of plans of British passage tombs top left Maeshowe, Orkney; bottom left Quoyness, Orkney; top right Loch a'Bharp, South Uist; bottom right Achnacree, Argyll and Bute (after Henshall 1972)	163
6.8	Composite photograph of the massive passage tomb of Newgrange, Co. Meath. This is one of the largest passage tombs in Ireland	164
6.9	The kerb at the main site at Knowth, Co. Meath (right). One of the smaller satellite tombs can be seen to the left	164
6.10	The highly decorated stone found at the entrance to Newgrange, Co. Meath	165
6.11	One of the stone basins in the chamber at Newgrange	166
6.12	The passage tomb of Bharpa Langass, North Uist, Outer Hebrides, which is set in an elevated position and has wide views out over the landscape	167
6.13	Profile (top) and plan (bottom) of the chamber at Newgrange showing the location of the winter solstice solar alignment. The sunlight enters Newgrange through the roof-box and travels down the passage to hit the back of the chamber (after Stout and Stout 2008)	168
6.14	Decoration on the back-slab of the rear chamber at Loughcrew, Co. Meath	169
6.15	The passage tomb of Fourknocks I, Co. Meath, showing the location of decoration panels at key threshold points within the monument (after Eogan 1986, Robin 2010)	169
6.16	Two of the Carrowkeel passage tombs, with wide views out over the Co. Sligo landscape	173
6.17	The inhumations at Barrow Hills, Radley, Oxfordshire (after Bradley *et al.* 1992)	176
6.18	The Dorset cursus in its wider landscape setting (after Johnston 1999)	178
7.1	Sites mentioned in this chapter	182
7.2	The exceptionally well-preserved late Neolithic village at Skara Brae, Orkney, showing the stone 'dresser' at the rear, two 'box-beds' to the left and right and a central hearth in one of the houses	183
7.3	Composite plan of the houses at Barnhouse, Orkney (after Richards 2005). Note the large House 2 and Structure 8	184
7.4	Plan of the late Neolithic settlement at Skara Brae, Orkney (after Childe 1931)	186
7.5	Aerial view of the Ness of Brodgar, Orkney	187
7.6	The remains of a late Neolithic house at Durrington Walls	188
7.7	Grooved Ware	192
7.8	Matting impression on the base of a Grooved Ware pot from Barnhouse, Orkney	195
7.9	The visible remains of flint extraction at Grime's Graves, Norfolk	196
7.10	A finely polished macehead from the Tomb of the Eagles, Orkney	197
7.11	Two deliberately broken maceheads from Sanday, Orkney	198

7.12	The carved stone ball from Towie, Aberdeenshire	199
7.13	One of the Folkton Drums	200
7.14	Late Neolithic arrowheads (after Richards 1990, Whittle *et al*. 1999)	201
7.15	Achnabreck rock art panel, Argyll	202
7.16	Rock art panel at Rydal Park, Cumbria	203
8.1	Location of the sites mentioned in the text. For detailed maps with individual sites see: Figure 8.15 Brodgar/Steness; Figure 8.21 Calanais; Figure 8.24 Brú na Boinné; Figure 8.2 Avebury; Figure 8.26 Stonehenge/Durrington Walls	207
8.2	Plan of the henge complex at Avebury illustrating the different architectural components (after Gillings *et al*. 2008)	209
8.3	Part of the henge at Avebury	209
8.4	Silbury Hill, Wiltshire	210
8.5	Plan of North Mains (Perth and Kinross) timber circle and later encircling henge in grey (after Millican 2007)	213
8.6	The monumental complex at Hindwell in the Walton Basin (after Gillings *et al*. 2008)	214
8.7	The excavated shafts at the Maumbury Rings, Dorset (after Harding 2003)	215
8.8	The stone circle at Castlerigg, Cumbria	215
8.9	Plan of the stone and timber components of The Sanctuary, Wiltshire, showing the primary timber phase (top) and the secondary stone phase (bottom: after Pollard 1992)	217
8.10	The Ring of Brodgar	218
8.11	The Rollright Stones, Oxfordshire	219
8.12	Plan of the henge at Mount Pleasant, Dorset, with an internal palisade and timber setting (after Gillings *et al*. 2008)	219
8.13	Plan of the stone features at henge at Avebury (after Pollard and Reynolds 2002)	221
8.14	The henge at Avebury	222
8.15	The late Neolithic architecture in the Brodgar-Stenness complex (after Richards 2013)	223
8.16	The Stones of Stenness looking out towards the Loch of Stenness and the hills of Hoy	224
8.17	Barnhouse Structure 8	225
8.18	The Ness of Brodgar in its wider landscape context, with the Stones of Stenness visible in the distance	226
8.19	Structure 27 at the Ness of Brodgar: one of the most elaborate structures at the site, which uses very large stones in its construction	227
8.20	One of the decorated stones from the Ness of Brodgar	227
8.21	The location of the stone circles in the Calanais complex (after Richards 2013)	228
8.22	Plan of the main circle and avenues at Calanais (after Henley 2005)	228
8.23	The main circle at Calanais site looking down the avenue to the north	229
8.24	The Brú na Boinné landscape in the late Neolithic (after Cooney 2000)	230
8.25	Reconstruction of the timber circle at Knowth, Co. Meath	231
8.26	The Stonehenge/Durrington Walls complex, showing the main late Neolithic monuments as well as the distribution of later round barrows (after Pollard 2012)	232

8.27	The first two phases at Stonehenge, phase 1 (left) and phase 2 (right)	233
8.28	Stonehenge	234
8.29	Plan of Durrington Walls (after Harding 2003)	235
8.30	Woodhenge – concrete bollards are positioned where timbers once stood	236
8.31	The large stone circle at Machrie Moor, Arran, part of a complex of monuments at this location	237
8.32	The location of the Thornborough henges and associated monuments in relation to the River Ure and earlier cursus monuments (after Gillings *et al*. 2008)	240
8.33	The location of the complex of monuments at Mount Pleasant/Maumbury Rings, Dorset (after Gillings *et al*. 2008)	241
8.34	The stone circle at Swinside, Cumbria	243
8.35	The Ring of Brodgar	244
8.36	The small stone circle at Gamelands, Cumbria	247
9.1	Location of the sites mentioned in this chapter	255
9.2	The Amesbury Archer Beaker burial, with the location of some of the grave goods illustrated (after Fitzpatrick 2011)	256
9.3	The material found with the Amesbury Archer when on display at the British Museum	257
9.4	Schematic diagram showing different Beaker styles in relation to their appearance in Britain (after Needham 2005)	258
9.5	A selection of Beakers (after Shepherd 2012)	259
9.6	Distinctive barbed and tanged arrowheads found with the Amesbury Archer (© Wessex Archaeology))	260
9.7	Food Vessels from Barns Farm, Fife (after Watkins 1982)	261
9.8	The two archers' wristguards found with the Amesbury Archer	261
9.9	Copper knife from Dorset (image courtesy of Portable Antiquities Scheme	263
9.10	Copper dagger from Lancashire (image courtesy of Portable Antiquities Scheme	266
9.11	Gold lunula from Dorset. Part of the object is missing (image from Portable Antiquities Scheme	266
9.12	Copper alloy flat axehead from Cumbria (image from Portable Antiquities Scheme (www.finds.org.uk) LANCUM-3324F7)	267
9.13	Hemp Knoll Beaker burial (after Fokkens *et al*. 2008)	269
9.14	The grave goods found in the Ferry Fryston Beaker burial, Yorkshire	272
9.15	The Giant's Leap wedge tomb, Co. Cavan, with the cupmarks on the front capstone illustrated	274
9.16	Plan of Island wedge tomb, Co. Cork (after Jones 2007)	275
9.17	Broomend of Crichie	276
9.18	The recumbent stone circle at Easter Aquhorthies, Aberdeenshire	277
9.19	Balnuaran of Clava	278

CHAPTER 1

Introducing the Neolithic of Britain and Ireland

INTRODUCTION

The Neolithic of Britain and Ireland covers the period from approximately 4000 cal BC to 2500 cal BC, around 1500 years, or 60 generations. It is the first time that people in these islands kept domesticated cattle, sheep and pigs and grew cereals. It is also the period when people first started making pottery and building large monuments from stone, timber and earth, although they had not yet started using metals. It was a time that saw significant clearance of woodlands and the permanent utilisation of landscapes from the southern tip of Cornwall right up to the Shetland Islands, from Co. Cork up to Rathlin Island. Neolithic people were highly skilled, as some material culture is exquisite, from beautifully polished stone axes through to carved stone balls and maceheads. Moreover, Neolithic monuments are architecturally sophisticated, quite extraordinary in their use of enormous stones, clearly indicating a massive investment of time and energy. These agricultural people had their origins in mainland Europe. In coming over to Britain and Ireland, they set up a completely new way of life from what had been here before when people made a living by hunting and gathering. To introduce you to this fascinating period of prehistory, this introductory chapter presents summaries of findings from three key sites from Neolithic Britain and Ireland. These sites, in turn, provide introductions to some of the key themes which will be highlighted throughout the book.

HAZLETON NORTH CHAMBERED TOMB, GLOUCESTERSHIRE

Sometime early on in the 37th century cal BC people returned to an existing clearing in the woodlands in the area we now call the Cotswolds in Gloucestershire. This clearing had, in previous years, been the location of a small settlement, and some of the remains

DOI: 10.4324/9781003387329-1

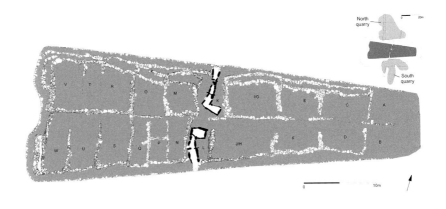

FIGURE 1.1
Plan of the chambered tomb of Hazleton North, Gloucestershire (after Saville 1990)

of that occupation were almost certainly still visible (Saville 1990). This time, however, people were here to conduct very different activities: the construction of a chambered tomb of which there are many examples from the early Neolithic in Britain and Ireland. The chambered tomb consisted of a cairn of stones which, when finished, was over 50m long and nearly 20m wide. Within the cairn two stone chambers were constructed, linked to the exterior of the monument by short, low passages (Figure 1.1). Well-preserved human remains were located in both chambers and passages, and a total of 41 individuals were identified through osteological analysis (Figure 1.2). Three of those individuals were cremated, but the rest were inhumations and were probably left in the chambered areas to decay before becoming disarticulated and mixed together over time.

This monument and the associated burial deposits are exceptionally well preserved but not unique. There are many chambered tombs with intact burial deposits in Britain and Ireland, as we shall see in Chapter 5. What is distinctive about Hazleton North is the additional information which has been acquired through the subsequent scientific analysis of the human remains. First the modelling of the radiocarbon dates from Hazleton North indicates that the monument only saw the deposition of human remains over a short period of time, perhaps two to three generations (Meadows *et al.* 2007). Instead of being the resting place for people over hundreds of years, it appears that the tomb was only in use for less than a century. Isotope analysis of the human bone revealed that people ate a high-protein diet, indicating a reliance on the new domesticated animals which were introduced into Britain at the start of the Neolithic (Neil *et al.* 2016). The analysis of other isotopes established that over the course of their lifetimes, people did not live exclusively in the landscapes immediately around Hazleton North and instead spent some of their time in other locations, potentially a good distance away (40km or so). This means that these early farmers were not settled in one place, then, but moved around a wider area.

The most recent analysis of the Hazleton North remains has examined the ancient DNA of the people interred at the site, and this has shown that the vast majority of those sampled, 27 in total, were biologically related to one another (Fowler *et al.* 2021). These results indicate that five generations of people were buried at this site, descended from a single male and the four females with whom he reproduced (Figure 1.3). Virtually all

FIGURE 1.2
Excavations of the two chambers at Hazleton North produced well-preserved skeletal remains in both chambers (after Saville 1990)

of the males placed in the tomb were descended from the same first-generation male through their fathers, with a few exceptions discussed subsequently, and this indicates that membership of the same male descent group was an important factor in deciding whose remains would be placed in the tomb. The overall absence of adult females from the later generations, in contrast, suggests that female descendants of this lineage married outside their communities. A small number of people not related through blood were also interred at Hazleton North, and it is possible to suggest that these individuals may have been adopted into this bloodline (Fowler *et al.* 2021).

The ancient DNA analyses also enable us to see other patterns of behaviour. The descendants from two of the first-generation women were deposited predominantly in the northern chamber, while descendants from the other two first-generation women were placed in the south chamber. Archaeologists have long speculated on the architectural configurations of chambered tombs, which are very varied both within traditions – such as the Cotswold–Severn tradition of which Hazleton North is a part – and more widely across Britain (see Chapter 5). We can now say for certain that architectural form, at

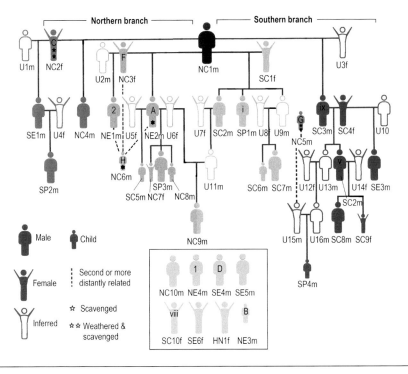

FIGURE 1.3
The biological relationships between people deposited at Hazleton North as demonstrated by the aDNA study at Hazleton North

least in this case, reflects family and kinship relationships that were either in place or anticipated when the tomb was built (Fowler 2022).

There are many more insights to be gleaned from the different investigations of material at Hazleton North (see Cummings and Fowler 2023), but here I wish to highlight one aspect, as it is a key theme which runs through the book: the importance of **kinship** to people in the Neolithic. At its most basic level kinship refers to the relationships between members of the same family or group. We often tend to think of biological relationships as the main way of defining families, but there are many examples where this is not the case; there is considerable variation in who people call their mother, father, brother, sister and so on, which may not relate to a biological relationship at all. The same may well have been the case in the Neolithic, but the identification of people who were biologically related at Hazleton North and buried together does suggest that people in the early Neolithic also placed considerable emphasis on biological relationships in terms of assigning kinship. Whom you are related to is one of the most important aspects of being human – it defines what you can and cannot do (for example whom you can and cannot marry), and it permeates all aspects of life from food production and resource ownership through to group allegiance. The insights from Hazleton North also suggest that it was a driving factor in the design and creation of monuments such as chambered tombs as well as defining who could, and could not, be deposited at the site. Kinship appears to have been an important component of both life and death in Neolithic Britain and Ireland, which we will pick up again at many points throughout the book.

KNOWTH PASSAGE TOMB, CO. MEATH

The next site to which we now turn is one of the most remarkable sites dating from the Neolithic period. Knowth passage tomb in County Meath, Ireland, is another chambered tomb, but it is on a wholly different scale from Hazleton North. It consists of a massive circular mound around 85 metres in diameter, many times larger than that at Hazleton North. Encircling the foot of the mound are a series of large slabs, many of which are covered with intricate designs. Distinctive black and white stones quarried from many kilometres away were also strewn around the perimeter of the monument. Within the enormous mound are two chambers. The eastern chamber was so large that it was able to contain two large stone basins, again carved and decorated with incised motifs, which were also found on stones in the chamber. These chambers contained burial deposits and were connected to the outside of the mound by long passages roughly 35m length and again containing stones covered with rock art. This was, quite simply, monumental architecture on a whole new scale. What is extraordinary is that this site dates only a few hundred years after Hazleton North to the middle Neolithic; it was probably constructed around 3200 BC (Eogan and Cleary 2017).

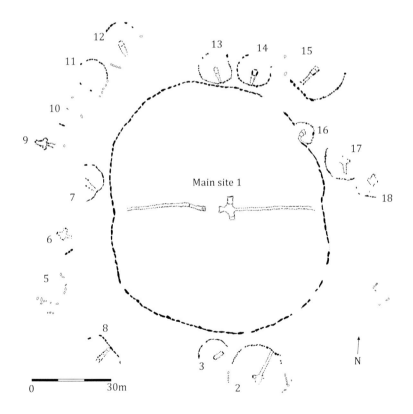

FIGURE 1.4
Plan of the main mound at Knowth, showing the large central passage tomb surrounded by smaller tombs (after Eogan 1986)

FIGURE 1.5
One of the intricately carved designs on the kerbstones encircling the mound at Knowth

Knowth has been extensively investigated and excavated over the past few decades, and we therefore have a good understanding about how the site was constructed and then used. The site was not constructed in a single phase, as we think was the case for Hazleton North, but was built over time and perhaps reusing stones from an earlier monument (Eogan and Cleary 2017, pp. 47–276). The mound in particular reveals multiple different construction events, showing people returning to the site and adding another layer of material to the mound. At some point in the construction people deposited the remains of the dead in the chambers, both inhumations and cremations. Alongside the human remains were different objects, often fragmented, including objects associated with personal ornamentation such as pendants and pins made from bone. The famous Knowth macehead was found in the eastern chamber and is one of the most exquisite and beautifully crafted items from the Neolithic (Figure 1.6). A second macehead was also found under the western chamber (Eogan and Richardson 1982).

The main mound at Knowth is an extraordinary and massive construction, and yet it is one of many passage tombs found at this location. Knowth is encircled not just by a kerb of large, often decorated stones but also a series of smaller passage tombs, often referred to as satellite tombs. Many of these actually pre-date the main mound, and one had to be partially destroyed in order to squeeze the main mound into its present position. These smaller monuments represent a significant investment of time, and some may have been intended to be incorporated into the main monument. The smaller

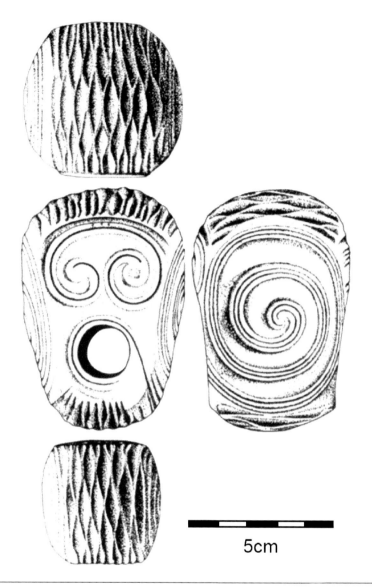

FIGURE 1.6
The Knowth macehead recovered from the eastern chamber (after Eogan and Richardson 1982)

tombs themselves contained burial deposits. The complex at Knowth thus consists of multiple passage tombs, and what is perhaps even more extraordinary is that there are many other monuments in the wider vicinity, including two more massive passage tombs at Newgrange and Dowth (see Chapter 6). These monuments, alongside others, created an entire landscape altered by monumental architecture. It is known as the Brú na Bóinne, as the sites are centred around the bend in the River Boyne, itself likely to have been an important landscape feature at the time.

The size and complexity of Knowth indicate that this is not a site that could realistically have been constructed by an extended family group as we might argue for the monument at Hazleton North. Instead, the sheer scale of the enterprise must have involved much larger groups of people coming together. This would have involved what we might term **corporate negotiations** – the aggregation of larger groups of people, perhaps more distant kin, or perhaps people not related by kin at all, to work together on larger projects. These sorts of negotiations must have taken place from early on in the Neolithic at sites such as causewayed enclosures (see Chapter 5), but the size, scale and frequency of these projects seem to have intensified as time went by and must have been a common features in the lives of many Neolithic people. In some instances, these were places, such as Knowth, that involved the deposition of the dead, but there were also plenty of sites which were not primarily about burial. Instead, many of these sites drew upon people's **belief systems** and provided arenas where they could undertake ritual practices. This may have been about ensuring both their everyday but also their spiritual wellbeing. What is key is that people invested huge amounts of time in projects concerned with their religious beliefs. However, not all corporate building projects were monuments, and with that in mind we turn to another important Neolithic site.

THE NESS OF BRODGAR, ORKNEY

Our final site is located in Orkney in northern Scotland. The Ness of Brodgar is still being excavated, so we do not have a complete understanding of the site as yet. However, the findings here have been so remarkable that this site is key for thinking about life at the end of the fourth millennium and into the third millennium. Around about 3000 cal BC in a location which had been in use for 500 years or so, people constructed buildings on a monumental scale. As we shall see in the book, Orkney is unusual in the early Neolithic in the sense that people built and lived in permanent stone houses. This type of architecture is not found elsewhere in Britain and Ireland. What is even more unusual is that at the Ness of Brodgar people constructed a series of enormous versions of Orcadian stone houses set at the very heart of a much larger monumental landscape which included the passage grave at Maeshowe similar to that at Knowth, stone circles and other settlements at Barnhouse and Buckan (Card *et al*. 2020a). At the Ness of Brodgar people were living in these monumental houses, as occupation layers and associated rubbish accumulated in nearby middens attest. For example, the massive Structure Eight was 18 metres long and 9.5 metres wide (Figure 1.7). It was built over two earlier houses, virtually covering both of these smaller structures. Its vast interior space was divided by stone piers, and four different hearths were uncovered. The walls had both painted surfaces as well as incised art designs (Thomas 2020). There is evidence for different activities happening within the structure such as cooking and storage and some high-quality artefacts such as maceheads and polished stone axes (Card *et al*. 2020b). It would have been a monumental undertaking just to build the structure. However, after only a short period of time the structure partly collapsed, and the remaining part of the building was repurposed for different activities.

The Ness of Brodgar was clearly not just a straightforward settlement, as the size and scale of the endeavour set it apart from other contemporary settlement sites in Orkney.

FIGURE 1.7
Structure Eight at the Ness of Brodgar, courtesy of Ness of Brodgar Trust/Scott Pike

Moreover, occupation at the Ness seems to have been episodic and punctuated, suggesting people coming together for specific occasions or at times of important negotiations. The buildings were not all contemporary, with some being built and rebuilt in quick succession and others lasting for a longer duration. This seems to have been a particularly special place, marked out by not only massive structures but these themselves being part of a wider and important landscape. As such, the Ness of Brodgar can be described as a 'luminous place', a phrase which I think captures the sense that some places, for whatever reason, drew people back over and over and became vital for historically specific reasons such as ongoing negotiations of kinship, of community and of beliefs. These places were clearly important within the local context, in this case Orkney, but it is also clear that these places were significant beyond the local area. There is evidence from the Ness of Brodgar which indicates connections with the wider world – further afield in Scotland but perhaps further still, with connections of some sort with Ireland and to southern Britain (see Carlin and Cooney 2020). Yet the Ness of Brodgar also illustrates another key point that I will return to throughout the book; there were significant **regional differences in Neolithic practices across in Britain and Ireland**. Right from the start, people across Britain and Ireland were doing things differently. There was no homogenous set of Neolithic practices found consistently and repeatedly across Britain and Ireland. Some places seem to have attracted certain types of activity over extended periods, while other areas were less intensively occupied or altered by monuments. It is perhaps unsurprising that there were regional trajectories in the Neolithic and that people chose to do things differently in different places when we consider that even though on a world scale Britain and Ireland are quite small, for people moving around by foot or boat, these are still significant landmasses. I now move on to consider how it may have been the landscapes of Britain and Ireland themselves that had an influence on how and why people did things differently in the Neolithic.

LANDSCAPES OF THE NEOLITHIC

In 1932 Cyril Fox published *The Personality of Britain*, a book which considered how land and environment influenced people living in the past. A few decades later Estyn Evans (1973) wrote *The Personality of Ireland*, which examined the landscapes of Ireland in the shaping of the use of this island. These books are important because they highlight the role that the landscape plays in relation to various aspects of people's lives. For example, looking after domesticated cattle and growing cereals is fundamentally affected by the region of Britain or Ireland in which you live. But these books were not simply environmentally deterministic: they both argue that the landscape is more than just a backdrop to how you make a living. Instead, the character of Britain and Ireland would have been a fundamental part of people's identity, tied up with stories, with family and kin, with belief systems and myths and legends (see Bender 1993, Ingold 2000, Tilley 1994, Ucko and Layton 1998), key themes I have already highlighted as important. Moreover, the landscapes of Britain and Ireland are very diverse. The west coast of Ireland often feels the full force of the Atlantic, in contrast with the east of Britain, sheltered from the rain and the wind by the Pennines but as a result often much cooler than the west. The south-east corner of Britain is frequently influenced by warmer Continental weather, whereas the north coast of Scotland can be battered by storms from the north. The weather of course influences where people want to live and how easy it is to make a living, but there is considerable variation in topography too. There are high mountains, not on the scale of the Alps, but sizeable enough to completely transform the surrounding area. The spectacular Mourne Mountains in north-east Ireland dominate the landscape for miles around, and movement around Britain is affected by the Grampian and Cambrian mountains in particular. There are also areas of extensive lowlands, such as the Fens. Indeed, the differences in topography were significant enough for Fox (1932) to suggest that Britain could be divided up into two quite different zones: the highlands and lowlands. While cereal agriculture and the keeping of domestic animals are the easiest in the lowland zone, it would be quite wrong to think that people in the Neolithic were only interested in these areas. Upland areas were most notably used for the extraction of stone for axes (see Chapter 4) and monumental constructions (see Chapters 5, 6 and 8) and seem to have been a draw to people for religious reasons.

Particular landscapes would also have been imbued with meanings; this tradition is well recorded in Irish mythology, as discussed by Evans (1973), where stories tell of how features were formed in relation to great heroes or important events. This demonstrates not only the depth of knowledge that people had of their local landscapes but how significant those landscapes were to understanding their place in the world. Of course while we can never know the exact stories told about landscapes in the Neolithic, we can find material remains which indicate the potential significance of particular features and create stories ourselves of how these may have been important. We have already seen

FIGURE 1.8
The dramatic mountain of Benbulbin, Co. Sligo, Ireland

how passage tombs in County Meath in Ireland were focused on a bend in the River Boyne. In the often densely forested landscape, the coast and sea may have been more intensively occupied than inland areas, particularly because from these areas it was easier to move around. Indeed, the maritime nature of the Neolithic appears to be one of its defining characteristics not just in terms of the start of the Neolithic but throughout this period. Waterways and rivers, as well as the sea, would have been conduits for movement and keeping in touch with other people (Cummings 2009, Cummings and Robinson 2015, Garrow and Sturt 2011).

FIGURE 1.9
The rock outcrops around Garn Turne in Pembrokeshire, Wales

The landscapes of Britain and Ireland today are, in many cases, quite different from the landscapes of the Neolithic. Both Britain and Ireland have seen intensive occupation and agriculture for thousands of years, as well several hundred years of industrialisation in many areas. This does not just relate to the presence of towns and cities but the drainage and reclamation of vast swathes of landscape which were previously marginal. Woodland was once ubiquitous but has been systematically removed. Fields have been created, patiently cleared of stone, ploughed, and enclosed by walls or hedges. Of particular note here is that glacial debris deposited as the last ice sheets retreated at the end of the Ice Age would have been substantial in the Neolithic. Virtually none of this stone survives untouched into the modern age (see Figure 1.9). Indeed, in some instances quarries and mines have altered entire landscapes in the quest for stone, coal, iron and other precious resources – an entire mountain summit utilised by people in the Neolithic has been mined away in recent decades at Penmaenmawr in North Wales, for example. Not all changes are the result of human action. Much of the upland peats were formed after the Neolithic, and coastal erosion has seen the loss of significant landmasses, particularly in the south of Britain and Ireland but also in island chains (e.g. the Scilly Isles and Orkney). Quite simply, the landscapes of modern Britain and Ireland are radically different from those of the Neolithic. The landscape would have looked quite different back then.

It is also worth briefly considering both the size and scale of Britain and Ireland. On a world scale, these are small land masses, but prior to the transport infrastructure of roads, rail and canal, and before any form of assistance with travel across land – not even horses were present in Britain and Ireland in the Neolithic – Britain and Ireland would have taken time and effort to move around. It may not have been the case that people in Britain and Ireland would have comprehended, as we do, their precise location within these islands. However, we should not think that people lived only in one small part of Britain or Ireland with no understanding of the world beyond them. As we will see throughout this book, there is plenty of evidence which suggests people had an awareness of distant places. Certainly people appear to have been aware of other parts of Britain and Ireland and communities living in them, and there are hints throughout the Neolithic that those networks extended to Mainland Europe, specifically the Low Countries and along the Atlantic façade. There may have been knowledge of other places, too, perhaps as far as the Alps to the south and Scandinavia to the east. There is also tantalising evidence that individuals were moving around, predominantly within Britain and Ireland but sometimes beyond. These wider connections are difficult definitively to demonstrate, but kinship ties, exchange networks and the lure of knowledge and gossip must have been powerful motivators for people to be in touch, even when it may have involved a risky sea crossing (Callaghan and Scarre 2009).

There would have been differences in environment too between now and the Neolithic. In summer temperatures would have been, on average, a few degrees warmer and in winter a few degrees cooler. After a period of sustained land loss due to rising sea levels, the Neolithic sea levels would have been, more or less and with a few notable exceptions, much as they are today (see Sturt *et al*. 2013). As already noted, one of the biggest differences between now and the Neolithic was in terms of vegetation, as most of Britain and Ireland was wooded at the start of the Neolithic. The focus of this book will not be the environment, although here it has been stressed that it would have played an important role in people's lives. Instead the focus will be on archaeological remains and what that can tell us about the lives of people at the time.

A BRIEF OUTLINE OF THE BOOK

The book has been written in chronological order, dividing the Neolithic into three periods:

- The early Neolithic, from roughly 4000 to 3400 cal BC
- The middle Neolithic, from 3400 to 3000 cal BC
- The late Neolithic, from 3000 to 2500 cal BC

In order to set the scene, Chapter 2 deals with the late Mesolithic of Britain and Ireland, specifically the thousand years prior to the start of the Neolithic around 4000 BC. Chapter 3 then considers the transition from the Mesolithic to the Neolithic not just in Britain and Ireland but within a wider north-west European context. Chapters 4 and 5 then deal with the early Neolithic, divided up between settlement, subsistence and material culture (Chapter 4) and mortuary practice and monumentality (Chapter 5). Chapter 6 summarises both life and death in the middle Neolithic. The late Neolithic chapters are divided up in the same fashion as those covering the early Neolithic, so Chapter 7 considers settlement, subsistence and material culture in the late Neolithic, and Chapter 8 covers mortuary practice and monumentality. Chapter 9 covers the very end of the

Neolithic period, with the arrival of Beakers and material associated with Beakers, and summarises new practices and forms of monument introduced up to around 2000 BC. Finally, Chapter 10 provides a broad overview of the period and considers the future of Neolithic studies. Since themes and topics are often split over several chapters (for example, pottery, which is discussed in Chapters 4, 6, 7 and 9), the reader is pointed to the index to follow up specific areas.

RECOMMENDED FURTHER READING

Neolithic overview

Bradley, R., 2019. *The prehistory of Britain and Ireland*. Cambridge: Cambridge University Press.

Hazleton North

Fowler, C., Olalde, I., Cummings, V., Armit, I., Buster, L., Cuthbert, S., Rohland, N., Cheronet, O., Pinhasi, R., and Reich, D., 2021. Complex kinship practices revealed in a five – generation family from Neolithic Britain. *Nature*, 601, 584–587.

Saville, A., 1990. *Hazelton north: The excavation of a Neolithic long cairn of the Cotswold – Severn group*. London: English Heritage.

Knowth

Eogan, G. and Cleary, K., 2017. *Excavations at Knowth 6. The passage tomb archaeology of the great mound at Knowth*. Dublin: Royal Irish Academy.

The Ness of Brodgar

Card, N., Edmonds, M., and Mitchell, A., eds., 2020. *The Ness of Brodgar: As it stands*. Kirkwall: The Orcadian.

CHAPTER 2

Britain and Ireland in the fifth millennium cal BC

The calm before the storm

INTRODUCTION

In order to truly understand the magnitude and nature of change brought about by the onset of the Neolithic we need to consider what was happening in Britain and Ireland beforehand. This chapter will therefore consider the last thousand years of the preceding Mesolithic. Indeed, in a recent consideration of the entire Mesolithic of Britain, Chantal Conneller (2022) defined the period from 5200 to 4000 cal BC as the Final Mesolithic, a discrete and distinct period which differs from earlier phases of the Mesolithic and conveniently coincides with the period under discussion here. Conneller (2022) defines the Final Mesolithic as seeing the uptake of distinctive forms of material culture, notably styles of microlith as well as other tool types. However, this uptake was not uniform across Britain, indicating regional differences – differences that are important in their own right for understanding the Mesolithic sequence but also useful for us in considerations of what came next. In Ireland the last thousand years of the Mesolithic are part of the broader Later Mesolithic as defined in Graeme Warren's recent account (2022), but here, too, the fifth millennium saw the development of distinctive tool types and other practices, setting it apart from what came before. This was thus a distinctive period of time with regionally specific practices occurring in both Britain and Ireland which demonstrate this was a dynamic period with people negotiating a changing world.

In many ways we can consider this period the calm before the storm caused by the arrival of the Neolithic, often referred to as the Neolithic or agricultural revolution. However, the title of this chapter is somewhat tongue in cheek, because, in reality, it may have been something of a storm before the calm. This may have been quite literal in the sense that this was actually a period of increased storminess after about 4500 cal BC (Tipping *pers. Comm.*). This would make moving around by boat, and there is significant evidence of a maritime way of life at this time, much trickier for people. It is also becoming increasingly clear that the occupants of Britain and Ireland were not living in

DOI: 10.4324/9781003387329-2

isolation from communities on the Continent, and many of these European communities by this point were practising Neolithic ways of life. As such there may have been considerable concern or unease amongst British and Irish hunter-gatherers faced with new ways of making a living such as agriculture alongside many other new practices. This could well mean that activities and practices in the Final Mesolithic were reactions to broader events elsewhere, essentially causing a real storm in terms of social cohesion and an understanding of one's place within the world. As we shall see, the Neolithic way of life was significantly different from a Mesolithic one in a number of important ways, not just in terms of what people ate but also how society was organised and what they believed in.

The aim of this chapter, then, is to focus on the archaeology dating only from the last thousand years of the Mesolithic, and here I only include sites which have radiocarbon dates confirming that each site dates to this phase. It is also worth noting that there are a few limitations to our understanding of the fifth millennium. First, sea levels have changed just enough that many coastal areas which were above water in the fifth millennium are now submerged under the sea. As we will see, coastal areas were extensively utilised in the Mesolithic, so this is a genuine problem – although this issue affects some areas of Britain and Ireland more than others. Stone tools from the fifth millennium survive well in the archaeological record, but these can only give us insights into some aspects of life at the time, especially since it seems clear that organic material was used extensively during the Mesolithic. Unfortunately, there is only limited organic preservation on most sites in Britain and Ireland, which means most Mesolithic material culture simply does not survive for us to find. This is in marked contrast to some Mesolithic sequences elsewhere, such as in Scandinavia, where there is excellent organic preservation, especially in waterlogged contexts (see, for example, Tilley 1996). Nevertheless, there have been some important new finds and sites in recent years, which alongside the new syntheses (Conneller 2022, Warren 2022) mean we now have a much more detailed understanding of life before the Neolithic. I shall refer to this period in both Britain and Ireland as the Final Mesolithic as a shorthand for the fifth millennium cal BC.

HUNTER-GATHERERS OF THE MESOLITHIC: AN OVERVIEW

Broadly speaking, the Mesolithic started at the end of the last ice age with the onset of the post-glacial period which dates to around 9600 cal BC (or 10,000 BP). While there was no sudden change from what had come before, this was a period of rapidly improving environmental conditions, and from this point on various characteristics associated with utilising warmer environments started to be used. At a general level, people in the Mesolithic were hunter-gatherers. This means they acquired all their food by hunting, gathering or fishing. There were no domesticated plants or animals used in the Mesolithic, apart from the domesticated dog. The landscape was predominantly wooded throughout Britain and Ireland, even at the now-treeless extremes such as the outlying Scottish Isles. The changing woodlands became deciduous, comprising species such as oak, elm and ash, and the temperatures were slightly warmer than today. This all provided a rich range of resources for people to utilise (Zvelebil 1994). By about 5000 cal BC the landmasses of both Britain and Ireland were broadly similar to how they are today; the large expanse of land known as Doggerland which now lies under the North Sea had been present in the early Mesolithic but was virtually entirely submerged by this time; the English Channel was also fully formed (Sturt *et al*. 2013). Sea levels were a little lower than today in much of Britain and Ireland, although not all. Because people relied entirely on hunting, gathering and fishing for their food, we can suggest from parallels with contemporary peoples who make a living this way that Mesolithic people had belief systems which were tied up with the natural world and that they placed considerable emphasis on sharing and dealing with the environment in specific ways (Bird-David 1990, Ingold 2000). The Mesolithic continued until the onset of the Neolithic, which began in Britain and Ireland around 4000 cal BC (but see Chapter 3, where the precise start date of the Neolithic is discussed in more detail).

AN ISLAND OF THE LIVING AND THE DEAD: ORONSAY

The tiny island of Oronsay is found to the south of Colonsay, itself a small island which is part of the Inner Hebrides in western Scotland. What is now a remote location on Scotland's Atlantic façade has produced some of the most fascinating Final Mesolithic remains found anywhere in Britain. Five shell middens are located on the old Mesolithic shoreline (Figure 2.1). These are the remains of discarded shells and other food refuse associated

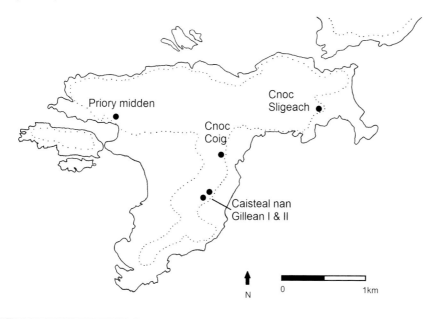

FIGURE 2.1
The five main late Mesolithic midden sites on Oronsay in relation to the present coastline (solid line) and the coastline at the time of occupation (dotted line: after Mellars 1987)

with activities such as animal, shell and fish processing, tool manufacture and occupation (Mellars 1987). Small quantities of human remains have also been found in the middens, rare examples of human bone from the Final Mesolithic. When Oronsay was occupied in the fifth millennium cal BC, the sea levels would have been higher than their present-day levels, with the sea very close to the middens. However, with the weight of the ice caps which once lay over much of Britain and Ireland now gone, this area of Scotland has seen the land continue to rise. This is known as isostatic lift, and it means that in some areas such as Oronsay, the old coastline is now inland as a result of this effect.

The Oronsay middens have been interpreted as the remains of subsistence practices which represent the activities of people who made a living by hunting, gathering and fishing. The middens themselves are made up from the remains of many thousands of shellfish, particularly limpets. Amongst these shells are the bones of other creatures which would have been caught or acquired nearby, including seals, small cetaceans (dolphins or porpoises), otters, sea birds, saithe (a cod-like fish) and even a whale. These would have provided a plentiful supply of food as well as hides, fats and oils. Indeed, later Mesolithic sites from across coastal north-west Europe show a heavy reliance on marine foods (see Bailey and Spikins 2008). These middens are more than just the remains of subsistence practices. There were also the remains of the making of various tools which would have been important for hunter-gatherer groups including bone objects and leather. Set amongst some of the middens were the remains of rather ephemeral hut-like structures, associated with hearths (Figure 2.3). These may have

FIGURE 2.2
The shell midden of Caisteal nan Gillean I, Oronsay, with the hills of Jura visible in the distance (© Crown Copyright: Historic Environment Scotland)

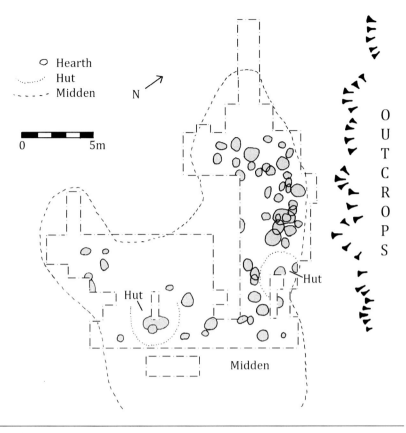

FIGURE 2.3
The excavation plan of the midden of Cnoc Coig, showing the location of the hearths, the huts and the midden in relation to the outcrops on the shore (after Mellars 1987)

been essentially tent-like structures, many elements of which could be transported for use elsewhere. These too can be considered typical for the Final Mesolithic, as there is good evidence that people were mobile, following seasonal resources, and therefore unlikely to invest in large-scale permanent settlements. Very little permanent architecture is known from this period, although people were more than capable of creating it and had done so in preceding phases of the Mesolithic (see Conneller 2022 Chapter 4, Warren 2022, Chapter 6).

However, Oronsay has also produced some rather surprising evidence. The shell middens also contained animal bones of deer and pig. Later Mesolithic sites elsewhere in north-west Europe have shown that hunter-gatherers would have regularly consumed these animals, but their discovery on Oronsay was curious because they could not have been acquired on this island. Oronsay would have been too small to sustain a population of these animals, so they must have been imported from other land masses nearby (Mithen and Finlayson 1991). This means that people were therefore going to considerable effort to import meat, and perhaps hides, to the island. Furthermore, it has been possible to ascertain which seasons of the year Oronsay was occupied: the fish otoliths (ear bones) show that Oronsay was in use in all seasons of the year (Wicks *et al.*

2014). Once again this was surprising because it was assumed that Oronsay would have only been suitable as a short-stay camp, not a location which was potentially occupied all year round.

The human remains from Oronsay are also important for understanding the Final Mesolithic because very few human remains are known from this period in Britain and Ireland (see subsequently). The Cnoc Coig midden produced the most material: 55 bones in total, including 30 bones from the hands and feet, three skull fragments, a patella (knee cap) and fragments from the clavicle (collarbone), maxilla (upper jaw), innominates (hip), vertebrae, fibulae and teeth (Conneller 2006, p. 143). Five bones were recovered from Caisteal nan Gillean II, and a single foot bone was also recovered from Priory midden. These bones have been subjected to radiocarbon dating and demonstrate a late fifth-millennium cal BC date (Wicks *et al*. 2014), while stable isotope analysis has revealed what kinds of food these people ate. The people from Cnoc Coig ate a diet overwhelmingly dominated by marine foods, while the individual from Caisteal nan Gillean II ate a mix of marine and foods from terrestrial sources (like red deer and pig: Richards and Mellars 1998). It is clear that these remains are not formal burials as have been found elsewhere in north-west Europe (see subsequently) because the bones were found singularly and widely distributed across the midden. It has been suggested that bodies may have been laid out on the middens prior to being moved elsewhere or as a deliberate act of excarnation (Pollard 1996). This, it has been argued, could explain the predominance of foot and hand bones on the middens, which would be the first bits to drop off once decomposition started.

On closer inspection, however, it was noted that some of the human bones were not incorporated into the midden as might be expected if excarnation was taking place. Instead, some of the hand bones were carefully and deliberately placed on top of seal flippers. The bones of both hands and seal flippers look remarkably similar, and people would certainly have been familiar with the bones of seals as they butchered and cooked them and may have noted the similarity between humans and seals. This suggests, then, a more careful and deliberate mixing of human and animal bones and has led to suggestions that people and animals were discarded in a similar fashion (Chatterton 2006, p. 115 and see subsequently). The excavator argued that parts of human bodies were defleshed elsewhere and were then collected and deliberately incorporated into the midden (Mellars 1987, p. 299). This suggestion is supported by the long-standing practice found throughout Europe of turning human remains into objects, which dates right back to the Upper Palaeolithic. It seems more likely, then, that at least some of the human bones found on the Oronsay middens were deliberately incorporated and deposited there, having decomposed and fragmented elsewhere. The bones were carefully placed in the midden, sometimes highlighting similarities between humans and animals.

It is worth considering the possibility that Oronsay would actually make an ideal location for the excarnation and disarticulation of human remains into dry bones. This is because Oronsay could not support populations of large predators such as wolves and foxes which could seriously damage or remove bones. While the act of excarnation may not have been occurring on the middens themselves, it may be that other locations on Oronsay were used as places for turning fleshed human bodies into bones. Some

FIGURE 2.4
The location of sites from the fifth millennium cal BC mentioned in the text

skeletal elements ended up being incorporated into the shell middens, while others, presumably, were taken elsewhere. This may mean that Oronsay could actually have been conceived as an 'island of the dead', and it may explain why people returned there over hundreds of years and during all seasons of the year. The middens also created permanent places in the landscape (Pollard 2000), providing a fixed location for people to return to when dealing with the dead.

The evidence from Oronsay may seem remarkable, but this chapter will now go on to explore the use of 'persistent places' in the landscape, particularly small islands, which was repeated across Britain and Ireland in the fifth millennium cal BC.

YOU ARE WHAT YOU EAT

People in Britain and Ireland in the fifth millennium cal BC were hunter-gatherers, and there is plentiful evidence which indicates which species people were exploiting. In Britain, there were a number of large land mammals which would have provided meat and other useable components such as bone, fat, sinew and antler. There were numerous species of mammal in the forests of Britain, including red deer, roe deer, wild boar (pig) and wild cattle (aurochs). Bones of these animals occur on occupation sites showing that people were hunting and eating them. For example, excavations at the site of Goldcliff, Gwent, had the butchered remains of deer, wild pig and aurochs (Bell 2007, p. 74). At Misbourne Viaduct, Buckinghamshire, a Final Mesolithic site, produced the remains of aurochs and stone tools (Barton and Roberts 2004). As we have seen, deer and wild pig bones were also found on the middens on Oronsay. One remarkable find from the Final Mesolithic is the complete skeleton of a wild boar at Lydstep, Pembrokeshire, which was found with two small stone tools embedded in it (David 2007, p. 119). This find has been interpreted as an animal which was hunted and shot but got away from the hunters. It appears to have later died from its injuries and was preserved in submerged peat. What is curious, however, is that the skeleton was covered by a tree trunk (Figure 2.5). It is possible that the tree trunk fell on top of the dead boar, but it is also possible that this

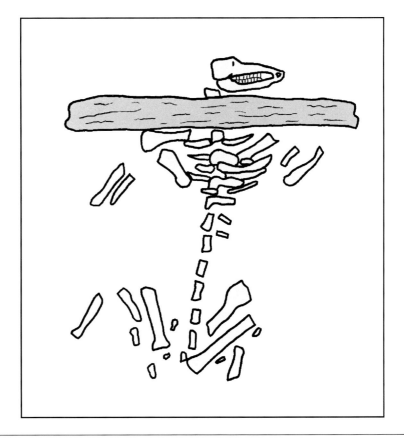

FIGURE 2.5
The late Mesolithic Lydstep boar covered by a tree trunk (after Chatterton 2006)

was a ritual deposit and that both the boar and the trunk were placed there by people. In Ireland a more restricted range of animals were available for people to hunt: aurochs and red deer were not present here. Instead the largest land mammal available in the later Mesolithic was wild boar, and this is found on fifth-millennium cal BC sites such as Moynagh, Co. Meath (McCormick 2007, p. 81). While a wide range of larger prey animals were available for hunting, there is also evidence for the hunting of smaller animals such as otters and pine marten.

In addition to land mammals, a whole range of other animals and birds were hunted in the fifth millennium. There is substantial evidence for the utilisation of the intertidal zone, rivers and lakes; these zones provide a wide range of foods, including fish, seals, shellfish and birds. A whole series of shell midden sites have been found across Britain and Ireland. The middens on Oronsay are one of a number of fifth-millennium middens found in this part of western Scotland, including sites such as Carding Mill Bay (Connock et al. 1993) and Port Lobh, Colonsay (Finlay et al. 2019). Indeed, middens containing fifth-millennium cal BC material have been found more widely in Scotland, including the site of An Corran on Skye (Wickham Jones 2009) and Tarradale, Highland (Conneller 2022, p. 363). In England and Wales, fewer middens have been identified, but this is probably due to sea level rise since the Mesolithic. There are nevertheless known examples as sites such as Westward Ho! (David 2007, p. 123); Nant Hall, Prestatyn (Conneller 2022, p. 404); and Portland, Culverwell (Palmer 1999). Likewise in Ireland there is good evidence for fifth-millennium cal BC middens, and examples are recorded at Rockmarshall, Co. Louth, and Fanore More, Co. Clare (Lynch 2014, p. 172). Middening, therefore, appears to be a widespread practice around the shores of the British and Irish Isles. These middens generally consist of a range of shellfish such as limpet, dogwhelk, periwinkle and oyster alongside mammal remains. It has been suggested that these middens were the remains of people collecting shellfish to eat, but it is also likely that the shellfish were used as bait to catch other species such as fish or seal. We will consider other aspects of these middens again subsequently.

It seems that fish may have played a significant role in the diets for many people in the fifth millennium. Salmon may have been important in Britain but may not have been as significant in Ireland, where eels may have been used more extensively (Meiklejohn and Woodman 2012, p. 27). Fish bone has been found on Irish sites, however, such as at Belderrig, Co. Mayo (Warren 2009). Likewise, seals and other sea mammals were used by groups, and bones from these are found in middens and on occupation sites. It has also been estimated that there were around 450 edible wild plant foods available in the Mesolithic (Zvelebil 1994), which would have been important sources of carbohydrate and nutrients. Of these, burnt hazelnut shells survive very well in the archaeological record.

There are two other forms of evidence which help us reconstruct fifth-millennium diets. First, there is increasing evidence from the foreshore zones which seems to indicate a substantial reliance on marine/water resources. There are an increasing number of known wooden platforms dating to the fifth millennium cal BC. On the foreshore in front of the MI6 building in London timbers have been found alongside lithics. These timbers appear to be a structure relating to fishing (Milne et al. 2010). In Ireland at Clowanstown, Co. Meath, a wooden structure was found standing on the edge of a lake. In association with this platform were four conical baskets which are likely to be fish traps (Mossop 2009, Figure 2.6). A series of scorched timbers from the site may indicate people were fishing at night, and a layer of burnt timbers in association with a hearth on the platform

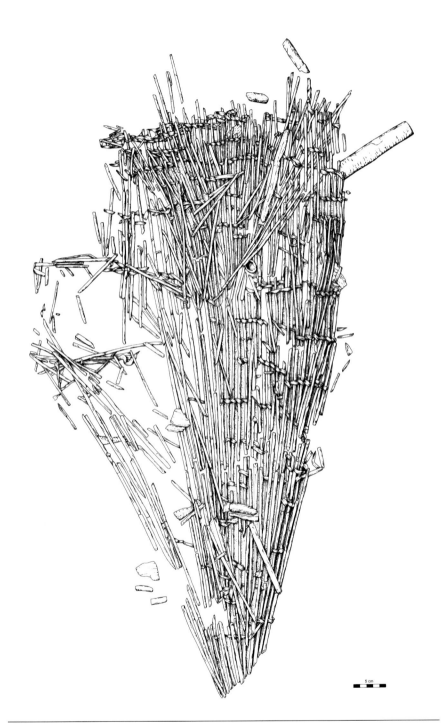

FIGURE 2.6
One of the baskets from Clowanstown, Co. Meath (image reproduced courtesy of Archaeological Consulting Services)

suggests people were smoking fish here as well. There is also the direct evidence of people utilising the foreshore from Goldcliff in Gwent and Low Hauxley in Northumberland, where human footprints have been preserved in the intertidal zone (Bell 2007, Eadie and Waddington 2013).

Second, stable isotope analysis of bone can also be used to ascertain the type of diet people had, specifically whether they relied more on marine or terrestrial foods. This approach is hindered by the overall lack of human remains from the fifth millennium cal BC (see subsequently), but bone from both Cnoc Coig, Oronsay, and Ferriter's Cove, Co. Kerry, indicates these people relied heavily on marine resources. However, the remains from Rockmarshall, Co. Louth, and Caisteal nan Gillean II demonstrated a mix of marine and terrestrial foods (Schulting and Richards 2002).

There is the tendency to assume that each community utilised a broad spectrum of foods, procuring both marine and terrestrial foods from across the landscape. Some accounts offer interpretations of the evidence which suggest that people utilised inland areas (for hunting and gathering) in the summer but moved to coasts (fishing) in the winter as part of a seasonal round, a strategy which has been identified anthropologically amongst contemporary hunter-gatherer groups. This may well have been the case, but there is also the possibility that different groups in the fifth millennium specialised in exploiting one type of environment or specific species. There is a sense from the evidence that different communities may have placed a special emphasis on hunting particular species or utilising particular areas of the landscape. This may have been in part because of a desire for particular products such as fur from specific species. However, it also hints at an affinity between human and animal communities which goes beyond simple resource procurement and will be discussed again subsequently.

There is also intriguing and increasing evidence for practices we may not immediately associate with hunter-gatherers. There is good evidence for the careful maintenance of clearings in otherwise wooded environments, with burnt layers appearing in many parts of the Pennines and North Yorkshire Moors (Conneller 2022, p. 402). This could be to maintain areas for meeting and congregating, but equally it could hint at the management of some species in the later Mesolithic, such as wild boar (see McCormick 2007). There are also claims that people may have been cultivating domestic cereal species in the latter part of the fifth millennium. It has been suggested that barley has been identified in the pollen record from sites in the Pennines (Albert and Innes 2020) and perhaps from Bexhill, East Sussex (Lawrence *et al*. 2022). This may seem improbable, but there is other evidence that fifth-millennium people in Britain and Ireland were in contact with agricultural groups on Mainland Europe (see subsequently), so it is not impossible. There are also many ethnographic examples of people who predominantly make a living by hunting and gathering also keeping domesticated plants. Future studies will certainly help us clarify and confirm this possibility.

MATERIAL CULTURE

Fifth-millennium cal BC sites are most frequently located by the presence of struck stone assemblages, frequently of flint, but also of chert, quartz and various other types of workable stone. Final Mesolithic assemblages in Britain often contain a notable component of blades, which could then be turned into artefacts such as microliths and scrapers. Indeed, the microlith is considered the key type of Mesolithic artefact from Britain; these were probably multi-purpose and could have been used as composite tools and as the tips of hunting projectiles (Butler 2005). The Final Mesolithic saw the appearance of symmetric and asymmetric micro-tranchets, including Bexhill Points throughout the southern part of Britain as far north as Cumbria (Conneller 2022, p. 356). Bexhill Points in particular have notable similarities with later Mesolithic tools found in Continental Europe, in particular from sites in northern Spain and western France (Lawrence et al. 2022). In Ireland stone tools kits are quite different in the fifth millennium cal BC. One diagnostic object is the Bann flake, which has been used to describe a broader object class which have carefully trimmed butts (Kador 2010). Irish assemblages also comprise large flakes and blades (Warren 2022, p. 12). There is also evidence of stone tool innovation in the form of Moynagh and Kerry Points, appearing after 4500 cal BC (Warren 2022, p. 149).

One of the notable aspects of Final Mesolithic stonework is the sheer quantity of debitage (waste pieces produced while making artefacts) sometimes found on sites. At Stainton West, Cumbria, over 300,000 struck lithics were found, the majority from the fifth millennium cal BC (Fraser Brown *pers. comm*.). The site of North Park Farm, Bletchingley, Surrey, produced over a million struck flints, including 17,000 microliths, associated with a hearth and a fire pit which produced a fifth-millennium date (Jones 2013). These may represent intensely occupied locations and specific ways of turning the raw material into objects. However, it may also relate to a particular way of dealing with specific things, which seems to have involved the extensive fragmentation of substances down into smaller components (as we have seen previously with human bodies on Oronsay). Kador (2007) has shown that small quantities of stone tools were travelling quite long distances in the later Mesolithic (and see subsequently). It can be suggested, then, that small pieces of people (bones) and small quantities of struck stone were moving around with people, creating portable assemblages of people, places and events which moved around the landscape with communities (also see Cummings 2009, Chapter 2).

There are also a number of objects made from bone and antler that date to the fifth millennium cal BC. A number of T-axes (often referred to as antler mattocks) are known from Scotland, including those from Risga, Argyll and Bute, and Tarradale, Highland, both of which have a fifth-millennium cal BC date (Conneller 2022, p. 365, Elliott 2015). Made from red deer antler, these are shaped pieces of antler with a perforation through the main body of the tool (see Figure 2.7). These are likely to have been used for butchery, carpentry and woodworking (Elliott 2015). Although T-axes are not found in Ireland, it can be argued that polished stone axes, which are found in considerable quantities, fulfilled a similar role in the toolkits of later Mesolithic people. At least 40 complete axes, and numerous fragments, were found at Newferry, Co. Antrim (Woodman 1977). There is the possibility that some ground stone axes from Scotland may date to the fifth millennium (Saville 2009), and there are known examples from Wales (David 2007). A number of barbed points have been found, including some from the middens on Oronsay and one from Shewalton, North Ayrshire (Saville 2004). These appear to have been used for fishing. Another find on late Mesolithic sites with good preservation in Britain and Ireland is the bevel-ended tool. Made from bone or antler, these seem to have been used for leather working, although they could have been used to fulfil a variety of tasks (Saville 2004).

FIGURE 2.7
Antler mattock (T-axe) from Meiklewood, Stirling (© National Museums Scotland)

It is likely that many objects in the fifth millennium were made from organic materials that rarely preserve in the archaeological record. In the wooded landscapes of Mesolithic Britain and Ireland, people would have had an endless supply of wood, and there are clear indications that wood would have been a key material at this time (see Warren 2022, Chapter 4). Several wooden platforms are known in Ireland (see subsequently), and fifth-millennium trackways have been found in Lough Gara, Co. Sligo, and Lullymore Bog, Co. Kildare, which may suggest that wooden architecture was widespread (Driscoll 2009). There are also occasional wooden finds such as a digging stick from Goldcliff, Gwent (Bell 2007), and a plank of poplar from Carrigdirty Rock, Co. Limerick (Lynch 2014, p. 172). The basketry from Clowanstown, Co. Meath (see previously), shows the level of sophistication which can be achieved with organic material, and as yet we have no known fifth-millennium cal BC examples of netting, rope, hide, skins or boats which would demonstrate the range of material people would have made from organic material. It is these objects, rather than the small stone tools which are so well preserved, which better represent fifth-millennium material culture and which may well have been the medium for expressions of social identity and kin relations.

SETTLEMENTS

Fifth-millennium lithic scatters have already been discussed, and most of these are likely to be the remains of settlement of some form, from a short-stay camp to locations occupied for longer periods of time. The presence of different stone tools can give us an indication of what kinds of activities were taking place at these sites; scrapers, for example, may indicate hide working, although they could have been used for a variety of tasks, and evidence of large-scale microlith manufacture may represent the remains of a base camp or more permanent occupation site. A few sites in Britain and Ireland, however, have produced more extensive evidence of settlement activity. It is worth noting that there are no known examples of large or permanent houses from the fifth millennium cal BC. It should be emphasised that this was a deliberate choice – earlier in the Mesolithic people had built large and enduring structures, but clearly at this point in time this was not how people chose to live.

The coast was clearly a significant draw for people in the fifth millennium, and some coastal occupation sites were marked out by the presence of middens like those on Oronsay. There and at other examples such as at Prestatyn, Denbighshire (Bell 2007); Fanore, Co. Clare; and Ferriter's Cove, Co. Kerry, people returned many times, collecting shells and depositing them on the middens. This was a deliberate practice and created highly visible markers in the landscape. Middening, then, may have been more than simply dumps of occupation rubbish but a practice which made visible occupation, perhaps associated with particular family groups or kinship groups.

People in the fifth millennium did not only utilise the coastal zone. Where fieldwork has been done inland, Mesolithic sites have also been found. In south-west Scotland, for example, numerous Final Mesolithic sites have been found on the coast, but fieldwork has also demonstrated inland occupation around Clatteringshaw Loch, Dumfries and Galloway, and Loch Doon, East Ayrshire (Edwards 1996). Smittons, Dumfries and Galloway, is typical of the kind of site found in these areas, producing flint and chert artefacts, hazelnut shells, hearths and stakeholes (Affleck 1983). There are some good examples of short-stay hunting camps in the archaeological record. In northern England a series of inland and upland sites have been located in both the North Yorks Moors and the Pennines, where lithics, small hearths and stakeholes associated with vegetation disturbance are likely to indicate the remains of hunting camps (Chatterton 2003, Tolan-Smith 2008, p. 148). At Waun Fignen Felen, Powys, a series of small lithic scatters have been found, some dating to the fifth millennium, which show this location was used for hunting over thousands of years (Barton *et al*. 1995).

Another striking feature of fifth-millennium cal BC occupation is that people were attracted to living on small islands. These islands come in a number of different forms and are not the same across Britain and Ireland. Nevertheless, the evidence seems to indicate a genuine preference for island living. We have already seen previously the occupation of the tiny island of Oronsay in the fifth millennium cal BC. Another well-known late Mesolithic Scottish site, that of Morton in Fife, has produced evidence of nearly 14,000 struck stone pieces, hearths, stakeholes and windbreaks which indicate a settlement of some kind (Coles 1971). However, at the time of occupation, the site would have been a low island linked to the mainland only at low tide. Further south, Stainton West in Cumbria produced a massive lithic assemblage as well as hearths, cooking pits and the remains of structures represented by stakeholes. Again, when this site was occupied, it was located on an island in a river. At Goldcliff, Gwent, the fifth-millennium cal BC occupation was on an island which was connected to the mainland at low tide (Bell 2007). And at Runnymede Bridge, fifth-millennium occupation was focused on a silt island (Conneller 2022, p. 406).

In Ireland there is also evidence for the use of islands, but here they were often artificially enhanced or constructed. Clonava Island in Lough Derravaragh, Co. Westmeath, is an island around 2km long which saw later Mesolithic occupation. The island seems to have been enhanced by a platform structure (Little 2009). A series of fifth-millennium artificial wooden platforms have been found in lakes. For example, at

Lough Kinale, Co. Longford, people built an artificial platform so that they could live on the interface between land and water (Fredengren 2002, 2009). Moynagh Lough, Co. Meath, saw occupation on a brushwood platform in the lake (Bradley 1991). These named examples are the best known, but island occupations may have been quite common, as lithics have regularly been found eroding out of lake edges and islands (Fredengren 2009).

Why were people attracted to these small islands? It would be possible to argue that people lived there as a defensive strategy. For this to be the case in the fifth millennium cal BC, we would need to envisage high population density; interpersonal violence and warfare are easily avoided in sparsely populated landscapes, as people can simply move to another area to avoid conflict. It remains exceptionally difficult to make anything other than a guess at population levels in the Mesolithic (and see Warren 2022, Chapter 8). There have been suggestions that population levels were low, most recently implied by the genetic evidence (Cassidy *et al*. 2020), but it may be that the archaeology is fooling us; for people who potentially relied extensively on organic material culture which rarely survives, or lived in coastal areas or islands which are now inundated, we simply may be unable to identify all the places fifth millennium hunter-gatherers worked, lived and died. Furthermore, population levels more broadly would perhaps have changed considerably over time, and there are known examples of hunter-gatherers carefully controlling their populations (Cannon 2011) as well as examples of hunter-gatherer populations which fluctuated over time (Habu 2014). Certain places may have been intensively occupied and returned to many times, but other areas may have seen virtually no late activity at all. Conneller (2022) notes, for example, that the English Midlands have an overall lack of Final Mesolithic sites. Islands may not, therefore, be occupied for defence but rather represent nodal points in the landscape, fixed locations for communities to congregate at particular times of the year. The potential significance of dwelling on islands in terms of identity will also be discussed in more detail subsequently.

CONNECTIONS WITH THE WIDER WORLD

For many years the seemingly idiosyncratic nature of the lithic evidence was used to suggest that Britain and Ireland were isolated from one another and from mainland Europe in the fifth millennium cal BC (e.g. Sheridan 2016a, also see Cassidy *et al.* 2020). In particular it was suggested that the different styles of stone tools found in Britain and Ireland meant there was very little contact between people on these islands (Kimball 2006, Saville 2004). The suggestion was that people were therefore insular in the later Mesolithic and did not regularly maintain long-distance contacts across the water. One anomaly to this perceived pattern has long been known about, and this is the Bann flake, a characteristically Irish tool type (see previously) which is also found on the Isle of Man. For example, the site of Rhendhoo has produced both Bann flakes and a fifth-millennium cal BC date (McCartan 2004). The Isle of Man, roughly equidistant between Britain and Ireland, is around 30 miles from both landmasses, and has long demonstrated that people were in contact across this area, at least between Ireland and the Isle of Man, and certainly enough for people to make the same kind of tool on both islands.

However, in the last few years there have been increasing amounts of evidence for widespread contact networks for people within Britain and Ireland, potentially with each other but also further afield. All of this suggests that connectivity was much more widespread. The recent excavations in advance of the Carlisle Northern Development Route at Stainton West in Cumbria have produced many stone tools which demonstrate wider connections across the landscape. Tuff and pebble flint were brought to the site from nearby, along with stones from further afield, including Arran pitchstone and Southern Scottish uplands chert (Fraser Brown *pers. comm.*). Likewise in Ireland there is good evidence for raw materials moving over distances of 50km or so, with some objects moving very large distances (see Warren 2022, p. 130).

There may be further indications of broader networks at this time. Kador (2010) suggests the late Mesolithic Irish polished stone axe was inspired by similar objects on mainland Europe which were being manufactured from the start of the fifth millennium cal BC. Indeed, Thomas (2013) has taken this argument a step further by suggesting that some axes were actually being imported from mainland Europe in the fifth millennium cal BC. Thomas suggests that jadeitite axes, which have been found exclusively in early Neolithic contexts, were actually already old when deposited and as such were therefore imported in the Final Mesolithic, when they were being made on continental Europe. This is an intriguing possibility, but a find of a jadeitite axe or axe fragment from a fifth-millennium context is needed to corroborate this suggestion.

There is, however, some securely dated evidence of connections between Britain and mainland Europe. Bexhill Points are a distinctive type of microlith, named after a site in East Sussex in south-east England. This site produced 124 Final Mesolithic scatters

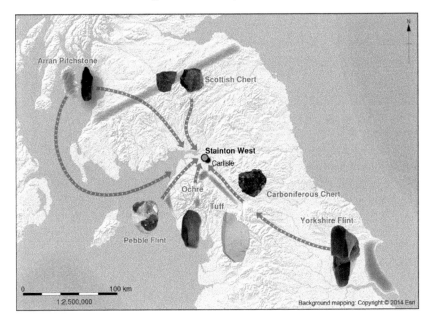

FIGURE 2.8
The movement of stone tools in northern Britain as evidenced from the excavations at Stainton West (copyrighted and reproduced with the kind permission of Oxford Archaeology Ltd)

and many hundreds of thousands of flints (Lawrence *et al.* 2022). The scatters seem to represent the remains of open-air knapping activity around hearths. It is the Bexhill Points which are of particular interest here, as they can quite clearly be paralleled with similar tools found in continental Europe and must therefore be indicative of long-standing contact between people in southern Britain, at least, and the Atlantic façade of Europe (Conneller 2022, p. 419). Moreover, we have already seen that T-axes were a distinctive form of tool found in what is now Scotland, and these objects are best paralleled with similar axes found in north-west Europe more widely in the fifth millennium cal BC, most notably in Denmark. The presence of T-axes in Britain may thus indicate much wider networks and connections beyond Britain at this time, possibly 'a large network of contact and communication, linking hunter-gatherer groups around this area of north-west Europe' (Elliott 2015, p. 240). While the landmass known as Doggerland would have been virtually entirely flooded by the fifth millennium cal BC, it does not mean to say that pre-existing contacts between people to the east and west (Denmark and Britain) did not maintain some form of contact, perhaps utilising the few small islands surviving in the North Sea as stop-over points. This evidence hints at the possibility that cultural affinities and connections may not have been expressed only through stone tool styles but potentially through other mediums, such as wooden objects, basketry or even designs on the human body. These latter objects, of course, rarely, if ever, survive.

There is further intriguing evidence of contact. Bearing in mind that there were no native cattle in Ireland in the Mesolithic, two fifth-millennium cal BC sites in Ireland have produced domesticated cow bones is of significant interest. The sites are Ferriter's Cove, Co. Kerry, and Kilgreany Cave, Co. Waterford, with a possible third site pending publication (Lough Kinale, Co. Longford: Fredengren 2009). This indicates of some sort of contact with mainland Europe, which would be the nearest source of domesticated cattle at this time. It is not necessarily the case that entire cows were shipped over; the bones could equally be the remains of joints of meat. As outlined previously, people clearly had good maritime skills, evidenced by travelling to small islands like Oronsay and catching fish. While no boats have been found from Mesolithic Britain or Ireland, people clearly used them, and would have been able to travel to mainland Europe and back relatively easily (see Callaghan and Scarre 2009, Garrow and Sturt 2011). People on mainland Europe would also have had boats and could also have travelled over to Britain and Ireland. Precisely what these contacts may have involved is unclear – everything from pioneer farmers making first incursions to these shores to exchanges of meat and furs could be envisioned. But we have also seen that there is also now perhaps evidence of fifth-millennium cereal cultivation (see previously). This evidence combined may well indicate hunter-gatherers in Britain and Ireland were in contact with farmers on mainland Europe and experimenting with agricultural practices themselves prior to the full onset of a Neolithic way of life (see next chapter).

Thus, material remains now indicate broad connections for people in the fifth millennium, and definitely across the water to mainland Europe. There are ethnographic parallels which demonstrate the kinds of contacts we might be envisioning. More recent hunter-gatherers in many continents maintained broad-scale contacts, as kin networks and exchange partners, and there would have been plenty of desirable products in Final Mesolithic Britain and Ireland that early Neolithic people on the European mainland would have wanted. Furs and seal fat may have been valuable commodities and were clearly being exchanged across other hunter-gatherer-farmer frontiers in northern Europe (Damm and Forsberg 2014). Family connections may have been equally, if not more, important.

IDENTITY, BELIEF SYSTEMS AND TREATMENT OF THE DEAD

Burials have long been used by archaeologists to provide insights into belief systems. The human bones found amongst the middens on Oronsay has already been described. At present, these are the only known human remains from the fifth millennium in Britain. It is worth noting that human remains are found in caves in Britain in earlier parts of the Mesolithic (see Conneller 2006), but there are notably no known examples from after 5000 cal BC. Ireland has produced a few more examples which indicate the treatment of human remains. The midden of Rockmarshall in County Louth contained a fragment of thigh bone and a fifth-millennium date (Meiklejohn and Woodman 2012). Seven human teeth and five fragments of long bone were also recovered amongst the occupation layers at Ferriter's Cove, Co. Kerry, demonstrating that loose human bone was deposited in a variety of settings. Fragmentary human remains have also been found in Killuragh Cave, Co. Limerick, dating to the fifth millennium cal BC, but here there is the possibility that they were washed into the cave from outside (Dowd 2015, p. 82). The cave of Sramore, Co. Leitrim, has also produced three human bones (fragments from a femur, mandible and humerus), but these have very late fifth-millennium dates and they may actually be earliest Neolithic (Dowd 2015, p. 86). The only other human remains fall into a similar time period; in a peat bog in Stoney Island, Co. Galway, a largely complete human skeleton was recovered at the base of the bog (Meiklejohn and Woodman 2012, p. 32). This find could easily be earliest Neolithic as late Mesolithic.

These finds seem to hint at differences in burial practice between Britain and Ireland in the fifth millennium. The use of caves in Ireland is not, at present, paralleled in Britain, although more evidence needs to be produced in Ireland to confirm their use (Dowd 2015). In both Britain and Ireland it is possible to argue that human bodies were reduced to single loose bones which appear to have become objects which were then deposited in domestic, and presumably other, settings. It is worth noting here that other parts of late Mesolithic Europe have cemeteries which saw the formal burial of the dead, for example, at Skateholm in Sweden and on the island of Hoëdic in Brittany (Schulting and Richards 2001). These cemeteries contain multiple whole burials of men, women and children, often with associated grave goods, and are fifth millennium cal BC in date. These are conspicuously absent from Britain or Ireland.

It is possible, therefore, to suggest one or two possibilities for the treatment of the dead after 5000 cal BC in Britain and Ireland. First, it seems that some people practised excarnation, that is, the reduction of the human body via natural processes such as predation or exposure, down to single, loose bones which may then have circulated with the living and been deposited in particular locations. This practice has a long tradition in Europe dating back into the Upper Palaeolithic and seems to explain the evidence found on shell middens. It also seems possible that people were depositing the dead in watery places, such as rivers, lakes, bogs or the sea. In the case of people with a strong maritime identity, this could have been in a boat, but equally bodies could have been formally disposed in other ways. If people were aware of communities and practices on mainland Europe, which has been argued previously, then they were making a conspicuous decision not to follow this practice, maintaining older or other ways of doing things.

The Oronsay evidence outlined previously also suggested that human bodies were being disposed of in similar ways to animal bodies. Many studies have shown that hunter-gatherers have very particular ways of understanding the animal world, which can be quite different from most agricultural societies (Kent 1989). For example in many hunter-gatherer societies, humans and animals are understood as being analogous and interchangeable; that is, they are regarded as similar beings, albeit with different external appearances. In some hunter-gatherer societies it is thought that humans can be reborn into animal bodies, and animals can become humans (Viveiros de Castro 1998). If this is how people understood animals, then it has quite far-reaching implications for how they dealt with animals, particularly if hunting them, eating them and then disposing of their remains. This is why some hunter-gatherer groups ask the permission of an animal before it is killed for meat, and thanks are given to each animal for giving up its life to sustain people. The remains of an animal once it has been killed are then subject to very specific treatments so as not to offend the dead spirit.

These are general observations about hunter-gatherers which are likely to be relevant for understanding the British and Irish Mesolithic, but it is also possible to suggest some specific relationships. It is hard to imagine that people in the fifth millennium did not have stories or beliefs involving the large mammals that were present in Britain. Deer and pig were clearly being consumed in Britain, and the extensive use of both antler from deer and bone from a variety of mammals indicates that these were important for making material culture. There is less evidence for the utilisation of aurochs (wild cattle), which would have been one of the largest and most powerful animals in British woodlands. Perhaps this animal held a special place in Mesolithic cosmologies. There must have been different cosmologies in place in Ireland, simply because there were no deer or aurochs present. Here it was the brown bear which was the largest mammal in the woods, and there are suggestions that Mesolithic populations actually imported bear to Ireland (Warren *et al*. 2014), demonstrating just how important this animal was in people's ritual lives. There may well have been much closer connections between individual communities and specific animal species, relating in part to what was hunted (see previously), for either meat or other products such as fur. In Brittany, for example, the burials there reveal different animals being used for personal ornamentation between different groups (see Schulting 1996).

It is possible to argue that people living near the coast in Britain and Ireland had the closest affinity with marine animals, perhaps seals. It is easy to envisage people identifying similarities between human and seals, and human and seal communities. Indeed, if it was the case that shell middens were in fact the leftovers after sealing, then people dwelling amongst these remains and leaving parts of human bodies amongst these remains reinforces the significance of these animals. On Oronsay human hand bones were left on top of seal flippers, highlighting the similarities between human and animal. It may well have been the case that these were people whose identities were most closely associated with sealing, fishing and maritime life, and in such a scenario boats would have been particularly important. It is a shame that no boats dating to the Mesolithic have been found in Britain or Ireland. The occupation of islands and the presence of marine resources demonstrate that people must have been competent sailors. Amongst maritime communities boats take on a special significance, and social prestige can be closely linked to seafaring ability (Robinson 2013).

Against this background it is important to remember that the later Mesolithic period saw significant periods of environmental change. Some of these would have been slow and imperceptible within a person's lifetime. Others, however, would have had instant and catastrophic effects, such as the flooding of Doggerland, which would have seriously affected communities and permanently disrupted broader kin and maritime networks in northern Europe. Such a major event would likely have lived on in folk memory and oral tradition. As suggested previously, there is a tendency to describe hunter-gatherers as being in a close and sharing relationship with the natural world. Of course people's lives were bound up with the natural world, being entirely reliant on its bounty for their food, shelter and material possessions. This does not preclude the possibility that, after events such as the rapid loss of key hunting grounds and associated animal and human populations, this relationship with the natural world was somewhat altered. Perhaps giving the dead to the sea may have been seen as placating angry spirits or returning people to a collective ancestral group.

CONCLUSIONS: LIFE IN THE LATE MESOLITHIC

Evidence from Britain and Ireland from the thousand years prior to the onset of the Neolithic demonstrates that people made a living hunting and gathering in very particular ways. They were deliberately mobile, and there was a particular emphasis on the utilisation and occupation of marine, lacustrine or riverine environments. There was a strong emphasis on the repeated use of specific 'persistent' places in the landscape. Some of these places were carefully maintained through the clearance of vegetation. In other instances people marked out lake edges by building wooden platforms. The creation of artificial platforms at some of these sites would have required a big investment of time, entirely unnecessary for simply gaining access to the water. Instead, these platforms can be viewed as the formalisation of the occupation of these places, presumably after many years of use. In addition to this people were attracted to small islands, and it may be that people used islands as much for reasons connected to identity and belief as they did for subsistence or resource purposes. It has been suggested that these islands were thought of as being situated at key interface points, essentially between the land and the water (Bell 2007, p. 335, Fredengren 2002, p. 129). These are certainly the zones occupied by other animals, in coastal locations by seals and inland by birds. We can suggest different groups had particular affinities with certain species, perhaps through resource specialisation or related more to their belief systems. What is becoming increasingly clear is that these were communities who were in contact with people more broadly in north-west Europe. Various innovations appear throughout the fifth millennium demonstrating those broader connections, including new tool types and perhaps even experiments with agriculture. People in the fifth millennium, then, were part of a wider set of communities in north-west Europe. What is intriguing is that many of these people were Neolithic agriculturalists or in contact with these groups. It is this transition to agriculture in Britain and Ireland which we consider in more detail in the next chapter.

RECOMMENDED READING

There are two terrific and new syntheses of the Mesolithic, one on Britain and one on Ireland.

Conneller, C., 2022. *The Mesolithic in Britain*. London: Routledge.
Warren, G., 2022. *Hunter-gatherer Ireland*. Oxford: Oxbow.

You might also want to consider my own very short summary on what ethnography can tell us about past hunter-gatherers. This is designed as an introduction to the cultural anthropology of hunter-gatherers.

Cummings, V., 2007. *The anthropology of hunter-gatherers: Key themes for archaeologists*. London: Duckworth.

CHAPTER 3

All change

The transition to the Neolithic in Britain and Ireland

INTRODUCTION

In the last chapter I looked at the evidence from Britain and Ireland in the fifth millennium cal BC. Archaeological remains suggest that late Mesolithic hunter-gatherers may have specialised in exploiting specific resources which impacted where they lived and how they thought about the world. It appears that late Mesolithic people in both Britain and Ireland were particularly attracted to the coast and often drawn to small islands or marginal locations. It was also suggested that these groups which had previously been considered insular may well have been in contact with people on mainland Europe and therefore might have been aware of what life was like for people who had already adopted agriculture and other Neolithic practices. There were also suggestions that people may have been experimenting with growing cereals, and they may also have imported, or been brought gifts of, domestic animal meat.

The onset of the Neolithic is one of the most profound changes in the history of these islands, as people stopped hunting, if not gathering, and adopted agricultural practices. This chapter focuses on the start of the Neolithic, and in particular on the question of how a new Neolithic way of life appeared in these islands around about the start of the fourth millennium cal BC. After decades of speculation the new ancient DNA evidence has provided unique insights into the mechanisms behind this change. The genetic analysis of peoples across Europe has shown that early European farmer groups from Anatolia dispersed across Europe along two main routes: the Mediterranean or the Danube (Brace and Booth 2022). As they went, they mixed with Mesolithic populations. As such, we now know that the Neolithic was introduced into Britain and Ireland by people from continental Europe, bringing knowledge of the Neolithic practices with them. Moreover, there is limited evidence for the addition of native British and Irish Mesolithic peoples into the genetic pool. This evidence has had to made us rethink this critical period and the processes involved.

SETTING THE SCENE: THE NEOLITHIC OF BRITAIN AND IRELAND

To the east of the River Medway in Kent, two rectangular structures made from timber posts were constructed in the early Neolithic. These structures were not built by the very first Neolithic people in this area, but a few centuries in, presumably once they had established themselves successfully in this area. The structures were kept meticulously clean, and any rubbish from activities undertaken there seem to have been deposited elsewhere, although archaeologists do not know where. However, a few remnants of activity were missed – a cattle tooth, a few crumbs of pottery, some cereal grains and a few stone tools (Hayden 2007). Not far away, to the west of the River Medway, people in the early Neolithic constructed a stone monument now called Coldrum. Built from large slabs of stone set within a mound, the chambered area of the monument then received deposits of the dead (Wysocki *et al*. 2013). These two sites epitomise all of the key elements of a new Neolithic way of life as introduced in Britain and Ireland around the turn of the fourth millennium BC.

The term Neolithic means New Stone Age and is a shorthand term for a period of time which is defined by the first appearance of a characteristic range of objects and material in the archaeological record. The British and Irish early Neolithic can be characterised by the presence of these key elements:

1. Domesticated animals, specifically cattle, sheep, goats and pigs. Apart from the domestic dog, which was present in the Mesolithic, this is the first use of domestic animals in Britain and Ireland. All these animals were domesticated elsewhere and were imported from existing domestic stock on the continent (see subsequently and Chapter 4).

2. Domesticated cereals, specifically domesticated varieties of wheat and barley as well as flax. These were also domesticated elsewhere and thus imported from the continent (see subsequently and Chapter 4).

3. Bowl pottery. This represents the first use of ceramic technology in Britain and Ireland, as there is no evidence of any form of pottery from Mesolithic contexts in Britain or Ireland, unlike in other parts of Europe. Once again this indicates that the knowledge of how to make pottery was imported into these islands by peoples familiar with this technology on the continent (see Chapter 4).

4. Monumental architecture in wood, stone and earth. A wide range of monument forms are found in Britain and Ireland from the start of the Neolithic, including chambered tombs and dolmens, long barrows, causewayed enclosures and cursus monuments (see Chapter 5). We might also include large timber houses, which were constructed in much smaller numbers in Britain and Ireland and undoubtedly had at least partly a domestic function. Once again, these were types of architecture not constructed by the preceding Mesolithic peoples.

5. Distinctive forms of stone tool, including leaf-shaped arrowheads and ground stone axes. The early Neolithic also saw the first utilisation of flint mines and stone axe extraction sites, often high in the mountains (see Chapter 4).

Taken together, these objects and materials are often referred to as the Neolithic 'package' because suites of material from the early Neolithic onwards contain a combination of these items, as we have seen at the two sites in Kent. However, in some areas of Britain and Ireland people adopted some of these elements before others, and in some parts of Britain and Ireland some aspects of the package, especially monument construction, never took place at all. As such, we should be wary of the idea that all people in the Neolithic utilised the entire package just as much as we should be aware that the term Neolithic is also shorthand for a diverse and complex period of time. The Neolithic period ends with the first appearance of metals in the archaeological record, notably copper and bronze (see Chapter 9).

WHERE DID THESE NEOLITHIC THINGS ORIGINATE?

None of the elements of the Neolithic package were first developed in Britain and Ireland – all had continental precursors and were imported from Mainland Europe. We have already seen in Chapter 2 that people prior to the Neolithic had domesticated dogs. However, the key animal species utilised in the Neolithic were domesticated in western Asia. It appears that sheep (*Ovis aries*) and goats (*Capra hircus*) were the earliest herd animals to be domesticated, with domestication events taking place in several different areas of western Asia (Larson and Burger 2013, Zheng *et al*. 2020). A bit later on, around 8500 cal BC, pigs (*Sus scrofa*) were also domesticated from wild boar, and finally aurochs were domesticated to be smaller and more manageable cattle (*Bos taurus*). It seems that all these domestication events took place over a 1000-year period in the landscapes north of the Fertile Crescent (Zeder 2008, Figure 3.1).

Roughly 10,000 years ago the Fertile Crescent became the centre of wheat and barley domestication. At this time people were already collecting wild plant species for food, but they took some of these, notably wheat and barley, and selectively tended and cultivated them (Barker 2004, Chapter 4). Over time this changed key characteristics of these plants so much so that they can be identified archaeologically as morphologically different from their wild progenitors (Salamini *et al*. 2002). It is these domestic plant species, alongside the domestic animal species, which would eventually spread across Europe and become a key part of the Neolithic way of life in both Britain and Ireland (Shennan 2018).

Ceramic technology is older still, and while in Britain and Ireland it first appears in the Neolithic, it is found in a multitude of earlier contexts, ostensibly associated with a variety of different hunter-gatherer populations. Fired clay in the form of both pots and figurines was definitely used in the Upper Palaeolithic/late Pleistocene, and Holocene hunter-gatherers in many different parts of Eurasia also developed ceramics (Jordan and Zvelebil 2009). In contrast to this, in the earliest agricultural communities of the Fertile Crescent, pottery was *not* part of the repertoire; hence the earliest Neolithic peoples there are described as pre-pottery (Pre-Pottery Neolithic A and B). Closer in both space and time, late Mesolithic hunting and gathering populations in northern Europe also incorporated pottery into their repertoire of material culture in multiple different contexts.

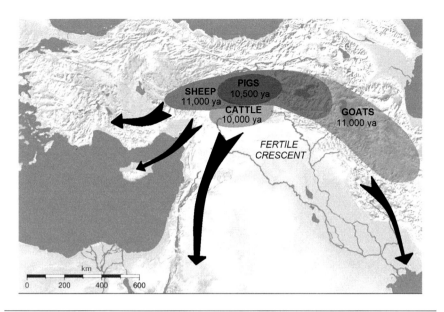

FIGURE 3.1
The estimated locations and dates of different domestic animal species in the Fertile Crescent in western Asia (after Zeder 2008)

It seems likely, therefore, that Mesolithic people in Britain and Ireland were aware of ceramic technology but chose not to make or use it. In the British and Irish record, then, ceramics are one of the earliest of the elements of the Neolithic package to be adopted (see subsequently).

It is important to note that in these three instances from across the globe, the domestication of animals, the domestication of cereals and the first use of ceramic vessels, it was hunter-gatherer populations who were doing the innovating. Moreover, these were not one-off instances of innovation, but hunter-gatherers elsewhere around the globe domesticated other species, both plant and animal (see, for example, Shennan 2018). This is important because the debate around the start of the Neolithic in Britain and Ireland has previously focused on whether or not it was Mesolithic hunter-gatherer populations who were responsible for the onset of the Neolithic. We will see this debate in more detail subsequently, but here it is just worth stressing that hunter-gatherers are more than capable of adopting new ways of doing things – indeed, it was hunters and gatherers elsewhere who came up with these practices in the first place.

The origins of monumentality are also quite difficult to tie down. One site, that of Göbekli Tepe in modern-day Türkiye, is generally regarded as one of the precursors of Neolithic monumentality. The site was in use from 9500 cal BC in the Pre-Pottery Neolithic A, so people were using domesticated cereals and also domestic sheep and goats but also supplementing this with wild resources. Carved and decorated limestone pillars were set upright in circles and with walls running between them. Two larger slabs were erected at the centre, and it is possible the whole thing was roofed (Dietrich *et al*. 2012). This exact form of monumentality did not spread beyond this area, but it is evidence that building monuments in some form is, very broadly, contemporary with the start of the use of domesticated plants and animals. Different monumental forms then make an appearance over the subsequent millennia as Neolithic practices spread into Europe: monumental longhouses in the latter part of the sixth millennium in Central Europe and monuments using large stones in north-western Europe in particular in the fifth millennium cal BC onwards (see subsequently). At the very least we know that the concept of monumentality originated elsewhere before the construction of similar, if not identical, sites in Britain and Ireland (Schutz Paulsson 2017).

New ways of working with stone and a fascination in particular with strikingly coloured stones from remote locations also clearly had origins on Mainland Europe. From the sixth millennium onwards, perhaps from as early as 5500 cal BC, a series of Alpine jadeitites were extracted from the Italian Alps and distributed widely in western Europe (Sheridan *et al*. 2019). These strikingly coloured and distinctive stones were used to make new forms of material culture, including beautiful polished stone axes. This practice thus significantly pre-dates the appearance of stone axe extraction sites and polished stone objects in Britain, although a small number are known from late Mesolithic contexts in Ireland. Likewise, flint mining is documented on Mainland Europe, most notably in Belgium in the fifth millennium, and thus predates the same practice found at a later date in these islands.

This very brief summary of the different aspects of Neolithic practices demonstrates that every element had a distant origin, mainly, in the case of domestic plants and animals, in the Near East. In addition to this archaeological evidence, we can now add the ancient DNA results to this picture. Ancient DNA shows that three distinctive groups of hunter-gatherers in the Near East were those initiating and developing domestication while sharing technological innovations (Fernández-Domínguez 2022, p. 68). Early farming populations predominantly had this Near Eastern genetic signature but with the addition of some genetic input from Anatolia (eastern Türkiye), and it was from this point that the Neolithic spread into Europe. Ancient DNA studies have shown that the first farmers across many parts of Europe have an Anatolian genetic signature, albeit with the addition of varying amounts of hunter-gatherer genes in different areas (see, for example, Allentoft *et al*. 2022, Rivollat *et al*. 2020). These results have demonstrated that people moved out of the Near East and in doing so took with them agricultural practices which then spread across Europe. With this very broad-brush introduction to the distant origins of the Neolithic package, we now turn our attention in more detail closer to home.

THE PICTURE IN NORTHERN EUROPE IN THE FIFTH MILLENNIUM

We have seen, then, that the different elements of the Neolithic package had their origins in different times and places but most pre-dating the onset of the Neolithic in Britain and Ireland by many thousands of years. Over time, and from origins with people from the Near East, Neolithic communities spread into Europe. By the fifth millennium cal BC, while Britain and Ireland were still practising a hunting and gathering lifestyle, Neolithic people with associated agricultural practices were edging ever closer into northern Europe. We are now going to consider, albeit briefly, three key sequences from northern Europe: Northern France, the Low Countries and southern Scandinavia. Each of these areas provides an interesting contrast to the nature of the Neolithic in Britain and Ireland. These case study regions also highlight that there was no single and predetermined Neolithic sweeping across Europe but localised and regionally specific transitions involving different combinations of things and people (cf. Cummings and Harris 2011, 2014). This will set the scene for what subsequently happened in Britain and Ireland.

Northern France

It was during the fifth millennium cal BC that the first evidence for Neolithic practices appeared in northern France. We have good evidence for how this change to the Neolithic took place, and it is clear that there were two main spheres of influence affecting this key area. To the south-east, farming groups known as the *Bandkeramik* moved out of their core central European homeland to the north and west of the Paris Basin. These groups are known to archaeologists as the 'Villeneuve-Saint-Germain', and they spread out into Normandy and western Brittany, as well as to Jersey and Guernsey, from 5000–4700 cal BC (Scarre 2011, p. 46). These were groups of people who used domesticates, pottery and polished stone rings made from jades, and they built distinctive trapezoidal houses (as evidenced at the site of Le Haut-Mée, for example: Cassen *et al*. 1998). They would have encountered groups practising hunting and gathering in the new regions they moved into, and a number were subsequently incorporated into this Neolithic society (Rivollat *et al*. 2020).

At the same time to the south on the Atlantic façade, another distinctive Neolithic society was spreading northwards. These Cardial, then Epicardial, groups did not build long houses, but they did use domesticates and pottery (Scarre 2011, p. 53). We now know from the ancient DNA that these groups were quite a complex mix of incoming farming populations who could trace their genetic ancestry to Anatolia and native hunter-gatherers, both at source and as they spread into western France (Rivollat *et al*. 2020). It seems that in addition to these incoming Neolithic groups, on the very north-western fringes of Brittany, Mesolithic hunting and gathering groups persisted. The two best-known sites from these surviving hunter-gatherer groups are the coastal sites of Téviec and Hoëdic in the Morbihan. These are shell middens associated with burials which date to 5200–4800 cal BC (Schulting and Richards 2001). At the time of occupation, Hoëdic was an island, while Téviec was situated on the coast of the mainland. Other middens are known in the region, such as Beg-er-Vil, dating between 5200 and 4700 cal BC (Scarre 2011, p. 67), and inland sites have also been recorded. It seems, then, that there were some hunter-gatherers in western Brittany who retained a Mesolithic way of life well into the fifth millennium cal BC, while people to the south and east were making a living through agriculture, incorporating some hunter-gatherers into their Neolithic communities as they went.

Somewhere between 4800 and 4700 cal BC, it seems that people on the north-western fringes of Brittany started practising a Neolithic lifestyle. This involved a change from hunting and gathering to cereal cultivation and keeping domesticated animals, making

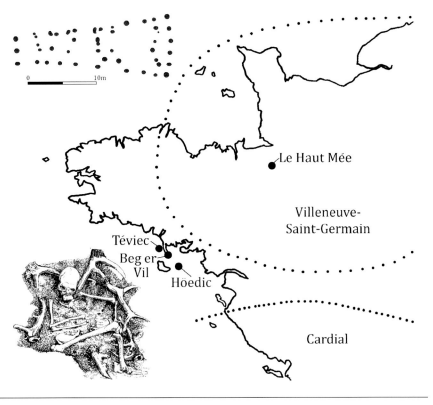

FIGURE 3.2
Northern France at the start of the fifth millennium BC, showing the location of farming groups (Villeneuve-Saint-Germain and Cardial) and hunter-gatherers, and sites named in the text (after Scarre 2011). Plan of the house at Le Haut Mée (top left, after Cassen et al. 1998) and Grave K at Höedic (after Péquart and Péquart 1954)

pottery and polished stone axes and building monuments. This is known as the Castellic, which then became the Late Castellic towards the end of the fifth millennium cal BC (Cassen 2009). What we do not know at present due to the scarcity of preserved human remains is if this change was the result of the substantial movement of Neolithic people into the area, as occurred in many other parts of Europe at the onset of the Neolithic, or whether this was an entirely indigenous uptake of the Neolithic. If it was the latter it would be rather unusual in Europe: future aDNA studies might be able to confirm the sequence of events, but the overall lack of human remains from this period is currently hindering research in this area. If this switch to the Neolithic did see the movements of people into north-western Brittany, we still do not know why this happened at this exact time.

While there is much we still do not know, the monuments of Brittany survive particularly well and have been studied in depth. These monuments are also distinctive from early Neolithic sequences elsewhere because they involve the substantial use of large stones to create distinctive monuments. The earliest form of monument constructed in Brittany seems to have been the menhirs (large standing stones: see Tilley 2004, Chapter 2,

Whittle 2000). The most exceptional example of a menhir is the Grand Menhir Brisé, which weighed somewhere around 300 tonnes (Cassen 2009): today it lies broken in four pieces, but if it ever stood upright, it would have been a phenomenal sight. Menhirs were often shaped and/or decorated and often resemble axes. Long mounds (*tertres*) and long cairns, often with cists, were also constructed in the early Castellic. Massive Carnac mounds, huge accumulations of earth and stone (Laporte *et al.* 2001), were also built: some of these were so large that chapels have been built on top of them in more recent times. Some of these monuments contained fantastic deposits of polished jadeitite artefacts, including stone axes, such as Mané er Hroëck. From around 4200 BC stone passage graves were built in large numbers in Brittany, and it seems likely that circular stone settings and enclosures along with some smaller stone rows were also built at this time (Scarre 2011, p. 118). The end result is a plethora of monuments built from stone and earth in western Brittany in the fifth millennium cal BC.

The sequence of monument construction in the latter part of the fifth millennium alongside the collection of large numbers of distinctive forms of material culture such as the objects made from jadeitite is particularly striking. It is the stone monuments in particular which are important for considering the origins of similar forms found in Britain and Ireland (see Chapter 5), but otherwise the sequence in Brittany is quite different from that on our islands. Instead it is the sequence of Neolithic peoples found to further to the east, in coastal Normandy and the Nord-Pas-de-Calais regions, which may have more bearing on the origins of the Neolithic in Britain and Ireland. In these areas the Villeneuve-Saint-Germain groups dating from the earlier part of the fifth millennium cal BC emerged from peoples who had moved into the area descended from Central European groups who made a living on good-quality (loess) soils and built long houses. Over time

FIGURE 3.3
Breton monuments from the fifth millennium BC. Top: Barnenez; bottom: Le Grand Menhir Brisé

these groups moving away from the longhouses of their predecessors to a much wider variety of domestic structures and also started to build long mounds/enclosures known as 'Passy type' of timber and earth up to 300m long which contained a single burial with associated grave goods (Chambon and Thomas 2010). This distinctive Neolithic phase is known as the 'Cerny' and occurred in the middle part of the fifth millennium BC. In the latter part of the millennium these people changed practices again and became the 'Northern Chasséen', with changes to material culture, especially pottery. There are also passage graves in Normandy, likely to be similar in date to those in Brittany, and further east still, people chose to build large earthen enclosures instead, such as at the site of Balloy, located adjacent to a mass of Passy burials (Bostyn *et al.* 2011). The Northern Chasséen groups also created clusters of pits with associated deposits (Vanmortfort 2001). Many authors have identified this sequence as being important for understanding the Neolithic sequence in the east of Britain in particular, and while it does not provide a direct comparison for what we find in Britain and Ireland, there are elements of this repertoire which are found once the Neolithic reaches our shores (see, for example, Sheridan 2016b, Thomas 2013, Whittle *et al.* 2011).

The Low Countries

There was a different sequence of events in the Low Countries (modern-day Belgium and the Netherlands) in the change from hunting and gathering to agriculture. In the southern parts of this area, *Bandkeramik* farming communities had arrived from the later sixth millennium cal BC, but instead of continuing to spread northwards, a hiatus occurred. This resulted in agriculturalists living to the south of the area, occupying the best agricultural soils, and hunter-gatherers to the north in the lower river valleys, estuaries and coasts. This did not mean that there was a strict boundary across which people did not move: in fact, it was quite the opposite. There is evidence from these areas that over a thousand-year period, agricultural people adopted elements of their neighbours' hunting and gathering lifestyles, and vice versa (Louwe Koojimans 2007, Thorpe 2015, p. 219). Thus the transition from hunter-gatherer to farmer, from Mesolithic to Neolithic, was slow and drawn out and not a straightforward change from one way of life to another.

The agricultural groups in the Low Countries after 5000 cal BC who were descended from *Bandkeramik* farming communities are known in the literature as the Rössen/Blicquy and Michelsberg cultures (Louwe Koojimans 2007). These were groups who relied on agricultural produce, built substantial wooden long houses and used pottery (Crombé and Vanmortfort 2007). To the north by the coast and around the Rhine Delta, late Mesolithic hunting and gathering groups are evidenced at sites like those around the type site of Swifterbant: like other late Mesolithic coastal groups, they relied on a variety of resources and did not live permanently in any one place. However, these Swifterbant groups began to incorporate Neolithic things into their otherwise hunting and gathering lifestyles. From about 5000 cal BC this included adzes and perforated stone wedges probably exchanged with farming groups (Raemaekers *et al.* 2021, Thomas 2013, pp. 76–77), as well as pottery (Figure 3.4). The pottery, however, was made by the foraging groups themselves, mainly for processing fish (Raemaekers *et al.* 2021), and there is the possibility this was a technology acquired primarily from hunter-gatherers to

FIGURE 3.4
Distinctive fifth-millennium BC hunter-gatherer pottery from northern Germany (left) and Belgium (right) (after Hartz et al. 2007 and Crombé and Vanmortfort 2007)

the east as opposed to from the agriculturalists to the south (Jordan and Zvelebil 2009, Shennan 2018, p. 160). From around 4500 cal BC small quantities of domesticated animals started to appear in Swifterbant contexts. This may mean that hunting and gathering groups began to keep a few domesticated animals while predominantly still hunting for their meat, but equally it may be that joints of meat were exchanged with farming groups to the south (Louwe Koojimans 2007, p. 297).

Another change is noted around 4300 cal BC. It is at this point that both the Swifterbant foragers and the encircling agricultural groups both changed practices. Amongst the Swifterbant groups there was the first use of cereals alongside the more visible presence of pig (Raemaekers et al. 2021), suggesting an increased interest in Neolithic practices. However, amongst the agricultural populations surrounding this area, people seem to have become much more dispersed in the landscape, in this instance indicating the ongoing and changing nature of Neolithic groups. It seems that while the Neolithic groups relied on pastoral economies, they now started to supplement this with the hunting of wild species. People also started building large ditched enclosures, which were likely to have been centralised ceremonial centres (Crombé and Vanmortfort 2007, Thomas 2013, p. 77). It was only around 3400 cal BC that all groups across the entirety of the Low Countries switched to a fully agricultural way of life after utilising elements of both foraging and farming for nearly 2000 years. This sequence is interesting because it does genuinely seem to be an instance of where hunting and gathering peoples adopted, piecemeal and over an extended period of time, Neolithic practices and material culture from neighbouring agricultural people (Shennan 2018, p. 152). At the time of writing there are no results from ancient DNA analyses, and of course these may change the picture once again. This sequence also offers an interesting contrast to the last area of north-west Europe we will consider: northern Germany and southern Scandinavia.

Northern Germany and southern Scandinavia

The last area in north-west Europe to be considered here is northern Germany and southern Scandinavia. This part of northern Europe may seem to be too far away from Britain to be relevant for thinking about connections in the fifth millennium cal BC. However, areas which now lie under the North Sea, in particular the Dogger Bank ('Doggerland'), had only recently been submerged at the start of the fifth millennium, and so people may well have had strong connections across this area which they may have tried to maintain even after parts of the land were inundated. Even if this was not the case, in terms of timings, the sequence of Neolithisation is very similar to that for Britain and Ireland, so this makes an interesting area to consider. As we saw previously, *Bandkeramik* farming communities had moved into the Northern European Plain prior to 5000 BC, but they did not expand beyond the good agricultural soils. This means that by the start of the fifth millennium cal BC there were established post-*Bandkeramik* farming groups to the south and numerous late Mesolithic hunting and gathering populations in northern Germany and in southern Scandinavia (Hartz *et al*. 2007).

The late Mesolithic in this area is known as the 'Ertebølle' culture. As in the Low Countries, there is some evidence that the foraging Ertebølle groups were in contact with their farming neighbours to the south, so Ertebølle people also acquired components from their Neolithic neighbours' material culture sets. Some Neolithic objects were imported into northern Germany and southern Scandinavia – shafthole adzes in particular, alongside a few other exotic items (Larsson 2007, Thomas 2013, p. 66). It is also interesting that there was the production of pottery amongst Ertebølle groups, but this seems to have been a technology which was imported from other hunting and gathering groups to the east (Jordan and Zvelebil 2009), and as a result the pots themselves were made locally and in a distinctive Ertebølle style used for fish processing (Figure 3.5). Unlike the Low Countries, however, there is little evidence for foraging groups beginning to use domesticates, so it seems that the Ertebølle people continued to hunt and gather in order to make a living.

By the end of the fifth millennium cal BC, the TRB (*Trichterbecherkultur*) followed on from the post-*Bandkeramik* farming groups to the south of northern Germany. The TRB, like the Michelsberg to the west, appears to have seen a more dispersed occupation of the landscape, probably involving transhumance and the movement of livestock, and new forms of pottery were also introduced (Larsson 2007, p. 603). However it seems that the TRB did not involve substantial amounts of hunting (Midgley 2005). The TRB also saw an increased emphasis on monumentality, especially long barrows, megalithic dolmens and enclosures as well as the production of polished flint axes (Wunderlich *et al*. 2019). The TRB, then, is in keeping with the broad evolution of Neolithic societies in north-west Europe in the late fifth millennium cal BC. However, it is also at this time that these groups began to expand again, moving this time into northern Germany and southern Scandinavia between 4100 cal BC in northern Germany and 4000 cal BC in southern Scandinavia (Hartz *et al*. 2007). The genetic evidence indicates that this involved more or less complete population replacement, with very few native hunting and gathering peoples marrying into the incoming Neolithic groups (Allentoft *et al*. 2022). This seems to represent the sudden and abrupt end to a lifestyle based on foraging which had been

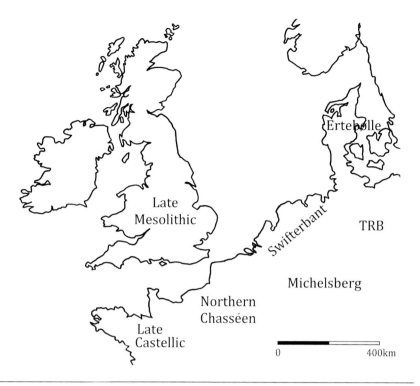

FIGURE 3.5
North-west Europe towards the end of the fifth millennium BC, indicating the main cultural groups discussed in the text

so successful in this area for many millennia and the rapid adoption of an agricultural way of life around 4000 cal BC. However, the continued use of shell middens into the Neolithic hints at the possibility of a more complex picture than the complete replacement of Neolithic peoples (Allentoft *et al*. 2022). Again, further genetic work alongside continued archaeological investigations will, no doubt, shed further light on this in due course.

In this brief summary of the development and spread of a Neolithic way of life into areas bordering Britain and Ireland, it is clear that the Neolithic arrived through a range of different processes. First, it is clear that the actual movement of people occurred in a number of areas, bringing agriculture and associated Neolithic practices with them. However, while this was overwhelmingly the case in most areas, it did not happen everywhere, and there is evidence that in the margins of northern Europe it was the native hunting and gathering peoples who adopted elements of the Neolithic. This brief review also highlights that a range of different Neolithic lifestyles emerged during the latter part of the fifth millennium cal BC. None of these were identical, with slightly different versions of a Neolithic way of life emerging in each area. All involved the use of pottery, and some included the construction of some form of monumentality. Some included a mix of hunting and gathering and farming, while others relied almost entirely on agriculture. What is crucial for understanding the British and Irish sequence is that none of these versions of the north-west European Neolithic were directly imported onto these shores.

Instead, the Neolithic of Britain and Ireland is different again. First, however, we consider the mechanisms by which the Neolithic arrived onto the shores of Britain and Ireland.

HOW DID THE NEOLITHIC ARRIVE INTO BRITAIN AND IRELAND?

We know in the late fifth millennium cal BC people on Mainland Europe were practising a Neolithic way of life, albeit one that varied from place to place. We also know that there were hunter-gatherer populations living in both Britain and Ireland, and there is some evidence of contact between those groups and farmers in Europe. While there is very little evidence for imported material culture, as we saw in the Low Countries and southern Scandinavia, there is evidence that at least some domesticates (either as animals or as joints of meat) were brought over, and there is also the possibility of some very small-scale and localised experimentation with cereal cultivation (see previous chapter). Unlike hunter-gatherer populations to the south-east, however, Mesolithic peoples in Britain and Ireland did not use pottery. The picture, therefore, seems to be that Britain and Ireland were not completely isolated from Mainland Europe in the fifth millennium BC, but equally they did not regularly engage with contacts with Neolithic peoples there. The one fundamental difference between Britain and Ireland and the other areas we have examined so far is that there is a substantial waterway to cross in order reach our islands: the English Channel to reach Britain and the Celtic Sea to reach Ireland.

If you read anything written predating 2018 you will see that there were two main models for how the Neolithic arrived into Britain and Ireland (and see Cummings 2014, Thomas 2013). The first was known as the *indigenist* approach and suggested that the native peoples of Britain and Ireland played a significant role in the uptake of the Neolithic (e.g. Thomas 1988, Zvelebil 2000). It was suggested that there could have been a period of time when people in these islands knew about domesticates in particular but did not chose the adopt them, slowly choosing to integrate them into their subsistence practices before finally 'going over' fully to an agricultural way of life (Zvelebil and Rowley Conwy 1984, 1986). Other authors highlighted the importance and desirability of other elements of the Neolithic package, arguing that it was monuments and artefacts that played a more prominent role in hunter-gatherers choosing to become Neolithic agriculturalists (Thomas 1988, 1996a, 2013, pp. 152–157). These models proposed that small numbers of Neolithic people may have crossed the waters around these islands, but it was the native peoples that were the prime movers in the process.

Earlier accounts beginning with Childe (1925) and Piggott (1954) had considered that it was the movement of people from Europe which had been the main way that the Neolithic arrived into Britain and Ireland (and also see Ammerman and Cavalli-Sforza 1984 and Rowley Conwy 2004). These broad considerations were replaced by a much more specific account of the specific origins of colonisation. In a number of papers, Sheridan (e.g. 2004a, 2010b) has argued that there were several separate strands of colonisation from Mainland Europe into Britain and Ireland. After an initial but failed attempt in south-west Ireland (as evidence by the domesticated cattle bone from Ferriter's Cove), the first successful wave, an Atlantic Breton strand, saw people leaving southern Brittany and moving to the west coast of Britain and the north coast of Ireland prior to 4000 BC (Sheridan 2010b, pp. 91–95). It is argued that subsequent to this people using a Carinated Bowl tradition arrived into large parts of Britain and Ireland from northern France, bringing with them much of the Neolithic package. Sheridan argues that the final colonisation was from Normandy, marked by the emergence of distinctive pot styles and the presence of rotunda graves (Sheridan 2010b, pp. 100–101). The prime movers in Sheridan's model were therefore various continental groups.

We have already seen that there is now genetic evidence that people originating in Anatolia moved into Europe, bringing Neolithic practices such as agriculture with them from their origins in and around the Fertile Crescent. The genetic evidence from those individuals sampled in Britain and Ireland shows the same Anatolian ancestry, albeit with signatures which suggest they probably came via the Mediterranean (Brace *et al*. 2019, Brace and Booth 2022). This evidence does not imply that peoples from Iberia moved directly into Britain and Ireland. Instead, it is likely that the generations of people whose ancestors originated in Iberia spread into north-western Europe in the fifth millennium BC, and from there people moved across the seas into Britain and Ireland (Brace *et al*. 2019). There is limited evidence for the addition of native Mesolithic peoples into the genetic pool – there may be a small amount of hunter-gatherer genetic input in western Scotland (see Mithen 2022), but otherwise the data suggest the replacement of population with the onset of the Neolithic. The genetic evidence therefore indicates that agricultural peoples on Continental Europe moved into Britain and Ireland, bringing with them Neolithic practices and ultimately replacing the hunting and gathering Mesolithic people on these islands.

WHEN DID THE NEOLITHIC START?

For many years archaeologists estimated that the Neolithic arrived into Britain and Ireland somewhere in the centuries around 4000 cal BC. As we have seen, it was generally considered a package of things which included domesticates, pottery, monuments and new stone tools. In the last few years, however, our understanding of the precise date for the start of the Neolithic has been greatly enhanced by a project which has used new techniques which enable us to estimate much more precisely the beginning of the Neolithic in Britain and Ireland. Using Bayesian statistics to model radiocarbon dates, a new chronological framework has been produced (see Whittle *et al*. 2011). One key result of this work is that it has demonstrated that the first appearance of Neolithic things and practices did not occur simultaneously across Britain and Ireland. Instead, it was a *staggered start*, with people arriving into south-east England initially from where Neolithic people and material culture spread north and west of this area (Whittle *et al*. 2011, pp. 833–843, Figure 3.5). The speed at which the Neolithic spread into different parts of Britain and Ireland can also be estimated from this work, suggesting that Neolithic practices took about 100 years to appear beyond south-east England, but beyond that point, the Neolithic began in most other areas after another hundred years, somewhere around 3800 cal BC (see Figure 3.6). The only problem area in the estimates for the start of the Neolithic is western Ireland. Whittle *et al*. (2011) suggest that it likely began between 3850 and 3740 cal BC, but the enclosure site of Magheraboy in County Sligo

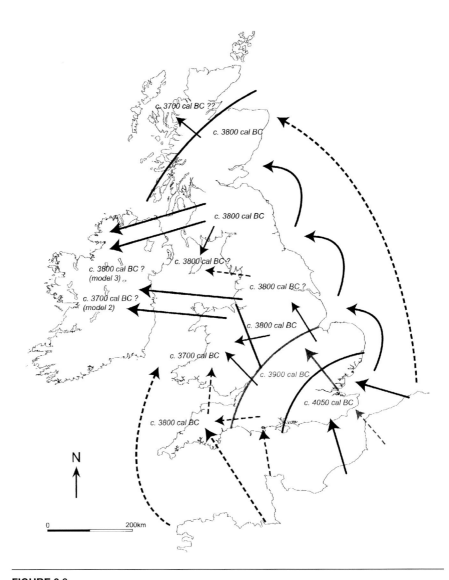

FIGURE 3.6
Suggested dates for the first appearance of Neolithic things in Britain and Ireland (after Whittle et al. 2011, figure 15.8)

has produced dates which are several hundred years before this date. This is likely to be an issue with the charcoal dates, but more work is required in western Ireland to resolve this (also see Whittle *et al*. 2011, Chapter 14).

This work has also revealed that not all elements of a full Neolithic package appeared right at the onset of the Neolithic in each area. In the south-east of England where the Neolithic first appeared, the work by Whittle *et al*. (2011) has suggested that the Neolithic package did not all appear at the same time. Instead, pottery and domesticates were the first Neolithic things to be used, presumably the key elements needed

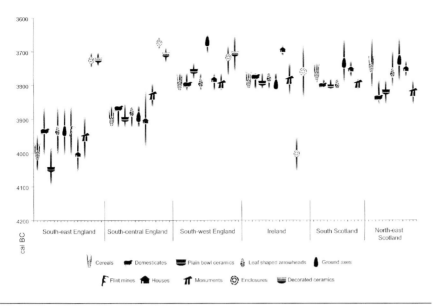

FIGURE 3.7
Diagram indicating the appearance of elements of the Neolithic package in parts of Britain and Ireland (reproduced from Whittle *et al*. 2011, figure 14.179 with the permission of the authors)

by migrating groups as they set up new communities on these shores. It took a few generations before people started building monuments and houses (Whittle *et al*. 2011, p. 840). However, in northern and western areas, where the Neolithic began a few hundred years later, it appears that there was genuinely a Neolithic package which was imported and utilised simultaneously (Figure 3.7). Included alongside the genetic data, we can now argue that people on Mainland Europe left in a series of small boats (see Garrow and Sturt 2011) and settled in the closest point to the Continent – south-east England. From there populations prospered and grew and a few generations later spread into southern Britain more widely, perhaps bolstered by more incoming peoples from the Continent with whom we might assume they retained some level of contact or from new streams of incomers. The success of this endeavour seems to have initiated further incursions of people from the Continent, perhaps from different source areas but now supported by local and successful agricultural groups. We might argue for a similar situation in Ireland, with primary incoming groups choosing the western coast of Ireland for their settlements, from where they spread east, bolstered in numbers by people who were born on Mainland Europe.

WHAT WE DO NOT YET KNOW ABOUT THE TRANSITION TO THE NEOLITHIC

It might appear that the debate that once raged about the Mesolithic-Neolithic transition is now consigned to history. Certainly, we know *who* was implicated in the transition to the Neolithic in Britain and Ireland: for the most part it seems to be agricultural groups

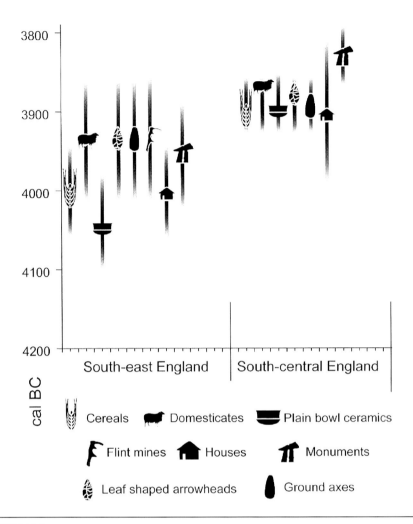

FIGURE 3.8
Diagram indicating the appearance of elements of the Neolithic package in south-east and south-central England (after Whittle *et al*. 2011, figure 14.179)

on the Continent moving over to Britain and Ireland, not native peoples choosing to go over to a Neolithic way of life. We also know *when* those Neolithic people moved into these islands from Mainland Europe: a staggered start which began and focused on south-east England initially before involving other parts of these islands. There remain, however, quite a few questions that we cannot, as yet, answer fully in relation to this fascinating period of prehistory.

First, what was the precise nature of contact between Mesolithic people in Britain and Ireland and the groups in Europe in the latter part of the fifth millennium cal BC? We have seen in the previous chapter that there is evidence of some form of contact between

Britain, Ireland and continental Europe. Were these random encounters? We know that Mesolithic people were proficient sailors who would have been more than capable of crossing, for example, the English Channel. Did they occasionally set sail only to encounter unknown peoples the other side of the water? If so, were these encounters friendly or hostile? Of course it is entirely possible that Mesolithic people in Britain and Ireland remained in contact with other hunting and gathering groups on the Mainland, and we have seen evidence for these in the later part of the fifth millennium cal BC. They may also have been in contact with farming groups there. The other possibility is that Neolithic people, perhaps contemplating larger-scale colonisations, travelled over to Britain and Ireland, perhaps scouting out new lands to occupy. This is certainly the argument made by Sheridan (2010b) for the early occurrences of domestic animal bone in south-west Ireland at places like Ferriter's Cove. They may also have brought over cereals which hunting groups could have encountered and perhaps even experimented with. All of these situations could be the case: there is good evidence to suggest complex, dynamic and multi-directional migrations of people at times like this (see Cummings *et al.* 2022, Thomas 2022).

The next question is – what happened once Neolithic people arrived into Britain and Ireland? The genetic evidence suggests there might have been some low-level integration of native people into Neolithic groups, but not everywhere consistently. Did Mesolithic people simply move away from core areas of colonisation into different landscapes less suited to farming? Did they attempt to carry on making a living hunting and gathering? If the native hunting and gathering populations of Britain and Ireland had survived and carried on practising their existing way of life, we might ultimately expect those groups to coalesce with Neolithic people, as is evidenced elsewhere in the European sequence. In some areas of Mainland Europe there appear to be two populations present in the landscape immediately after initial colonisation by incoming Neolithic groups, albeit with the hunter-gatherer groups leaving little material trace. After a few centuries multiple different groups of hunter-gatherers seem to re-emerge and become integrated with the now-settled Neolithic people, as evidenced in the genetic data (e.g. Brace *et al.* 2019, Fernandez *et al.* 2019, Fraser *et al.* 2018, Rivollat *et al.* 2020). However, this does not occur in the British and Irish sequence, with only one possible exception – that of Western Scotland (and see Mithen 2022).

This might mean that there were really quite low levels of population in the late Mesolithic and that these groups simply died out over a relatively short time scale. It has been argued that this was concomitant with a population boom at the start of the Neolithic, where incoming peoples were extremely successful (Shennan 2018). We must also not rule out a less pleasant end for the native peoples of Britain and Ireland. As we will see in the following chapters, there are surprisingly high incidences of violence amongst early Neolithic groups (e.g. Schulting and Wysocki 2005) – there is an implicit assumption that this was interpersonal violence amongst competing agricultural groups. This may well be the case, but it does not rule out the possibility that once native people had outlasted their usefulness to the incomers (knowledge of the local environment), they were deliberately targeted and driven from their lands (and see Gron *et al.* 2018). This, of course, is not without precedent in more recent times in other parts of the world.

CONCLUSION

The transition to the Neolithic has been debated at length for years. Thanks to the genetic data we are now confident that the beginnings of agriculture and concomitant Neolithic practices, which in Britain and Ireland include making pottery and building monuments were introduced into these islands by peoples from Mainland Europe. Their arrival on our shores seems to have taken place over a period of several hundred years and may have involved Neolithic people from different parts of northern Europe, as well as groups already here growing their numbers rapidly and expanding out from pioneer settlements. At such times of profound change for migrating people, it is therefore no great surprise that their material expressions such as pottery and monuments were also quite different from their origin points on the continent and rapidly took on regional differences. The fate of the native hunter-gatherers is less clear at present, but it seems that apart from some enclaves such as western Scotland, this way of life did not continue much past the first few hundred years after the arrival of the Neolithic. As such, this was one of the most dramatic changes to these islands in their history – the change from people making a living hunting and gathering to one based on agricultural production.

RECOMMENDED FURTHER READING

The origins of the Neolithic across Europe overview

Shennan, S., 2018. *The first farmers of Europe: An evolutionary perspective*. Cambridge: Cambridge University Press.

The genetic evidence

Brace, S., Diekmann, Y., Booth, T. J., *et al*., 2019. Ancient genomes indicate population replacement in early Neolithic Britain. *Nature Ecology and Evolution*, 3, 765–771.

Whittle, A., Pollard, J., and Greaney, S., eds., 2022. *Ancient DNA and the European Neolithic*. Oxford: Oxbow.

The dating and spread of the Neolithic in Britain and Ireland

Whittle, A., Healy, F., and Bayliss, A., 2011. *Gathering time: Dating the early Neolithic enclosures of southern Britain and Ireland*. Oxford: Oxbow.

Models for the transition

Sheridan, A., 2010b. The Neolithization of Britain and Ireland: The 'big picture'. *In:* B. Finlayson and G. Warren, eds. *Landscapes in transition*. Oxford: Oxbow, 89–105.

Thomas, J., 2022. Neolithization and population replacement in Britain: An alternative view. *Cambridge Archaeological Journal*, 32 (3), 507–525.

CHAPTER 4

A brave new world

Life in the early Neolithic of Britain and Ireland

INTRODUCTION

In the previous chapter we saw how the Neolithic was introduced into southern England by people from Mainland Europe. However, it probably took several hundred years before Neolithic people and practices had spread throughout the whole of Britain and Ireland (Whittle *et al*. 2011). This chapter picks up the story by discussing various aspects of how people lived in the early Neolithic, with a particular emphasis on material culture, subsistence and settlement. This includes a consideration of the new types of material culture introduced into Britain and Ireland at the start of the Neolithic, such as polished stone axes and pottery, alongside new plants and animals, including domesticated cattle, sheep, goats and pigs and cereals. It also considers the evidence for settlement and houses from the early Neolithic. This is not to suggest that monumentality in early Neolithic Britain and Ireland was not an essential part of everyday life for people at the time, but monuments and mortuary practice are dealt with separately in the next chapter. As we will see in this chapter, while a new range of things, animals and architectures were clearly introduced into Britain and Ireland, they were not adopted consistently, either in space or time, although it is fair to say our evidence is somewhat uneven from across Britain and Ireland. Certain traditions were adopted with more vigour in some places than others and at certain times. Moreover, while the early Neolithic here is defined as the start of the Neolithic in each area (see previous chapter) up to between 3500 and 3400 cal BC, this does not mean ways of doing things were homogenous throughout this period. Instead, there are important horizons or peaks in activity. As will be shown throughout this and the next two chapters, there is also often no clear end to particular ways of doing things or distinctive types of material culture. Instead there were considerable elements of continuity into the middle Neolithic and beyond. This means that there was a mosaic of related yet varied practices across these islands.

DOI: 10.4324/9781003387329-4

MATERIAL CULTURE: INTRODUCTION

It appears that Neolithic people admired symmetry and fine finish in their artefacts, respected tradition and valued things from far away. At a time before metals, they seem to have been attracted to objects with polish and sheen as well as making things from materials in a range of distinctive colours. The first section of this chapter considers the different types of material culture used in the early Neolithic. This includes some objects which would have been ubiquitous at this time, most notably stone tools and objects made from organic materials such as leather, wood and bone; many of these items would have been used on a daily basis. Within this broader category of everyday items, some would have been more important than others for expressions of social identity (clothes, for example) or status (perhaps basketry or textiles). Other early Neolithic objects seem to have been less common and may have been prestige items, not available for everyone in society to possess. There is evidence for the very early digging of flint from extraction sites, but in southern England only. Small-scale stone axe production found in many different parts of western Britain and northern Ireland also started early, showing that these practices were key ways of 'being Neolithic' in a new land. Pottery also appeared early on in the take-up of Neolithic things in each region (see Chapter 3), but it was only later on that people started to make a variety of regional pot styles which were employed in specific regional settings. While material culture is discussed here separately, it is important to note that there are significant cross-overs with other parts of the Neolithic world. For example, pottery seems to have been used for the preparation and serving of food, and it was also deposited in significant quantities at some monuments (covered in the next chapter). In this regard objects can operate at multiple levels – they can have a practical use but still be employed as a material expression of broader relationships and be used in ritualised actions.

MATERIAL CULTURE: STONE QUARRYING AND AXES

The Langdale Pikes in Cumbria are visually very striking mountains – two great domes of rock protruding into the sky (Figure. 4.2). In the early Neolithic people walked into the Langdale valley, and on looking up through woodland they would have seen these two rocky peaks sticking out above the trees (Topping 2021, p. 70). People had come to extract a distinctive green-blue stone – a fine-grained volcanic tuff found in this part of the Cumbrian mountains. This was a practice with European origins – their forefathers had possessed green axes extracted from distant mountains – and this practice was now being enacted in a new location. They passed good-quality stone in the valley, deliberately putting in the effort to walk up the mountain to the very top. Once there people carefully extracted small quantities of stone from steep and inaccessible locations particularly focused on Harrison Stickle (Bradley and Edmonds 1993). Having roughly shaped the stone, they then retreated down the mountainside to further work and polish these stones into beautiful stone axes.

A BRAVE NEW WORLD **57**

FIGURE 4.1
Location of sites named in this chapter, excluding houses, middens and pits

Polished stone axes are one of the most striking objects from the early Neolithic. These objects can be made from both flint or stone; some are roughly shaped by flaking (knapping) the stone, but many were then ground and polished, which created a smooth and shiny outer surface (Figure 4.3). Some of the most spectacular polished stone axes are very beautiful objects and were never used, but there is no doubt that many axes were hafted functional tools which would have been used for woodworking (Roy *et al*.

FIGURE 4.2
The Langdale Pikes, Cumbria, source of Group VI axes (mountains to the right). The picture is taken from the Copt Howe rock art site in the Langdale valley

2023). For example, the wooden trackway, the Sweet Track, discussed in more detail later on in the chapter, had tool marks which indicated axes had been used to procure wood for the trackway and then shape the timbers (Coles and Coles 1986). The vast majority of stone axes have been found as stray finds, which means we are not sure of the precise context in which axes were originally deposited. For those examples which come from secure archaeological contexts, they have been found in significant numbers from causewayed enclosures (see next chapter) and contexts such as pits, settlements, rivers and bogs (Cooney 2000, 208, Edmonds 1995, Topping 2021).

Considerable research has been conducted over the years on those axes, which are made of stone in particular. Unlike with flint examples, these axes can be sourced

FIGURE 4.3
A polished stone axe from near Hayscastle, Pembrokeshire (© Tenby Museum and Art Gallery)

through petrological analysis which enables us to pinpoint the location from where that type of stone originated (Clough and Cummins 1988). A number of major extraction sites have been identified and numbered (by 'Group'), the most productive stone axe sources being the site we have already seen: Langdale in Cumbria (Group VI, which actually incorporates 566 distinct working sites in the Cumbrian Fells: Edinborough *et al.* 2020). There are other important axe extraction sites: Group I from Cornwall, Group VII from Graig Lwyd in north Wales and Group IX from Tievebulliagh and Rathlin Island in northern Ireland (Figure 4.4). The largest of the axe extraction sites, Group VI centred around the Langdale Pikes in Cumbria, produced many thousands of stone axes (Bradley and Edmonds 1993); around a third of all stone axes found in Britain originated from the Langdale Pikes (Topping 2021). In Ireland the largest source of stone axes was from Tievebulliagh and Rathlin Island, which produced a distinctive type of stone known as porcellanite. It appears that many of these stone sources started being used right from the beginning of the Neolithic, predominantly for stone axes but also to make other stone tools (Edinborough *et al.* 2020). The production of objects from these sources declined towards the end of the early Neolithic, although it picked up again later on (Whittle *et al.* 2011, p. 794).

Because we are able to source individual stone axes, it has been possible to demonstrate the distribution of axes made from specific stone types. Langdale axes are found widely throughout Britain, with significant numbers (over 100) in Ireland (Cooney 2000, p. 205). Likewise, Group IX axes from Tievebulliagh and Rathlin Island are found widely throughout Ireland, and around 200 are also known from Britain (Cooney 2000, p. 205). This is good evidence for contacts between different communities in the early Neolithic, which extended across the Irish Sea. It is also worth noting that there are examples of stone axes which originate from beyond Britain and Ireland. Over 100 axes from the Alps have been found in both Britain and Ireland, including one found alongside the Sweet Track and a fragment of another from the monument at Cairnholy I, Dumfries and Galloway (Piggott and Powell 1949). These axes are made from distinctive green stone in the Alps known as jadeitite, although they used to be referred to as jade or jadeite; these axes are found on mainland Europe, primarily dating to the later part of the fifth millennium cal BC (Sheridan and Pailler 2012). It was suggested in the previous chapter that there is the possibility that these may have exchanged by late Mesolithic populations in Britain who were in contact with Neolithic peoples on the continent (Thomas

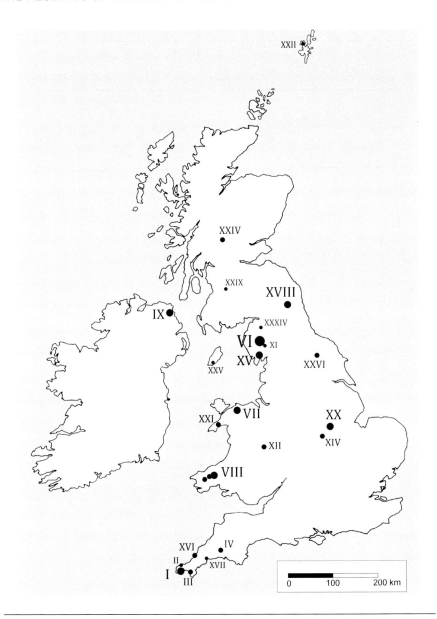

FIGURE 4.4
The known extraction sites for stone axes in Britain and Ireland (after Clough and Cummins 1988). The size of the dot and text relates to the quantities of axes known to have come from these sources: the larger the dot, the more axes produced

2013). Equally, they may have still been in circulation on mainland Europe at the start of our Neolithic and were imported alongside incoming peoples (Sheridan and Pailler 2012). Whichever of these scenarios is correct, these spectacular green axes must have been highly prized objects, and their exotic source must have added to their potency. A small number of Breton axes were also imported into Britain in the Neolithic (Walker 2014), further evidence of ongoing cross-channel connections.

A BRAVE NEW WORLD 61

FIGURE 4.5
Jadeitite axes on display at the recent World of Stonehenge exhibit at the British Museum

As we have already seen at the Langdale Pikes, these are steep mountains in the Cumbrian fells, and tuff was taken from exposed outcrops close to the summit of these peaks (see Bradley and Edmonds 1993, Topping 2021). This is a feature repeated at other stone axe extraction places in Britain and Ireland where stone was quarried from sources high in the mountains (Figure 4.6). Indeed, some tuff was quarried from the summit of Scafell Pike, England's highest mountain, and this has led to suggestions that Neolithic people were deliberately choosing to acquire stone from perilous locations, the extraction of which would have been potentially quite dangerous. Gabriel

Cooney (2000, p. 191), among others, has noted that a number of stone axe sources are in similar locations to that of Langdale, including the mountain of Tievebulliagh, Co. Antrim (Group IX); Penmaenmawr, north Wales (Group VIII); the Preseli mountains, south Wales (Group VII); and Creag na Caillich, Perth and Kinross (Group XXIV). This has led to suggestions that the mountain location was considered a critical part of the stone extraction process, an idea which originated with the quarrying of stone to make axes in Mainland Europe (see Topping 2021). Moreover, people wanted visually distinctive stones to make into axes; the remote source of that stone may have further added to its potency and significance. Indeed, it seems that over time the source of the stone may have become an important location in its own right. People were essentially taking bits of those remote and inaccessible places and turning them into objects, the source of which people could visually identify. So significant may these places have become in Neolithic cosmology that people may have understood them as 'gifts from the earth' (Bradley 2000a, Whittle 1995), or perhaps gifts from the sky (we saw how the Langdale Pikes were visible on the skyline above the trees when people stood in the valley looking up). It has been argued that mountains more generally held a special place in the belief systems of people in the early Neolithic, perhaps understood as the home of gods, spirits or ancestors (see, for example, Cummings and Whittle 2004, Cummings 2009, Tilley 1994) or as wondrous and magical places (Cummings and Richards 2021). If mountains were understood in this way, to possess an axe made from such a source would have been to have a powerful object indeed. Axes, it seems, were potent symbols, intimately tied up with notions of 'being Neolithic'. It was likely that not everyone in early Neolithic

FIGURE 4.6
Tievebulliagh mountain, Co. Antrim, one of the sources of Group IX axes

Britain and Ireland possessed such an object; if this was the case, the beautifully polished and exotic axes from mountain or upland locations may well have been objects of status, perhaps owned and displayed by those in power in society.

As we have seen, one of the most distinctive aspects of a number of these axes is that they have been polished. It has been estimated that it would have taken at least 40 hours to polish a large stone axe (Butler 2005, p. 142), so this was a time-consuming process. There is some evidence for how this was done in the form of polissoirs, stones which were used in the polishing process. These stones would have been used in combination with sand and water to remove the rough flaked edges of an axe. Polissoirs were sometimes portable, and examples have been found deposited along with other forms of material culture, for example, at Etton causewayed enclosure (Pryor 1999) and Ehenside Tarn, Cumbria (Evans 2008). Polissoirs have also been found on larger stones, including on outcrops, and there is one incorporated into the monument at West Kennet. However, it is worth considering that there was little technological benefit to the all-over polishing of an axe: it does not make it a more efficient cutting tool and certainly does not justify the amount of time required to polish the axe. This has led to debates as to precisely why people in the early Neolithic expended so much time polishing axes. It certainly added to the overall visual effect of the axe if they were used as objects of status. It has also been noted that polishing brings out the character of the stone, so that it is much easier to identify its origin. All that effort, therefore, may have been to enhance the visual character of the stone and to emphasise it as an item of prestige (Pétrequin *et al*. 1998, p. 308).

Finally it is worth considering how these objects were used over time. Mark Edmonds in particular has written about the kinds of life histories that individual stone axes may have had. First, these were objects that originated from very specific sources, and places such as the high mountains were not places that people were living but visiting occasionally, probably on a seasonal basis (Topping 2021, p. 70). Once the stone was extracted from these very particular places, the stone was moved away and further worked and polished – usually in the lowlands, perhaps at specific (including monumental) places. Axes were usually, although not always, used – for cutting down trees and woodworking. But it seems that part of this process also involved these objects passing from person to person over both space and time, in some cases travelling considerable distances involving both land and sea travel. They may have acquired associations with the people who owned them and perhaps events they attended (Edmonds 1995, 1998). It may have been the case that they became more powerful as time went on, acquiring a biography as they passed from person to person. Eventually axes were taken out of circulation, deposited at causewayed enclosures or in rivers or wetlands, and this in itself must have been quite a significant act. There is evidence that in some cases axes were broken up and fragmented to reduce them down to smaller pieces, effectively taking them out of circulation permanently (cf. Whittle 1995). All of this indicates that axes were powerful mediums in the early Neolithic for they demonstrated an affinity with particular ways of doing things, harking back to Continental origins (real or perceived). Those Neolithic practices were multiple – visiting mountains, extracting stone, working stone and clearing the land. They were therefore statements in stone of belonging, but also of knowledge and ultimately of descent – a theme will shall see throughout this book.

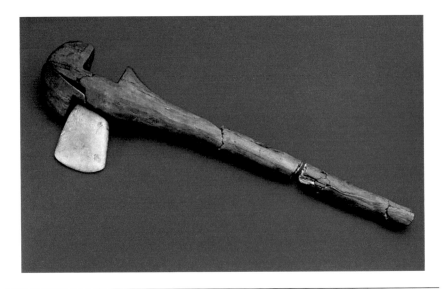

FIGURE 4.7
The Shulishader axe, Lewis, was found hafted (©National Museums Scotland)

MATERIAL CULTURE: LITHICS

One of the most common finds on any early Neolithic site are stone tools and stone tool production waste (debitage). This form of material culture is extremely durable and can be retrieved not only through excavation but also through fieldwalking ploughed fields and from eroding surfaces. As a result stone tools form a prolific and invaluable record of settlement and activity. In the early Neolithic many stone tools were made from flint, a strong and easily worked stone which occurs both in areas of chalk and as secondary deposits on beaches. In addition to this, and especially in areas with limited flint supplies, other types of stone were also used, notably chert, quartz, pitchstone from the island of Arran and felsite on Shetland (Cooney et al. 2019). These different types of stone were used to make a number of distinctive early Neolithic objects. In Britain these include leaf-shaped arrowheads, along with laurel leaves, sickles, scrapers, knives, serrated flakes, points, borers and retouched flakes (Butler 2005). In Ireland lithic assemblages are broadly similar, but in addition to the types already noted, hollow scrapers are also found, predominantly from the northern half of Ireland (Nelis 2004, p. 162).

Stone tools were clearly important everyday objects which would have been used for a variety of different tasks. Arrowheads would have been used for hunting animals, perhaps for food (see subsequently) but certainly for fur and to kill predators which would otherwise attack domestic stock. Arrows could also be used as weapons against people, for which there is some evidence in the early Neolithic (Chapter 5 discusses examples of skeletal remains with arrowheads embedded in them). It seems likely that not everyone was skilled with a bow, and there are suggestions that archers may have held a special role in early Neolithic society (Edmonds 1995, p. 46). Other tools such as scrapers, knives and piercers would have been used to make and work leather. Studies

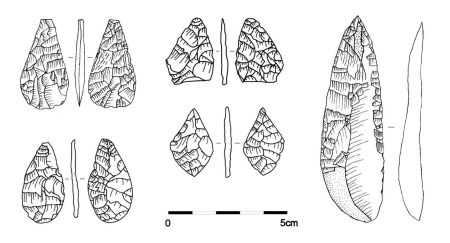

FIGURE 4.8
A selection of early Neolithic stone tools

have also shown that stone tools, particularly those with serrated edges, would have been used to work with various types of vegetation (Hurcombe 2014) and would have been important in both processing food such as cereals and making organic containers such as baskets (see subsequently). Essentially the early Neolithic stone toolkit could have been used for a variety of tasks, and the quantity of material recovered from the archaeological record suggests in most areas this was a technology that was disposable (discarded once it had been used, perhaps as people moved between settlements). Indeed, some stone tools were made very quickly, possibly on an *ad hoc* basis and perhaps being made in only a couple of minutes (Edmonds 1995, p. 40).

Making more complex stone tools such as arrowheads, however, requires skill and two basic stages of production. First the raw material must be turned from a large block of stone into smaller, usable flakes or blades. This was achieved by using a hammer to break up the larger block, a technique known as knapping. By repeatedly striking a block of flint, much waste (debitage) would have been produced but also some flakes and blades which could then be turned into objects. The second phase of making a tool was more close and fine work, involving pressure flaking or invasive retouch which carefully shaped a flake or blade into an object (Edmonds 1995, p. 45). It may have been the case that everyone in a community could knap stone and make basic tools but that fine work was done by a smaller number of specialists.

MATERIAL CULTURE: FLINT EXTRACTION SITES

As we have seen, both stone tools and axes are made from flint which occurs as surface outcrops or nodules in certain parts of the country, most notably in southern and eastern England, north-east Scotland and north-east Ireland as well as on beaches. However, one of the most extraordinary features of the early Neolithic in Britain is the first use of digging deep shafts into the earth as a way of acquiring flint. Flint extraction sites, often referred to as mines, are found in southern England and appear to be a feature of the very earliest Neolithic in this area (Edinborough *et al*. 2020, Whittle *et al*. 2011, p. 257). These flint extraction sites comprise a series of vertical shafts sunk into the ground in order to get at seams of flint underground (Barber *et al*. 1999, Russell 2000). Once a vertical shaft was excavated, a series of horizontal galleries could then be dug, which enabled the flint to be extracted (Figures 4.9 and 4.10). The largest early Neolithic flint mine is Cissbury, where 270 shafts are recorded, but there was also activity at Harrow Hill, Blackpatch, Long Down, Stoke Down and Church Hill (see Russell 2000). It seems likely that only a few shafts were open at any one time, and there is evidence that after flint had been extracted from galleries around one shaft they were then quickly backfilled, suggesting excavation, extraction and refilling in a single season (Holgate 2019, Whittle *et al*. 2011, p. 255). In the early Neolithic flint mining only seems to have taken place in southern England, although there are later Neolithic extraction sites beyond this area, including in Scotland (see Chapter 7). There is good evidence from the continent which shows that Neolithic communities there were already mining for flint, so this appears to be an innovation introduced into Britain from Europe at the start of the Neolithic.

Once flint had been excavated from the earth it was then removed from the extraction site. Knapping floors have been found around the shafts which demonstrates that people were shaping the flint within the mines' vicinity. However, there is no evidence for grinding or polishing near the mines, so this seems to have taken place elsewhere (Baczkowski 2019, Thomas 2013, p. 382). Furthermore, there is very little evidence for long-term settlement around these extraction sites, suggesting that only short-term camps were used when flint was being mined, although more investigation is required to demonstrate this conclusively (Russell 2000, pp. 121–128). There is good evidence, however, that the products of these early Neolithic mines were exported more broadly into southern England, which may suggest that people came to the mines to extract flint from occupation areas elsewhere, perhaps on a temporary and seasonal basis, and predominantly to make axes (Holgate 2019).

One of the intriguing aspects of these sites is that a series of deposits have been recovered from them. Notable quantities of antler picks were left behind in the mines, particularly red deer antler (Russell 2000, pp. 84–90). These would have been used for digging and breaking up the chalk. Ox scapulae (shoulder blades) were found which may have been used as shovels. Human skeletal remains have also been recovered, including a whole articulated body at Cissbury as well as isolated skull fragments. Animal bones, both articulated and incomplete, were also deposited in the mine shafts and include a complete ox skeleton which had been cooked and partially eaten (Russell 2000, p. 115). These deposits are clearly ritualised and can be paralleled with depositional practice taking place in early Neolithic Britain more broadly (see subsequently and next chapter). There are also incised lines marked above some of the galleries; similar incised chalk blocks have been found in the ditches of causewayed enclosures, and scratch marks are also found in passage graves (see Chapter 6). Precisely what these incised lines mean in the context of these flint mines currently remains unclear (Russell 2000, p. 113).

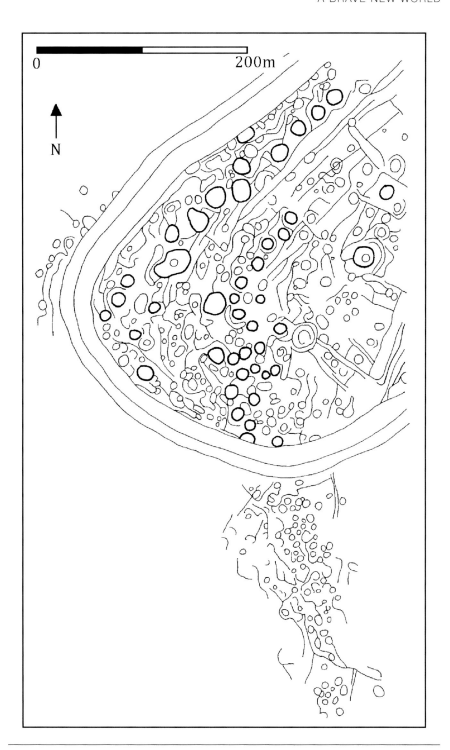

FIGURE 4.9
Plan of the features of the flint mines at Cissbury. The edge of the flint extraction area is obscured by a later Iron Age rampart (after Russell 2000)

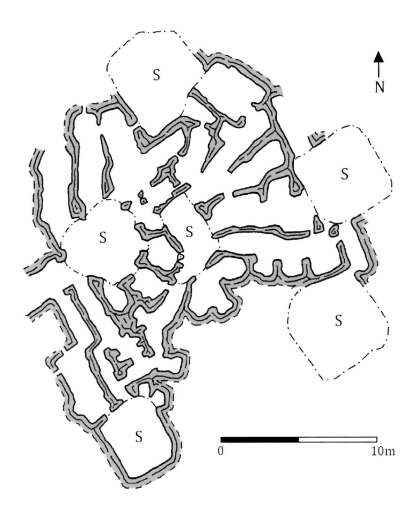

FIGURE 4.10
Plan of some of the galleries of the flint mines at Cissbury (after Russell 2000). S marks a vertical shaft from the surface

Since flint was easily accessible above ground, one question is why people went to so much effort in order to acquire flint from these extraction sites. Certainly the flint taken from deep in the earth is high quality, easy to work and visually distinctive (Edmonds 1995, p. 66). However, as with digging the ditches for long barrows or causewayed enclosures, digging a flint mine may have been a community endeavour which resulted not only in the practical acquisition of flint but also fulfilled a social role where communities came together to work (Edmond 1995, 1998, Russell 2000, p. 142). It can be suggested, as it has been for Neolithic monuments more broadly (see Chapters 5, 6 and 8), that these community projects were as much about bringing people together to renegotiate social relations as anything else (Thomas 2013, p. 383). In the case of flint mines, the product of this labour was manifest in an object or series of objects which may have represented specific kinship groups, or perhaps new alliances and networks.

Tools made from these sources, then, may have been used only by specific groups of people. In some ways the mine workings were as distinctive in the southern England landscape as early Neolithic monuments such as causewayed enclosures and long barrows found elsewhere, as well as potentially fulfilling a similar role in terms of social negotiations. They may have been considered special places where procurement was highly ritualised; this would also explain the deposits found within the mines which are more than just the practical left-overs of digging (Teather 2016, Topping 2011). The closing up of each shaft at the end of each season of work also hints at the potency of opening up the earth and extracting material and the need to mark the end of each extraction event.

MATERIAL CULTURE: POTTERY

One of the new types of material culture which is found in Britain and Ireland at the start of the Neolithic is pottery. Unlike in some parts of northern Europe where pottery was used by hunting and gathering groups prior to the adoption of agriculture (see Chapter 3), there is no evidence from either Britain or Ireland of pottery from Mesolithic contexts. Instead pottery appears to be one of the first Neolithic elements which was produced in most areas as Neolithic people arrived and spread across our islands (see previous chapter for the details on this). Thus, pottery was probably first made in south-east England between 4055 and 3995 cal BC (Whittle *et al*. 2011, p. 744ff).

Over the years considerable effort has been invested in understanding the different types of Neolithic pottery, in particular in relation to regional and chronological differences. This has left the literature full of a bewildering array of pottery types. While these regional names are useful for researchers, early Neolithic pottery can most simply be described as bowl pottery. The earliest type of pottery in Britain and Ireland is the Carinated Bowl (Müller and Peterson 2015, p. 588, Sheridan 2007). These early bowls were very finely made, but only a very restricted range of vessels were produced (Gibson 2002a, p. 70). Broadly speaking, after the onset of the Neolithic, a series of modified or developed bowls were then produced (this includes regional pottery styles such as Unstan Ware, Hebridean Ware and Beacharra Ware). These early Neolithic bowls include a wider range of vessel forms and in some regions also include a decorative element (Copper and Armit 2018, Müller and Peterson 2015, Sheridan 2016a). Towards the end of the early Neolithic, the Impressed Ware tradition began. This pottery style has particular currency in the middle Neolithic and so will be discussed in more detail in Chapter 6. It is worth noting here, however, that some of these individual pottery styles did not stop being made and used abruptly but have a long currency and overlap significantly with one another (for more specific details on regional pottery styles, see Sheridan 1995 for Ireland, Peterson 2003 for Wales, Cleal 2004 for England, Sheridan 2007 and 2016a for Scotland, Gibson 2002 for an overview and Whittle *et al*. 2011, pp. 759–778 for the precise date ranges of each type).

Pottery is found in a variety of early Neolithic contexts, and again there seem to be important regional variations. In southern England pottery is often found in pits, pre-barrow contexts and causewayed enclosures but is less common in the primary burial phases

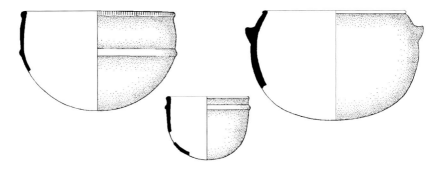

FIGURE 4.11
Early Neolithic bowl pottery from Windmill Hill, Wiltshire (after Keiller 1965)

of the chambered tombs (Whittle et al. 2011, p. 759). This has led to suggestions that perhaps the earliest Neolithic pottery was reserved for use at special occasions in southern Britain, especially prior to its more widespread use later on in the early Neolithic (Thomas 2013, p. 370). In northern Britain and Ireland bowl pottery is commonly found in early Neolithic chambered tombs (Figure 4.12), although in small quantities, and significant numbers have also been found at settlement sites (see Smyth 2014 and Thomas 2013, p. 369). This could suggest that pottery was in more everyday use in these areas (Sheridan 2007). Archaeologists are yet to find a pottery production site in Britain or Ireland, so we remain unsure whether ceramics were made at or close to settlement sites: they may have been made at special locations. We do know, however, that when pottery has been sourced it appears to have been predominantly made and then used within the local area (Cooney 2000, p. 186, Thompson et al. 2015). One clear exception to this is the gabbroic wares of Cornwall, which moved significant distances from their source between 3700 and 3500 cal BC (Whittle et al. 2011, p. 794).

A considerable amount of knowledge is required to make pottery – not only with regard shaping and decorating the pot itself, which usually involved many different stages, but also how to prepare the clay properly and how to fire it successfully. Neolithic people on the Continent were themselves making pottery, so the knowledge of ceramic production travelled over with them at the start of the Neolithic. Indeed, the earliest pots were very finely made, so clearly people knew exactly what they were doing, although of course they would have to locate new sources of clay. All pottery was hand-built in the Neolithic and fired using the 'bonfire' technique: this is where you stack the pottery within an upstanding bonfire instead of using a kiln (Müller and Peterson 2015, p. 591 Sheridan 2004a); again, both of these techniques require considerable skill. As such it has been suggested that not everyone in each community knew how to make pots, so this may well have been knowledge restricted to a small group of people. Ethnographic examples show that women traditionally make pots in many societies (e.g. Crown and Wills 1995, p. 247). Perhaps, then, from the beginning of the Neolithic, pottery production was connected with only a specific group of people who had the knowledge to turn clay into pottery.

While the style of early Neolithic pottery clearly varied in Britain and Ireland, it has been demonstrated that pottery was used ubiquitously for cooking food. The bases of pots

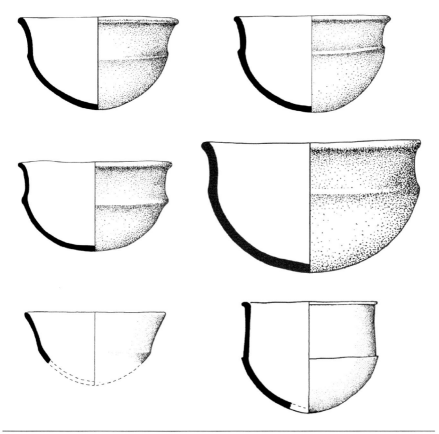

FIGURE 4.12
Carinated bowls from Ballintaggart, Co. Armagh and Cairnholy I, Dumfries and Galloway (after Thompson *et al*. 2015)

have distinctive spalling or charring which indicates that vessels were placed on or above a fire (Müller and Peterson 2015). In addition to this pots are often found with charred residues, and where no residues survive pots can be chemically analysed for lipids or fatty acids which can indicate which foodstuffs had been cooked in the vessel. There is growing data on this, and early Neolithic pottery seems to have been used to cook animal products as well as heating milk (see subsequently). In Ireland lipid analysis of early Neolithic pottery vessels indicates that most were used for processing dairy products, with only a small number used for meat (Smyth and Evershed 2015a, 2015b).

Pottery did not just enable the cooking of food but also more complex sequences of food production. Pottery can be used for storing food, and some forms of pottery were probably used to enhance existing practices, including salting, smoking and drying. Pottery also enables people to cook foods in distinctive ways, including over an open fire. It has even been suggested that pottery enabled the brewing of alcohol for the first time (Dineley and Dineley 2000), which has interesting implications for its presence in ritualised contexts such as monuments. Moreover, the significance of pottery may have been particularly important in relation to the serving of food and drink. In many societies

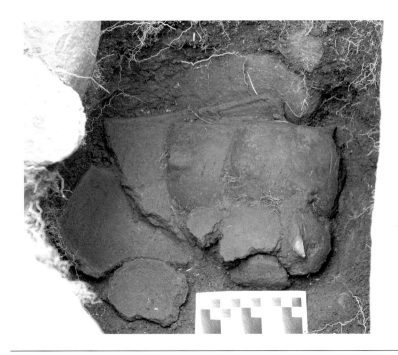

FIGURE 4.13
Early Neolithic bowl found in the chambered tomb of Blasthill, Kintyre. It has been flattened by material subsequently placed on top of it. Residue on the pot was radiocarbon dated to 3630–3360 cal BC (Cummings and Robinson 2015)

the exchange, preparation and consumption of food are often a crucial part of ritualised activity. Certain foods can only be served in certain dishes and particular foods eaten in a specific order. This frequently relates to everyday life but is even more pronounced in special, ritualised contexts (Counihan 1999, Lysaght 2002). New foodstuffs introduced at the start of the Neolithic, most notably dairy products, may have been inextricably connected with new material culture with cultural practices dictating their use. Ethnographic examples also show how the throwing of feasts is a way of gaining social status (see Hayden 2014, Chapter 5). The issue of feasting is discussed in more detail subsequently (and see Copper and Armit 2018).

The significance of pottery in the Neolithic is likely to have gone beyond the ways in which it was used for cooking and serving food and drink. The production of pottery involves a long process which may have made all sorts of connections with people and places. First, the source of materials in the Neolithic seems to have been significant to people, exemplified by the taking of particular stone from specific mountains and outcrops and turning them into stone axes (see previously). The source of the clay used to make pots may have been equally important (A. Jones 2002), associating the finished pot with a specific location in the landscape. Neolithic pottery also contains temper, which helps with the firing process, but it has been shown that a wide variety of tempers were used, including in some instances cremated bone (Müller and Peterson 2015). This would have added another significant element to each pot. Equally, the making

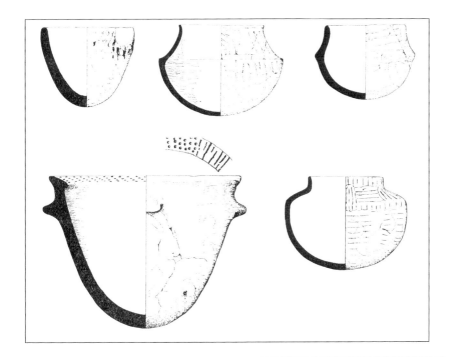

FIGURE 4.14
Beacharra bowls from Beacharra, Argyll and Bute (after Scott 1969)

of the pot may have been an important event in people's lives. A considerable amount of preparation would be required before a firing took place. This would involve not only making of the pottery but also the collection of wood and the making of charcoal. A firing would also have been quite a visual spectacle. It can be suggested that the investment of time in making pottery may have meant that a community would have made and fired pots only once or twice a year, perhaps making it a seasonal event involving the coming together of kin groups, as has been suggested in relation to other events in the Neolithic such as building monuments. The style and decoration on pottery which evolved as throughout the early Neolithic may equally have been ways of visually indicating kin affiliations and wider social networks.

We should be careful not to assign a single meaning or use to pottery, either throughout the early Neolithic or throughout Britain and Ireland. There were likely to have been significant temporal and spatial differences in pottery use, production and deposition. There seems little doubt that pottery was intimately tied up with dealing with some of the new foodstuffs that were available from the start of the Neolithic. While pottery was made locally, shared styles and decoration on pottery indicate wider networks of contact, which are evident through other forms of material culture. This suggests that pottery was deemed an appropriate form of material culture for communicating broader connections or networks with other people and places in the Neolithic. Pottery, however, was only one type of material culture that people used, and it would have sat alongside many organic objects. It is to these which we now turn.

MATERIAL CULTURE: ORGANIC MATERIALS

At the start of the Neolithic much of Britain and Ireland was wooded, providing an invaluable material which would have been used to make a variety of objects. We have already seen that stone axes were used to cut down trees, not just to clear the land for agricultural practices but also to provide a supply of an invaluable raw material: wood. Timber would have been extensively used to make many different types of object, including the frames for the skin boats needed to bring over people and things from mainland Europe. Boats would also have been used for transportation along rivers and maintaining social networks including over the Irish Sea and to the Western and Northern Isles. Other everyday objects could easily be fashioned from wood, and a few of these are occasionally recovered from the archaeological record. There are few examples of wooden bowls from the Neolithic of Britain and Ireland such as from Warren Field, Aberdeenshire, although many examples are known from mainland Europe, for example, the settlements of the Alpine foreland. A wooden stirrer was found in one of the pots along with other wooden objects deposited along the Sweet Track in the early Neolithic (Coles and Coles 1986, p. 59), and a wooden club was found on the Thames foreshore in Chelsea (Lewis 2000). Several bows were found alongside the Sweet Track, and another was recovered from a bog at Rotten Bottom, Dumfries and Galloway, which dates to the early Neolithic (NMS 1992). Occasionally, axes are found with wooden hafts, such as the Shulishader axe found on the Isle of Lewis (see Figure 4.7). Timber was also important for building structures, and these are investigated in more detail subsequently alongside practices of dealing with woodland (coppicing). The next chapter also discusses the monuments which were constructed from wood. It is also worth noting that wood was an essential fuel for fires which would have provided both warmth as well as heat for cooking. Wood was also a necessary component of making other forms of material culture such as the firing of pottery, and it was required for other Neolithic practices such as cremation. All in all, wood was an essential material in the early Neolithic (and see Brophy and Millican 2015, Noble 2006), and there was an abundant supply across most of Britain and Ireland (the exception being Shetland, where the woodland, once felled, does not seem to have grown back).

Other components of trees and plants would have been significant. Bark would have been an important product which could have been used for making cord, containers, canoes, clothing and matting (Hurcombe 2014, p. 30). Birch bark boxes were found at Horton, Berkshire and Runnymede, and a mat of birch bark and another folded piece were recovered from the ditches at Etton (Pryor 1999, p. 157). Baskets may well have been much more commonly made and used than ceramics in the early Neolithic, so much so that that there have been suggestions that pottery forms mimicked baskets or other organic bags: some decoration may also have been to replicate the design of basketry (Hurcombe 2014). Unlike pottery, which was restricted in form in the early Neolithic to bowls (see previously), basketry can produce a wide range of forms, including watertight baskets, large containers, serving bowls, trays for winnowing, large mats and even walls for dwellings (Hurcombe 2014, p. 52). Basketry has been recovered from the Carrigdirty foreshore in Co. Limerick, which produced a woven reed basketry fragment (Cooney 2000, p. 74), and another example was found in a bog at Twyford, Co. Westmeath. Comparable examples from elsewhere show that baskets can be very

FIGURE 4.15
A fragment of Neolithic basketry from Twyford, Co. Westmeath (© National Museum of Ireland)

finely made in a variety of striking colours and designs (Hurcombe 2014). Furthermore, baskets were much lighter and more easily transportable than ceramics, all of which suggests that this form of material culture may have been much more extensively used than pottery.

Cordage made from fibrous plant material would have been essential in a variety of different contexts in the early Neolithic. It is rarely preserved in the archaeological record, but its presence can be demonstrated, as some pottery has twisted cord impressions (particularly on impressed wares, although there are earlier examples: Gibson 2002, p. 78). A rare piece of cord was found at Etton causewayed enclosure, Cambridgeshire (Pryor 1999). It is worth noting here that flax was introduced into Britain and Ireland in the

Neolithic and is recorded on several sites (Harris 2014). Not only did it produce seeds which could be consumed, but flax can be used to create fibres which could be made into both cord but also high-quality fabrics (Hurcombe 2014, p. 144). The desirability of such fabric can be highlighted when contrasted with the clothes found associated with the 'Iceman', the remains of a man recovered in the Alps and dating to 3350–3100 cal BC. The clothes found with the Iceman are exceptionally well preserved and give us an insight into the kinds of clothing people would have worn in Britain and Ireland in the early Neolithic. He wore garments of leather, fur and possibly woven grass (Spindler 1995). However, flax and other vegetable matter such as nettles can be processed to make bast fibres which can be woven into soft fabrics (Harris 2014, Hurcombe 2014). Woven fabric is now known from late Neolithic contexts (see Chapter 7) and may well have been made in the early Neolithic too.

Antler was clearly an important material in the early Neolithic. The evidence from the flint mines has already been presented and shows that these were dug using antler picks, which in some instances were left behind after use. Antler picks have also been found at other early Neolithic sites such as causewayed enclosures and long mounds (see next chapter), where they would have been essential tools for construction. Antler can also be worked, and there is evidence for this at sites such as Windmill Hill in Wiltshire (Whittle *et al.* 1999, p. 233). Antler is a strong and durable material with which to make objects. For example, a red deer antler comb was recovered from the Thames near Battersea which might have been used to strip hair from animal hides (Museum of London ID A10683). Animal bone would also have been used to make different objects and was widely available as a by-product of domestic waste. Likewise, animal hides and leather would have been used extensively not only for clothes and shoes but also as part of structures (tents). Other animal by-products which could have been used were the hooves and horns for making glue and the brains for tanning leather (Hurcombe 2014, p. 68).

Organic materials only survive in the archaeological record in exceptional circumstances, so we rarely get to study these objects. However, they were almost certainly used extensively by people in the early Neolithic and alongside other forms of material culture may have been important mediums for the expression of social identity or affiliations. The reality may have been that belonging to a particular kin group was expressed through stone tools or pottery styles (the things we commonly find in the archaeological record) as well as in clothing and hair styles. The discovery of a site with excellent organic preservation like Must Farm (which is late Bronze Age in date) but dating from the Neolithic could radically change our view of how people dressed and what material objects they used on a day-to-day basis.

YOU ARE WHAT YOU EAT. DIET AND SUBSISTENCE IN THE EARLY NEOLITHIC

Food is of fundamental importance to people, vital of course for survival but also tied up with social identity and deeply embedded in day-to-day practices. This section explores the different types of evidence which give an indication of what people were eating in the early Neolithic. Domesticated animals, specifically cattle, seem to have been of particular importance beyond their calorific contribution to people's diets. Domesticated crops were certainly introduced and grown across Britain and Ireland from the early Neolithic onwards, but it seems that some communities were less enamoured with cereals than others, and there is now good evidence that in some areas cereal cultivation fell out of favour after a time. As such, wild plant foods would have been important in some parts of Britain and Ireland.

Domesticated animals

On Salisbury Plain sometime between the years of 3800 and 3700 cal BC there was a gathering of a fairly substantial number of people. We cannot be sure quite how many people there were, but they brought with them ten cows, two pigs, seven roe deer and two red deer (Richards 1990). What followed appears to be the remains of a single large feast – the animals were butchered and eaten, served in a range of ceramic bowls and cups, and then a large pit was excavated and remains of the feast along with stone tools were deposited within (Figure 4.16). This site is known as the 'Coneybury Anomaly' – it

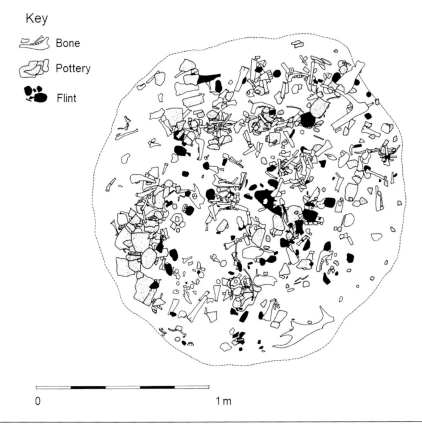

FIGURE 4.16
The Coneybury Anomaly showing the mass of animal bones and stone tools deposited

was discovered as a geophysical anomaly on a survey of the area, but it remains an apt name, because such a deposit is unique in Britain and Ireland. It is unique because it contains a large number of wild animal remains – as we shall see the early Neolithic of both Britain and Ireland is dominated by domestic animals, and there is very little evidence for the use of wild animal species which would have remained plentiful in most parts of these islands. This leads to the question, then, of what the Coneybury Anomaly might represent. It has recently been argued that this may be remains of a feast involving multiple families or groups from the surrounding area coming together and reinforcing communal ties. However, in this instance some of the people who belonged to this group still practised the old ways of doing things – hunting and gathering (Gron *et al.* 2018). This is an intriguing prospect and may indicate that some (native?) hunter-gatherers survived into the Neolithic. It also illustrates how unusual the presence of wild animals is in the archaeological record of the early Neolithic, showing the overall importance of domestic stock to these people.

At the start of the Neolithic four new domesticated species were introduced from mainland Europe into Britain and Ireland. These were domesticated cattle, sheep, goats and pigs. Of these, two wild equivalent species were already present: in Britain, wild cattle (aurochs) and wild boar/pig and in Ireland, wild boar only. It is clear, however, that people in Britain and Ireland did not domesticate cattle themselves; instead, domestication took place elsewhere, and domestic stock was introduced at the start of the Neolithic from mainland Europe (Bollongino and Burger 2007, Tresset and Vigne 2007). With regard to pig, we know that people in mainland Europe had domestic pigs prior to the appearance of this animal in Britain and Ireland, but the DNA evidence suggests that there is the possibility of localised domestication events (Ottoni *et al.* 2013). At present, we cannot rule out the possibility that some wild pigs were domesticated in Britain and Ireland. Sheep and goat were never found in the wild in north-west Europe; these species were native to, and therefore domesticated in, the Near East and subsequently introduced into Europe (Pedrosa *et al.* 2005). It is worth noting here that Neolithic people also used domesticated dogs. This domestic animal was the only species that had been present in Britain and Ireland in the preceding Mesolithic period. There is now substantial evidence that new breeds of domestic dogs were introduced into Britain and Ireland with incoming Neolithic people and that these then mixed with native dog populations once here (Olliver *et al.* 2018). These new dog breeds may have been bred for managing domestic stock such as cattle. It is also intriguing to note that red deer were introduced into Ireland at the start of the Neolithic alongside domesticates (see subsequently).

A range of domestic animals were therefore introduced into Britain and Ireland from mainland Europe right at the very start of the Neolithic (see Whittle *et al.* 2011, pp. 840–841), and there is good evidence for the widespread adoption of domesticates across both Britain and Ireland with a concomitant and widespread decline in the use of wild animals for food. There are several different strands of evidence which support this view. First, there are animal bones from the archaeological record. Domesticated animals dominate the faunal assemblages from the early Neolithic, making up between 90% and 95% of bones recovered from a variety of contexts (the Coneybury Anomaly being the exception). Significant quantities of animal remains have been recovered from the causewayed enclosures in southern Britain as well as from a number of long barrows and chambered tombs in Britain and Ireland (Thomas and McFadyen 2010). In most of these instances cattle remains dominate the record from the early Neolithic, with much smaller numbers of sheep, goat and pig (Serjeantson 2011). There have been questions regarding how representative these assemblages are because so many of them are 'special' or found in ceremonial contexts such as long barrows or causewayed enclosures. These particular assemblages might be seen as unrepresentative of what people would have been eating on a more regular basis and could be seen as the remains of special feasts (see next chapter). However, more recent work on animal bone assemblages from a range of contexts has shown a similar pattern among more domestic, everyday assemblages such as middens, occupation sites and pits (Serjeantson 2011 and see Schulting 2008, figure 4.2).

Our understanding of the use of domesticated animals in the early Neolithic has been enhanced by the results of stable isotope analyses; this technique investigates diet via bone chemistry.

Studies on early Neolithic human remains have shown that a high percentage of the protein in people's diet in the early Neolithic was from animal products (Hamilton and Hedges 2011, Hedges *et al*. 2008, Richards 2003). These studies also show that people did not use marine foods, a stark contrast to the results of stable isotope analysis of late Mesolithic people, many of whom had a very high marine component in their diets (Schulting and Richards 2002). Clearly incoming Neolithic people did not draw on the marine foods widely available on British and Irish shores, instead maintaining a reliance on terrestrial resources throughout the early Neolithic (Smyth and Evershed 2015b). Indeed, while there have been issues regarding the preservation and retention of fish remains from archaeological sites, where excavators have used methods for recovering fish bone, little has been found. Only at times of extreme stress do people seemed to have been willing to use marine resources (see Montgomery *et al*. 2013)

Quite clearly animals would have been used to provide meat. Sheep, goats and cattle, however, also produce milk, and there is good evidence for the use of this from the early Neolithic onwards. Fatty acid residues (lipids) are left behind in the fabric of ceramic vessels and can be identified scientifically. The analysis of early Neolithic ceramics has shown that between 50% and 60% of ceramics in Britain and virtually all Irish early Neolithic pottery have dairy lipids present (Copley *et al*. 2005, Smyth and Evershed 2015a, 2015b). This suggests that milk, or milk-derived foods such as cheese and yogurt, were an important food right from the start of the Neolithic. The cattle bone evidence shows the maintenance of mature female cows, which is a characteristic trait of a dairying economy (Serjeantson 2011, pp. 23–25). It has also been suggested that cattle in particular could be used for traction since the start of the Neolithic also saw the first use of cereals. There is good evidence from later periods of prehistory for ploughing and that animals were used to assist with this. There is only limited evidence from the Neolithic, however, and it may have been the case that cows were as likely to be used to help move material possessions around, perhaps with the help of carts (Serjeantson 2011, p. 15), or assist in the moving of large objects such as stones used in monuments than they were with ploughing, especially the small garden plots we think people kept in the Neolithic (see subsequently).

One of the most important elements relating to the use of domestic animals is that this would have created a distinctive set of relations between people and animals. In the keeping of domesticated animals there is a level of care and closeness to those animals, as domestic stock needs tending all year round (Edmonds 1998, pp. 27–28 and see Ingold 2000). These animals, especially with young, need protecting from predators, and in early Neolithic Britain, cattle herds would also need to be isolated from wild aurochs to prevent interbreeding. While there was no need to provide winter fodder for animals in southern Britain, in upland and northern areas communities would have needed to provide shelter and food throughout the winter months (Schulting 2008, p. 97). We may envisage the practice of transhumance in the early Neolithic where people moved animals around different landscapes throughout the year. As part of this care of domestic stock, domesticated dogs would have been vital in the early Neolithic for herding and keeping predators away.

The keeping of domestic animals may also have enabled important social interactions between groups of people. Cattle in particular provide a significant quantity of meat when slaughtered – certainly more than a small group of people could consume (this is how we know the Coneybury Anomaly represents the coming together of a larger group of people). The meat from a single cow could therefore feed many people. Large numbers of cattle, then, would have enabled people to accumulate surplus animals, the meat from which could feed large numbers of people. This is important, as one of the ways that people are able to enhance their social position is by throwing lavish feasts. The work of Brian Hayden in particular has highlighted how feasting can be used to have significant social benefits for the person, or people, who provide the feast. It has been shown that feasting enables the consolidation of kinship networks, it has huge social advantages such as acquiring marriage partners or desirable material culture and it creates a sense of debt which can be drawn on at a later date: essentially significant social, economic and political advantages (see Hayden 2014). Feasts can include the consumption of high-quality meat but also the conspicuous non-consumption of food, for which there is some evidence from the archaeological record. At Windmill Hill causewayed enclosure, for example, a whole pig and goat were placed in the ditches along with joints of beef (Whittle *et al*. 1999). Domestic animals, then, could have been desirable to those wishing to enhance their status, and cattle in particular may have been an important form of wealth in the early Neolithic which enabled social aggrandisement for individuals or groups of people through feasting or displays of consumption (Ray and Thomas 2003, Schulting 2008, p. 109).

If people in the early Neolithic almost exclusively used domesticated animals for food, what role did wild animals have and how might people have understood these animals? At present there is only limited evidence for the use of wild animals for meat, with only 5% of animal bone assemblages coming from wild animals (Serjeantson 2011, p. 33). Deer antler is found on many Neolithic sites, but the animal does not need to be killed to acquire it, as deer shed their antlers once a year. Smaller animals may have been hunted for their fur. It would seem, therefore, that wild animals played a small role in dietary terms in the early Neolithic. However, it is worth bearing in mind that red deer were introduced into Ireland at the start of the Neolithic alongside domesticated animals (Woodman and McCarthy 2003), as well as into Orkney and the Outer Hebrides (Stanton *et al*. 2016). This has interesting parallels with the introduction of the bear into

Ireland in the Mesolithic, which has been suggested was for cosmological reasons (see Chapter 2). If wild animals such as red deer were significant in belief systems, we might anticipate that people would actively avoid eating them. People may only have eaten wild animals at times of dire need, and their remains, recovered only in small quantities, may have been less to do with subsistence and more an indication of ritual practice (and see Sharples 2000). The importance of wild animals is discussed again in the next chapter in relation to mortuary practice, which also supports the idea that animals played a role in belief systems.

Domesticated plants

Alongside domesticated animals, the early Neolithic saw domesticated plants in the form of cereals introduced into Britain and Ireland (Fairbairn 2000, Jones and Rowley-Conwy 2007). The knowledge of how to grow and process cereals was already well-established in Mainland Europe and was imported into Britain with incoming people. The three main types of crop introduced were wheat, barley and to a lesser extent flax; other domesticated plant species found on the continent such as peas, lentils and chickpeas were not brought over, probably because they would not do well in our climate (Fairbairn 2000, McClatchie *et al*. 2014). Moreover, there seems to be regional variation in the use of different cereals in Britain and Ireland, with barley favoured over wheat in the north (Bishop *et al*. 2009). There is some evidence for the use of cereals, but it has its limitations, mainly because small organic material like cereal grain is poorly preserved in the archaeological record (McClatchie *et al*. 2022). Quantities of cereal grains have been found when charred, however, and while we do not know whether these were accidental charrings or deliberate burnt offerings, they do give us some insight into cereal production in the early Neolithic. Notable quantities of charred grain have been found at timber halls such as Balbridie, Aberdeenshire (Fairweather and Ralston 1993, and see Bishop *et al*. 2022), and Yarnton, Oxfordshire (Hey and Barclay 2007), and 1000 cereal grains were recovered from the house at Tankardstown South, Co. Limerick (McClatchie *et al*. 2014, p. 211). Notable quantities are also found at causewayed enclosure sites such as Hambledon Hill and Windmill Hill, and smaller amounts are found on occupation sites and in pits (Brown 2007). Quantities of cereal have also been found in early Neolithic contexts in both Orkney and Shetland, showing that even in northern climes, people were growing cereals (Cummings *et al*. forthcoming; Richards and Jones 2015b).

Apart from the cereal grains themselves there are other types of evidence which can assist in understanding the role of cereals in the early Neolithic. Recent research has conclusively demonstrated that some Neolithic pottery was used for preparing cereals (Hammann *et al*. 2022). Very occasionally there are cereal grain impressions on pottery which are a proxy for cereal cultivation. For example, an impression of wheat chaff was found on a pot from Dooey's Cairn, Co. Antrim (E.E. Evans 1938), and cereal impressions were found on some of the pottery from Hurst Fen, Suffolk (Helbaek 1960, pp. 228–240). A very rare example of charred bread was found in fragments at Yarnton (Hey *et al*. 2016), but it seems more common that cereals were added to stews instead of being ground to make flour (McClatchie *et al*. 2022). Chaff, the leftovers from the threshing process, could also be helpful in assessing the contribution of cereals to the early Neolithic diet, but it does not always survive well in the archaeological record. There are examples of chaff from early Neolithic sites such as Lismore Fields and Hambledon Hill (Bogaard and Jones 2007, p. 364). It is entirely possible that it was an important by-product of cereal cultivation, perhaps used as fodder for domestic animals (McClatchie *et al.* 2014, p. 212). The excavation of the South Street long barrow revealed ardmarks underneath the monument. This may be evidence for ploughing but equally may be the result of the careful ritual preparation of the ground prior to monument construction, as has been evident elsewhere in Neolithic Europe (Bradley 2005a, p. 24).

For many years field walls and enclosures have been considered important for understanding cereal agriculture. This form of evidence is prolific in Britain and Ireland from later in prehistory but much rarer in the Neolithic. The best-known of these are the Céide Fields, Co. Mayo (Figure 4.17). These remarkable field walls extend for miles over the landscape and have been preserved since the Neolithic by blanket bog (Caulfield 1988). Work has shown that many of these walls date to the early Neolithic, but this area seems to have been primarily used for keeping livestock, with only limited amounts of pollen which indicate limited cereal cultivation (Malloy and O'Connell 1995). The construction of walls was clearly not a pre-requisite for keeping livestock, so the proliferation of these fields in this area of Ireland remains something of an enigma. They certainly do not inform our understanding of cereal cultivation.

Another type of evidence used in discussions on Neolithic agriculture is the pollen evidence and most notably the elm decline which seemed to occur at the start of the Neolithic. Originally it was envisaged that this decrease in woodland, clearly visible in pollen records and particularly obvious in relation to the decline in elm, was the result of

FIGURE 4.17
A portion of the Céide Fields, Co. Mayo, exposed by removing the overlying peat

clearing trees for cereal cultivation (e.g. Piggott 1954, p. 5). However, it is now recognised that it was not this straightforward. First, the elm decline varies in date from area to area, and while pollen from weeds, which we might expect to accompany cereal cultivation, were found in post-elm decline pollen samples, cereal pollen itself is uncommon (Batchelor *et al*. 2014). This has led in recent years to suggestions that patterns of elm decline detected in local pollen sequences was not, primarily, about clearing the land for cereal cultivation. Instead, reduction in elm may relate to the use of woodlands by people keeping cattle or by a prehistoric equivalent of Dutch elm disease (Perry and Moore 1987), although this as a single causal factor may be too simplistic (Batchelor *et al*. 2014). Tree ring evidence from the Sweet Track and its immediate predecessor the Post Track has shown that woodland management was in place prior to the construction of the trackway in the late 39th century cal BC (Coles and Coles 1986, Whittle *et al*. 2011), and here the decrease in woodland may be as much to do with the careful management of the forest via coppicing as for cereal cultivation. It may also have been the case that hazel was also carefully managed for its yearly crop of hazelnuts (Schulting 2008, p. 94), which are found on most early Neolithic sites (see subsequently). Broadly speaking, then, there is evidence for significant landscape clearance in the early Neolithic, but precisely what this clearance was for remains a matter of considerable debate. It may have been to do with clearance for animals, monument building, the careful managing of trees to produce specific products or simply a desire to clear away trees to open up the landscape (see Tilley 2007).

Because of the limitations of the evidence, it remains difficult to conclusively demonstrate the role of cereals in the early Neolithic. They do seem to have been adopted widely across both Britain and Ireland. As we will see in subsequent chapters, this initial enthusiasm for cereal growing waned in the middle and later Neolithic. While there is virtually no evidence for people in the early Neolithic having large fields of cereals, it is now suggested that people in the early Neolithic maintained 'garden plots'. This was not short-lived swidden agriculture but carefully cultivated plots which were maintained over many years (Bogaard and Jones 2007, McClatchie *et al*. 2014). While these were probably used for growing relatively small quantities of cereals, it does nevertheless appear that cereal agriculture was an important part of the early Neolithic, and the use of these garden plots over a number of years shows an investment of time and effort in specific parts of the landscape which drew people back time and again.

While it appears that people in the early Neolithic used very little wild meat, it seems clear that they continued to use wild plants. Hazelnuts are the most conspicuous of these, as charred hazelnut shells preserve very well in the archaeological record (Jones 2000). For example, quantities of hazelnuts were found in pots deposited alongside the Sweet Track, Somerset (Coles and Coles 1986, Figure 4.18). Other plant remains have also been found, including crab apple, raspberry, blackberry, tubers and leafy greens (McClatchie *et al*. 2014, Robinson 2000, Treasure *et al*. 2019). The 500 or so edible plants estimated to be present in Britain and Ireland at this time would have supplemented cereal consumption on a seasonal basis (Zvelebil 1994). Just like uncharred cereal, however, these do not always survive in the archaeological record, so it can often be difficult to fully assess their contribution to early Neolithic diets.

FIGURE 4.18
Reconstruction drawing of the pottery found alongside the Sweet Track, one of which contained hazelnuts (copyright Somerset Levels Project)

Neolithic foodways

Having identified the range of foods that people were eating in the early Neolithic, it is worth considering precisely why these foods were utilised. This is particularly significant because the agricultural production of the early Neolithic marks a major step-change for Britain and Ireland from the preceding late Mesolithic when people acquired all their food from hunting and gathering. At first glance it may appear that farming offers a much more secure way of making a living than hunting and gathering, but this is actually not the case. It has been demonstrated that the adoption of domesticates is not about increasing resource reliability; in fact the switch from hunting and gathering to farming can be a riskier strategy because if one source of food fails for hunter-gatherers, they have a wealth of alternatives to use instead. The small range of foods grown by agriculturalists, however, means that the failure of one just one of these can be more problematic. However, the adoption of agriculture may have been perceived as a more secure way of acquiring food (and see Zvelebil 2000), and certainly it enabled the production of large quantities of produce, which was rarely possible from gathering. There were clearly other reasons why people adopted domesticates too.

First and foremost, since we know that Neolithic people who looked after domestic crops and animals moved into Britain and Ireland from the Continent, they were simply bringing with them established ways of making a living. There was no need to alter this subsistence strategy when they moved – indeed, agricultural products would have been both familiar and also desirable. Milk could only be acquired in significant quantities from domestic animals, and dairying seems to have been one of the defining characteristics of the early Neolithic. Likewise, we should also not underestimate the significance of carbohydrates in the diet. Cereals offered an opportunity to create foods such as bread, porridge and even beer (Milner 2010): again, these kinds of carbohydrate could not have been so easily produced by gathering (Barton 2014). As we have already seen, cattle in particular may quickly have become symbols of status and wealth which could be converted in high social standing (see previously). They may also have represented connections with other communities, particularly on mainland Europe. We have considered the importance of kin relations amongst humans, but animals could also have been conceived as coming from particular family groups with their own histories and biographies.

It is also worth considering the importance of food as an expression of social identity. Food can be a strong statement of affiliation. It appears that ways of cooking and serving food were not the same across Britain and Ireland. In Ireland milk fats were found in pottery with only a small number showing evidence for both milk and meat (Smyth and Evershed 2015b). In contrast, in Britain pots have the signature for cooking both meat and milk (Copley *et al*. 2005). Likewise barley was more commonly grown than wheat in northern Scotland, and people could have quite quickly developed regional ways of using this, from making different breads and soups through to different flavours of beer. Particular types of cooking specific foods may quickly have established identities for newcomers in these lands.

There is often the assumption that people in the early Neolithic practised broad-based agriculture (i.e. that each group or community kept animals, grew crops and gathered wild plants). While this may have been the case, we should also consider the possibility that particular groups specialised in the production of one type of food, so one group may have kept cattle, and another was involved in plant production and collection, which were exchanged at particular times of the year; this has been documented among other groups (Spielmann 2014). Equally, different age or gender groups may have undertaken specific jobs in relation to the production of different types of food. Such a model of production enables expertise to develop and may have translated beyond just subsistence into other areas of specialisation (for example, in the production of particular types of material culture). Thinking back once more to the Coneybury Anomaly, the remains found there could represent some people practising hunting and gathering (i.e. surviving Mesolithic peoples), but equally the presence of roe deer at the site could be resource specialisation by one sector of society, in this case the rather unusual choice of hunting wild animals.

SETTLEMENT

This final section considers the evidence for settlement in the early Neolithic of Britain and Ireland. This evidence is quite diverse and suggests a complex picture of occupation which was quite variable both across space and time. Clearly, some aspects of the early Neolithic were shared consistently by communities across Britain and Ireland, like making pottery and using domesticated plants and animals. However, the nature of settlement seems to have varied considerably. Evidence from lithic scatters, middens and pits will be considered first, followed by the more enduring forms of architecture evidenced through halls and houses. Finally, these different strands of data will be used to consider how settled or indeed how mobile people were in the early Neolithic.

Lithic scatters, middens and pits

Lithic scatters and stone axe finds have already been considered, but it is worth reiterating here that these are often the only remnants of early Neolithic settlement. In areas that have been intensively or deeply ploughed, any structural evidence may be long gone, and the stone tools are all that remains (and see Gibson 2003). However, it is also clear that some early Neolithic sites which have produced lithics were never associated with substantial structures, and often just the occasional stakehole, scoop or area of burning (hearth) is found. From this evidence it is possible to suggest that much early Neolithic occupation of a landscape involved transient settlement in most parts of Britain (Whittle 1997) and probably in Ireland (Cooney 2000). Precisely what lithic scatters represent is potentially problematic, because they could be the remains of anything from a quick knapping event while on the move to activity areas deliberately set aside from where people were living, for example, for the processing of hides. However, we can begin to make some educated guesses about what Neolithic settlement might entail. As we have seen, there is good evidence for people keeping cattle in the Neolithic. In addition to this people probably used a wide range of wild plant foods and maintained small garden plots of cereals. We might, therefore, suggest that people would have been moving around with their animals to use different pastures, perhaps between lowlands in the winter and uplands in the summer in some areas. Garden plots and favoured wild plant resources would need careful tending in the spring and summer in particular and thus would draw people back to particular places in the landscape at certain points of the year. Add to this the presence of monuments in the landscape, dealt with in detail in the next chapter, which saw the repeated investment of labour alongside ritualised acts also drawing people back to specific places. It is therefore possible to suggest that people remained mobile to a greater or lesser extent, with variability over time for much of the year. People were probably tied to specific landscapes from very early on in the Neolithic and might have returned to particular places on a cyclical basis, possibly every year. We might consider this a form of logistical mobility which is likely to represent the bulk of settlement patterns in the early Neolithic (Whittle 1997 and see Evans *et al*. 2016).

Middens are also found in the archaeological record and are the remnants of occupations of some sort, probably temporary but often repeatedly focused on one location. Middens are the accumulations of pottery, flint, animal bone, burnt material and organic material, and they seem to represent the gathering up and careful deposition of this material at a particular point in the landscape. In this sense they are deliberate and visible remnants of occupation, not just the casual discard of rubbish, and evidence suggests that they were places returned to and reworked over many decades. Early Neolithic middens have been found at both Ascott-under-Wychwood and

Hazleton North, preserved under subsequent monuments (Benson and Whittle 2007, Saville 1990). Both of these middens were also associated with small timber structures although these are not houses as described previously. Spreads of midden material were found at Eton rowing course, Buckinghamshire, in hollows; the thousands of pot sherds, lithics, animal bone fragments and quernstones led the excavators to suggest that the site had been used over a long period of time, even though no buildings were found (Allen et al. 2013). Early Neolithic middens have also been found in the far north. In Orkney, midden material pre-dated the construction of stone houses at the Knap of Howar, for example (Ritchie 1984). It is also interesting that some of the late Mesolithic shell midden and occupation sites in western Scotland also have early Neolithic material on them, including Ulva Cave, Carding Mill Bay, and Raschoille Cave, Argyll and Bute. At these sites both pottery and early Neolithic human bone have been found (Schulting and Richards 2002), showing an ongoing significance of middening and the continued use of certain places in the landscape across the Mesolithic-Neolithic transition.

Another form of evidence commonly found during excavations which offers additional evidence for understanding settlement are pits. For the most part single or small clusters of pits have been found, except in East Anglia, where very large numbers of pit clusters have been uncovered, with over 200 examples in some cases (see papers in Anderson-Whymark and Thomas 2012). In the early Neolithic of both Britain and Ireland, pit digging was a common practice, where it seems that material accumulated from occupation was then subsequently deposited in pits (Brophy and Noble 2012, Garrow 2007, Smyth 2014). Most pits contain the remnants of everyday occupation debris – stone tool knapping debris, pot sherds, hearth sweepings, plant remains and animal bone – and it seems that pits were dug and then rapidly backfilled with this material (Garrow 2007, p. 14). However, these pits should not simply be understood as the casual discard of rubbish. Instead it seems that there was a delay between the formation of the material and its subsequent deposition in a pit, suggesting this was a careful and considered act which took place at appropriate times only (Thomas 2012, p. 5). For example, the large pit clusters at Hurst Fen, Spong Hill, Kilverstone and Broom Heath in East Anglia clearly represent persistent places where this practice continued in the same place over time (see Garrow 2007). So far, this practice has not been found on this scale in other areas of Britain or Ireland, but there are also a few examples of larger pits which may represent the remains of larger gatherings. One of the best-known examples of these is the Coneybury Anomaly in Wiltshire, which we have already seen.

Timber halls in Britain

We now turn our attention to a rather different form of evidence for settlement: halls. In Britain a small number of large timber halls are now known, many discovered as the result of developer-led archaeology over the last two decades. These wooden timber structures were over 15 metres in length and would have been large and impressive buildings (Figures 4.19 and 4.20). They all date to the earliest centuries of the Neolithic. There are a small number of sites in England (for example, White Horse Stone, Kent; Yarnton, Oxfordshire; Horton, Berkshire; Cat's Brain, Wiltshire; Dorstone Hill, Herefordshire; and Lismore Fields, Derbyshire), Wales (Parc Cybi, Gwynedd) and Scotland (Claish, Stirling, Doon Hill in East Lothian; Lockerbie Academy, Dumfries and Galloway;

FIGURE 4.19
The timber hall at Claish (© Crown Copyright: Historic Environment Scotland)

and Balbridie and Warren Field in Aberdeenshire), although it seems likely that more will be found in due course (Barclay *et al*. 2020). These halls used massive timbers to create a long building which would have been roofed; to fell these trees and construct the hall would therefore have involved a significant investment of time and effort. Some were kept clean and therefore have not produced much in the way of material culture (Thomas 2013, p. 299); others have produced more, including large assemblages of cereal grains (in comparison with other early Neolithic sites), such as Balbridie, where 20,000 cereal grains were recovered (Fairweather and Ralston 1993). At the end of their use these timber buildings seem to have been carefully decommissioned, which often involved burning them down – another event which would have required considerable investment of time as well as being a spectacular visual spectacle (Noble 2006 and see Tringham 2005).

These sites have been called halls because they are very significant structures comparable with halls found from different periods. This does not mean, however, that people

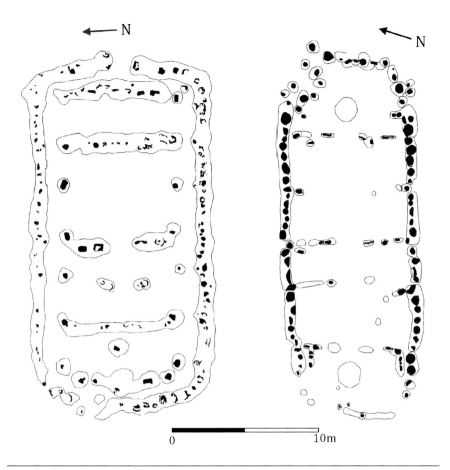

FIGURE 4.20
The timber halls at Warren Field and Balbridie, Aberdeenshire (after Brophy 2007 and Murray *et al*. 2009)

were not living in these structures, but clearly they were large enough to accommodate a considerable number of people (Thomas 2013, p. 306). Whether or not people lived in these structures all year round is a different matter altogether. Some have argued that they may have acted as places for congregation for otherwise dispersed kinship groups (Brophy 2007, Cooney 2000), which may also have involved seasonal activities such as the processing and storing of cereals. There has also been the suggestion that these structures acted more like feasting halls where people congregated for special events or ritualised activities (Brophy 2007, Cross 2003). Julian Thomas (2013, 2015b) has recently argued that these halls were essentially symbols of a new Neolithic way of life which were constructed as part of the creation of new social groups and thus the foundation of new lineages. He argues that these were places where people not connected by blood ties could come together to form new social groupings, or 'house societies', as they are known from anthropological parallels (and also see Richards and Jones 2015b). While we do not have an accurate understanding of the original numbers

FIGURE 4.21
The location of houses, middens and pit sites discussed in Chapter 4

of these houses, they certainly have not been found in as large numbers as chambered tombs, for example – so while they may have been a powerful architectural symbol standing for broader affiliations, it was a symbol that did not have the same resonance as other forms of architecture, nor the uptake of construction as seen in other parts of Neolithic Europe. Instead, there was a short burst of construction of halls at the start of the Neolithic only.

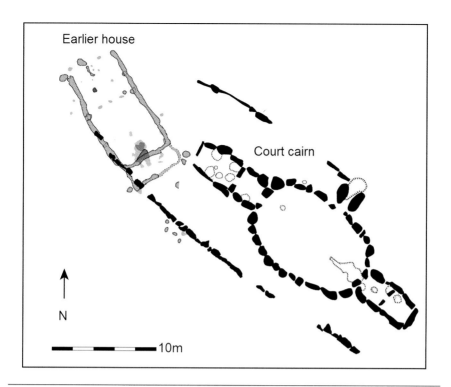

FIGURE 4.22
The house at Ballyglass, Co. Mayo (after Smyth 2020)

Irish house horizon

Over in Ireland at a site called Ballyglass in County Mayo, people constructed a smaller timber building (Figure 4.22). Measuring 13 by 6m, this was still a substantial timber building, and there is good evidence that the house was used from the remains of pottery which contained food remnants and burnt areas probably representing hearths (Smyth 2020). What is slightly more unusual is that at a later date the house at Ballyglass was replaced with a chambered tomb, helping preserve the earlier remains of the house. The structure at Ballyglass is in keeping with other examples from Ireland (Figure 4.23). Typically less than 10m long but occasionally up to 15m in length, over 90 rectangular timber houses have now been found in Ireland (Smyth 2014). Many of these houses have been found and excavated in the last 20 years as part of the boom in developer-funded archaeology, particularly to the east of the island. One of the most remarkable aspects of these houses is that they were constructed in a very specific period of the early Neolithic: these houses were built between 3730 and 3660 cal BC and were used until between 3640 and 3605 cal BC (Whittle *et al*. 2011). This is a restricted period of time focused either side of 3650 BC and has been called the 'Irish house horizon' (Smyth 2014). These Irish timber houses are slightly smaller than the British examples described previously, but there are nevertheless a number of parallels with those timber halls. Some have evidence of domestic assemblages, including

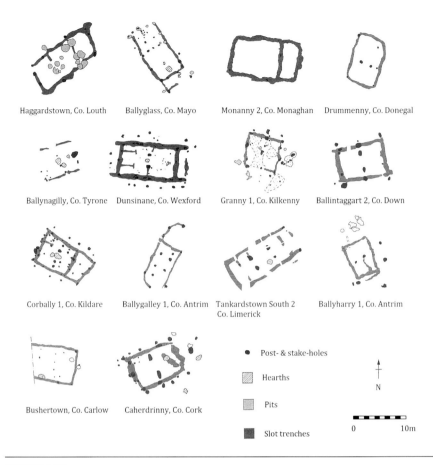

FIGURE 4.23
Examples of early Neolithic houses from Ireland (after Smyth 2014)

pottery, stone tools and cereals, meaning that domestic activity took place in many of these structures. At Ballygalley, Co. Antrim, for example, there were large amounts of carbonised grain, as well as stone tool working debris (Simpson 1996). Other sites, however, show evidence of little or no use, and some sites do not have hearths, which suggests limited occupation (Smyth 2014). There are some examples where multiple houses are found in one location (as at Corbally, Co. Kildare), and there are also examples which were constructed over previous activity, represented particularly in the form of pits (Smyth 2014, p. 22). These two factors are different from the timber halls in Britain, which were located in previously unoccupied parts of the landscape. However, just like the timber halls in Britain, many of these houses were deliberately and systematically burnt down at the end of their lives.

These houses may simply be smaller versions of the timber halls of Britain, fulfilling the same set of roles as those structures (see previously). What is so striking about these Irish examples, however, is the rapidity with which they were constructed across the entire island of Ireland. This suggests strong and wide-ranging contacts in place across, and beyond, Ireland in the early Neolithic and that this particular form of architecture had real resonance at this particular moment in time (and see Whittle *et al*. 2011, pp. 665–669). It has been argued that these structures were material metaphors for a bigger change in society (Smyth 2014, p. 41), an architectural expression of an agricultural way of life with strong connections to other places in Neolithic northern Europe (Thomas 2013, p. 290).

Other known houses

Outside the restricted early Neolithic hall and house horizon, there are other examples of houses, but they are much less common: it remains difficult to assess whether this is a genuine pattern or a reflection of different land uses and developments in Britain and Ireland. A few examples have been found recently in north-west Wales, and these could be understood as part of the early Neolithic tradition of house building seen in Ireland: the site at Parc Bryn Cegin, Llandygai, near Bangor was constructed and used between 3760–3700 and 3670–3620 cal BC (Kenney 2008, p. 26) and is therefore contemporary with the houses the other side of the Irish Sea. More early Neolithic houses have also been found at Llanfaethlu, Anglesey (Rees and Jones 2015). Occasional other examples have been found, such as the smaller houses at Horton, Berkshire, where there is also a large timber hall (Barclay 2014), and Gorhambury, Hertfordshire (Darvill 1996, p. 104). In Ireland the excavations at Tullahedy, Co. Tipperary, have produced houses which date to the tail end or just after the house horizon (Cleary and Kelleher 2011). There are also a range of possible sites where postholes and stakeholes may represent the remains of a structure of some sort (see Darvill 1996). However, other known houses are found in rather unusual settings. The site of Clegyr Boia in Pembrokeshire produced the remains of two possible early Neolithic houses, but these are positioned on the summit of a rocky outcrop, an unusual location for a settlement (Williams 1953). Early Neolithic occupation has also been found on hilltop enclosures such as Carn Brea in Cornwall (Mercer 2003). Small sub-circular timber buildings with central hearths have been found at Cowie near Stirling, one of a number of similar structures which have been discovered recently in Scotland (see Brophy 2016a).

Early Neolithic structures with associated occupation were also found at Eilean Dhomnuill, North Uist: this site is unusual as the houses are located on a small islet in a loch, a different setting than most other examples (Armit 2003, Figure 4.24). However, a recent research project has shown that Eilean Dhomnuill is not unique, and more of these islets were constructed in the early Neolithic in this part of the world (Garrow and Sturt 2019). These sites illustrate that people used a wide range of different locations, but there is the real possibility that some of these sites were not 'typical' settlements. The placing of structures on small islands or on top of rock outcrops may have been in order to isolate or remove some people from everyday life; there are plentiful ethnographic examples of certain members of a community being isolated at particular times of their lives, including for rites of passage (for example, from childhood to adulthood). It may well be the case that these structures, placed in liminal parts of the landscape, were set aside for people undergoing transformation; in this sense these are houses where people lived but can also be understood as playing a part in ritual life (also see Cummings and Richards 2013). The evidence from Eilean Dhomnuill supports this interpretation; the houses were shielded from view by screens, and the dominant activities at the site

FIGURE 4.24
Eilean Dhomnuil, North Uist. This islet was occupied in the early Neolithic

were eating and drinking, not day-to-day craft or subsistence activities. Other islets also seem to have been special locations more than simply places to live (see Garrow and Sturt 2019).

Orcadian and Shetland settlement evidence

One area of Britain where there is good evidence for the continued construction and use of houses is from the very north, incorporating the island groups of Orkney and Shetland. Orkney is well known for its stone houses at sites like Skara Brae, but these are late Neolithic, and it seems that in the early Neolithic, people in Orkney, like other parts of Britain and Ireland, built their houses from wood (Richards and Jones 2015a). At Wideford Hill, for example, an early Neolithic timber house was constructed associated with large quantities of cereal grain (Richards and Jones 2015a). Other timber houses have been found, for example at Ha'Breck, Wyre (Farrell *et al*. 2014, Lee and Thomas 2012, Figure 4.25). It is in later centuries (the middle Neolithic in this volume) that people in Orkney started building from stone (see Richards and Jones 2015b and Chapter 6).

On Shetland an early Neolithic house was excavated at the Hill of Crooksetter. A stone house along with two more ephemeral structures were found dating to 3635–3515 cal BC (Cummings *et al*. forthcoming). Just 20m to the north-east of the house, a contemporary feature was found; this was an area roughly 6 × 4m of intense burning which contained the burnt remains of stakes, wattle and posts along with three polished felsite

FIGURE 4.25
Timber house 4 at Ha'Breck, Wyre, Orkney (image reproduced courtesy of Dan Lee and Antonia Thomas)

axes, pot sherds from 25 vessels and nearly 3000 carbonised barley grains. This may well be a dismantled timber house which was decommissioned through burning (Cummings et al. forthcoming). This is the earliest example of house architecture, which, like in Orkney, continued to be built throughout the early Neolithic and beyond but which may also hint at primary wooden phases pre-dating those in stone.

Timber trackways

In the year 3807 or perhaps 3806 cal BC, people in the area now known as the Somerset Levels expended considerable energy building a wooden trackway. It was fairly simple in design but created a wooden walkway which stretched for nearly 2km across marshland, connecting up areas of more solid ground. We have already seen that stone axes were used to cut and shape the timbers used to build the trackway. What is extraordinary is that the Sweet Track overlaid an earlier timber trackway which had sunk into the marsh – the Post Track (Coles and Coles 1986). Once the Sweet Track had been constructed, there is evidence for repairs in both 3804 and 3800 cal BC. However, the entire structure was submerged shortly after the last repair, as the water levels in the marsh rose once again, preserving both the trackways for archaeologists to uncover. During the excavations a series of objects were found carefully deposited next to the trackway in the marsh, including a jadeitite axe, pottery, bows and arrows and other wooden artefacts (Coles and Coles 1986, pp. 57–62). The precise dates for the construction of this trackway come from dendrochronological dates on the timbers which are accurate to the year, and this provides us with a fascinating insight into life in this

FIGURE 4.26
The Sweet Track, Somerset, under excavation (copyright Somerset Levels Project)

part of Britain early in the Neolithic. What is so intriguing is why people went to such lengths to construct these trackways.

We now know that the Sweet Track is not unique – other examples are known: two early Neolithic trackways were recently discovered and excavated at Belmarsh, London (Hart 2015), and five at Wootton-Quarr, Isle of Wight (Loader 2007); one is recorded at Castle Donington, Leicestershire (Clay and Salisbury 1990), and an example was found at Storrs Moss, Yealand Redmayne in Lancashire (Powell *et al*. 1971). Indeed, Martin Bell lists 19 trackways from Britain dating to between 3800 and 3000 cal BC (Bell 2007, p. 337). There are examples in Ireland as well: Corlea 9, Co. Longford, dates to the early Neolithic (Raftery 1996). These wooden trackways seem to be about facilitating movement across wetlands or saltmarsh; these wetlands would be rich with a wide variety of resources, including fish, fowl and various species of plant, and may indicate that people lived on the edge of these areas in order to gain access to these resources. Wetlands, then, may have been used seasonally, but clearly they were important enough for people to expend energy building trackways across them. The presence of special deposits along the Sweet Track may also suggest that these sometimes saw ritualised activity and that a clear distinction between functional and ceremonial may not be relevant for the Neolithic (also see Bradley 2005a, Brück 1999). As with other aspects of the early Neolithic, it may well have been that this form of construction was one that was already established prior to the arrival of people into Britain. By building wooden trackways in their new home, people may well have been referencing European ways of doing things and their own origins on Mainland Europe.

All this evidence combined suggests that some people were mobile to some extent, at least for some of the year, probably following herds around the landscape (transhumance). However, it also seems to be the case that people were drawn to specific places at particular points in the year, perhaps points marked by architecture or by visible middens, and certainly in relation to plant food sources, grown or gathered. Timber architecture in the form of halls and houses, however, only seems to have had currency in the early Neolithic. The notable fall-off of hall and house construction after about 3600 cal BC seems to indicate that whatever function or functions they fulfilled, perhaps in the creation of new lineages, that after this point they were no longer necessary. Perhaps after this time other types of site, such as monuments, fulfilled the role that these houses and halls had at the onset of the Neolithic. It might, therefore, be fair to best describe early Neolithic settlement as tethered mobility, with people congregating at particular places at certain times of the year.

CONCLUSIONS: LIFE IN THE EARLY NEOLITHIC

This chapter has examined various aspects of life for people in the early Neolithic. New forms of material culture started to be produced at the start of the Neolithic, including pottery and new stone tool types. This clearly represents new technologies and ways of doing things that originated on mainland Europe and were brought over as existing technologies as people moved into these islands. In addition to this, pottery styles and the extensive distribution of stone axes indicate that there were wide networks of contact in place in the early Neolithic, not just within Britain and Ireland but also out to Europe. From this evidence it is possible to suggest that these were communities that may have maintained far-reaching networks, probably involving kinship ties. These networks, it can be argued, were important for the adoption of these new technologies. Yet people did not make things exactly as their predecessors had, and moving to a new land inspired new forms of material culture from the outset. Equally important, but rarely surviving in the archaeological record, are perishable objects, which seem to have been important in many areas. What is clear is that not all types of early Neolithic material culture were adopted simultaneously across Britain and Ireland and then used throughout this period. Pottery was one of the first new technologies to be used, and it continued to be made throughout the Neolithic, albeit in increasingly regionalised styles. In contrast, stone axe production seems to have peaked between 3700 and 3500 cal BC, indicating more restricted production of this type of object.

Many types of material culture may well have been intimately tied up with the subsistence practices introduced into Britain with the onset of the Neolithic, specifically domesticated animals and crops. Cattle and cereal seem to have been widely used by people in the early Neolithic throughout Britain and Ireland. Domesticated plants and animals enabled highly desirable foodstuffs to be produced, including carbohydrates, dairy foods and beer, which could be accumulated and distributed through feasting. This would have been critical for growing social networks and for the sponsorship of large-scale building projects. At the same time, the care of domesticated animals in particular may well have created very specific relationships between people, animals and persistent places in the landscape which had far-reaching implications played out across the rest of the Neolithic. In contrast, after an initial enthusiastic uptake of cereal cultivation, as we will see in Chapter 6, some Neolithic communities may have ceased growing cereals by the middle Neolithic.

Houses also seem to have been important at a specific point in the early Neolithic, but they were not constructed consistently throughout the period. Instead there are distinctive 'house horizons' in both Britain and Ireland which saw the sudden, but not long-lasting, construction of wooden structures. These houses and halls almost certainly functioned not only as dwelling places but may, in some cases, also have operated in much the same way as some of the monuments discussed in the next chapter: fixed locales in the landscape where populations could congregate at particular times of the year to conduct everyday as well as ritual affairs. This seems particularly fitting for the large timber halls which have been found in southern and central England and lowland Scotland and may have been about new kin networks making a statement about belonging in that place. Beyond this initial construction of timber house architecture, people may have been involved in tethered mobility settlement patterns, following their animals as well as using a whole range of different parts of the landscape for tools, resources and food. Occupation was not a casual act, however; it seems to have involved the careful orchestration and sometimes deposition of the remains of occupations in both middens and pits. Certain places seem to have drawn people back time and again, and sometimes those places became formalised in other ways, such as through the construction of monuments. It is fitting, then, that the next chapter considers the range of early Neolithic monuments which were constructed in Britain and Ireland, and it is worth highlighting here that monuments themselves were not just ritual sites which stood apart from everyday life and activity. These were places which would have themselves structured movements and occupations of the landscape. They were as much a part of life as pottery, food and cattle.

RECOMMENDED FURTHER READING

There are lots of good books on the different types of evidence presented in this chapter.

Stone tools, axes and flint mines: these are a few years old but are the best overviews.

Edmonds, M., 1995. *Stone tools and society*. London: Batsford.
Russell, M., 2000. *Flint mines in Neolithic Britain*. Stroud: Tempus.

Pottery: likewise, dated but still a good place to start

Gibson, A., 2002. *Prehistoric pottery in Britain and Ireland*. Stroud: Tempus.

Also see

Müller, J. and Peterson, R., 2015. Ceramics and society in northern Europe. *In:* C. Fowler, J. Harding, and D. Hofmann, eds. *The Oxford handbook of Neolithic Europe*. Oxford: Oxford University Press, 573–604.

Organic material culture

Hurcombe, L., 2014. *Perishable material culture in prehistory*. London: Routledge.

Subsistence

Serjeantson, D., 2011. *Review of animal remains from the Neolithic and early Bronze Age of southern Britain*. Swindon: English Heritage.

Houses and timber halls

Barclay, A., Field, D., and Leary, J., eds., 2020. *Houses of the dead?* Oxford: Oxbow.
Smyth, J., 2014. *Settlement in the Irish Neolithic*. Oxford: Oxbow.

Overall accounts of early Neolithic life can be found in

Thomas, J., 2013. *The birth of Neolithic Britain: An interpretive account*. Oxford: Oxford University Press.
Whittle, A., Healy, F., and Bayliss, A., 2011. *Gathering time: Dating the early Neolithic enclosures of southern Britain and Ireland*. Oxford: Oxbow.

CHAPTER 5

Of earth, bone, timber and stone

Mortuary practice and monumentality in the early Neolithic of Britain and Ireland

INTRODUCTION

On the banks of the River Thames roughly 6000 years ago, people dug a shallow grave in the sand. To stop the sand collapsing into the freshly dug grave, they shored up one side with an oak plank; then they laid the remains of a young adult women in the grave. She was carefully positioned, flexed and placed on her side, and she was accompanied by stone tools, including a polished flint axe and pot sherds. One pot rim was from a finely made Carinated Bowl which was deliberately placed near her head. In amongst the backfilled sand were cereal grains, indicating, along with the pottery and stone tools, that this person was buried by people practising agriculture. The site is now known as Yabsley Street in London, and is a fine, if unusual, example of an early Neolithic burial (Coles *et al*. 2008). This burial sets the scene for us, as this chapter will begin by examining the diverse range of mortuary practices that have been documented from the early Neolithic period. Yabsley Street is actually fairly unusual for the early Neolithic, and human remains, when recovered, suggest that, for the most part, people were not buried in formal graves or monuments but underwent what was often a complex series of rites. The chapter then moves on to consider the range of different structures built from earth, timber and stone in the early Neolithic of Britain and Ireland. These monuments includes the well-known chambered tombs of the Cotswold-Severn region and the court cairns of Ireland through to dolmens and causewayed enclosures. These monuments were constructed from a range of materials including wood, stone and earth, and some, but not all, involved the treatment and deposition of the dead. Moreover, there are significant regional differences, which means that some monuments are

DOI: 10.4324/9781003387329-5

OF EARTH, BONE, TIMBER AND STONE **101**

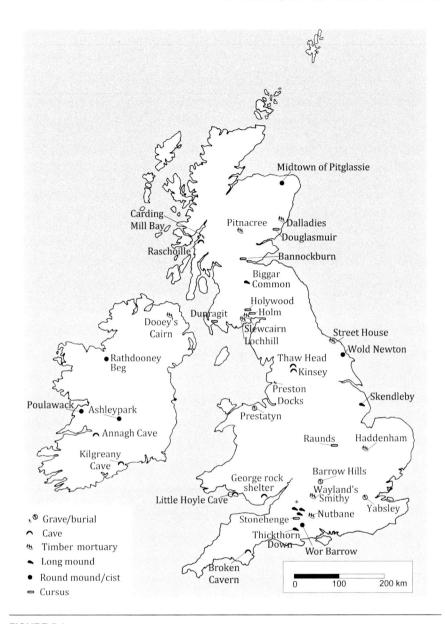

FIGURE 5.1
The location of sites discussed in this chapter, except chambered tombs (see Figure 5.4) and causewayed enclosures (see Figure 5.27) *=Norton Bevant, Beckhampton Road and South Street

found in dense concentrations in some parts of Britain and Ireland while being entirely absent in others. This will paint quite a diverse picture of monument building and mortuary practice in the early Neolithic. Finally, it is worth noting here that the early Neolithic is defined as the start of the Neolithic in each area (see Chapter 3), up to around about 3400 BC.

MORTUARY PRACTICE IN THE EARLY NEOLITHIC

We began with a consideration of the grave at Yabsley Street, London, and there are a small number of similar burials known from the early Neolithic. For example, a grave containing an articulated female skeleton was found in Prestatyn, north Wales (Schulting 2007, p. 583), and at Barrow Hills, Oxfordshire (discussed subsequently in relation to its mortuary enclosure), beyond the enclosure were three flat graves, which are early or middle Neolithic in date (Barclay and Halpin 1997, Figure 5.2). Single graves are also found as part of mortuary practice at some causewayed enclosures (see subsequently), but beyond this context this does not seem to have been a common practice. This can be considered rather unusual because many parts of mainland Europe in the Neolithic have produced evidence for inhumation cemeteries, but this does not occur in Britain and Ireland.

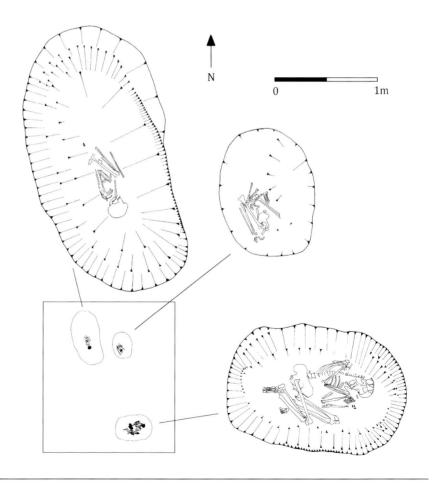

FIGURE 5.2
The flat graves at Barrow Hills, Oxfordshire (after Barclay and Halpin 1997)

While individual graves are unusual, and cemeteries unknown, caves and fissures in rock seem to have been used more extensively for a range of mortuary practice in the early Neolithic. There are a number of sites in Britain and Ireland which have produced human remains which have radiocarbon dates from the early Neolithic, and it is likely that many more undated deposits are from this period as well (see Peterson 2019, Schulting 2007). There is good evidence for caves receiving a series of successive burials. A number of sites in south Wales, for example, have skeletal material, including the remains of at least 18 individuals from Little Hoyle Cave in Pembrokeshire which were located beneath the central chimney feature: some of these are definitely early Neolithic (Peterson 2019). At Cave Ha 3 in North Yorkshire, four individuals were deposited fleshed in the niches at the back of the cave. Other good examples of this practice include Kinsey Cave and Thaw Head Cave, both in North Yorkshire, and Hay Wood Cave, Somerset. As we shall see, this practice of adding burials to a known location is replicated in built architecture, particularly in the form of chambered tombs. Other practices took place in caves, however, including single burials, and Dowd (2015) has argued that in Ireland, at least, this was a burial practice that was distinct from those occurring contemporaneously in monuments. In Ireland good examples of human remains in caves include Annagh Cave, Co. Limerick, and Kilgreany Cave, Co. Waterford (Dowd 2015, p. 95).

In Britain, caves also seem to have been used as places to store bodies before elements were retrieved, perhaps, but not necessarily, for burial elsewhere. At George Rock Shelter, part of the Goldsland Caves located just outside Cardiff, the remains of at least two early Neolithic people were recovered, with clear evidence that this was a location for the exposure and fragmentation of human remains (Peterson 2012 and see Figure 5.3).

FIGURE 5.3
Excavations at George Rock Shelter which produced the disarticulated remains of two early Neolithic individuals (photo by Rick Peterson)

A similar situation may have occurred at Broken Cavern in Devon where human teeth were found associated with material including animal remains, pottery and stone debitage (Peterson 2019, p. 108). In addition to this, caves (alongside middens) seem to have been used as places for excarnation in the early Neolithic. A mass of disarticulated human remains was recovered from Raschoille Cave near Oban. The early Neolithic Carding Mill Bay midden, also located in a rock shelter, has produced early Neolithic human remains which had clearly been left on the midden, and the suggestion is that whole bodies were placed here to deflesh. There is also evidence for another extraordinary practice in the early Neolithic represented in caves but also at other monumental sites: the head only removed from the body and deposited. This practice could well be understood as a 'head cult' (see Peterson 2019, p. 125), and examples include Sewell's Cave, North Yorkshire, and Robin Hood's Cave, Derbyshire. This again indicates complex burial practices because in these instances a body would need to be buried or stored somewhere prior to sufficient decomposition in order to easily remove the head. The evidence from caves, therefore, paints a picture of varied and mixed burial practices taking place in early Neolithic Britain and Ireland (Peterson 2019).

As already noted, the treatment of skeletal remains in caves sometimes bears a striking resemblance to that found in chambered tombs (see subsequently). In both cases it is clear that bodies were laid out in either the cave or tomb, which could enable the body to be defleshed; in some cases the defleshed bones could then be removed or ordered. It also seems to be the case that both caves and chambered tombs were used for the deposition of already disarticulated remains, including heads. This has led to the suggestion that chambered tombs and caves may have used interchangeably; certainly both provide secluded spaces for the deposition and subsequent disarticulation of bodies (see Barnatt and Edmonds 2002). The closeness of sites such as Goldsland Cave and nearby Tinkinswood chambered tomb, for example, also lends weight to this argument. But while caves and chambered tombs may have been used in similar ways in terms of enabling different types of primary and secondary mortuary practices, people are unlikely to have thought about the two in the same way, with caves being unaltered natural places, while monuments were clearly constructed by people. The caves may have been known and possibly special places prior to burial in the early Neolithic. However, as noted in Chapter 2, caves were not used for burial in the preceding late Mesolithic period, so their use in the early Neolithic was clearly a new practice which, like other aspects of the Neolithic, originated on Mainland Europe (Peterson 2019, Chapter 5, Schulting 2007, p. 588). Cave burial also took place where there are no chambered tombs, and there is also variation across Britain and Ireland in the exact ways in which caves were used. Caves, then, were probably incorporated into localised but distinctly Neolithic mortuary practice.

Other natural places have produced human remains. There are occasional skeletal remains recovered from rivers which date to the early Neolithic. An early Neolithic skull was recovered from the River Thames (Bradley and Gordon 1988), and four human skulls dating to the earlier fourth millennium cal BC were dredged from the docks in Preston, Lancashire (Smith and Brickley 2009, p. 42). From this extremely limited evidence it might be possible to suggest that people were regularly cast into watercourses; archaeologically it would be unusual to expect the vast majority of these to survive. However, there may have been other practices and processes in place which resulted in these remains, for example, swollen rivers washing away human remains left or buried near a river. There is also evidence that mortuary practice may also have involved deliberate predation; some early Neolithic human bones found in a variety of contexts have evidence of gnawing, which suggests that some bodies were left out to be skeletonised by predators such as wolves and foxes (Smith and Brickley 2009, p. 44). Again, if this was a common practice, we would not expect to find much evidence of it in the archaeological record since in most cases it would result in all the remains being destroyed. The only other rite we have not considered here is that of cremation. Cremated remains are commonly found in monumental contexts, particularly chambered tombs and wooden mortuary structures (see subsequently). In most cases it is clear that the cremation event did not take place within the monument, and this must mean that the pyre firing took place elsewhere and the cremated remains collected up before deposition in a monument or elsewhere. There is only limited evidence at present for where these cremation events may have taken place, and cremation may have been practised widely.

It may well be the case, then, that a considerable proportion of the deceased in the early Neolithic were disposed of in rivers, caves, trees or other natural places, or their bodies reduced to bones through excarnation or predation. Certainly, as we will see, very few ended up in the constructions we call monuments. What, then, does this tell us about belief systems at the time? In many ways, the early Neolithic can be seen as a continuation of practices which took place across Europe from the Upper Palaeolithic onwards, where the vast majority of people were disposed of not through formal burial but by being deposited in natural places or by the removal of the flesh from the body so that the skeleton could be used in depositional practice or as artefacts in their own right.

It is documented ethnographically that the vast majority of people believe that the process of dying involves the spirit or soul leaving the body, and that a component of that spirit or soul goes on to be reborn or to the afterlife (e.g. Metcalf and Huntington 1991). In order for the spirit to successfully get to its destination, many rituals are performed, often involving the remains of the dead. This is because the transition from life to death is a potentially drawn-out and tricky transformation, which if handled incorrectly can have disastrous consequences for the living. Spirits or souls can lose their way and potentially come back and cause many problems for their living descendants. Mortuary rituals are often, therefore, concerned with making sure that the soul or spirit is properly separated from the mortal remains. The defleshing of bodies via a variety of natural and cultural processes is well documented in the anthropological record and is often part of the rituals which enable a soul to leave this world and make its way to its new destination. Quite clearly the process of defleshing bones through natural processes was a key practice in the early Neolithic, and we could perhaps interpret this as the freeing of the spirit. If the freeing of the soul was achieved through predation, for which there is some evidence, then it would be possible to argue that perhaps people believed that those predators took on part of the soul of the deceased (Fowler 2010, p. 15). In this respect it would be possible to argue for wild animals playing an important role in Neolithic belief systems, and this could easily explain why these animals were not consumed even though abundantly available. It is also suggestive that early Neolithic belief systems were concerned with the ancestral dead (Fowler 2021). It is also clear is that these early Neolithic mortuary rites evoked rites and practices which had their origins on Mainland Europe which were well established prior to the arrival of the Neolithic on our islands and which included the use of caves and also the construction of various types of monument where mortuary rituals were incorporated. In order to further understand early Neolithic belief systems, it is to these monuments that we now turn and consider in some detail.

EARLY NEOLITHIC CHAMBERED TOMBS

At some point in the later part of the 38th century cal BC, people on the western side of the Black Mountains constructed a large chambered tomb. They chose a location which had already been used for transient occupation, perhaps by their forebears

FIGURE 5.4
The distribution of early Neolithic chambered tombs and dolmens

(Whittle *et al.* 2022b, p. 258). This clearing in woodland then saw the construction of at least four chambers: one large compartment built from slabs of stone and three much smaller cells (Figure 5.5 top middle). These chambers were then enclosed in an enormous cairn over 50m long end to end. To the south-east the builders constructed a forecourt where people could gather, and the whole monument was encased in high-quality walling, creating a visually stunning stone monument which would have stood out in the wider landscape. Over the course of the next few hundred years (between 200 and 500 years), human remains were then deposited in the chambers (Whittle *et al.* 2022b, Wysocki 2022). The remains of these people may have been added as whole skeletons, but over time their bones became mixed, as perhaps some bones were removed or added in bursts of activity and deposition. Three of the people deposited had been victims of violence, two involving arrowhead wounds (Figure 5.19) and one a blow to the head. It has been suggested that this monument represents early Neolithic people (although not the very earliest) laying claim to this particular location and its wider landscape (Whittle *et al.* 2022b). It shares some similarities with chambered tomb we saw in Chapter 1 (Hazleton North) but also has important differences, notably being built earlier and staying in use for longer. This site is now known as Penywyrlod, and it is an excellent example of a chambered tomb (see Britnell and Whittle 2022), raising many of the key aspects of this kind of monument, which we will now explore in more detail.

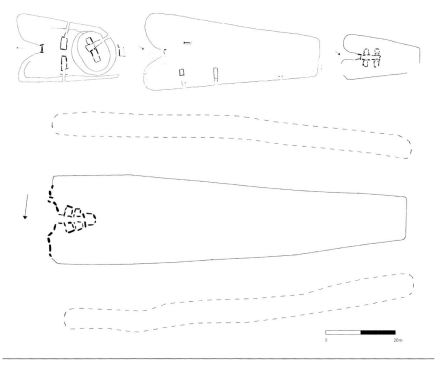

FIGURE 5.5
Plans of a selection of Cotswold-Severn chambered tombs. Top from left to right: Ty Isaf, Powys; Penywyrlod, Powys; Parc le Breos Cwm, Glamorgan. Bottom: West Kennet, Wiltshire (after Corcoran 1969a)

Chambered tombs are one of the most recognisable monuments dating from the early Neolithic. They are found in discrete regional clusters and are often referred to by these regional names. The chambered tombs under consideration here are: (1) the Cotswold-Severn chambered tombs found predominantly in Gloucestershire, Wiltshire, Oxfordshire, Somerset and into south Wales including the Black Mountains and the Gower (Figure 5.5–7); (2) the Clyde cairns of western Scotland found mostly in Argyll and Bute but also occurring as far south as Dumfries and Galloway and as far north as the Western Isles (Figure 5.8 and 5.9); (3) the stalled cairns of northern Scotland found in Caithness, Sutherland, and in the Orkney Islands (Figure 5.10 and 5.11); and (4) the court cairns of Ireland, which are found in the northern half of the island of Ireland (Figure 5.12 and 13). These monuments will be considered here as a whole, as they share many key similarities, and will be referred to as early Neolithic chambered tombs from here on. I also want to point out that there are some chambered tombs which are considered elsewhere in the book: in particular the monuments known as portal dolmens, portal tombs and passage graves/tombs are not included here (dolmens are considered separately in the following, as they are a different form of monument entirely, and passage graves in the next chapter because they are later). It is also worth noting that the early Neolithic chambered tombs are not found everywhere in Britain and Ireland but only in some parts of these islands (Figure 5.4). The distribution is predominantly western and northern; significant parts of eastern Britain and southern Ireland do not have any early Neolithic chambered tombs, although they have other types of monument (see subsequently in relation to long barrows).

FIGURE 5.6
West Kennett Cotswold-Severn monument

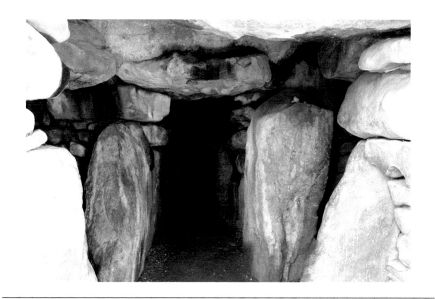

FIGURE 5.7
View looking into the chambers at West Kennet

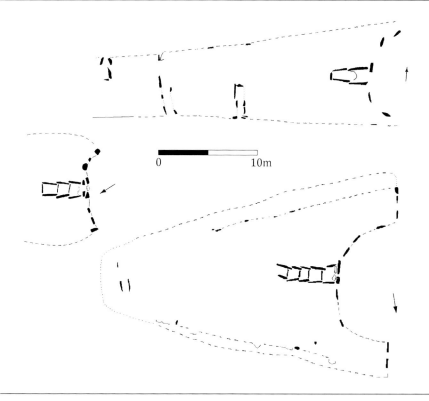

FIGURE 5.8
Plans of a selection of Clyde (western Scottish) chambered tombs. Top: Gort na h'Ulaidhe, Kintyre, middle: Monamore, Arran and bottom: East Bennan, Arran (after Henshall 1972)

FIGURE 5.9
Blasthill chambered tomb, Kintyre, looking at the façade

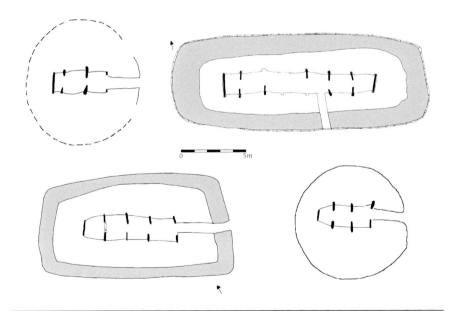

FIGURE 5.10
Plans of a selection of stalled (northern Scottish) chambered tombs. Top left: Warehouse North, Caithness; top right: Blackhammer, Rousay; bottom left: Knowe of Yarso, Rousay; bottom right: Kierfea Hill, Rousay (after Henshall 1963)

FIGURE 5.11
Midhowe stalled cairn, Rousay, Orkney, showing the stalls which divide up the chamber

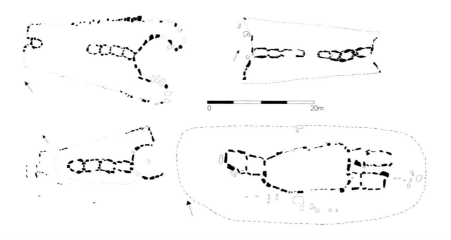

FIGURE 5.12
Plans of a selection of court cairns (Irish chambered tombs) Top left: Ballymarlagh, Co. Antrim, top right: Audleystown, Co. Down (dual court cairn), bottom left: Browndod, Co. Antrim, and bottom right: Deerpark, Co. Sligo (central court cairn) after de Valera 1960

FIGURE 5.13
The court cairn at Ballymacdermot, Co. Armagh

Monumental form

Early Neolithic chambered tombs exhibit some regional variation, but all share several key features in their final form. As their name suggests, one of these features is the presence of a chamber or chambers. The chambers on these monuments are built using slabs of stone, which essentially create a box or series of boxes. The chamber is then roofed with a slim capstone or series of capstones and in some cases layers of overlapping stones called corbels. The vast majority of chambered tombs have quite small chambers, which may most easily have been accessed from above; this would involve removing the capstone or capstones and placing deposits in the chamber from above. There are examples, however, where it would be possible to actually walk into the chamber because they are sufficiently large the chambers are sufficiently large to accommodate people. A number of the Cotswold-Severn monuments could have been accessed via a small entranceway and passage which led to chambers large enough to fit both the remains of the dead and several living participants. One of the largest chambers is that at West Kennet, Wiltshire (Figures 5.5 and 5.7), but this is not typical for these monuments (Darvill 2004, p. 102). Penywyrlod, which we have just seen, is more typical, where the smaller chambers are much more modest in size, although still accessible by crawling along the passage. Some of the larger stalled cairns and court cairns could also have been accessed in this way.

The chambers of these chambered tombs are usually rectangular or sub-rectangular, and there is a sense of space being divided up into discrete units. Amongst the Cotswold-Severn monuments, smaller chambers are sometimes clustered around a central passage, as at West Kennet and Parc le Breos Cwm on the Gower (see

Figure 5.5). Multiple single chambers can also be found within these monuments, situated at the side of the long cairn (lateral chambers), as at Penywyrlod or the front end of the monument (terminal chambers). The stalled cairns of northern Scotland are also rectangular or sub-rectangular, but in this case the chamber is divided up by standing uprights which effectively create smaller chambers or stalls, hence the name (see Figure 5.10). Both Clyde and court cairns typically consist of a series of small boxes in a row, accessed from the terminal end of the monument, but with some variations. Some Clyde cairns have small lateral chambers such as at Gort na h'Ulaidhe, Kintyre, and there are variations amongst the court cairns as well. At Audleystown, Co. Down, two chambers are set back-to-back, with a gap between the two chambers, accessed from either end of the cairn. At Aghnaglack, Co. Fermanagh, there is a single chamber, divided into four, but with a court at either end of the long cairn. Another variation of the court cairn is the central or enclosed court. At Deerpark, Co. Sligo, for example, chambers are found on opposing sides of the central court (see Figure 5.12). As discussed in the following, these chambers were uniformly used for the deposition of the remains of the dead.

Another shared key element of these chambered tombs is that the chambers are usually enclosed within a long cairn or mound (sometimes referred to as a 'barrow'). The stalled cairn tradition has a slight variation from this, in that stalled cairns are set within both round and long cairns. These cairns or mounds not only enclosed the chambers within but also created a substantial presence in the landscape, as already seen at Penywyrlod. In many cases these cairns and mounds are trapezoidal in shape, which means that they are wider at one end than the other. The widest end also contained a forecourt, another key feature of these monuments (see subsequently). Less attention is often paid to the cairns or mounds at these chambered tombs since the chambers saw the most significant deposits, but the cairn/mound was an important component of the monument and, most critically, provides an area of significant overlap with another form of monument which is the unchambered long cairn/mound. These are discussed separately subsequently, but there are similarities with those and the cairns/mounds of chambered tombs. Cotswold-Severn sites which have been excavated have often produced evidence that the mound was built in a 'modular' fashion so that the mound comprised what were essentially a series of interlocking sections. At Ascott-under-Wychwood, Oxfordshire, for example, the barrow was constructed from 21 separate bays, each defined by lines of stakes and stones and filled with earth, stone and turf (Benson and Whittle 2007). Such features may have also occurred in cairns but would be harder to identify in stone. The cairn or mound also often saw significant alteration over time, with elements being added or altered in several different periods of construction (and see subsequently).

The final key element of early Neolithic chambered tombs is the presence of a forecourt. This provided a focal area for people to gather and potentially conduct rituals associated with the use of these monuments. The forecourt area varies considerably amongst these monuments. Some are extremely well defined and create a distinctive enclosed area. This is particularly obvious at many of the court cairns in Ireland and Clyde cairns in western Scotland (Figure 5.14). Forecourts are rarely as monumental amongst the Cotswold-Severn group, with the shaping of the mound or cairn and presence of the chamber entrance (or dummy entrances in some cases) being sufficient. Amongst

FIGURE 5.14
The distinctive façade at Cairnholy I, creating a forecourt at the front of the chambered tomb

the stalled cairns the forecourt was simply the area in front of the entrance to the chamber and often does not seem to have been formally marked out at all, although one end of the cairn being horn shaped created a forecourt in some examples. The construction of a chamber or chambers set within a cairn or mound with the presence of a forecourt would appear to make these fairly simple monuments. However, these were actually complex, multi-phase monuments, with some of these components only being added on much later in the life histories of these sites.

Sequences of construction

A number of excavated chambered tombs have revealed evidence for quite complicated sequences of construction, indicating that this type of monument was not always designed and built in one phase of activity. Instead, chambered tombs were often constructed in places where activity had already taken place and then altered and expanded once built.

In some instances there is evidence for occupation and/or activity prior to construction of the chambered cairn (known as pre-cairn activity). This has led to the suggestion that these monuments were built in known locales in the landscape or at the very least in pre-existing clearances. At Ascott-under-Wychwood, Oxfordshire, there was both early Neolithic as well as late Mesolithic activity underneath the monument (Benson and Whittle 2007). The early Neolithic evidence is particularly interesting, as it seems to have involved various activities, including the creation of a midden. A small timber structure was built, flint was knapped and food was consumed; over time a midden formed. Pre-cairn occupation was noted at other Cotswold-Severn monuments, including Gwernvale, Penywyrlod and Hazleton North, involving, amongst other things, small quantities of human remains (Darvill 2004, p. 93). Pre-cairn activity has also been found under both Clyde and court cairns. For example, a small shell midden was found underneath the monument at Glecknabae, Argyll, and hearths, pots, tools and cremated human bone was found underneath the court cairn of Ballybriest, Co. Derry. In the previous chapter we saw that at Ballyglass, Co. Mayo, the remains of an entire house were found underneath the later court cairn. It is also worth noting here that some monuments have pre-cairn wooden components. At Gwernvale, Powys, the stone monument had postholes which would have held wooden posts creating a timber structure (a house?) in the area pre-dating the construction of the forecourt (Britnell 2022). The court cairn at Rathlackan, Co. Mayo, had a series of timber stakes or posts in the forecourt (Byrne *et al.* 2009). While there is some evidence for pre-cairn activity prior to the construction of some monuments, this did not occur at all sites. Therefore occupation or earlier activity was not a pre-requisite for monument construction, although where it did occur it would have added to the significance and life history of the monument.

While the final form of these chambered tombs has been described previously, it is important to note that in a number of cases these sites began life as much smaller monuments which were subsequently altered. In western Scotland there is good evidence that some Clyde cairns began life as small and simple 'boxes' (sometimes described as cists) set within small circular cairns. Scott (1992) described these as 'proto-megaliths' to indicate the phase before the main construction of a chambered tomb. A good example of this is Mid Gleniron I in Dumfries and Galloway, which began as a small simple chamber set within a small oval cairn. Next another chamber was added in front of the first chamber and again set within its own small oval cairn. At a later date a third chamber was added between the earlier chambers, and the whole monument was incorporated into a long cairn with a façade built at one end (Figure 5.15). A similar sequence of

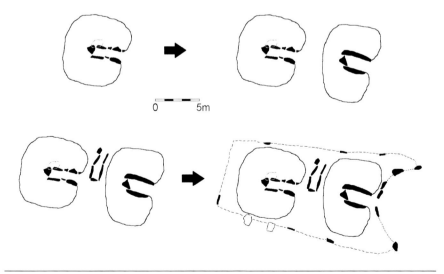

FIGURE 5.15
The sequence of construction at Mid Gleniron I, Dumfries and Galloway (after Corcoran 1969b)

construction was documented at Mid Gleniron II just a short distance from the first site (Corcoran 1969b). A similar sequence has been proposed for the chambered tomb at Blasthill, Kintyre, and here it appears that the first phase monument dated close to the start of the Neolithic in this area (Cummings and Robinson 2015 and see subsequently).

There is similar evidence amongst the Cotswold-Severn group where the early phase of a chambered tomb is often known as a 'rotunda'. At Notgrove, Gloucestershire, the primary phase consisted of a central cist surrounded by a circular cairn roughly 7m in diameter (Darvill 2004, p. 60). Similar primary phases have been noted at Sale's Lot, Gloucestershire, and Ty Isaf, Powys (but see Whittle *et al*. 2022b, p. 269). The same is found in northern Scotland, with a small number of little box-like structures found in stalled cairns such as Holm of Papa Westray North in Orkney (Ritchie 2009). There is little evidence for simple, stand-alone box chambers amongst the Irish court cairns at present, although further excavation in the future might reveal similar cases to those in the Clyde series. This does not mean that the court cairns are single-phase monuments, however, as the enclosed court cairns in Ireland are almost definitely built in several phases. The majority of these sites appear to have started off as single court cairns to which another court cairn was added. By building the horns of another court cairn up against the horns of a pre-existing monument, this would create the central court area (Figure 5.16). In other examples, horn-work was added, and additional chambers were also inserted into existing cairns (Jones 2007). The precise date of this work is unclear. It is worth considering that the first phase of some of these early Neolithic chambered tombs was a timber mortuary structure. These are dealt with separately subsequently, but there are documented timber mortuary structures under court cairns, Clyde cairns and Cotswold-Severn monuments.

FIGURE 5.16
Creevykeel, Co. Sligo, looking into the enclosed court

At this point it is worth briefly considering the few examples of very early Neolithic chambered tomb which cannot be paralleled with sites anywhere else in Britain or Ireland. These unusual sites have all been securely dated to the early Neolithic and are stone-built chambered tombs, but they do not resemble the set of sites we have otherwise been considering. One of the earliest dated chambered tombs is that of Coldrum, Kent. Here the chamber is made from massive slabs but set on the edge of a natural terrace (Wysocki *et al*. 2013). It is close to a small number of monuments known as the 'Medway group', which are dolmens (see subsequently); Coldrum itself could conceivably be a dolmen which has lost its capstone. Broadsands in Devon has also produced early dates for the monument there (Sheridan *et al*. 2008). It has been described as a passage grave, but it seems likely that, like a number of sites in Britain and Ireland, it was converted into a passage grave at a later date (post-3500 BC). Without the passage it is a rather peculiar monument in an area with very few chambered tombs. Burn Ground, Gloucestershire, also has an eccentric plan where the primary phase is likely to be a long passage which was later converted into a Cotswold-Severn monument: this also has early dates (Thomas 2013, p. 317). Finally, the site of Mull Hill on the Isle of Man has produced early Neolithic pottery, but the arrangement of six chambers in a circle does not resemble any other monument. If we consider these peculiar monuments and the first phase of other types of chambered tomb, it seems that there was considerable diversity amongst these primary-phase chambered tombs. Thus it seems that it was only later that the style of building became homogenised, and people started to follow specific 'rules' when building these monuments.

Mortuary deposits in chambered tombs

As their name suggests, one of the key elements of these chambered tombs is that they were used for mortuary practice, that is, as a place for the deposition of human remains. One of the key characteristics of the mortuary deposits found in chambered tombs is that they usually comprise a mass of skeletal remains containing multiple individuals. Less common are the remains of the dead found as complete individuals with skeletons still remaining articulated. This has led scholars to describe these remains found in chambered tombs as collective deposits, as it is hard to identify individuals amongst the mass of bones. At West Kennet, Wiltshire, for example, the remains of 34 individuals were found. Not far away at Hazleton North, the remains of disarticulated individuals were found spread between two chambers, most a collective mass of bone. However, in the entranceway of one of the passages, a near-complete skeleton was found associated with a flint core and a hammerstone known as the 'flint knapper' (Meadows *et al*. 2007, Figure 5.17). This individual was added at the end of the use of the monument and was not subject to later alterations. Multiple burials are found in the other chambered tomb traditions. At the stalled cairn of the Point of Cott on Westray, Orkney, the disarticulated and partial remains of 13 people were found in the monument (Barber 1997), and on the island of Arran, the Clyde cairn at Clachaig contained the mixed and incomplete remains of 14 individuals (Henshall 1972, p. 392). And while there are issues surrounding the preservation of bone in Ireland, some sites have still produced evidence of similar practices in the court cairns there. At Audleystown, Co. Down, the excavator found a mixed deposit of disarticulated remains of 34 individuals which were probably also interred fleshed and subsequently rearranged (C. Jones 2007, p. 127).

FIGURE 5.17
The complete burial at Hazleton North of the 'flint knapper' (Photo Alan Saville)

There is evidence to suggest that bodies were going into chambered tombs in a variety of different states, from fully fleshed and articulated, as was the case with the flint knapper at Hazleton North, through to fully disarticulated. In many instances it seems that chambered tombs saw the deposition of fleshed bodies which decayed within the monument. Once they had lost their flesh and disarticulated, they may then have been reordered and rearranged (Smith and Brickley 2009). For example, at the Knowe of Yarso, Rousay, Orkney, the skulls were placed around the edge of the rear of the chamber and the other bones placed in the middle of the chamber (Richards 1988, Figure 5.18). Just a short distance away at Midhowe on Rousay, nine articulated skeletons were found crouched or sitting on the stone benches along the right-hand side of the chamber; earlier deposits, now disarticulated, had clearly been pushed out of the way to make room for the new additions (Richards 1988, p. 46). At Audleystown, Co. Down, ten small long bones and ribs were carefully laid out in parallel rows on a flat stone slab in chamber one (Collins 1954, p. 17). In some cases there is some evidence that when bones were rearranged within chambered tombs, some parts were removed, as sometimes skeletal components are missing; for example, at the Knowe of Yarso, no mandibles were found (Richards 1988). However, it is also clear that missing skeletal components can also be a product of the original fieldwork (i.e. some were missed or not kept) or post-depositional processes (Wysocki 2022). In some instances, for example, in the chambered tombs of the Black Mountains, there was also an attempt to reconstitute skeletons by piling bones together which had been previously disarticulated; in many of these cases the reconstituted individuals are made up of bones from multiple people (Fowler 2010, Smith and Brickley 2009, p. 67, Wysocki 2022). There is also evidence that in some examples, people were placed in the monument in relation to age or gender differences. At West Kennet, Wiltshire, for example, the remains of 34

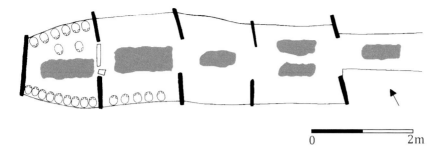

FIGURE 5.18
The position of skulls at the Knowe of Yarso, Rousay, Orkney (after Richards 1988). The grey indicates patches of human bone. As found in some caves, this may represent a particular interest in skulls

individuals were found in the five chambers of the monument; four out of the five chambers contained a mix of people, but the western chamber contained only adult males (Bayliss et al. 2007). For the most part, however, skeletal remains in chambered tombs are a mixed mass of bones from men, women and children, although there are typically more males than females represented (Fowler et al. 2021, Smith and Brickley 2009 and see Rivollat et al. 2022).

Cremations are also found in early Neolithic chambered tombs, and in some areas where unburnt bone does not survive in the acidic soil, it is the only type of skeletal material found. Cremations may have been more commonly deposited in chambered tombs than is currently recognised, as they may not have been retained during older excavations. While cremation deposits are found within the chambers, there is little evidence that the cremation event took place within the chambered tomb: this would be clear from burnt stones, but these are not found. This must mean that the cremations took place elsewhere. The remains of a cremation pyre were found in the court at Ballymarlagh, Co. Antrim (Davies 1949), and at Creggandevesky, Co. Tyrone (Bell and Foley 2005), which may indicate a wider trend of the cremations being held in the general vicinity.

Recent re-examinations of older excavations have revealed that a considerable number of people buried in chambered tombs suffered traumatic injuries. Schulting and Wysocki (2005) note that 7.4% of crania have evidence of both blunt-force and sharp-force trauma. There are also examples of arrowheads being embedded in the remains found in chambered tombs. Tips of arrowheads have been found in bone from Ascott-under-Wychwood, Oxfordshire; Penywyrlod, Powys (Figure 5.19); Poulnabrone, Co. Clare; and Tulloch of Assery B, Caithness (Schulting 2012, Smith and Brickley 2009, p. 104). Other, potentially fatal injuries would not necessarily show up in the bone record, which may mean the number of people who died from a violent death was even higher than this, but we should be aware of possible regional variations of this across Britain and Ireland (Schulting 2012).

Early Neolithic chambered tombs, then, seem to ubiquitously contain the remains of the dead, from small numbers of bones from a few individuals to a mass of bones from

FIGURE 5.19
Rib fragment with embedded leaf-shaped arrowhead tip from Penywyrlod. Photo Michael Wysocki

many people. These remains were sometimes accompanied by small amounts of material culture, usually pottery and stone tools, but rarely in any quantity. It seems likely, therefore, that these monuments were built with burial in mind, and this is, of course, what has led to them being called chambered tombs. However, as noted previously the vast majority of people were not buried in a chambered tomb in the early Neolithic. So why were certain people buried in this way? One idea is that these were founder families: Neolithic people in an area laying claim to the land by building a monument and burying their dead there. This idea is in part inspired by an original and influential paper by Renfrew (1973), but also the new aDNA data we have from a small number of sites. At Hazleton North, which we first saw in Chapter 1, the monument contained the remains of a single 'founding' male and his four female partners (Fowler *et al*. 2021). Also buried at the site were the male offspring from those partnerships and some of their offspring (see Figure 1.3). It can be suggested that this monument represents a powerful lineage in this area laying claim to this place and in doing so creating a new kinship line (and see Cummings and Fowler 2023). What is also interesting about Hazleton North is that dates from this and other chambered tombs shows that these monuments were not always built at the start of the Neolithic in each area. In the case of Hazleton North, then, the expression of a new lineage was created several hundred years into the Neolithic, suggesting that these processes of social negotiation did not just occur with initial occupation of an area but continued throughout the period (and see Britnell and Whittle 2022).

It is also possible to suggest that chambered tombs could have been introduced as a novel way of containing and controlling the transformation process from the living to the dead. No longer reliant solely on predation or excarnation to manage the remains of the deceased, chambered tombs could have acted as containers which isolated the potentially dangerous soul or spirit away from the living (which could also have worked with caves: see previously). Chris Fowler (2010, p. 15) has argued that chambered tomb mortuary practices were about dealing with 'difficult' deaths: people who should not be afforded more typical burial rites. This could include people who died a violent death, as has been noted from chambered tombs, but also other inauspicious circumstances which may not be archaeologically detectable (e.g. illness or perceived witchcraft). Following this line of thought, it has been argued that chambered tombs are set up away from areas of settlement on the sides of hillsides: within sight of the living but positioned at a safe distance. In this sense, then, chambered tombs should not be thought of as being sited at the centre of territories but on the edge of inhabited areas in more liminal zones.

In a slightly different interpretation of the mortuary remains from chambered tombs, it has also been suggested that the bones of the deceased remained accessible to the living and were regularly reordered by them, as they were the remains of important founding forebears (Whittle *et al*. 2007, 2022). Others have suggested that these were important ancestors being commemorated at these sites (e.g. Edmonds 1998). Again drawn from ethnographic parallels there are some communities, most notably those in Madagascar, that believe the spirits of the dead remain with their mortal remains and that these ancestral spirits can have a powerful effect on the living; they must be treated carefully and reordered and organised on a regular basis in order to pacify the spirits (and see Whitley 2002). Thus chambered tombs may have been places where the living engaged with the dead, either as founders or ancestors. However, a new dating programme (see subsequently) has demonstrated that some chambered tombs were actually not in use for that long and may well have been sealed up after a fairly short period of use. Whatever the driving force or forces were for their creation, and this might have been quite different across time and space, this suggests that these deposits of human remains were a response to a specific, but often short-lived, social requirement at this point in the early Neolithic.

The dates of early Neolithic chambered tombs

For many years, the dating of chambered tombs was based on radiocarbon samples which indicated that these monuments were early Neolithic. However, until the advent of Bayesian modelling, the precise dates of chambered tombs could not be refined. Typological studies, therefore, continued to be employed to suggest the order in which different monument types were built. Certain forms of monument were thought to precede other types of monument, as one form developed into other forms over time. There was much debate in relation to the Cotswold-Severn sites, for example, regarding the dates of monuments with lateral chambers and terminal chambers (see Darvill 2004, pp. 80–83), with similar discussions in relation to the Scottish and Irish monuments. However, advances in dating in the last 15 years, specifically in a technique which enables archaeologists to narrow down date ranges (known as Bayesian modelling), have changed this, and we can now offer much more precise dates for different monument types (see Bayliss and Whittle 2007, Whittle *et al*. 2011). In particular the detailed study of the dates of five long barrows in southern Britain have provided an impetus to re-examine the dates from a range of sites and produce more accurate chronologies for early Neolithic chambered tombs. The only caveat is that in some instances we are dating the *use* of sites, not their actual construction date. This is because there is usually a wealth of material which can be used for radiocarbon dating from the chamber or burial deposits, such as human remains, but not always material from the construction or pre-construction phase.

A study used Bayesian modelling to reconsider the dates of five monuments in southern Britain which had been excavated (Bayliss and Whittle 2007). Prior to this study these monuments were considered broadly comparable, but it was suggested that the lateral chambered monuments pre-dated those with terminal chambers. This picture has now been significantly refined. First, this study showed that monuments were not apparently constructed as part of the very first Neolithic activity in the area but a little later on once the Neolithic had been established (Whittle *et al.* 2007, pp. 126–137, and see Whittle *et al.* 2022b). Where we have dates, this seems to be the same for most, if not all, areas of Britain and Ireland. This means that monumentality, at least in most areas, was not something the very first Neolithic settlers did upon arrival on our shores. Second, it appears that these many of these monuments saw fairly short build and deposition phases; in some cases only a generation of people were deposited in the chambers (as at West Kennet). This would mean that many of these monuments these were 'quick builds', constructed, used and abandoned much quicker than had previously been thought. This has serious implications for how we interpret these sites (see subsequently). This has now been shown to be regionally variable – sites in other areas, including Cotswold-Severn monuments in east Wales, did see the deposition of human remains over extended periods of time, so some chambered tombs were quick builds, fulfilling the needs of just a few generations of people, while others remained in use for much longer. Third, these monuments were not all built at the same time. Broadly similar monuments were actually constructed hundreds of years apart; West Kennet and Wayland's Smithy II are architecturally very similar yet were built several hundred years apart (West Kennet was built 3670–3635 cal BC and Wayland's Smithy II was built 3460–3400 cal BC: Bayliss *et al.* 2007, Whittle *et al.* 2007). Cotswold-Severn monuments, then, appear to have been built once the Neolithic had been established in this area. There are some examples of earlier sites: Coldrum in Kent appears to be one of the earliest megalithic monuments built in Britain. This monument saw the deposition of human remains somewhere between 3980 and 3800 cal BC (Wysocki *et al.* 2013). However, it is also worth noting that the Neolithic started in Kent around 4050 cal BC (see previous chapter), so this monument too is later than the initial uptake of Neolithic practices.

The dating of chambered tombs beyond the south of Britain is much more limited, and we do not, as yet, have a good number of dates which could then be subjected to Bayesian modelling. Amongst the Clyde cairns, the recent excavations at Blasthill have produced some early dates (Cummings and Robinson 2015). The three earliest dates from the primary chamber fall between 4040 and 3710 cal BC, and these date either primary use or possibly pre-cairn land clearance. Whichever is the case, these dates do suggest that Blasthill was potentially one of the earliest chambered monuments to be constructed in southern Scotland. The use of the chamber clearly continued into a later

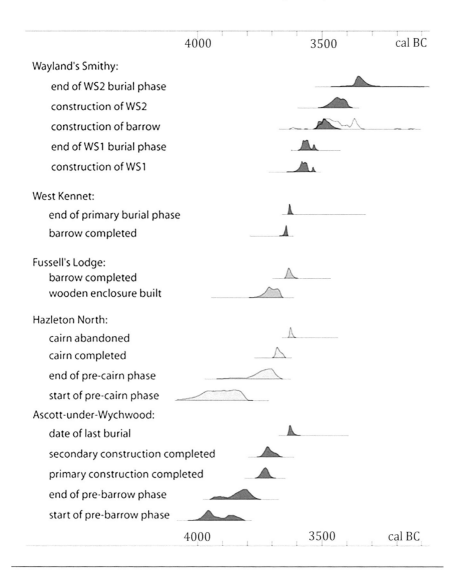

FIGURE 5.20
The key dates in the construction and use of five Cotswold-Severn chambered tombs (Bayliss and Whittle 2007)

phase, with dates of 3650–3360 cal BC showing deposition in this period. The monument also seems to have been remodelled somewhere in the period 3777–3654 cal BC. Blasthill, therefore, is a good example of the complex history of construction and use for this kind of monument, potentially covering the whole of the early Neolithic. The chambered tomb of Cladh Aindreis, Highlands, has been excavated recently and has also produced some dates. A pre-monument cremation deposit dates to 3783–3656 cal BC, with the primary deposits from the chambered tomb itself dating to 3639–3507 cal BC (Harris *et al*. 2014). These dates are much more precise than older dates from Clyde cairns and suggest that this example was constructed sometime after 3650 cal BC.

A recent re-dating programme of court cairns has shown that these monuments appear to have been constructed and used between 3700 and 3550 cal BC (Schulting *et al*. 2011). This would mean that people were building Cotswold-Severn, Clyde cairns and court tombs simultaneously, although it appears that court cairns were the last of these monuments to appear. Some court cairns also show use into the middle Neolithic (see next chapter). Of all of the types of early Neolithic chambered tombs, the stalled cairns lack high-precision radiocarbon dates, and where dates have been acquired, many are later, indicating that many of these monuments continued to be used not only through the latter part of the fourth millennium but also into the third millennium cal BC, unlike many of their southern British counterparts (Griffiths 2016).

The interpretation of early Neolithic chambered tombs

When these monuments were first discussed in any detail, they were generally considered the burial places for Neolithic people arriving into Britain and Ireland at the start of the Neolithic. They were tombs for generations of people which stood in the landscape as markers of lands being colonised and new communities being established (Piggott 1954). Clearly, we now have a more nuanced chronology and sequence for these sites which suggests that these ideas may need refining. So how should we now interpret this particular type of early Neolithic monument?

One of the most important elements of these chambered tombs was that they involved a significant investment of time and effort in their construction. Renfrew (1973) estimated that such a monument would take around 10,000 hours to construct. Communities would need to come together with a food surplus and raw materials such as rope, rollers and stone and work as a group for a sustained period of time on the project; all of this would take considerable planning and investment of time and resources before the monument had even been started (Richards 2004). McFadyen (2006) has written about how the act of construction was an important part of the monument, because it brought together people and materials at a particular place; chambered tombs were thus carefully 'composed' with materials, people and place being brought together and reconstituted at a specific point in the landscape. This made the act of construction very important in its own right, regardless of the final architectural outcome. On top of this, we know from ethnographic examples (e.g. Hoskins 1986) that situations which brought people together to build monuments were also important social events, involving feasts and celebrations. Add to this the evidence from the recent dating programmes which suggests that some monuments were quick builds with the equally rapid deposition of bodies, and this could suggest that chambered tombs were the architectural remains of important social gatherings where founding lineages were created, marked and then sealed up (Cummings and Fowler 2023).

Another potentially important part of the monument was its location. It has already been noted previously that chambered tombs do not seem to have been located amongst settlements but were set up and away from the valley areas which would have been occupied in the early Neolithic. Work on the setting of these monuments has shown that they appear to be located in remarkably similar parts of the landscape, and this is consistent amongst all of these early Neolithic chambered tombs in Britain and Ireland. The sites are positioned with views out of particular landscape features, most notably views of hills or mountains and waterways and the sea (Cummings 2009, Tilley 1994, Whittle *et al*. 2022b). They are never positioned on the summit of hills or mountains (in complete contrast to many middle Neolithic passage graves: see Chapter 6) or tucked away out of sight next to streams (unlike dolmens: see subsequently). This suggests that the landscape setting was an important component of the monument, as significant as the stones which made up the chamber. Mountains and waterways are likely to have been important in belief systems. We have already seen previously how mortuary practice involved the use of natural places, and it is likely that such places were also thought of as the source of power or the home of deities or spirits (and see Bradley 2000a). Waterways would also have been an important way of moving around the landscape which in many places would be wooded: movement by boat, therefore, would have been much easier.

The early diversity in form of chambered tombs (see previously) does suggest that people were not following a clear blueprint for these monuments. Instead there seems to have been the desire to create a monument with a chamber which was clearly designed for the deposition of particular combinations of the dead. Later on, these sites were homogenised; early sites were altered so that they were broadly similar to sites which were being constructed elsewhere. Early construction at sites, therefore, might be understood as localised versions of monuments, drawing on both wider ideas of building and dealing with the dead but also incorporating more localised practices and beliefs. Later on, people seem to have conformed to specific architectural practices, so much so that we are now able to talk about 'Cotswold-Severn' chambered tombs or court cairns. This must indicate wide social networks and contact at this time between people across quite broad areas of Britain and Ireland. Other forms of monumentality, other types of material culture and other practices all support this idea as well. People in the early Neolithic maintained broad-scale contacts with other Neolithic communities across Britain and Ireland (and see previous chapter).

Once constructed, what role did these monuments then play within society? As discussed previously, it is becoming increasingly clear that these monuments were not all built at the same time, so they are not all contemporary. We should, therefore, move away from the idea that each community had its own chambered tomb and that tombs fulfilled an identical role in every instance. It could well be the case that a single community built multiple monuments spread out over both space and time; having one monument was not enough – it was the construction process that was significant and fulfilled a social need, and it may have needed to be repeated if circumstances were such that the construction of another site was deemed necessary (e.g. a new kinship group needed to be created). It is interesting that in the Cotswold-Severn examples discussed previously, some seem to have seen quite short episodes of deposition, while others were clearly in use for longer periods (see Chapters 6 and 8 for details on how chambered tombs were also in use in the middle and late Neolithic periods). Amongst some communities, then, monuments were built, the dead were deposited, and then the site went out of use quite rapidly. As discussed, this could have been to do with violent episodes (Schulting and Wysocki 2005), social upheaval or dealing with difficult deaths (Fowler 2010) or the creation of founder lineage groups (Cummings and Fowler

2023). In other instances communities returned again and again to a site, to deposit more remains, to reorder remains in the chambers, to rebuild or alter the monument and to carry out various ceremonies. These monuments may have been more concerned with ancestral rites or customs and controlling the transformation process from living to dead. This strongly supports the idea that chambered tombs fulfilled different social needs in each community and that their meanings and importance to a group varied considerably, both throughout the early Neolithic and in different regions of Britain and Ireland. It is also worth reiterating here that people in many parts of Britain and Ireland never built a chambered tomb, so clearly they had other ways of dealing with the issues that these monuments could fulfil (see subsequently for some of the other types of monument these communities constructed).

DOLMENS

Six thousand years ago in the county of Pembrokeshire at a site called Garn Turne, people decided to built a megalithic monument. This was not a chambered tomb as found further to the east of the country but a different kind of monument. They began by selecting one enormous stone – in this instance weighting 80 tonnes. They excavated it from the earth where it had been deposited by the last glacier, and then they slowly begin to elevate the stone. Even in the modern age it is hard to imagine how people armed only with rope and wooden levers were able to move such a vast stone, yet they did – setting it on top of vertically placed upright stones. This created a chamber of sorts, certainly an area where remains of the dead could be placed, but the sheer size and scale of this endeavour indicate that this construction was more than the creation of just a burial space. Instead, people at Garn Turne had constructed a dolmen – a different kind of monument altogether (Cummings and Richards 2021).

Most accounts of early Neolithic chambered tombs in Britain and Ireland include details on dolmens as if they are one and the same. What I am calling dolmens here are actually known by an array of names: portal dolmens (in west Wales), quoits (in Cornwall), portal tombs (in Ireland) and also in some instances as 'simple passage tombs'. However, there are two key things to note with these monuments

1. All of these differently named monuments share fundamental similarities, so much so that it is much easier to simply describe them as 'dolmens.'

2. They differ significantly from the other early Neolithic chambered tombs we have already considered so that they should not be considered alongside other chambered tombs, at least in their primary phase.

One of the key differences between early Neolithic chambered tombs found in Britain and Ireland and dolmens is the nature of the chamber. At the sites we have already considered, these were fairly straightforward constructions, which created a box or series of boxes using stone slabs. Dolmens do create a chamber of sorts, which is why they are sometimes considered alongside other early Neolithic chambered tombs, but this chamber was often not entirely sealed and open to the elements. Dolmen monuments

FIGURE 5.21
Excavations at Garn Turne, Pembrokeshire. The enormous capstone was quarried from a pit in front of where the monument now lies (Adam Stanford © Aerial-Cam Ltd)

also vary significantly from the chambers of other chambered tombs because of the magnitude of the capstone. Above it was argued that the small box-like chambers at chambered tombs could have been accessed by simply sliding off the capstone, but at dolmens, the capstones could never have been moved, as the builders used enormous capstones. Sites in both Britain and Ireland employ some massive stones in their construction (Figure 5.21). As we have seen at Garn Turne, this site has a capstone that weighs approximately 80 tonnes, the biggest stone used in a Neolithic monument in Britain. Carrickglass (the Labby Rock) in County Sligo has a capstone weighing 70 tonnes, and the largest is at the site of Kernanstown (Brownshill) in County Carlow, where the capstone weighs around 160 tonnes (Kytmannow 2008, p. 47). These capstones are not only massive stones but also very distinctive stones. The outer and upper surfaces of the capstones on dolmens are natural and weathered, but the underside is carefully shaped. This means that when people were quarrying large boulders, they were leaving the upper surface untouched, but shaping and dressing the underside of the stone. This was achieved in different ways: by flaking off large pieces of stone or by pecking.

Another key component of dolmens are the uprights which support the massive capstone. Again, these vary significantly from those found in other early Neolithic chambered tombs. Bearing in mind that many capstones weigh over 50 tonnes, people seem to have deliberately chosen slender stones to support the capstone. Furthermore, many uprights have pointed tops, which means that only the smallest points of the uprights support the capstone. Moreover, many dolmens are only supported by three uprights, even though there are more stones in the chamber. This suggests that people were

FIGURE 5.22
The dolmen at Brownshill, Co. Carlow, where the capstone weighs approximately 160 tonnes

trying to balance massive capstones on the smallest number of supporters and having the smallest areas of support touching. This creates the most extraordinary effect with these monuments, and has led several authors to suggest that one of the primary roles of dolmens was the display of huge stones (Figure 5.22), where stones seem to almost float above the ground (Richards 2004, Whittle 2004). A dolmen, then, is primarily the display of a large capstone, which was balanced on the smallest points of the supporting stones as possible, which did not always create a functional chamber.

At those sites which have only a small number of uprights, it would be hard to describe these monuments as having chambers at all because the area underneath the capstone would be open and unenclosed. There have been suggestions that drystone walling was used in between the uprights in order to create a chamber area (at Pentre Ifan, for example: Grimes 1948), although no evidence for this has ever been found. It has also been suggested that cairns would originally have been an important part of the monument. However, the vast majority of dolmens have no trace of a cairn remaining, and where they have been found, it was just a small platform around the monument (Cummings and Whittle 2004). It is highly likely that at some sites cairns were added at a later date, as some of these dolmens were 'converted' into other monument types (see subsequently). We certainly know that these sites remained the focus of activity for many millennia (Kytmannow 2008). At other dolmens in Britain and Ireland, the chamber area is different again. At sites such as Dyffryn Ardudwy in Wales, for example, the dolmen is essentially a sealed box, albeit with a large and heavy capstone (Powell 1973). These monuments may have included a chamber as an important part of the monument, but deposits would need to have been added either during construction or, once constructed, in very small quantities that were pushed through the cracks between stones.

One interesting site which has recently been excavated is that of Poulnabrone, on the Burren in Co. Clare. Essentially a stone box open to the elements over the millennia, the excavators were astonished to find significant quantities of human remains at this site, especially since they were directly underneath a layer of drinks cans and crisp packets! The dolmen at Poulnabrone is built in an area of limestone paving which has naturally occurring crevices amongst the large slabs of limestone, and the monument was built over one of these crevices in which the human remains were crammed and, incredibly, preserved. At this site a minimum of 35 people were deposited in the limestone paving over a 600-year period, starting in the early Neolithic, probably somewhere between 3885 and 3710 cal BC (see Lynch 2014). There was evidence for successive internments and some skeletal parts being removed.

Burial was a component of some of these monuments, then, but when compared to the chambers of chambered tombs in Clyde cairns, court cairns, Cotswold-Severn tombs and stalled tombs, where the chambers could easily have been accessed repeatedly for the deposition of human remains (see previously), dolmens clearly differ. Thus, it is possible to suggest that dolmens were not, in their primary phase, designed for repeated acts of mortuary deposition; instead these monuments were as much about creating a visually spectacular megalithic construction involving the balancing of massive stones as they were about creating functional burial spaces.

If the human remains found in these monuments suggest that these were token or foundation deposits only, as found at many different types of early Neolithic site from houses through to dolmens, how should we understand these monuments? The process of construction must have been a significant element, as moving stones up to 160 tonnes in weight would have been a phenomenal feat of engineering. It would have involved bringing together many people from different communities to be involved in the build. This is a tradition which probably had its origins in north-west France, where people were building with massive stones in the preceding fifth millennium cal BC (for example, the Grand Menhir Brisé, which it is estimated weighed 300 tonnes: see Chapter 3). In many ways, then, this could be similar to the bringing together of new kin groups, as has already been suggested for some chambered tombs like Hazleton North. However, the aDNA analysis at Poulnabrone indicates a lack of close kin buried at the site (Cassidy *et al*. 2020) and so indicates that the building of a dolmen was not about the creation of new descent groups defined by biological reproduction. Instead it seems more likely they were built by disparate groups working together but maintaining their own discrete kinship networks.

It is also worth considering that dolmens are not found throughout Britain and Ireland but only in western Britain (west Wales and south-west England predominantly, with the exception of the Medway group in Kent) and in clusters in Ireland (with no examples in south-west Ireland). This was clearly a tradition of building which was only relevant for some communities in the early Neolithic, and elsewhere it has been argued that dolmen architecture may have appealed particularly to people in those areas which were in significant contact with communities in north-west France who had a long tradition of building with big stones or people for whom big stones were already an important part of their belief system (see Cummings and Richards 2021). It has also been suggested that dolmens were only constructed around places in the landscape that were considered particularly special because of natural features such as distinctive outcrops or, in

FIGURE 5.23
Pentre Ifan, Pembrokeshire, where the capstone can be seen balancing on three supporting stones

particular, unique mountain forms. These places may quickly have become important in Neolithic belief systems, attracting stories about how such wondrous places came into being (see Cummings and Richards 2021).

One question that remains unclear is the date at which these dolmens were constructed. The primary Poulnabrone dates (see previously) are earlier than the suggested use date of court cairns, but Poulnabrone is the only securely dated dolmen in Ireland at present. Recent excavations at Garn Turne, Pembrokeshire, suggest that the last phase of primary construction here dated between 3800 and 3650 cal BC (Cummings and Richards 2021), but more excavations and dates are required to resolve this issue. Kytmannow (2008) notes that the few dates on dolmens from other sites date use, not construction, and these were monuments which were in use over several thousand years. Some of these dolmen sites, then, may be very earliest Neolithic but in a tradition which maintained potency well into the early Neolithic.

Another interesting element of these monuments is that dolmens were sometimes 'converted' into other monument types. This supports the idea that dolmens may have been one of the earliest forms of monument built in Britain and Ireland but also that the meanings and uses of these sites were not fixed in stone. At Tinkinswood, near Cardiff, a dolmen had a large trapezoidal cairn with an impressive forecourt added to make it in keeping with the Cotswold-Severn style of building chambered tombs. At Tanrego West, Co. Sligo, the dolmen had chambers and a cairn added to make it a functional court cairn. Some of the most interesting examples of converted dolmens at are the extraordinary site of Carrowmore, Co. Sligo, where a number of dolmen monuments were elaborated with different architectural components to make them into passage graves (see Chapter 6).

TIMBER MORTUARY STRUCTURES

Attention now turns to another form of monument from the early Neolithic which has distinct parallels with stone chambered tombs. Wooden mortuary structures typically consist of two or three upright timbers which may have created a timber box or chamber of sorts. This form of monument is primarily found in southern and eastern England, with some examples from Yorkshire and further afield. At Wayland's Smithy I, Oxfordshire, for example, the primary timber phase consisted of two large D-shaped posts plus a double row of small postholes, which appears to have created a lidded wooden box (Whittle *et al*. 2007). At Fussell's Lodge, Wiltshire, the remains of three large pits were found which would have contained large timbers, surrounded by a timber revetment; a wooden 'porch' was also found at the eastern end (Wysocki *et al*. 2007). An extremely well-preserved example was excavated at Haddenham, Cambridgeshire. Here a wooden structure was found which consisted of two wooden cells or chambers built from planks. The planks were held in place by three large vertical posts, as seen at other examples, and a clay bank (Field 2006, p. 91). The entire wooden structure was covered by a wooden roof which would have created a sealed wooden chamber. A wooden façade was also found to the north-east of the wooden chamber. At Street House, North Yorkshire, three pits would have held timbers, and a substantial timber façade which held closely set posts was found at the eastern end (Vyner 1984, Figure 5.24). These timber chambers and wooden façades, therefore, are very similar in form to the chambers of early Neolithic chambered tombs discussed previously. In some, but not all, of these cases, a stone phase replaced the timber monument. For example, at Wayland's Smithy, the timber box was covered by an oval mound and then

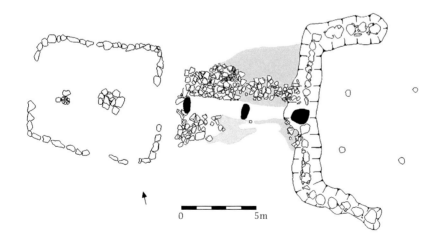

FIGURE 5.24
The timber mortuary structure at Street House, North Yorkshire (after Vyner 1984). The three large posts of the timber mortuary structure are marked in black: note postholes are also present in the forecourt. The façade consists of a bedding trench which had timbers set upright in it. The grey indicates the presence of a clay and earth mound, and the rest are contemporary, or later, stone elements

in due course superseded by a stone chambered tomb not dissimilar in form from West Kennet. In other cases the timber monument was sealed beneath an unchambered long mound or cairn (see subsequently). It remains difficult to assess how widespread this monument form may originally have been: free-standing examples not sealed by a later monument may be difficult to locate or not preserved in the archaeological record.

Split timbers and three large post structures are found in smaller numbers beyond southern and eastern England. At Lochhill and Slewcairn, Dumfries and Galloway, both had primary wooden phases which consisted of three large upright timbers creating a wooden chamber; Lochhill also had a timber façade (Masters 1973). Both were subsequently replaced and therefore sealed by stone monuments. At Pitnacree, Perth and Kinross, a pair of D-shaped postholes were found under a barrow which are likely to date to the early Neolithic, and at Dalladies, Aberdeenshire, three large pits would have once held enormous split timbers (Noble 2006, 73–86). Likewise, in Ireland, the primary phase at Dooey's Cairn, Co. Antrim (Ballymacaldrack), consisted of three large timber posts over which a court cairn was later constructed (Evans 1938). So far, this form of monument has not been found in the very north of Scotland, but it would be no surprise if examples were located here; as we saw in the previous chapter, the earliest houses in Orkney were built from timber, and monuments may have been too.

We will see that these timber structures were used for burials, although it remains unclear whether they stood as timber structures without burials for a period before becoming mortuary sites or whether they were used from the outset for mortuary deposition (see Noble 2006, p. 93, Thomas 2013, p. 324). There was probably variation between sites. At Fussell's Lodge a total of 34 individuals were placed between the timbers. Some were buried fleshed and subsequently disarticulated and then stacked up, but others were clearly added already disarticulated (Wysocki *et al*. 2007, p. 80). The mortuary deposits were added sometime between 3700 and 3640 cal BC, after which a barrow was built over the whole site. At Wayland's Smithy I, 14 individuals were buried, again the majority being deposited as fleshed corpses, but here there was also evidence that some of the bodies had been scavenged by canids before deposition (Whittle *et al*. 2007, p. 114). Furthermore, one individual had an arrowhead embedded in bone which would have killed them: two more arrowheads found alongside bodies, although not embedded in them, may have pierced flesh and been a cause of death. The mortuary deposits appear to represent a single event or perhaps generation of people, predominantly men, after which a mound was again built over the structure. An interesting feature of some of these mortuary structures is that some were deliberately burnt down after the deposition of skeletal remains had taken place. The wooden structures at Haddenham and Nutbane, Hampshire, for example, were both burnt down prior to the construction of a long mound over the area of activity. At Street House the timber mortuary structure was burnt down along with human remains, which effectively cremated these remains.

There are a number of radiocarbon dates from material associated with wooden mortuary structures which can give us a general sense of when these monuments were being built and used. They appear to be part of a wider monument-building phase, with deposition at these sites occurring mainly in the second quarter of the fourth millennium cal BC. The three large posts at Haddenham have been dated to the 38th century cal BC, but the planks of the timber chamber date to around 3600 cal BC: this may mean that different parts of this site were built at different times (Thomas 2013, p. 325, Whittle *et al*. 2011, pp. 288–290). At Dooey's Cairn, Co. Antrim, dates suggest construction sometime in the first half of the fourth millennium (Whittle *et al*. 2011, p. 613). Mortuary deposits are likely to be a bit later; the human remains at Fussell's Lodge were added sometime between 3700 and 3640 cal BC. Mortuary practice may have been quite short lived; Wayland's Smithy I appears to have only seen human remains being deposited there for a generation or less (Whittle *et al*. 2007, p. 129).

One of the most interesting elements of these sites is they seem to use split timbers, that is, enormous timbers which had been split down the middle to create 'D-shaped' posts. The splitting of large timbers and placing human remains between these timbers is particularly evocative and is reminiscent of the same practice amongst chambered tombs, where bodies were placed in between stones which had been split through quarrying. It may well be that these monuments were understood in much the same way as their stone equivalents, and the two may have been considered broadly interchangeable in terms of use and function within society. If the suggestion is that human remains were only added at some sites *after* the timbers had rotted away, however, then the power of the place may have been the primary wooden monument which potentially had nothing to do with burial (Noble 2006, pp. 93–94). If this is the case, these wooden mortuary structures actually share elements with dolmens, where it was the acquisition of a large stone its subsequent dressing and display that were important; only later were these sites used for the deposition of human remains. It can be considered that the felling of an enormous timber and splitting it down the middle would have involved as much labour as the quarrying of a dolmen capstone, and the best way to display this would have been to stand the posts upright in the ground. The choice of wood in eastern Britain and stone in western Britain and Ireland may reflect broader belief systems focusing on the significance of these two substances (see subsequently).

UNCHAMBERED LONG MOUNDS/CAIRNS

So far this chapter has considered early Neolithic chambered tombs and wooden mortuary structures, both of which appear to have been constructed with the deposition of human remains in mind, as well as dolmens, the builders of which appear to have been concerned more with the act of construction and displaying large stones. Another form of monument also commonly found dating from the early Neolithic has both notable parallels with chambered tombs but also striking differences. This is the form of monument known as unchambered long mounds (these sites are also sometimes referred to as non-megalithic barrows, which denotes the absence of a stone chamber). Whereas chambered tombs are predominantly found in the west of Britain, unchambered long mounds are usually found to the east. In some instances timber mortuary structures have long mounds constructed over them at a later date, but it would be a mistake to think that all unchambered long mounds simply had a wooden, instead of a stone, chamber. Unchambered long mounds and cairns might be considered a monument form in their own right, but perhaps the most significant element of these sites is not the long mound or cairn which is usually the last act of construction but what lies underneath the mound or cairn, and in this regard there is some overlap with other monuments such as chambered tombs.

When long mounds or cairns have been excavated, they have revealed a whole variety of pre-mound features using a variety of forms of wood and stone, the digging of pits, the creation of above-ground deposits such as middens and the manipulation of human remains. For example, at Giant's Hill I, Skendleby, Lincolnshire, there were a number of features underneath the long mound. At the eastern end was a trench which would presumably have held wooden posts creating a façade and forecourt area; this is comparable with a similar feature found at Street House discussed previously. But unlike Street House, no wooden mortuary structure was found at Skendleby. Instead, behind the façade, a pit and stone platform with human bones on it were enclosed by a low wall. The area was divided up by a series of hurdles, and stake holes were found marking out the perimeter (Field 2006, p. 84, Figure 5.25). The human remains were a mix of crouched inhumations from four individuals and disarticulated bones from another four individuals (Field 2006, p. 86); this mortuary deposit mirrors that found in both chambered tombs and wooden mortuary structures but in this case was not contained by an enduring structure. At Norton Bevant, Wiltshire, the remains of 18 individuals were found tightly packed into an area 2.4 × 1 × 0.5m; these remains must have been disarticulated when deposited, as they would not have fitted into this space if fleshed (Field 2006, pp. 136–137). This raises the distinct possibility that the remains were contained in something which does not usually survive in the archaeological record, such as a basket, which may have been widely used in the Neolithic (see previous chapter). While mortuary practice is commonly found under long mounds, it is important to note that some long mounds produced no human remains at all, including Thickthorn Down, Dorset, and Beckhampton Road, Wiltshire. These sites, therefore, should not just be considered another location where the remains of the dead were dealt with, rather that dealing with the dead was one of a suite of practices which took place at these locations prior to long mounds being constructed.

Common practices found under long mounds also included the careful dividing up of space. The hurdles at Skendleby created bays, and each bay seems to have been

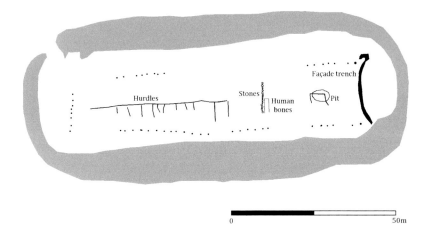

FIGURE 5.25
The excavation plan of Giants Hills 1, Skendleby, Lincolnshire (after Field 2006)

partly filled with different types of material. Similar bays were found at South Street long mound, Wiltshire, and incorporated both stone and wood. This use of bays is paralleled at Cotswold-Severn monuments which used the same construction method in some of the cairns and mounds surrounding the chambers (see previously). In some areas of Britain, then, there was a tradition of creating long mounds and cairns, regardless of the presence or not of a stone or wooden chamber. This may indicate that while we place considerable emphasis on the presence or absence of a chamber in our classification of these sites, people in the Neolithic may not have done so.

The creation of bays and their infilling with different materials was not simply a convenient way of creating a long mound. Indeed, this form of building would have been more time-consuming than creating an amorphous and undifferentiated mound. So how can we interpret this evidence? It has been suggested that the creation and filling of separate bays were representative of different communities coming together in the act of construction (see Benson and Whittle 2007, Cummings and Fowler 2023). Separate bays or areas are found in chambered tomb architecture as well, with the dividing up of the chamber into discrete units (see previously). The idea of individual communities contributing to a bigger project is also reflected in the architecture of causewayed enclosures (see subsequently). The division of space, then, through separate acts of construction and deposition, is found in a variety of early Neolithic monumental contexts. Julian Thomas (2013) argues that this is the start of a preoccupation with framing space in a particular way and creating hidden spaces. Equally, it may be the material expression of different social or kinship groups, who were brought together in a collaborative act of construction but still wished to maintain separate identities at one level. The long mound/cairn, therefore, was both a literal and figurative coming together of different kinship groups into a broader community. They could be seen as the founding act of the fixing of social affiliations amongst the living (Thomas 2013, p. 329). Extensive fieldwork around the long barrow at Biggar Common, south Lanarkshire, has revealed substantial evidence of occupation around the monument (Noble 2006, p. 213), which supports the idea that long mounds and cairns represented the foundation of new social groups and alliances set in proximity to areas of settlement.

On top of very variable earlier activity, long mounds or cairns were then constructed which essentially masked previous activity. This act of construction, therefore, hid a diverse set of practices and turned that location into a form of monument found very widely, on the outside at least. In their final form unchambered long mounds and cairns were striking monuments. They vary in size but some are as large as 70m long and up to 3m tall (Field 2006, p. 22). These were clearly monuments meant to stand out in the landscape, and they would have taken considerable effort to build. Many accounts of these monuments have highlighted the importance of the long mound/cairn in terms of referencing architecture found elsewhere in Neolithic Europe, most specifically the long houses of the LBK and long mounds of the post-Bandkeramik cultures of northern Europe (see Whittle *et al*. 2011, p. 872). In Chapter 3, the evidence from these areas was briefly summarised and the importance of the long house highlighted. Abandoned long houses would rapidly take on the appearance of a long mound, which then seems to have been constructed as a monument in its own right (see Hodder 1990, Thomas 2013). Long mounds are found in the Cerny culture of the Paris Basin, Normandy, and the TRB in the northern European plain and southern Scandinavia. This powerful

ROUND MOUNDS/CAIRNS AND CISTS

The characteristic early Neolithic monument is the chambered long cairn, but there are a surprising number of monuments which are round. We have already seen a few examples previously – the primary phases of some chambered long cairns were often set within a small round cairn *before* being turned into long cairns or mounds. However, the best-known round mounds are those from the Yorkshire Wolds. At Wold Newton round barrow excavations revealed that the primary deposit on site was the disarticulated remains of six people covered with a peat and turf mound; this primary deposit was made sometime in the 38th century cal BC (Gibson and Bayliss 2010, p. 84). Another burial was inserted sometime between 3645 and 3520 cal BC, showing its continued significance after the main deposition and construction event. Other barrows in the area such as Duggleby Howe are of a similar date, although some are certainly early Bronze Age (Gibson and Bayliss 2010). One of the most interesting elements of the sites in the Yorkshire Wolds is that long barrows are also found here and the two monument types are broadly contemporary.

There are other examples from elsewhere in Britain, and there are likely to be more waiting to be identified, as round mounds are usually classified as early Bronze Age, and only excavation would reveal otherwise. Wor barrow, Dorset, appears to have been a wooden mortuary structure in its primary phase. The second phase saw bundles of skeletal material being placed on the old ground surface, which was then covered by a circular mound of turf (Field 2006, p. 85). In Scotland at Midtown of Pitglassie, Aberdeenshire, an individual was cremated, and their remains, along with pottery sherds, flint and quartz, were placed in three pits. The pits were sealed by a ring cairn or round cairn; material from the pits indicates an early Neolithic date for this activity (Sheridan 2010a, pp. 36–37). In Ireland a round mound was demonstrated to be early Neolithic in date at Rathdooney Beg, near Ballymote, Co. Sligo (Whittle *et al.* 2011, p. 613).

Since round mounds were clearly associated with mortuary practices, which is a common feature at long mounds, were there any meaningful differences between round and long mounds? They certainly seem to have been deployed in similar ways, that is, as coverings over activities associated with a whole variety of depositional acts and usually burial practice. If long mounds have been interpreted as representations of collapsed long houses on mainland Europe, then it could equally be argued that round mounds could be considered representations of round houses. This would place a slightly different origin point for these as the idea is that the long house/long mound metaphor stemmed from the LBK and post-LBK peoples of the northern European plain. The round house (or moveable circular tent-lie dwelling) is likely to have had considerable use in many parts of Europe but also late Mesolithic Britain and Ireland as well and may hint at different origins for Neolithic ideas in areas where round mounds were being built. Another possibility is that round mounds referenced a completely different part of the material world in the early Neolithic: boats. Upturned coracles/currachs would be roughly the shape of these mounds, and if we follow this logic, long cairns and mounds may not be referencing long houses of far-distant Neolithic peoples but the vessels by which Neolithic things and practices arrived on these shores (long boats). It is also worth considering here that long mounds are often located in relation to water, especially rivers, streams and springs (Field 2006, p. 104), which may strengthen this argument. Equally, they may be new expressions of identity or references to new ideas created as part of the act of building monuments in a new part of the landscape. Ultimately we might never know why some mounds were round and some long, but it is worth bearing in mind that it is very straightforward to turn a round mound into a long one, yet obviously this was not done in many cases. As such, the choice of building round or long was deliberate and may well have been a strong expression of affinities with particular groups or places as much as origin points.

Another interesting variation to the monument types already discussed here are the Linkardstown cists of Ireland. These monuments are found only in the southern half of Ireland and consist of one or more inhumations placed in a central cist covered by a round mound (Cooney 2000, p. 97). The inhumations were accompanied by a highly decorated pot and date from the latter part of the early Neolithic, from 3500–3300 cal BC. Ashleypark, Co. Tipperary, is the best-known example of a Linkardstown cist. The chamber was constructed by splitting open a large limestone block, and the monument held the disarticulated remains of an elderly male, a child and an infant (Jones 2007, p. 177). The human remains were accompanied by decorated pottery and animal bones which have been interpreted as the remains of a feast (Cooney 2000, p. 98). The cist was then covered with a large cairn. Another excavated example is Poulawack, Co. Clare (Jones 2007, pp. 120–124).

CAUSEWAYED ENCLOSURES

Between the years 3680 and 3630 cal BC, people in Dorset gathered on the hilltop of Hambledon Hill and began the first of what would prove to become a long series of constructions (Figure 5.26). They dug a series of segmented ditches around the edge of the hilltop, close to a pre-existing long barrow (Mercer and Healy 2008). This created a central area encircled by ditches. These acts of digging into the earth and working together undoubtedly brought disparate communities from the wider landscape together to work on this communal project (cf. McFadyen 2006). Communities probably returned over many seasons, to dig a new ditch segment and renegotiate their place amongst this wider corporate group. Yet alongside these acts of monument construction and social negotiations, other practices occurred at Hambledon Hill. Within the main enclosure the remains of 44 weathered and disarticulated people were recovered (McKinley 2008, pp. 504–505, Figure 5.26). It appears that both whole and partially fleshed bodies had been placed in the ditches and left to be broken down into bone by natural forces. Bones were then moved around, deposited, redeposited and carefully placed, with a notable emphasis on skulls (Harris 2010). Indeed, there is good evidence of skulls being deliberately placed and deposited within the ditches and around the site, suggesting that people came together here not just to work on the construction of a new monument but also to commemorate specific individuals while also weaving in other materials

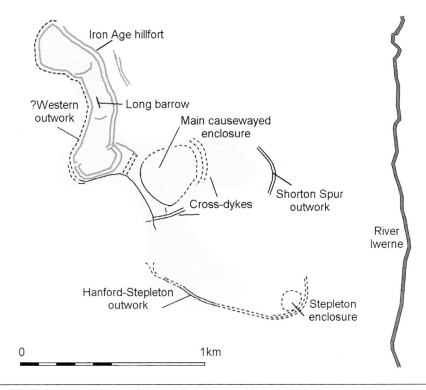

FIGURE 5.26
The monumental complex at Hambledon Hill, Dorset. The earliest monument is the main causewayed enclosure in the centre – further earthworks were added later on

from different places and events (Harris 2010). This site is thus an excellent example of a causewayed enclosure: a complex and varied construction often involving mortuary practice found in the early Neolithic.

Like other early Neolithic monuments, causewayed enclosures are not found everywhere in Britain and Ireland but predominantly in southern England, although there are a few outliers in Wales, northern England and Ireland (Figure 5.27). So far only 'possible' causewayed enclosures have been found in Scotland. Unlike upstanding chambered tombs, causewayed enclosures are often no longer visible above ground so are identified through survey, aerial photography or excavation. Even after a century of research into these monuments, new sites are regularly found, for example at Thame, Oxfordshire; Dorstone Hill, Herefordshire (Ray et al. 2023); Whitewell in Lancashire; and Caerau on the edge of Cardiff (and see Last 2022). This may mean many more are waiting to be discovered. Some of the best-known examples such as Hambledon Hill, Dorset, which we have already seen, and Windmill Hill, Wiltshire, are located on hilltops, but causewayed enclosures are also found on the side of valleys and in low-lying locations close to rivers (Oswald et al. 2001, p. 24). At present there are over 70 definite and probable causewayed enclosures known in Britain and Ireland, with lots of 'possible' sites (Whittle et al. 2011, p. 5, 2022).

OF EARTH, BONE, TIMBER AND STONE **139**

FIGURE 5.27
The distribution of definite and probable causewayed enclosures in Britain and Ireland (after Oswald *et al.* 2001 and Whittle *et al.* 2011). Circles are causewayed enclosures, squares are tor enclosures

Monumental form

Generally speaking, causewayed enclosure are roughly circular and consist of one or more discontinuous circuits of ditches and usually banks encircling an interior area (Figure 5.28). Earlier enclosures were simpler, and later ones were typically larger and more complex. Causewayed enclosures are variable in size, usually covering an area from 1–8 hectares. The ditches are cut into the ground and are flat-bottomed and typically 1–2m deep, while the causeways in the name refer to the gaps between the ditches.

FIGURE 5.28
The plans of selected causewayed enclosures in Britain and Ireland. Left Donegore Hill, Co. Antrim; centre Freston, Suffolk; right Haddenham, Cambridgeshire (after Oswald et al. 2001)

Some causewayed enclosures also have a timber component, usually a palisade (a fence or line of wooden stakes or posts). Within this broad definition, however, there is considerable diversity. In some instances the ditches are more or less continuous, while other examples have ditches which are more like extended pits. In some cases the ditches do not create a complete circuit, instead using the local topography to create a boundary, or in some cases because they were probably never completed. Some ditches appear to be outlying works away from the main enclosure (see Figure 5.26 at Hambledon Hill, which is one of the most complex of the causewayed enclosures found in Britain). The nature of the bank or banks at sites are often difficult to define because they have been ploughed away or have slumped into the nearby ditches; in some instances banks may have been continuous, but clearly in other instances they too had gaps between them like the ditches (Oswald *et al*. 2001). Compared with most of the other monuments we have considered from the early Neolithic, causewayed enclosures are big monuments requiring considerable effort to construct, comparable perhaps only with cursus monuments in terms of investment of labour and certainly many times more time consuming to build than chambered tombs.

There are other examples of monuments which date to the early Neolithic which draw on the broad notion of enclosure, but they are not causewayed. The best known of these are the tor enclosures of south-west England, especially Carn Brea and Helman Tor, Cornwall. In both these cases the enclosure was created by building a boulder wall between the granite outcrops on these hilltops. At Helman Tor a hollow behind the wall may have acted in a similar way to the ditches at causewayed enclosures; certainly it was filled with early Neolithic artefacts, as are the ditches of causewayed sites (see subsequently).

From their plans it may appear that these monuments could have been accessed from many different directions, but it has been argued that there are usually fewer than five entrances into the enclosed area, and often only one (Oswald *et al*. 2001, p. 49). The entranceways are also often marked out; some have earthworks, others timber passages, and at others, the side of the circuit with the entranceway was flattened, which would have presented anyone approaching from this direction with something not too dissimilar from the façades seen on chambered tombs and wooden mortuary structures. On top of all of this, some causewayed enclosures were clearly modified over time, with the addition of extra circuits of banks and ditches noted in a number of cases (Whittle *et al*. 2011).

For people encountering these monuments on the ground in the early Neolithic, they would have been striking and impressive. At those sites with multiple circuits, banks and timber palisades the centre of the monument would have been completely obscured from view as it was being approached. Since it seems that many of these sites had the ditches recut many times (see subsequently), they would probably have looked like construction sites with fresh earth or chalk piled up. Deposits in the ditches such as those at Hambledon Hill of human remains would have been visible as people moved past them. Many of the entranceways were aggrandised, so a façade of timber or extra earthworks may have indicated the way into the next circuit. Unlike chambered tombs, where only a relatively small number of people could have participated in activity, causewayed enclosures, even small ones, incorporated a much larger space; these were by far the largest constructions in the landscape at this time and would have been a much more impressive sight than can perhaps be appreciated today from their plans.

The dating of causewayed enclosures

A major dating programme reconsidered the dates of causewayed enclosures in Britain and Ireland, and we now have a much more precise understanding of the dating of these monuments. At the broadest level causewayed enclosures were built and in use from 3700–3500 cal BC, although a few may be slightly earlier than this and some continued to be used until around or just after 3300 cal BC (Whittle *et al*. 2011, p. 683, 2022). We now know that causewayed enclosures were first constructed around the southern coasts of Britain and then spread quickly inland from the coasts, although Helman Tor in Cornwall may also be very early (Whittle *et al*. 2022a, p. 215). The peak of building causewayed enclosures was around the decades of 3650 cal BC, with a renewed burst of building in the first part of the 36th century BC. There may be one exception to this broad pattern, and that is the site of Magheraboy, Co. Sligo, which has produced dates several centuries earlier than any comparable monuments in Britain; precisely why this is the case is subject to considerable debate. It may indicate very early connections between people on the west coast of Ireland and continental Europe (see Whitehouse *et al*. 2014, Whittle *et al*. 2011 Chapter 12) but equally, and perhaps increasingly likely, the result of dates from charcoal which may be misleading in terms of a construction date (Sam Moore *pers. comm*.).

The new dating programme has revealed other aspects of these monuments, particularly relating to the speed of construction and use. The interpretive Bayesian model would suggest that one of the biggest causewayed enclosures, that of Windmill Hill, was built rather rapidly. The entire monument took between 20 and 55 years to complete (Whittle *et al*. 2011, pp. 61–96), and this means that one person could have witnessed the construction of the whole enclosure. While the construction of Windmill Hill was rapid, deposition continued over a longer period of time, with the main phase of deposition ending between 3355 and 3325 cal BC (and there were more deposits made in later phases as well). Hambledon Hill, in contrast, took much longer to build, probably up to around 250 years (Whittle *et al*. 2011, p. 701). Deposition here also continued until later, between 3345 and 3305 cal BC (Whittle *et al*. 2011, pp. 117–150). These individual site histories can be contrasted with the bigger picture to assist with regional trajectories (note that some of the long barrows which have also been subject to these new dating programmes are found in the same area as causewayed enclosures, and therefore these different types of monument can be put into local sequences of construction and use).

The use of causewayed enclosures

Just as with the chambered tombs and long mounds discussed previously, some causewayed enclosures were constructed in locations which had already seen some previous activity. For example, Crickley Hill in Gloucestershire had evidence of occupation dating back to the fifth millennium BC: here the earlier 'banana barrow' was constructed prior to the construction of the enclosure (Whittle *et al*. 2011, p. 453), so clearly this was already a significant spot in the landscape which had seen some construction activity. Likewise, Hambledon Hill had already seen long barrow construction (Mercer and Healy 2008). In some cases, then, locations where causewayed enclosures would one day be built had already seen some modification and/or use. In most other instances, however, there appears to be only limited activity prior to the construction of causewayed enclosures; most sites have produced very little evidence of pre-enclosure building or deposition. It seems to be the case, then, that causewayed enclosures did not, for the most part, rely on these locations already having been important in terms of earlier significant occupation or activity. Instead, the first major event at many sites was the clearance of woodland and the cutting of a circuit of ditches. This might mean that virgin ground was ideally chosen for the location of such a monument.

The construction sequences at causewayed enclosures also vary. Some monuments seem to have only had a single phase; Haddenham, Cambridgeshire, comprised only a single circuit which seems to have been little used (Evans and Hodder 2006). Other sites saw multiple phases of construction, again with considerable diversity. At Windmill Hill the primary inner ditch circuit was small scale and short lived, while at sites like Hambledon Hill the first phase of construction was on a monumental scale and was longer in duration (Whittle *et al*. 2011, p. 95, 150). Both these sites then saw further alterations. At Windmill Hill after the modest inner ditch was built, a much larger outer ditch was constructed, probably a few decades later. Later still, the middle ditch was constructed. At Hambledon Hill there were at least five main phases of construction activity, with the two main peaks of building work taking place in 3675–3600 cal BC and again 3350–3325 cal BC. In addition to this, there is good evidence from those sites which have been excavated that even once a ditch had been created, people went back many times to recut the ditches. At Etton Cambridgeshire, the excavator noted up to eight episodes of recutting in some of the ditches (Pryor 1999). This suggests that the act of digging into the earth was one of the most important components for people creating and using these sites, and as such they were regularly sites where construction was ongoing.

There is also significant evidence for depositional events at causewayed enclosures and they have provided some of the richest evidence from the early Neolithic period. This is because there are numerous deposits in the ditches at these sites, including large quantities of animal bones (both complete and disarticulated individuals), pottery, stone tools including polished stone axes and human remains (which are dealt with separately subsequently). Many sites have produced numerous animal remains. Cattle in particular seem to have been important at causewayed enclosures but sheep, goat, pig, dog and some wild species are also represented. This has led to suggestions that these deposits are the remains of feasts, but there is evidence from some enclosures that live animals were brought into them as well. At Etton the beetle remains demonstrated that animals had been corralled inside the enclosure, and a similar argument was made for Northborough, Cambridgeshire, based on the phosphate evidence (Whittle *et al*. 2011, p. 893).

Significant quantities of pottery have also been found at causewayed enclosures. Around 1200 early Neolithic vessels were recovered from the excavations at Windmill Hill (Whittle *et al*. 1999, p. 257) and at Donegore Hill, Co. Antrim, the remains of 1500 pottery vessels were found along with over 23,000 lithics (Mallory *et al*. 2011). These are significant quantities of material culture, which contrast with other types of monument in the early Neolithic which usually only produce a small number of objects. Other notable deposits in the ditches at causewayed enclosures include stone tools as well as a polished stone axes. The latter in particular have received considerable attention as many are from exotic sources. At Windmill Hill, for example, there were eight stone axes from the Lake District, seven from south-west Wales, four from north Wales, two from Cornwall and two from Charnwood Forest, Leicestershire (Whittle *et al*. 1999, p. 340). At Hambledon Hill there were axes and flakes from Cornwall, the Lake District, Wales, possibly the Leicestershire source as well as two of continental origin. Many of these axes were found in a fragmentary state, suggesting that it was important to break them down into smaller parts; this is reflected in other types of material deposited at causewayed enclosures, including human remains, which were also fragmented prior to final deposition.

Some sites have produced evidence which suggests that they were used to make specific items. At Etton, Cambridgeshire, for example, the exceptional organic preservation revealed woodworking debris on the western side of the enclosure (Pryor 1999). In contrast, Maiden Castle, Dorset, produced evidence for the manufacture of flint axeheads (Whittle *et al*. 2011, p. 168). Polissoirs for polishing stone have been recovered from Etton, Abingdon and the Trundle (Pryor 1999, p. 266). But evidence for the production of material culture is not found at all sites and in many cases it was clear that material was predominantly being brought in from elsewhere. Certainly the deposition of material culture in the ditches was one of the key ways in which causewayed enclosures were used. It is worth noting regional variation here once again; broadly speaking, causewayed enclosures in the east of the country have much lower levels of deposition in the ditches than those found to in Wessex and the Thames Valley (Whittle *et al*. 2011, p. 701).

In contrast to the quantity of material found in the ditches, most causewayed enclosures have produced much less material from the centre of the enclosure; this has some important implications for the interpretation of these sites (see subsequently). The lack of material is probably a result of either the lack of investigation of the interior in some cases or a genuine reflection of the lack of use in others. There are exceptions; the interior of Donegore Hill, Co. Antrim, for example, has produced postholes, pits and hearths from the interior of the enclosure along with a substantial pottery assemblage, lithics and axeheads (Whittle *et al*. 2011, p. 564–574). This is a similar assemblage to that found at Lyles Hill a few kilometres away; Lyles Hill, however, is not a causewayed enclosure. This may suggest a significant regional difference in the creation and use of causewayed enclosures in Ireland.

One of the most extraordinary types of evidence from causewayed enclosure relates to what appears to be significant destruction events and acts of violence. At Hambledon Hill there are two episodes of burning where elements of the palisade were set on fire. Two burials at the site may be contemporary with one of these burning events, and at a later date two young men were killed by arrows (Whittle *et al*. 2011, p. 717–718). This may be evidence for violent attacks, but there are post-mortem cut marks on one man's skeleton, which suggests he was being defleshed on site like other bodies (see subsequently: Mercer and Healy 2008, p. 513). At Crickley Hill, Gloucestershire, there was also evidence of destruction and possible violence. Here hundreds of arrowheads along with a major episode of burning occurred between 3495 and 3410 cal BC (Whittle *et al*. 2011, p. 453). It has been suggested that at Crickley Hill the enclosure was attacked and the palisade burnt down in a violent attack. There is other evidence for violence in the early Neolithic from the chambered tombs and wooden mortuary structures (see previously), in particular in the form of interpersonal violence. It can be suggested that at causewayed enclosures what appear to be acts of aggression and violence were, in some cases at least, ritualised events (Mercer and Healy 2008, p. 761), but raids and killings were clearly taking place. Moreover, other timber structures in the early Neolithic were carefully burnt down, and this may be a way of decommissioning or ending the use of a particular site (see this and previous chapter on wooden mortuary structures and timber houses).

Mortuary practices at causewayed enclosures

Human remains are commonly found at causewayed enclosures, and this has led to suggestions that these sites were important locations for both dealing with and commemorating the dead. Like human remains found in other early Neolithic contexts, those from causewayed enclosures are found in a variety of states from fully articulated through to fully disarticulated. One of the most-discussed sites in terms of mortuary practice is Hambledon Hill in Dorset. As we have already seen, this site produced a wide range of human remains which clearly indicate that human bodies were undergoing complex mortuary rites in this location. Here the remains of 75 people have been found from all the different phases of use, predominantly fully disarticulated, with the occasional fully articulated example. It has been argued that bodies were deliberately excarnated on Hambledon Hill because there is evidence of canid gnawing on some of the bones, some are weathered and others have cutmarks on them, which suggests that is some cases bodies were carefully defleshed by hand (McKinley 2008). As discussed, crania in particular seem to have been selected for careful deposition, including at the base of the main ditch, and it was noted that many of the skulls at Hambledon were weathered, perhaps indicating they had been on display either at the site itself or elsewhere (Harris 2010, McKinley 2008, p. 492). At Hambledon, then, fleshed bodies were brought to site to be disarticulated, but defleshed bones may also have been brought to the site as well; bones may also have been taken away for deposition elsewhere. Mortuary practice, then, would have been a significant component of activity at the site, although evidence suggests that other activities took place at this site as well.

At other sites, only parts of the enclosure seem to have been associated with mortuary practice. At Etton, for example, half of the enclosure had small quantities of funerary deposits alongside pits with other carefully placed deposits; this was in contrast to the other half, which was associated with non-funerary activity (Pryor 1999, Figure 5.29). At Windmill Hill an adult male was placed in a grave which ultimately was covered by the outer bank (Whittle *et al.* 1999, pp. 80–81). The body would have been exposed in an open grave for a time before being sealed under the bank. At Offham Hill, Sussex, a crouched inhumation was found in a pit cut into the base of the outer ditch (Drewett 1977, p. 209). This evidence does not represent the casual discard of human remains or simply the remnants of disarticulation processes. Instead human remains, either complete or partial, were woven into the very fabric of the monument. The vicinity of other places associated with mortuary practice may have been relevant; many causewayed enclosures are close to long barrows, and it was noted that some enclosures are very close to rivers, which again may have been involved in a complex of early Neolithic mortuary practices (Oswald *et al.* 2001, p. 114). Causewayed enclosures were intimately tied up with ritualised acts involving the human body, although it is important to note that this happened at many other early Neolithic sites too.

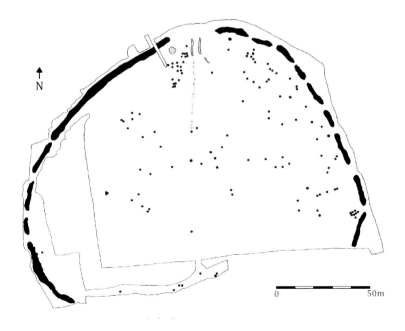

FIGURE 5.29
The internal features (pits) at Etton, Cambridgeshire (after Pryor 1999)

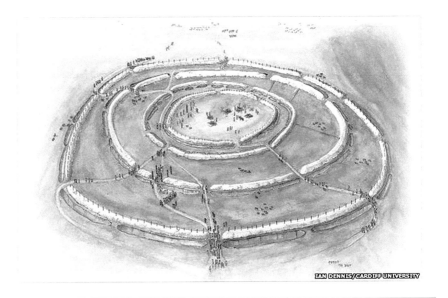

FIGURE 5.30
Reconstruction of Whitehawk causewayed enclosure (© Ian Dennis and reproduced with permission)

The interpretation of causewayed enclosures

With such a wide range of material having been recovered from causewayed enclosures, their use and function might seem clear. The presence of so much material culture in the ditches, especially animal bone and pottery, has been interpreted as the remains of feasting events. There is the strong possibility that these feasts were associated with the rites associated with dealing with the dead; as discussed, many sites have produced evidence for complex mortuary practices, including excarnation and the deposition of disarticulated bones. Causewayed enclosures, then, may have been places of transformation, particularly relating to the dead and ritual feasts associated with the dead. However, the explanation that these were places for the treatment of the dead does not account for all of the evidence.

Certainly it seems that one of the key roles of causewayed enclosures was the bringing together of people, both in the construction phase but also during their use. In the last chapter, issues of mobility and settlement were discussed, and it was suggested that people were probably still fairly mobile in the Neolithic, living for much of the year dispersed across the landscape, probably moving around with their animals (especially cattle). The building of a causewayed enclosure, then, may have tethered people to a central (neutral?) place where they could come together at specific times. In particular people may have been concerned with wider social relations and networks, which it is argued were wide ranging in the early Neolithic. Broader kinship networks may have required constant renegotiation once the Neolithic was established, so enclosures could well be places for the creation and negotiation of new genealogies or corporate groups; this may be among human participants (Whittle *et al.* 2011, p. 894) but equally could relate to animal populations too (Thomas 2015b). The dead could easily have been deployed as part of this, and this suggestion may also indicate why so many exotic stones, particularly in the form of polished stone axes from many different sources, were found at causewayed enclosures; they were brought and deposited as signs of wider social networks and lineages beyond the immediate area. The recutting of some of the ditches at some causewayed enclosures may be connected to the constant renegotiation of social relations over several generations. This could also explain the acts of violence (real or symbolic) at some sites which related to contested relations between different social groups.

This idea of kin or genealogical negotiation may also be useful in considering the fact that the form of the causewayed enclosure had its origins outside Britain and Ireland. This form of monument is found widely in other parts of north-west Europe. By building a monument which made explicit reference to people and practices beyond these islands, people were drawing on both external ways of doing things but also descent from that particular social order. By drawing on a monument form found on continental Europe, communities in Britain and Ireland may have been making strong statements about their origins (either real or conceptual). Causewayed enclosures may have been about the creation and subsequent negotiation of various groups into new corporate descent groups, with European origins especially being highlighted and evoked.

The precise location of causewayed enclosures may, too, have been important. About a third of causewayed enclosures occupy slight rises above river valley floors, and in some cases there is good evidence that, for some of the year at least, parts of the enclosure ditches were flooded (Oswald *et al*. 2001, p. 91). In these cases water may have been a powerful symbol being drawn on, evidenced elsewhere in the Neolithic world. Rivers functioned not only as navigable routeways though the Neolithic landscape but would also have been important in belief systems (Bradley 2000a); it was suggested previously that they may have played a significant role in early Neolithic mortuary practice. Other causewayed enclosures are set close to striking upland features such as hilltops, and there are arguments that these locations, too, may have been important, perhaps for communicating with spirits or deities which may have resided in such locations (e.g. Cummings and Whittle 2004). Unlike chambered tombs and long mounds/cairns, then, some of which seem to have been built on top of earlier activity and occupation, causewayed enclosures for the most part were built on previously unoccupied but significant locales which may have related to broader practices and belief systems in the early Neolithic (Whittle *et al*. 2011, p. 888). These places were set aside from everyday life for the activities outlined previously and then formalised through the digging of ditches, the creation of banks and the building of palisades. In this sense they could be understood as important places or conduits between the lands of the living and the dead, between the earth and the sky, and locations for dealing with the powerful dead. All of these elements may have been drawn upon for people renegotiating their place in the world and in the cosmos.

While archaeologists have sought an explanation which incorporates all the different types of evidence from the range of sites explored through excavation, we must also retain the real possibility that these sites were used in quite different ways in different parts of the country, as well as over time. A causewayed enclosure in one part of southern Britain may have been understood and subsequently used quite differently than one elsewhere; this may explain the diverse forms, locations and deposits found at these sites. Many sites were used over long time periods and so maintained a potency way beyond initial construction and use. It is also worth reiterating here that causewayed enclosures were not built in most parts of Britain and Ireland: they were a predominantly southern British phenomenon. Clearly in other parts of the country people felt no need to build this form of monument. In these areas social negotiations were clearly dealt with in other ways and at other places.

CURSUS MONUMENTS AND LONG ENCLOSURES

So far we have considered the wide variety of stone-built monuments along with natural places like caves, mainly used for the deposition of the dead along with causewayed enclosures. However, there is another form of timber monument that was built from the early Neolithic onwards, but in Scotland only: the cursus monument. In Scotland these monuments are defined by pits and posts, and known examples are concentrated exclusively in the Scottish lowlands (Brophy 2016). As their name suggests they were constructed either by digging pits into the ground or by erecting posts in pits, with double parallel lines of posts or pits creating a long and thin space between them (Figure 5.31). These early Neolithic pit and post-defined cursus monuments are relatively small when compared with other cursus monuments to the south, usually up to about 500m in length. A series of these monuments have recently been excavated in Dumfries and Galloway, including at Holywood, Holm and Dunragit, so we have a good understanding of this kind of monument (Thomas 2007a, 2015a).

These cursus sites would have been striking monuments in the landscape with double lines of massive timbers cutting a swathe across the landscape. They would have been

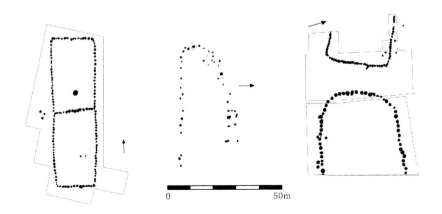

FIGURE 5.31
Plans of pit and post-defined cursus monuments. Left Douglasmuir, centre Holywood North, right Bannockburn (after Thomas 2007a)

large and prominent monuments, taking a considerable amount of effort to construct. Moreover, it is also notable that some of these sites were burnt down (Thomas 2013, pp. 337–340); Douglasmuir, Angus, and Cowie Road, Bannockburn, Stirling, for example, were both destroyed by fire. These were not accidents; it would take a mass of carefully laid kindling and fuel to fire the large timber posts at these monuments. Indeed, some sites were constructed then destroyed by fire multiple times, showing this was a deliberate act. At Hollywood North, Dumfries and Galloway, four separate phases of construction then destruction took place between 3778 and 3698 cal BC (Thomas 2007a). Clearly, the building and then destruction of these sites were significant and would have provided an incredible visual spectacle for those involved. Julian Thomas has argued that the pit and post-defined cursus monuments of Scotland related to another type of architecture – the timber hall (Thomas 2013, p. 338 and previous chapter), but they could equally be interpreted as an elongated form of long barrows, bank barrows and long enclosures (Brophy 2016). They also have parallels with natural features, especially rivers (see next chapter). This highlights, yet again, the interplay between different forms of monumentality in the early Neolithic.

Later on in the early Neolithic this form of monument underwent a change and started to be constructed from earth. Instead of digging pits, people dug continuous ditches and mounded up the soil from the ditch to create a bank. These parallel banks and ditches created a long, linear monument. Some of these were are many kilometres in length (see Barclay and Harding 1999). An avenue found at Raunds, Northamptonshire, is 60m long and may be one of the earliest southern British cursus-type monuments; it dates to between 3860 and 3620 cal BC (Harding and Healy 2011, p. 64). However, the Greater Stonehenge cursus is more typical in size, which was, in its final form, nearly 3km in length (Thomas *et al*. 2009). This has been dated to between 3630 and 3370 cal BC, While many of these cursus monuments are definitively early Neolithic in date (see Barclay and Bayliss 1999, Thomas *et al*. 2009), some also appear to have been built later on in the fourth millennium (see Chapter 6). One of the issues with these monuments is that, unlike other early Neolithic monuments, they saw virtually no deposition in their ditches, and as such it remains difficult to date them; this has also led to issues surrounding their interpretation. But since many of the earthen cursus monuments were probably built in the later part of the fourth millennium, they will be discussed in more detail in the following chapter.

CONCLUSIONS ON EARLY NEOLITHIC MORTUARY PRACTICE AND MONUMENTS

Throughout this chapter the treatment of the dead has been considered, both in relation to monuments but also from other contexts. It appears that there was considerable diversity in mortuary practice in the early Neolithic. Human remains have been found from a wide variety of contexts, not just monuments such as chambered tombs and causewayed enclosures but also in caves, rivers and single graves. One of the commonalities of early Neolithic mortuary practice is the reduction of the fleshed human body into disarticulated bones. In a number of cases there is good evidence that scavengers were involved in this process, so much so that it may have been normal practice for people to be left out for predators in the early Neolithic. Other processes may well have been involved in disarticulation, and we have seen evidence for cutmarks on bone which shows that, in some cases, people assisted with this process. The exceptions to this broad practice of exposure, predation and disarticulation are those people who ended up in long barrows or chambered tombs. We can no longer think of this practice as the 'norm' but the exception to the rule. These were bodies deployed for specific reasons in particular places at a particular moment in time.

Throughout this chapter I have emphasised that there are notable blank areas in the distributions of different forms of monument. For example, chambered tombs are only found to the west and north of Britain, although it could be argued that wooden equivalents are represented in the east. In Ireland chambered tombs are only found in the northern part of the island; dolmens have a wider distribution but are found in smaller numbers. So the question is: what was going on in areas where none of these monuments are found? It seems unlikely that every square mile of Britain and Ireland was occupied during the Neolithic, as some areas would have remained wooded. However, there is evidence for Neolithic occupation in areas which are blank of monuments, so it is clear that this form of architecture was not constructed by everyone in the early Neolithic, and even then not all the time by those who did build them. Monumentality, then, was not a given; keeping domesticates and making pottery in Britain and Ireland did not necessarily go hand in hand with the construction of monuments. It seems, then, that monuments fulfilled a role that not all communities in the early Neolithic needed. This makes their interpretation even more complex, because instead of understanding chambered tombs, for example, as functioning as burial chambers, this is clearly not the whole story. People could manage to dispose of their dead without recourse to the construction of such a monument. So, while these monuments were built to take human remains, their 'function' was rather different. They may have been places for containing dangerous spirits or built at times of serious social unrest when the souls of the dead needed to be used to effect a change in the lives of the living. It was suggested previously that chambered tombs may have been constructed in response to violent episodes, dealing with difficult deaths or in some cases as the creation of founder lineage groups as at Hazleton North. Likewise, causewayed enclosures were used by people predominantly in southern Britain with an initial burst of building and use focused starting in the 37th century BC. At one level the use of causewayed enclosures seems to have mirrored the use of chambered tombs, with the careful deployment of the dead at specific points in the landscape. However, it is clear that other practices took place within these monuments, again with important regional differences. It has been argued here that causewayed enclosures were places for the careful negotiation of social relationships, particularly relating to lineage and corporate descent, which may have been contested and open to negotiation in the early Neolithic. Monuments were places, then, were people and substances came together at crucial or critical points in time. They enabled people to work together on a project, employ powerful symbols including the dead and to renegotiate their place in the world, be that the cosmological world or the very real social networks of early Neolithic society.

RECOMMENDED FURTHER READING

There are some good books which deal with the different types of monuments discussed in this chapter. For chambered tombs and dolmens, try:

Cummings, V. and Richards, C., 2021. *Monuments in the making. Building the great dolmens of early Neolithic northern Europe*. Oxford: Oxbow.
Darvill, T., 2004. *Long barrows of the Cotswolds and surrounding areas*. Stroud: Tempus.
Field, D., 2006. *Earthen long barrows*. Stroud: Tempus.
Jones, C., 2007. *Temples of stone*. Cork: Collins.
Smith, M. and Brickley, M., 2009. *People of the long barrows*. The History Press.

For cursus monuments

Brophy, K., 2016. *Reading between the lines. The Neolithic cursus monuments of Scotland*. London: Routledge.

For causewayed enclosures

Last, J., ed., 2022. *Marking place: New perspectives on early Neolithic enclosures*. Oxford: Oxbow.
Oswald, A., Dyer, C., and Barber, M., 2001. *The creation of monuments. Neolithic causewayed enclosures in the British Isles*. Swindon: English Heritage.

For mortuary practice more broadly

Fowler, C., 2010. Pattern and diversity in the early Neolithic mortuary practices of Britain and Ireland: contextualising the treatment of the dead. *Documenta Praehistorica*, 37, 1–22.
Peterson, R., 2019. *Neolithic cave burials of Britain*. Manchester: Manchester University Press.

CHAPTER 6

Circles and lines

The middle Neolithic of Britain and Ireland

INTRODUCTION

This chapter considers the evidence from the middle Neolithic of Britain and Ireland. This can be differentiated from both the preceding early Neolithic and the subsequent late Neolithic in a number of ways, including the use of characteristic types of material culture, especially Impressed Ware pottery, and the construction of particular types of monument, most notably passage tombs in the west and north of Ireland and Britain, alongside the continued tradition of building earthen cursus monuments in many parts of Britain. This is a period which saw very clear regional trajectories, with significant differences between parts of Britain and Ireland. As we will see, there was an intensity of monument construction in some areas, while other areas saw no sites being built at all. Moreover, many of the elements of late Neolithic monumentality have their origins in the middle Neolithic, so it is an important period for exploring the development of later traditions of practice. The period is equally distinguished by the abandonment of earlier forms of monument, including chambered tombs and causewayed enclosures, again suggesting a shift or change in society at this time. However, while this evidence marks a shift in practice from what came before, the traits of the middle Neolithic do not appear in the archaeological record at a single moment in time across Britain and Ireland. Instead there was a series of varied trajectories towards these practices more broadly, which start to appear consistently between 3500 cal BC and 3400 cal BC in Britain, and perhaps even earlier in Ireland, but are widely evident from 3300 cal BC. Likewise, the end of the middle Neolithic period differs from region to region but will be taken here to date to around 3000 cal BC, although is almost certainly earlier in Orkney. Overall, the middle Neolithic can be characterised by mobile settlement practices probably associated with pastoralism and the decline of cereal agriculture, the beginning of the creation of monumental complexes which saw the transformation of entire landscapes and the use of distinctive types of material culture which utilised distinctive

DOI: 10.4324/9781003387329-6

decoration on both pottery and monuments. The most recent ancient DNA evidence is also suggestive of communities facing the effects of plague, which may have resulted in the decline of populations at this time: the evidence for plague, at the time of writing, has been mainly located elsewhere in northern Europe (Seersholm *et al*. 2024) but almost certainly affected communities in Britain and Ireland in the middle Neolithic. In short, then, the middle Neolithic is a convenient label to indicate the centuries between the early and late Neolithic but with a lot of fuzzy edges and regional trajectories in which not everything was in sync up and down the country.

LIFE IN THE MIDDLE NEOLITHIC: SUBSISTENCE, SETTLEMENT AND MATERIAL CULTURE

The middle Neolithic is not as well understood as the early and late Neolithic because other than the distinctive range of monuments discussed in the following, there is an overall lack of evidence from this period. In terms of how people made a living, evidence suggests that there was significant continuity from the early Neolithic in the keeping of cattle for both meat and milk (Serjeantson 2011), but it seems that people also kept significant quantities of pig in some areas (Worley *et al*. 2019). Wild plant foods continued to be used, but there are now suggestions that there may have been a distinct decline in the cultivation of cereals in the middle Neolithic period (see Stevens and Fuller 2012). This appears to have occurred around about the same time as a broader decline in environmental conditions along with forest regeneration (Whitehouse *et al*. 2014, Woodbridge *et al*. 2014), and it may have been the case that people choose to utilise the 500 or so wild plants available to them in Britain and Ireland instead of relying on one cereal crop which had the potential to fail in changing climatic conditions (Stevens and Fuller 2012, p. 718). Hazelnuts continued to dominate plant assemblages in many places (Worley *et al*. 2019). There is also now the intriguing possibility that there was a population decline at this time brought about by plague, which may have made cereal cultivation more challenging (cf. Shennan *et al*. 2013).

It seems that people used a wide range of environments at this time, including wetlands and floodplains, evidenced by wooden trackways of a middle Neolithic date. This includes the Parks of Garden trackway, Stirlingshire (Ellis *et al*. 2002), and the Silvertown trackway, London (Crockett *et al*. 2002). There may also have been some use of marine foods at this time – a middle Neolithic log-boat from Greyabbey Bay, Co. Down, has been found on the shores of Strangford Lough (Forsythe and Gregory 2007), and a middle Neolithic fish weir has been recovered from the Liffey estuary (Smyth 2014, p. 140). As discussed in relation to the early Neolithic, fishing may have been a supplemental addition to the diet at times of stress as opposed to a vital component of the diet. All of this paints a rather diverse picture of subsistence practices at this time.

Broadly speaking, there was also some continuity from the early Neolithic in terms of stone tool production and use, although chisel arrowheads were now commonly made. Moreover, stone axe production declined around 3500 cal BC (Whittle *et al*. 2011, p. 895),

FIGURE 6.1
Location of sites mentioned in this chapter, except passage tombs (see Figure 6.4)

but those already produced may well have been in circulation after this point. Some small-scale exploitation of stone axe quarries and flint mines probably continued in the middle Neolithic. While most material culture from the middle Neolithic had elements of continuity from the earlier Neolithic, pottery underwent an important change at this time. The pottery from the middle Neolithic is dominated by Impressed Wares, a type of pottery which is bowl shaped but, as the name suggests, is also profusely decorated

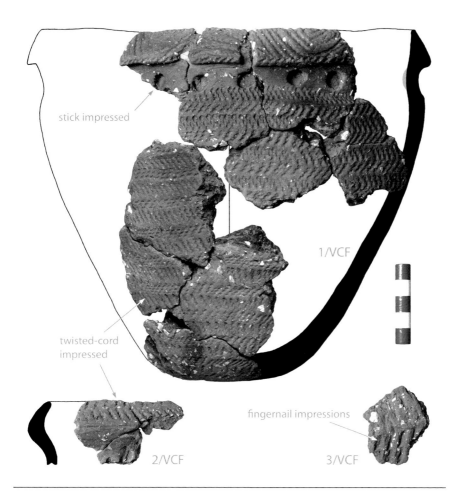

FIGURE 6.2
Impressed wares from Westbourne, Sussex (image by Mike Seager Thomas)

with impressions in the clay (Figure 6.2). There are many different regional variations of Impressed Ware, including the type of pottery often called Peterborough Ware in southern Britain (which itself has a range of regional variations) and Goodland and Carrowkeel Ware in Ireland (see Sheridan 1995). The precise date for the appearance of these different impressed wares varies from region to region and may have begun as early as 3600 cal BC (Gibson 2002a, p. 74, Sheridan 1995), but they were more widely established and used by 3400 cal BC or so (Müller and Peterson 2015); they continued in use well into the later Neolithic and overlapped with the appearance and adoption of Grooved Ware, which is the most common form of pottery from the late Neolithic (and as such discussed in the next chapter). The distinctive decorated pot styles from northern and western Scotland are also found in the latter part of the fourth millennium; these are known as Unstan and Hebridean Wares (Hunter 2000). While there is clear regional variety and diversity in both the form and decoration of Impressed Wares, there are also shared traits which indicate continued strong links between Britain and Ireland, especially western Scotland and Ireland (Gibson 2002a, p. 81, Sheridan 1995). This is suggestive of extensive and ongoing contacts at this time, which, it has been argued, were in place in the early Neolithic and continued into the middle Neolithic. These contacts are evidenced in other ways and are discussed again in the following.

In many ways Impressed Ware has elements of continuity with earlier Neolithic bowls. Impressed Wares retain the round-bottomed bowl form, and there is evidence that this pottery continued to be used for cooking and serving food; at Upper Ninepence, Powys, for example, cattle and sheep meat was cooked, and in Ireland, pottery continued to be used for processing dairy products (Smyth and Evershed 2015b). Pottery, therefore, remained firmly associated with the cooking of food. It continued to be used in a mix of domestic and monumental settings (Thomas 1999, pp. 106–112). The significant change from early Neolithic pottery production was the profusion of decoration now added to vessels. This new way of doing things was clearly understood and adopted as a wider tradition of practice and may relate to connections beyond Britain and Ireland and beyond this form of material culture (see subsequently in relation to decoration on passage tombs). Impressed Wares, therefore, can be understood as an expression of wider connections while at the same time displaying localised expressions of identity and authorship (and see Robb and Michelaki 2009). It is worth noting here again that Grooved Ware, a completely different style of pottery found predominantly in late Neolithic contexts, had its origins towards the end of the middle Neolithic (see Copper *et al*. 2023); this, once again, highlights the fact that pottery styles did not come and go rapidly but had long currencies of overlapping use.

Other forms of distinctive middle Neolithic material culture are known, but in smaller quantities. Antler maceheads have been recovered, mainly from the Thames foreshore but also from funerary contexts in the east of England, with a single example from a settlement site on the Outer Hebrides (Loveday *et al*. 2007). These are made from red deer antler beams with a central perforation through the centre; they are often ground and polished and in some instances are also decorated. These objects may be the inspiration for, or contemporary with, stone maceheads, the most simple of which may also date to the middle Neolithic but which are found in larger quantities from the late Neolithic onwards (see next chapter). A small number of jet belt sliders are also known from middle Neolithic contexts (Loveday 2009). Jet is a distinctive black shiny mineral found at Whitby, Yorkshire, which saw more extensive use in later periods, and its presence, along with other distinctive objects such as boars' tusks in single graves (see subsequently), hints at the development of new types of material expression relating to objects on the body in the middle Neolithic period. In some ways jet and maceheads can be seen in a similar way to the polished stone axes which were more prevalent in the early Neolithic. The source of jet is likely to have been known and understood, as was the source of polished stone axes (see Chapter 4).

In terms of middle Neolithic settlement, very little is known from most parts of Britain and Ireland. The Irish 'house horizon' and the early Neolithic timber halls discussed in Chapter 4 had been burnt down or were abandoned well before the start of the middle Neolithic. With some notable exceptions discussed subsequently, evidence of occupation from the middle Neolithic consists of spreads of material, middens, hearths and pits, which suggest dispersed and mobile populations practising pastoralism and transhumance (e.g. Gibson 1999). One exception are the middle Neolithic houses of the Northern Isles.

In Chapter 4 it was noted that early Neolithic timber houses had been found in Orkney. This was unexpected because it was thought there was little available wood in the Northern Isles for such architecture, and Orkney was well known for its stone houses. However, it seems that house architecture on Orkney mirrored what was going on elsewhere in Britain and Ireland. After an initial early Neolithic timber phase, there are a number of examples of middle Neolithic stone houses on Orkney, which is different from other parts of Britain. These structures are rectangular in shape, constructed from slabs of stone with a central slab-built hearth. They had slabs protruding on the internal space like the stalls of chambered cairns. These houses were constructed as single structures dispersed across the landscape, but additional houses or extensions were subsequently added over time (Richards *et al*. 2015). On the Orkney mainland, later fourth-millennium BC houses have been excavated at Stonehall, Wideford Hill, the Knowes of Trotty and Smerquoy (Figure 6.3), and similar stone houses are found further afield within the Orkney islands at the Knap of Howar, Papa Westray; Ha'Breck, Wyre; and Green, Eday. Towards the end of the fourth millennium, the larger, conglomerated settlements such as that found at Barnhouse was also founded. These mark a notable shift in settlement more typical of the late Neolithic and so will be dealt with in the next chapter.

Although not investigated to the same extent as Orkney, there seems to be similar evidence from Shetland. At Firths Voe, a middle Neolithic house was discovered preserved under the peat, and excavations produced a stone house that was constructed

FIGURE 6.3
The stone house at Smerquoy, Orkney (image by Colin Richards)

in 3415–3135 cal BC. Significant quantities of artefacts were trampled into the floor, including pottery, carbonised plant remains, worked quartz and polished felsite axe flakes (Lee and Reay forthcoming). Two more stone houses of a similar date are known at the Scord of Brouster (Whittle 1986).

What is so intriguing about these stone houses on Orkney is that they mark a significant shift from earlier, wooden constructions. Instead these houses were constructed to resemble the architecture of the earlier stalled cairns (see chapters in Richards and Jones 2015b). Long thought to be the other way round (i.e. that stalled cairns drew on the architecture of the houses), this sequence in Orkney demonstrates the importance of monumental architecture (chambered tombs) influencing the structures of the living. There may be a connection on Shetland too between houses and monuments; small passage tombs were constructed there in the latter part of the fourth millennium, and their circular form is also echoed in the shape of the houses in the area. This is a phenomenon that is not, so far, replicated anywhere else in either Britain or Ireland, and it suggests something rather different was going on in the Northern Isles at this time. This idea will be explored again in the following chapters, which deal with developments on these islands in the late Neolithic, and we will also see further examples of the interplay between monumental and house architecture in the structures of late Neolithic Orkney.

MORTUARY PRACTICE AND MONUMENTS

Monuments are the most visible remains of the middle Neolithic, and this period is characterised by the construction of a form of monument which appears to the west and north of Ireland and Britain: the passage tomb. In other parts of Britain, notably north-eastern England, round mounds were prevalent, and to the south earthen cursus monuments continued to be built across the landscape alongside new forms of enclosure (see subsequently). Some of these may appear to be new forms of monumentality, but all have their antecedents in the earlier Neolithic. Moreover, early Neolithic monuments would have been standing in the landscape for hundreds of years by the start of the middle Neolithic. It is therefore worth noting that early Neolithic monuments often continued to be used in the middle Neolithic; activity tailed off at most chambered tombs, but it seems clear that some monuments saw continued deposition or were altered at this time. At Skendleby 2, Lincolnshire, for example, early Neolithic activity continued into the middle Neolithic, with clear evidence for the destruction of a wooden façade (Field 2006, p. 87). Human remains may also have been placed in chambered tombs. However, where middle Neolithic burial has been identified, it is not in the same quantity as in the early Neolithic where multiple individuals seem to have been buried in one event or in rapid succession. Instead, the middle Neolithic saw single individuals added to pre-existing chambered tombs.

In addition to the occasional burial being deposited the blocking of façades and forecourts at Clyde cairns, court cairns and Cotswold-Severn monuments seem to have taken place in the middle Neolithic. The blocking of the forecourt essentially decommissioned these monuments both in terms of restricting deposition but also preventing the forecourts being used as meeting places (Darvill 2004, p. 184). Likewise, causewayed enclosures had mostly fallen out of use by about 3500 cal BC, but some activity was still ongoing at some sites until 3315–3280 cal BC (Whittle *et al.* 2011, p. 683). At Windmill Hill, for example, deposition in the ditches ceased between 3355 and 3325 cal BC and at Hambledon Hill, Dorset, after a surge of activity in 3350–3325 cal BC, the site then went out of use (Whittle *et al.* 2011).

With chambered tombs and causewayed enclosures seeing only limited use or being decommissioned in this period there is less detail on mortuary practice at this time in comparison to the early Neolithic. In south and central Britain there are some examples of inhumations in flat graves, cists and pits, and in East Yorkshire individuals and groups of individuals were placed in graves with a distinctive set of grave goods in episodic bursts of activity (Cooper *et al.* 2022, pp. 326–329, Greaney and Whittle forthcoming). There was also an increase in cremation, with examples appearing at the early enclosure sites such as Stonehenge and in Scotland in stone settings such as Balbirnie and Forteviot (Noble and Brophy 2017). As with the early Neolithic there is evidence for the use of caves as places for the deposition of human remains, although as with the use of chambered tombs, this appears to be on a smaller scale than in the early Neolithic. In Ireland fragmentary human remains have been recovered from caves dating to the middle Neolithic including Barntick Cave, Co. Clare, and Carrigmurrish Cave, Co. Waterford (Dowd 2015). This is suggestive of ongoing processes of excarnation and fragmentation. There is a similar pattern in Britain; there are examples of middle Neolithic human remains from caves such as the Totty Pot, Somerset although more remains recovered from caves require dating to establish how widespread this practice was (see Schulting *et al.* 2010). Thus from the evidence we have it is clear that both inhumation and cremation were used, but clearly the vast majority of people did not receive formal burial in a monumental setting.

It is also possible to argue that mortuary practices which rarely leave a trace in the archaeological record were in use in the middle Neolithic. This could include the exposure of bodies which were then skeletonised by predators (see last chapter). Disarticulated human bone on the midden at An Corran, Skye, for example, dates to the middle Neolithic and is suggestive of the ongoing use of exposure at this time. This may indicate that wild animals were an important part of belief systems, particularly relating to the freeing of spirits to go to the afterlife (see Chapter 5). Equally, bodies could have been placed in rivers; there was a link between monuments built in this period and rivers which may strengthen this suggestion (see subsequently). As discussed in the next section there were also the beginnings of an interest in celestial bodies in the middle Neolithic, most notably the sun. This increased referencing of celestial events is suggestive of changing belief systems and may indicate a re-orientation away from natural places and beings to the heavens (and see Fowler 2021).

MONUMENTS: PASSAGE TOMBS

Passage tombs are a distinctive type of monument found in Britain and Ireland. In a period which is often notable for its lack of sites, passage tombs provide a wealth of evidence for us to consider. This is not a type of monument which is found throughout

Britain and Ireland, however; these monuments are only found in very specific parts of the landscape. Passage tombs are distributed across Ireland, predominantly in the northern and eastern parts of the island, with a general absence in the south-west (Herity 1974). The best-known of these are the complexes of passage tombs at Brú na Bóinne and Loughcrew, Co. Meath, and Carrowkeel/Keshcorran and Knocknarea/Carrowmore, Co. Sligo. Another significant cluster is found in the Northern Isles (Orkney and Shetland) and the Western Isles (Outer Hebrides: see Henshall 1963, 1972). A small number of passage tombs are also known from mainland western Britain (Figure 6.4).

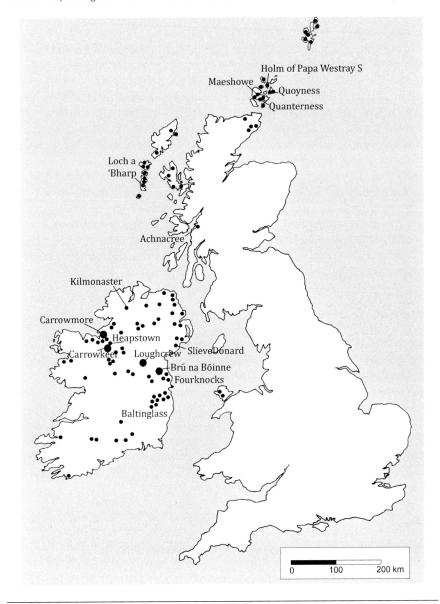

FIGURE 6.4
The distribution of passage tombs in Britain and Ireland, with sites named in the text

It is worth noting here that only middle Neolithic passage tombs are considered in this section. Some authors describe some early Neolithic monuments as 'simple passage tombs': those monuments are discussed in the previous chapter alongside similar dolmen sites (see Cummings and Richards 2021 for more details on the typology of these monuments).

Monumental form

Passage tombs get their name from the presence of a megalithic passage leading to a stone-built chamber. These passages vary quite considerably, however, from ones only a few metres in length to those at the largest sites such as Newgrange, where the passage is 19m long (O'Kelly 1982, Figure 6.5). Certainly some of these passages could have been used to access the chamber, but many are too small and narrow to ever have been used in this way. The presence of a passage was nevertheless a key component of these monuments.

The passages in these monuments lead to a chamber, and in this regard these monuments share some similarities with early Neolithic chambered tombs (see Chapter 5). The chambers of passage tombs create an enclosed area using a combination of upright stones (orthostats) and overlapping dry-stone walling (corbelling) to create a roofed chamber. This can often simply be a rectangular space located at one end of the passage, but there is some variation with this; some passage tombs have cruciform chambers whereby smaller side-chambers or recesses are located off the central chamber

FIGURE 6.5
Looking down the passage at Knowth, Co. Meath

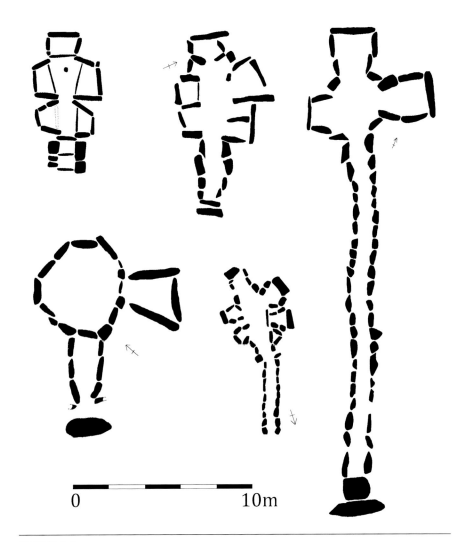

FIGURE 6.6
A selection of chamber plans from Irish passage tombs (after Powell 2016). Top left Carrowkeel F, Co. Sligo; top row middle Loughcrew L, Co. Meath; top right Newgrange, Co. Meath; bottom left Dowth South, Co. Meath; bottom centre Seefin, Co. Wicklow

area (see Figures 6.6–6.7). Those passage tombs with recesses have between three and seven (Hensey 2015, p. 35). Some of the large passage tombs have exceptionally well-built chambers which are considered the pinnacle of chambered tomb construction in the Neolithic. These monuments clearly indicate skill and precision in megalithic engineering. As will be discussed in more detail subsequently, some of the stones used in the chamber and passage were also decorated.

One of the most striking aspects of these monuments is the presence of a circular cairn or mound which covers the passage and chamber. It was noted in the previous chapter that the vast majority of early Neolithic chambered tombs are covered by a long cairn or

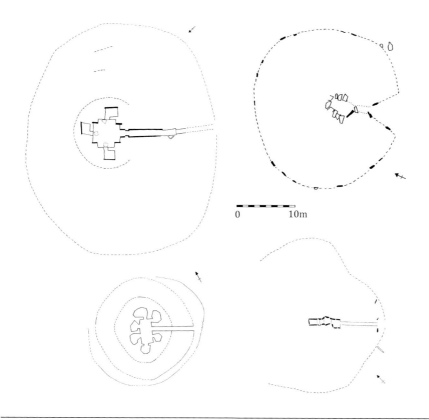

FIGURE 6.7
A selection of plans of British passage tombs top left Maeshowe, Orkney; bottom left Quoyness, Orkney; top right Loch a'Bharp, South Uist; bottom right Achnacree, Argyll and Bute (after Henshall 1972)

mound, so the presence of a round cairn/mound at passage tombs marks a significant change in practice (and is replicated with other middle Neolithic monuments elsewhere: see subsequently). While the chambers at passage tombs do not vary enormously in size, the covering cairns show considerable variation. Some of the smallest passage tombs have cairns only a few metres in diameter; for example, Site 16 at Knowth, Co. Meath (one of the smaller satellite tombs found around the main Knowth passage tomb known as Knowth 1) is only 4m in diameter (Eogan 1986). In contrast, the cairn on Site 1 at Knowth is 90m across at its widest point, and Heapstown, Co. Sligo, is 60m in diameter (Hensey et al. 2014). These enormous cairns make the largest of the passage tombs very striking and sizeable monuments (Figure 6.8).

Another feature of some of these passage tombs is the presence of a kerb. This is a circuit of stones around the outside of the monument which would have supported the cairn or mound but which also provided a clear boundary or edge to the monument (Figure 6.9). Kerbs are found on many, although not all, Irish sites but only some British sites. One of the most striking elements of some of the kerbs in Ireland is that the

FIGURE 6.8
Composite photograph of the massive passage tomb of Newgrange, Co. Meath. This is one of the largest passage tombs in Ireland

FIGURE 6.9
The kerb at the main site at Knowth, Co. Meath (right). One of the smaller satellite tombs can be seen to the left

stones can be decorated with motifs pecked or chiselled into the stone (Figure 6.10). This is the most prevalent at the Brú na Bóinne complex, especially Knowth. Decoration is also present on stones in the passages and chambers of some passage tombs, again notably in the Brú na Bóinne and Loughcrew complexes (Hensey 2015).

One of the most striking differences between passage tombs and early Neolithic chambered tombs is that passage tombs are sometimes found in complexes. These are large clusters of monuments situated close together, and this phenomenon only occurs

FIGURE 6.10
The highly decorated stone found at the entrance to Newgrange, Co. Meath

in Ireland. At Brú na Bóinne it is suggested that up to 45 passage tombs were once located here, clustered around three of the largest passage tombs in Ireland: Knowth, Dowth and Newgrange (Eogan 1986). Knowth in particular had multiple passage tombs around the larger monument in the centre (see Figure 1.4). At Loughcrew up to 30 passage tombs are located over and around four hilltops (McMann 1993). The Carrowkeel/Keshcorran complex consists of 30 surviving monuments, most located on prominent ridges and hilltops (Hensey *et al.* 2014). Also in County Sligo the Knocknarea/Carrowmore area has 30 surviving monuments; some of these are earlier dolmen monuments which have been converted into passage tombs, a theme that will be explored in more detail subsequently (Cummings and Richards 2021). Smaller clusters of passage tombs are also found at Kilmonaster, Co. Donegal, and Bremore/Gormanstown, Co. Dublin (Hensey 2015, p. 13). It is interesting, therefore, that the clustering of monuments is not a feature of these sites in western Britain where passage tombs are all found in isolation. This is suggestive of regional differences in terms of how these monuments were both built and understood.

Another key element of these monuments is their location. As already noted in relation to the large complexes, many are located on hilltops; this means that these passage tombs are visible for miles around, and they themselves command wide views out over the landscape. The most striking examples of this are the Carrowkeel/Keshcorran complex and the massive passage tomb on the summit of Knocknarea, both in County Sligo (Bergh 1995, Moore 2016). The Loughcrew monuments are highly visible in the Meath landscape, and there are many other hilltop passage tombs in Ulster, one of which can

FIGURE 6.11
One of the stone basins in the chamber at Newgrange

be seen from the Scottish mainland on the other side of the Irish Sea. The hilltop location is replicated with the passage tombs in Shetland, although those in Orkney and the Outer Hebrides do not follow this pattern. While not on hilltops, they are often positioned in commanding positions which overlooked routeways (see Cummings and Richards 2013; Figure 6.12).

It has been observed that some passage tombs are aligned on celestial alignments, specifically the rising of the sun. At both Newgrange, Co. Meath, and Maeshowe on Orkney the midwinter sunrise shines down the passage and illuminates the back of the chamber. This is particularly extraordinary at Newgrange because in order to achieve this effect, the builders had to incorporate a roof-box above the passage which enabled a ray of sun to enter the monument (see Figure 6.13); because the passage is sloping, the sunlight would not reach the chamber without the addition of the roof-box. At other examples the passage is oriented on the midsummer solstice, for example, at Townleyhall, Co. Meath (Hensey 2015, p. 70). The orientation of monuments on celestial alignments was deliberate and may have related to a celebration of these events. The longest and shortest days would have been significant in terms of the agricultural year but also in terms of cosmology (the rebirth of the year). The careful alignment of the passage in relation to celestial events at some of these monuments was a feature which appeared increasingly in monuments built in the later part of the middle Neolithic (cf. Bradley 1993), and is found at other forms of monument elsewhere (see subsequently).

A final and notable component of passage tombs is the presence of decoration. This is non-representational and comprises a series of abstract designs such as circles, spirals,

FIGURE 6.12
The passage tomb of Bharpa Langass, North Uist, Outer Hebrides, which is set in an elevated position and has wide views out over the landscape

lozenges, zig-zigs and cupmarks (Figure 6.14). Decoration is most commonly found at the County Meath complexes, although there are smaller quantities of decoration from Carrowkeel/Keshcorran, Co. Sligo (Hensey *et al*. 2014), the two passage tombs on Anglesey (Powell and Daniel 1956) and some of the Orcadian monuments (Bradley *et al*. 2001). Since the decoration is abstract it is difficult to interpret precisely what it may represent; it has been suggested it was produced by people in an altered state of consciousness (Dronfield 1996), but it has also been noted that it appears at key transitional points or thresholds both within and outside the monument (Robin 2010, Figure 6.15).

Dating and phasing

The dates from passage tombs place the majority of them in the middle Neolithic period, with most probably built between 3400 and 3000 cal BC. There are some early dates for passage tombs which suggest that their construction may have started in the mid-fourth millennium BC, perhaps as early as 3500 cal BC. Cremated bone from Baltinglass, Co. Wicklow, has been dated to between 3600 and 3400 cal BC (Whitehouse *et al*. 2014). The monuments at Carrowmore have long been contentious in understanding the dating of passage tombs. The excavator dated charcoal samples which returned extremely early dates (from the late Mesolithic), but these were problematic and have been since been dismissed by many (see Bergh and Hensey 2013). A more recent programme has dated some of the bone pins deposited as grave goods in the Carrowmore monuments, showing that those objects were probably deposited between 3685–3555 cal BC and 3275–3000 cal BC (Bayliss in Bergh and Hensey 2013). This is potentially an extended

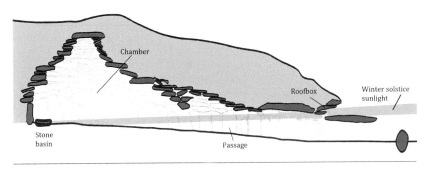
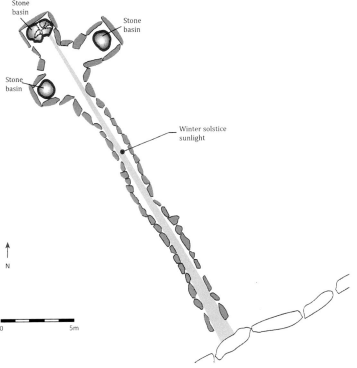

FIGURE 6.13
Profile (top) and plan (bottom) of the chamber at Newgrange showing the location of the winter solstice solar alignment. The sunlight enters Newgrange through the roof-box and travels down the passage to hit the back of the chamber (after Stout and Stout 2008)

period of use of these sites but still puts the main phase of their use in the middle Neolithic (also see subsequently).

The large complexes of passage tombs seem to indicate a sequence of construction. At Knowth some of the small tombs were constructed first, followed by the large tomb in the centre: some small tombs were added subsequently (Whittle et al. 2011, 650). The same sequence is suggested for Newgrange. The main phase of deposition in the main tomb at Knowth dates to 3200–3040 cal BC (Schulting et al. 2010), and recent

FIGURE 6.14
Decoration on the back-slab of the rear chamber at Loughcrew, Co. Meath

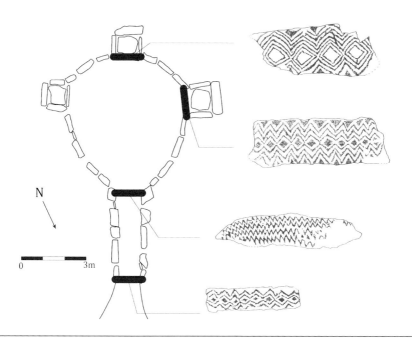

FIGURE 6.15
The passage tomb of Fourknocks I, Co. Meath, showing the location of decoration panels at key threshold points within the monument (after Eogan 1986, Robin 2010)

dates from Carrowkeel date the mortuary deposits as 3346–3097 cal BC (Kador *et al*. 2015). Dates from the Mound of the Hostages, Tara, indicate that the chamber, cists and cairn were first used between 3295 and 3120 cal BC, but burial continued into the later Neolithic period (Whittle *et al*. 2011, p. 654). This is mirrored at the Orcadian passage tombs such as Quanterness, which was constructed in the later part of the fourth millennium BC but continued to be used into the late Neolithic (Schulting *et al*. 2010).

One of the most interesting aspects of some of these monuments is that it appears that some earlier sites were 'converted' into passage tombs. Some of the Carrowmore monuments were earlier dolmens (see previous chapter) which appear to have been altered to create passage tombs, while other passage tombs proper were built in amongst these earlier monuments (see Cummings and Richards 2021). Elsewhere the Knowe of Lairo and Holm of Papa Westray South, Orkney, were converted from earlier monuments into passage tombs. It is clear, then, that passage tombs were built and used over an extended period of time, possibly originating at the end of the early Neolithic, but with the bulk of sites being built in the middle Neolithic. Moreover, some continued to be used into the late Neolithic period. Those passage tombs in complexes were not constructed all in one go but over time, with the larger and central passage tombs later in the sequence.

Use

For such large and impressive monuments, there is not always an equivalent wealth of material culture or burials from many of the sites, although it is worth noting that many sites have seen extensive exploration and sometimes destruction in historic times (Herity 1974, Chapter 1). In terms of the burial evidence, cremation seems to be the dominant burial rite at passage tombs in Ireland (Eogan 1986), with inhumation more prevalent in Orkney. Again there is evidence for considerable variation, with some sites producing smaller amounts of human bone, while others saw really large numbers of depositions. At Quanterness, Orkney, 59 individuals were found in the chamber which were deposited as whole bodies (Crozier *et al*. 2016). The Mound of the Hostages, Co. Meath, has produced the remains of over 100 cremated individuals, although these come from pre-monument, middle Neolithic and late Neolithic activity combined. Other sites have produced the remains of much smaller numbers of people (e.g. Eogan 1986). There are hints that some of the burials which were deposited in passage tombs were secondary; at Newgrange the excavator noted that some deposits were a mix of soil and bone and must have been exhumed from elsewhere (O'Kelly 1982). Potentially, then, complex and varied burial rites took place at these monuments, with some sites seeing considerable deposition and others only token deposits.

Grave goods have also been found in a number of passage tombs, most notably comprising bone and antler pins, beads, pendants, stone balls and pottery (Hensey *et al*. 2014). Occasionally more elaborate objects such as maceheads are found, which include the beautiful polished and carved macehead from Knowth (Eogan 1986, pp. 141–142). Perhaps one of the most extraordinary finds are the stone basins found within some sites in Ireland, with a total of 25 known (Hensey 2015, p. 100). This is not a feature of passage tombs beyond Ireland, however. What is interesting about these basins is that they would have had to have been in place prior to the construction of the monument, as they were too large to be added in later. This may indicate that these were one of the first components on site and effectively the focus of building.

The most recent addition to our narratives on passage tombs has been ancient DNA analyses. The genetic evidence indicated that one middle-aged male from Newgrange, Co. Meath, was the product of incest: his parents were either brother and sister or parent and child (Cassidy *et al*. 2020). Relatives of this individual were also found in other passage tombs 150km away to the west, and the authors of this study suggest that this indicates the presence of a dynastic elite in middle Neolithic Ireland, comparable to that found in ancient Egypt and elsewhere.

Interpreting passage tombs: construction sites

Monuments such as passage tombs represent the coming together of people at particular points in the landscape to work on a project. This would have involved the quarrying and dragging of large stones and careful and precise megalithic construction techniques. Smaller stones, turf, clay and earth would have been brought in baskets to the site to create mounds and cairns. This is the case for all these monuments, but the largest of the passage tombs would have involved a huge investment of labour and time, potentially over a number of years. It is interesting that there is now evidence that people may have started to use domestic cattle (oxen) to help build some of these enormous passage tombs (Pigiére and Smyth 2022) and suggestive of new technologies arriving alongside new traditions of practice in terms of monument construction. It is therefore not unreasonable to suggest that the large passage tombs were essentially locales for the focus of many different communities working together through construction (cf. McFadyen 2006, Richards 2004). As has been argued in relation to other large construction events, this may have been, in part, about the ongoing negotiation of lineages, identity and the social order (and see Cummings and Fowler 2023).

The idea that these were construction projects bringing together different communities is supported by the evidence that at some passage tombs, at least, people were bringing bits of distant landscapes to a single point and incorporating these into a composite monument. This is particularly obvious at the Brú na Bóinne complex because some of the stones used came from further afield, most notably quartz 40km from the Wicklow Mountains to the south, greywacke slabs from 5km to the east and north and granite and granodiorite from 35km to the north (Cooney 2000, p. 136). It is possible some of the carved stones were brought in from other places or possibly reused monuments elsewhere (Hensey 2015, pp. 120–136). The constructions of the large passage tombs, then, were probably projects involving many different communities working together, where the bringing together of people may have been in and of itself one of the key aims of these monuments. Group effort and distant kin groups were incorporated into a composite structure.

In this regard it is also worth reiterating the fact that passage tombs are located in very particular parts of the landscape. It has been noted that they are often, although not always, positioned on hilltops or in island-like locations, set up and away from everyday settlement. These could have been neutral spaces, essentially meeting places between different social groups or even liminal zones. Richard Bradley (2000a) has argued that it was possible that prehistoric people had an understanding of the world which saw it divided into three: the world of the living (the earth), the underworld (the sea, caves etc) and the upper-world (the sky). This can be described as a 'three-tier cosmology'. Early Neolithic chambered tombs avoided mountain tops altogether (Cummings 2009), instead echoing caves and the underworld in their architecture. Passage tombs, in contrast, emphasise a connection with the sky and the upper world. The most extreme example of this is the passage tomb on the summit of Slieve Donard, Co. Down, which is at a height of 848m OD (Moore 2012), making it the highest passage tomb in north-west Europe (Herity 1974, p. 230). In this sense these monuments may differ from their early Neolithic counterparts and were instead drawing on different sets of relations with otherworldly beings, and creating a connection between this realm and the upper-world. This may mark a significant shift in cosmological beliefs and may also explain the increased emphasis on celestial alignments as noted at a number of passage tombs (and see Fowler 2021).

Passage tombs for the living

Passage tombs, as their names implies, were places for the deposition of the dead. In Ireland many corpses were cremated prior to being deposited, but in Orkney it appears bodies were deposited whole. Passage tombs would therefore have been the final place of deposition for selected people, not a place where fleshed bodies underwent transformation to bones/relics as we saw in the early Neolithic. It can be suggested that the presence of the passage in the larger monuments facilitated repeated access to the chamber, so that people could go in and add more remains of people over time. However, there is now also evidence for these sites being places for the transformation of bodies; new evidence from Carrowkeel, Co. Sligo, indicates that fleshed remains were being dismembered at this site, with clear evidence of cut marks being found on a number of the bones (Geber *et al*. 2017).

However, these monuments should not simply be understood as repositories for the remains of the dead. While it is tempting to see the objects found in the chambers as 'grave goods', the lack of direct association with the remains of the dead invites alternative interpretations. Some authors have suggested that passage tombs created places for the living to use: to conduct rituals, to engage with the other world and perhaps even to undergo rites of passage. The remains of the dead and perhaps the processing of the dead may have been part of this, but the deposition of skeletal remains was simply part of other rituals taking place in these monuments. Robert Hensey, for example, has argued that passage tombs were for ritual training or the seclusion of the living (Hensey 2015). It could be envisaged that initiates went into these monuments where perhaps they remained for a period of seclusion before emerging; this could easily tie into transformation in the state of personhood, for example from a child to an adult (Fowler 2004b). Material culture such as bone pins, pots or maceheads may have been tokens of this transformative process.

There are certainly a number of extraordinary components of these monuments which suggest that they were more than just burial places. It has already been noted that

FIGURE 6.16
Two of the Carrowkeel passage tombs, with wide views out over the Co. Sligo landscape

passage tombs have a series of thresholds marked via the location of decorated panels (Robin 2010). While much of the decoration was definitely carved on the stone prior to construction, there is also evidence of some of it being altered once the monument had been built. In particular there is pick dressing which seems to have deliberately obscured earlier designs, suggesting the desire to eradicate existing designs (Hensey 2015, p. 47). This may suggest that some people went into passage tombs to alter or add to carvings. Another phenomenon noted at passage tombs is that sounds made within them, such as the hammering of stone, speaking or chanting, would have created specific acoustic effects (Watson and Keating 1999). Creating noise within passage tombs creates an effect known as Helmholtz resonance, which is similar to that created when blowing over the lip of a bottle; for participants within the chamber of a passage tomb the effects of chanting or drumming could have been unsettling and unpleasant and possibly understood as otherworldly (Watson and Keating 1999). All these different elements may suggest that passage tombs were used by the living for dealing with other worlds, perhaps for deliberately creating transformative effects. The small internal space of a passage tomb meant that only certain people could go inside, perhaps those undergoing transformation or ritual specialists.

Passage tombs for the dead

A completely different interpretation of passage tombs is that they were not designed to be used at all once constructed. It has already been noted that many passages are not actually passable by people, making them more of a conceptual connection from the outside to the inside than a functioning access point. Certainly burial deposits could have been added through the roof, as may well have been the case for many early Neolithic chambered tombs (Crozier et al. 2016). If this was the case, then, the passage could represent an access point for spirits, ancestors, the dead or otherworldly beings (Lynch 1973) and thus a conceptual, not actual, entry point into the chamber. It is also interesting to note that some really extraordinary architecture is employed at many passage tombs which involves the creation of multiple distinct layers around the monument. Robin (2010) has described these as a series of concentric spaces created by layers of stone, turf, sand, earth, clay, shell and animal bone within the mounds or cairns of passage tombs. Beyond the passage tomb are often additional boundaries especially banks and ditches (Robin 2010, pp. 374–384) but also spreads of quartz and platforms. These layers within the mounds are not just the by-product of building in stages as the interfaces between layers are also carefully marked out within the passage via sillstones, changes in angle, and rock art showing a deliberate and careful placement of distinctive layers around the chamber. This can be understood as a process of 'wrapping' – the careful addition of multiple layers around a central point (Richards 2013) using a wide variety of different materials and ways of enclosing space (Cummings and Richards 2017). Sometimes passage tombs are encircled or wrapped by more passage tombs, as at Loughcrew or Knowth (Figure 6.11), and in the later Neolithic other acts of wrapping were added to some passage tombs.

If the inside of passage tombs were spaces set aside for non-living beings, but carefully wrapped by multiple layers of different substances, this might suggest that passage tombs were all about containment, or keeping something dangerous inside. This could of course simply be the remains of the dead but could equally be something even more powerful. In the previous chapter it was suggested that early Neolithic chambered tombs were about the containment of bad deaths, the results of illness, perceived witchcraft or sorcery (Fowler 2010). If these monuments were understood as doorways to other worlds, essentially an interface between this world and another world for certain people deposited in these monuments, then the wrapping of such a powerful place both kept spirits contained within but also prevented contamination from outside (Cummings and Richards 2017).

It is also interesting that this idea of wrapping is something which already existed in the Neolithic world. In the previous chapter the evidence from causewayed enclosures was discussed. These monuments were constructed around a central area, sometimes, but not always, a hilltop. It is not entirely clear how the central area was used as the evidence from this is variable; in some cases the centre of a causewayed enclosure was used in the processing of the dead but also for gatherings of the living (see previous chapter). The central area, however, was encircled by a series of features including ditches, banks and palisades. Furthermore, access to the centre was restricted, usually to one or two ways through the encircling architecture. These elements were replicated at passage tombs, although realised in a radically different fashion. In this way, people could have been inspired both by earlier monuments in Britain and Ireland (causewayed enclosures) and monuments found elsewhere in Neolithic Europe (the passage tomb tradition of Atlantic Europe). What they created was a unique form of monument found in Ireland and Britain, where the central tenet was to wrap and contain.

With all these different interpretations, how then should we therefore understand the passage tomb tradition? We should be careful not to think of these monuments as part of a single phenomenon across Britain and Ireland. There was quite clearly some regional variation in form, location and use. These were certainly monuments which were set carefully away from living communities, possibly at the interface between worlds (cf. Richards 1992). In contrast to early Neolithic chambered tombs, passage tombs emphasise a connection with the sky and the upper world. In this sense they may well be drawing on different sets of relations with otherworldly beings and perhaps a new understanding of the world itself (see Fowler 2021). Whatever was contained within these monuments, however, required careful wrapping and seclusion from the outside world.

These were also monuments which seem to have been built over several hundreds of years, so again the meanings associated with them may well have changed over time. What is clear is that this was a tradition of construction which altered entire landscapes. The large complexes in Ireland demonstrate that whole hilltops could be altered through architecture (Bradley 1993). These were the forerunners for the larger late Neolithic complexes which appeared throughout Britain and Ireland in the late Neolithic (see next chapter). Even single passage tombs were placed so that they were highly visible in the landscape, meaning that they would have been seen by many people. These were monuments which drew on earlier traditions of doing things, albeit in a radically altered architectural form, while also anticipating what would happen in the later Neolithic. The presence of passage tombs along the Atlantic seaboard must also indicate wider connections beyond Britain and Ireland to European ways of doing things. Throughout this book it has been suggested that there were wide set of connections between people which were present in the late Mesolithic and continued throughout the Neolithic. This is further evidence of ongoing and widespread connections between people in different parts of the Neolithic world: in the case of passage tombs, this was firmly focused on the Atlantic façade.

MONUMENTS: ROUND MOUNDS

Another monument type often associated with the middle Neolithic is the round mound. However, as discussed in the previous chapter, round mounds are also a feature of the early Neolithic. In some ways the round mounds of the middle Neolithic can be considered a continuation of practice already established in the early Neolithic, but there are also marked differences between the two in terms of the style of burial. In contrast to the burials found in early Neolithic round mounds, those of middle Neolithic date are inhumations of single or paired individuals. Individuals are also typically accompanied by grave goods associated with personal or group identity, in some cases in considerable quantities. This was not a style of monument found throughout Britain, however. Only small clusters of this style of monument are found in southern England and Yorkshire although other examples may await discovery. Liff's Low, Derbyshire, for example contained a single burial associated with a large quantity of grave goods including an antler macehead and boars' tusks (Loveday and Barclay 2010). At Barrow Hills, Radley, Oxfordshire, two individuals were found, one with a jet belt slider and one with a polished flint knife (Bradley *et al*. 1992, Figure 6.17). The best-known example of a round mound is Duggleby Howe in Yorkshire; while many of the individual burials beneath the

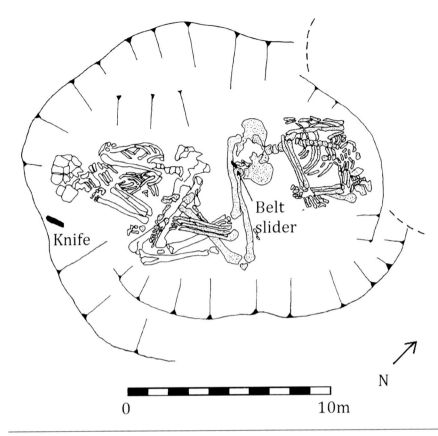

FIGURE 6.17
The inhumations at Barrow Hills, Radley, Oxfordshire (after Bradley *et al*. 1992)

round mound are both early and middle Neolithic in date the round mound itself was actually constructed in the late Neolithic (Gibson 2016).

It is also worth noting here that Linkardstown cists which were discussed in the previous chapter continued to be used into the latter part of the fourth millennium cal BC. They have similarities with both early Neolithic chambered tombs, particularly court cairns, and middle Neolithic traditions of practice focusing on the burial of an individual. They are one of several types of monument whose construction and use spans the early middle Neolithic divide, and it is to another of these monuments which we now turn.

CURSUS MONUMENTS AND ENCLOSURES OF THE MIDDLE NEOLITHIC

The previous chapter briefly considered cursus monuments. These are the long linear monuments which consist of opposing banks and ditches and which run through lowland landscapes, often for many miles. In that chapter it was noted that some cursus monuments were constructed in the early Neolithic, including various pit- and post-defined examples in Scotland and some of the earthen bank and ditch sites elsewhere, such as the Great Stonehenge cursus in Wiltshire (Thomas et al. 2009). While some of these sites began to be constructed in the early Neolithic, it appears that many may well date to the latter part of the fourth millennium BC (Barclay and Bayliss 1999, Brophy 2016b, Whittle et al. 2011, pp. 724, 907). The problem of dating these sites stems from the fact that the ditches were kept clear of material culture and complicated by the fact that these are enormous monuments. The largest example is the Dorset cursus, which is 10km long, and this means we can only ever excavate a tiny portion of these sites. Brophy (2016b, Chapter 6) notes that these are also monuments which seem, in many cases, to have been built piecemeal, and this means that they could have been under construction for long periods of time or added to and altered over many hundreds of years. It is fair to say that, at present, we have only a limited understanding of where these monuments fit in the overall chronology of the early and middle Neolithic. However, Whittle et al. (2011, pp. 907–908) argue that these were sites which were typically constructed later on than causewayed enclosures, in some cases overlying them, and as such they fit in more broadly with a middle Neolithic architectural tradition.

Earthen cursus monuments usually consist of two parallel banks and ditches rounded or squared off at the terminal ends but there are some variations on this. A few sites, including the Cleaven Dyke, Perthshire (Barclay and Maxwell 1999), and Stanwell C1 at Heathrow Airport (Brophy 2016b, p. 210, Framework Archaeology 2011), have two parallel ditches but only a single internal bank. There is also considerable variation in terms of size, from the smallest sites often referred to as long enclosures being up to 150m in length to the longest example (the Dorset cursus), a massive 10km long. Whether all these different types of monument would have been understood as being part of the same order of things is therefore highly debateable (Thomas 2006), and if they were built from the early Neolithic right through to the third millennium cal BC, as has been suggested (Whittle et al. 2011, p. 724), then their meaning and uses may well also have changed. Bearing all that in mind, how, then, should we understand this form of monumentality?

It has been noted that some cursus monuments appear to connect pre-existing monuments as well as potentially significant natural features, thus creating a physical structure which links these places together in an ordered fashion (e.g. Tilley 1994). In particular a relationship between cursuses and rivers has been discussed (Brophy 2000). These observations had been used to suggest that cursus monuments could therefore have acted as bounded routes, tied up, perhaps, with ritualised processions or formalising existing pathways. The potential use of rivers in middle Neolithic mortuary practice was discussed previously, and the connection between cursuses and places used for the deposition of the dead such as long barrows and causewayed enclosures further enhances this suggestion. However, it has also been noted that many cursus monuments do not have entrances into them; in this sense they may have been restricting access to specific parts of the landscape, perhaps routeways which were now no longer appropriate for use by the living (Johnston 1999). This could be a process which culminated in the late Neolithic with the creation of spaces and landscapes designed for the dead (see Chapter 8). It is also relevant that, like other middle Neolithic monuments,

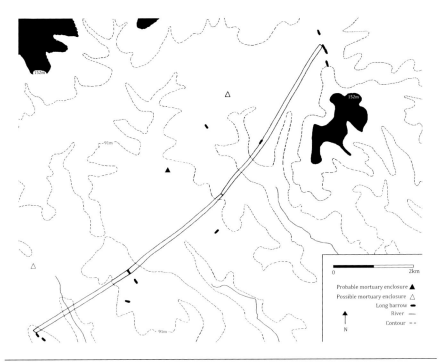

FIGURE 6.18
The Dorset cursus in its wider landscape setting (after Johnston 1999)

cursuses effectively altered entire landscapes, and they were also built in complexes like passage tombs. There are five cursuses at Stanwell, Heathrow; four at Rudston, Yorkshire; and four at Manor Farm outside Milton Keynes (Brophy 2016b, p. 137). It is also interesting that the Dorset cursus is aligned on the midwinter sunset (Bradley 1993, p. 51), since, as we saw previously, some middle Neolithic passage tombs are also aligned on celestial events (see previously). In the late Neolithic many monumental complexes occur close to existing cursus monuments, suggesting that whatever the initial purpose of these sites was, these locations had an enduring significance (see Chapter 8).

Finally, people also started building enclosures towards the end of the middle Neolithic. These are also sometimes known as formative henges and seem to mark the beginning of the henge tradition which gained much wider traction in the late Neolithic (see Chapter 8). A good example of an early enclosure is the site of Flagstones in Dorset, which was constructed around 3200 cal BC. This was a large but simple enclosure with shallow segmented ditches, again built in a location which had already seen some activity in the form of pits (Smith *et al.* 1997). Both enclosures and cursuses were monuments which took considerable effort to construct, and in this sense they can be understood as construction projects which brought disparate social groups together in the act of moving earth, as has been argued previously for passage tombs. These monuments, therefore, mark a step change in the scale and size of the monumental endeavour, a tradition which expanded even further in the late Neolithic.

CONCLUSION: LIFE AND DEATH IN THE MIDDLE NEOLITHIC

In many ways the middle Neolithic is the least-understood phase of the Neolithic. Overshadowed on either side by the architecture and material culture marking the beginning of the Neolithic and the large and impressive monumental complexes and rich material culture sets which appear in the late Neolithic, the middle Neolithic might seem a quiet period, lost somewhere in between. There is very little settlement evidence, and while people continued to keep cattle, it seems that some people may have stopped growing cereals. This suggests the continuation of a pastoral economy, and mobile, albeit tethered, settlement patterns. Intriguingly, there is the possibility that this may have been a result of the arrival and spread of plague into Britain and Ireland, which had an effect on population numbers and the success of individual communities. There is evidence that early Neolithic chambered tombs and caves saw some continued deposition in the middle Neolithic, particularly of single bodies, but excarnation or deposition in rivers may still have been the most common funerary rite. New forms of burial practice were also adopted in a localised manner, with round mounds of differing types with single inhumations in some parts of the country and cremation becoming prevalent in other areas. However, the larger monuments of the early Neolithic, specifically the causewayed enclosures of southern Britain, more or less went out of use at this time. It seems that the social dynamic which created the need for these sites, possibly involving the mediation of new lineages and seemingly sometimes violently negotiated, were no longer necessary in this area. However, a related form of architecture was constructed instead, this time in western and northern parts of Britain and Ireland. Here it has been argued that passage tombs fulfilled many of the social functions of the causewayed enclosures of the early Neolithic, albeit now relevant for different parts of Britain and Ireland. These were places where people could come together and resolve social tensions and negotiate identity and corporate groupings. They may have been places where dynamic leaders were involved in rallying local communities into building projects. Passage tombs could also be understood as the product of societies under stress where construction helped to resolve and renegotiate relations, both with living communities but also perhaps between the living and the dead. Moreover, the construction of passage tombs also hints at a change in belief systems with an increased focus on the heavens and the sky. In parts of lowland Britain the construction of cursus monuments may have marked a formalisation of routeways connected with particular peoples and lineages, now no longer open to negotiation.

There is a temptation to argue that the low level of monumental construction, particularly in Britain, marks a period of relative stability for people at this time. However, the climatic downturn, the move away from the use of cereal, the arrival of plague and the construction of monumental landscapes may represent a period of considerable readjustment for much of Britain and Ireland where social networks, yet again, needed to be renegotiated. While regional differences were clearly being stressed through material culture, it still appears to be the case that there were broad connections throughout Britain and Ireland and beyond to north-west Europe. There are arguments that an Atlantic connection may have been strengthened at this time, and the continued emphasis on rivers and waterways indicates the importance of connections by boat. Not only were people widely connected in the middle Neolithic, but here we find the beginnings of the inter-relatedness of things as well. This is demonstrated via the application of decoration onto material culture (such as antler maceheads) which also appeared on passage tombs. In the Northern Isles houses started to look like monuments. Therefore the middle Neolithic is a period when people began to explore new ways of doing things, renegotiate the old order and create connections between previously separate elements of life. The inter-connectedness of materials and places and the creation of monumental complexes in the middle Neolithic therefore set the scene for what would come to the fore in the late Neolithic.

RECOMMENDED READING

Passage tombs: lots written but start with

Hensey, R., 2015. *First light: The origins of Newgrange*. Oxford: Oxbow.

The Neolithic houses on Orkney

Richards, C. and Jones, R., eds., 2015. *The development of Neolithic house societies in Orkney*. Oxford: Oxbow.

For cursus monuments

Brophy, K., 2016. *Reading between the lines. The Neolithic cursus monuments of Scotland*. London: Routledge.

CHAPTER 7

Lines and landscapes of descent

Life in the late Neolithic of Britain and Ireland

INTRODUCTION

It was in the late Neolithic when some of the largest monuments ever built appear in Britain and Ireland, not in isolation but as part of massive and impressive monumental complexes covering entire landscapes. This culminated with the construction of perhaps the period's most famous site, Stonehenge, a testament to the sheer amount of time and effort people were willing to invest in creating a monument. By the middle part of the third millennium, however, another big change was on the horizon: the arrival of Beaker-using people from continental Europe. This would herald another era: the Bronze Age.

In this chapter we investigate life in the late Neolithic of Britain and Ireland, and the subsequent chapter considers the monuments for which the period is best known. As such this chapter will focus on settlement, material culture and subsistence. This is a period characterised by the presence of some quite distinctive types of material culture, many of which have decoration and were beautifully made on exotic materials. This includes Grooved Ware pottery as well as maceheads, carved stone balls and polished flint objects. Decoration was also important in the creation of rock art panels some of which were definitively carved during the late Neolithic. While it is clear that people were investing time and effort in the creation of distinctive forms of material culture, it seems that the majority probably made their living as pastoralists, following their animals around the landscape. There is very little evidence for reliance on cereals and only limited evidence for houses and settlements. Recent suggestions are that there were quite low population levels at this time. It should be noted that the late Neolithic is defined in this book as starting around 3000 cal BC, although practices discussed here clearly started earlier in northern Scotland. Indeed, northern Scotland appears to have been on a distinctive and different regional trajectory than most of Britain and Ireland at this time. The late Neolithic continues until between 2500 and 2400 cal BC when new types of material

DOI: 10.4324/9781003387329-7

culture began to appear, including Beakers and metalwork, and these are dealt with separately in Chapter 9. As with earlier divisions of the Neolithic used in this book, the boundaries for the start and the end of this period are fluid and different dependent on region. Instead, most forms of material culture, settlements and subsistence strategies continued with considerable elements of continuity from the middle Neolithic at the start of the late Neolithic and some continued practices into the early Bronze Age.

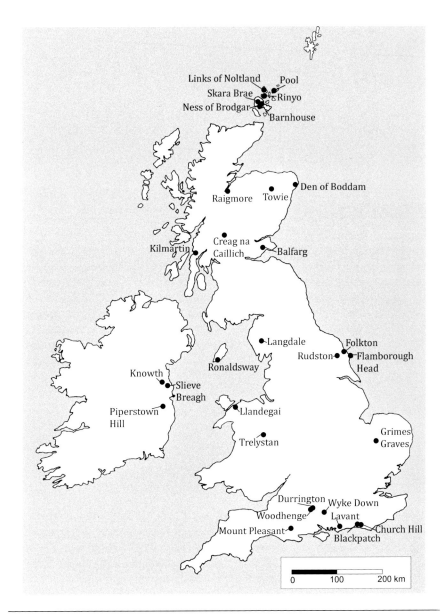

FIGURE 7.1
Sites mentioned in this chapter

FIGURE 7.2
The exceptionally well-preserved late Neolithic village at Skara Brae, Orkney, showing the stone 'dresser' at the rear, two 'box-beds' to the left and right and a central hearth in one of the houses

SETTLEMENT

We are fortunate in the late Neolithic to have a small number of exceptionally well-preserved examples of settlement. Perhaps the best-known example is the site of Skara Brae in Orkney. This site was revealed on the edge of the Bay of Skaill in the nineteenth century and partially excavated by Gordon Childe in the early part of the twentieth century. The houses at the site survive to roof height, and there is stone architecture surviving perfectly preserved within the houses, set around a central hearth (Figure 7.2). There are stone-lined 'box beds' which we think were used for sleeping, along with stone dressers looking remarkably like more recent dressers in houses used for storing kitchen utensils (Childe 1931). The houses are conjoined and linked by narrow passages. They would have been dark but warm in the Neolithic, built into midden material (or discarded material) produced by the settlement.

More widely the Orkney Isles have produced some remarkable settlement sites dating to the late Neolithic, including the site of Barnhouse close to the Stones of Stenness (Richards 2005 and see subsequently), Rinyo on Rousay, Links of Noltland on Westray and Pool on Sanday (Richards and Jones 2015b). We can describe these as 'nucleated' settlements, as they comprise multiple stone houses built in close proximity to one another. They usually have distinctive internal features including a central slab-lined hearth, two opposed 'box-beds' and a rear dresser, although there are variations depending on the size and shape of each house. Various other features are often found, including under-floor drains, which would have meant these sites essentially had water which could flow in and out of the house. It is important to note that while these conglomerated settlements are discussed here in relation to the late Neolithic, some of these begin life towards the end of the fourth millennium cal BC (such as Barnhouse: see Richards et al. 2016). Nevertheless, this is a way of dwelling which reached its apogee in the late Neolithic, and the broader implications of these sites were also felt elsewhere in the late Neolithic.

One of these conglomerated settlements is Barnhouse on the Orkney mainland, which has been excavated, subjected to recent intensive investigation and is fully published (Richards 2005, Richards et al. 2016). This site consists of 13 separate structures representing multiple construction events (see Richards et al. 2016 for details). All houses have produced evidence of domestic habitation (Figure 7.3), and it appears that much

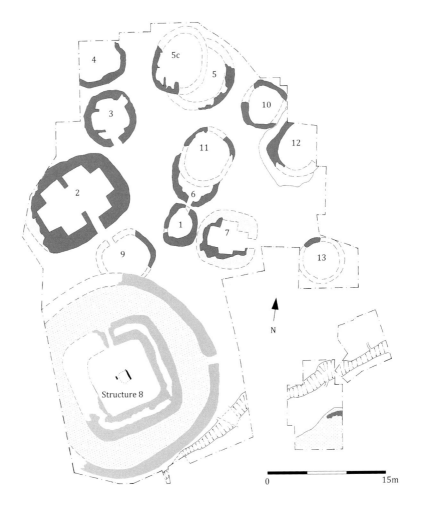

FIGURE 7.3
Composite plan of the houses at Barnhouse, Orkney (after Richards 2005). Note the large House 2 and Structure 8

of the craft-working such as pottery production, bone and hide working and hide preparation took place in a central area at the heart of the settlement. A detailed study of Grooved Ware from the site has also shown variation between houses which can be identified in relation to the type of material used to temper the pottery: different households used different tempers acquired from the local landscape (A. Jones 2002, p. 128). Barnhouse also produced the remains of two rather different structures. House 2 is twice the size of other houses on site; it also has two hearths and six large recesses. It was constructed using extremely high-quality masonry and appears to have been associated with the preparation and consumption of food, particularly beef, as well as the making and deposition of special objects, including maceheads (Richards 2005, pp. 130–153). Structure 8 is the biggest building on the site and was built over an area where people had previously gathered and feasted. It was also encircled by a large wall. While people clearly undertook activities within these houses, both have been interpreted as a ceremonial or gathering houses used for restricted and special practices (Richards and Jones 2015a). Whether this means they were houses in the purely domestic sense or whether they share more similarities with monuments is discussed again subsequently.

Colin Richards has argued that these conglomerated settlements on Orkney are the result of unique sets of social relationships which differed from those that existed elsewhere in Britain and Ireland (see various papers in Richards and Jones 2015b). It is suggested that membership of a social group was focused not on blood relations and lineages of descent, which is typical for most groups ethnographically, but on the house itself: to dwell within the house was to become part of a corporate group (see Richards and Jones 2015b, pp. 7–8). In these societies the house acted as an anchor or a mechanism which could be deployed within extremely fluid social conditions. The house effectively bound people together through close proximity as well as communal social practices. Therefore it was the act of doing things together which established relations, and social identity was expressed through claims to kinship or blood relations. The Orcadian conglomerated settlements, then, represent the coming together of disparate groups in specific social circumstances in an attempt to create social links and formalise their position within society more broadly. The individual houses at Barnhouse and Skara Brae represent individual groups or small communities of people, and the larger ceremonial houses were representative of that new unified group.

As such the conglomerated settlements in Orkney such as Skara Brae should not be seen as representative of settlement outside this specific context. However, this particular sequence does seem to have had a wider *influence* on Neolithic society in the early part of the third millennium cal BC. We will see that the distinctive late Neolithic pottery known as Grooved Ware originated in these settlements and was adopted across Britain and Ireland in the following centuries. Other material culture, in particular special and exotic items such as maceheads and objects with incised designs, were also associated with these Orcadian settlements (Richards 2005) and are found elsewhere, although this does not imply that the idea of maceheads originated in Orkney (and see Chapter 6). However, the next chapter will discuss how some monument forms of the late Neolithic also seem to have had their origins in Orkney, drawing heavily on the notion of a house. While it is easy to observe the uptake of material culture and monuments from Orkney across Britain and Ireland, it is harder to explain precisely *why* this

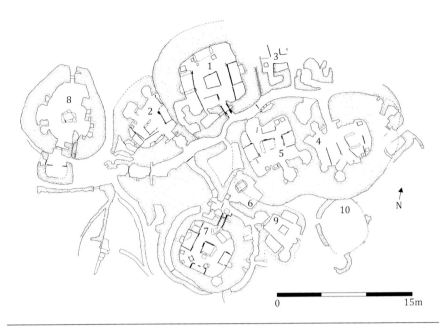

FIGURE 7.4
Plan of the late Neolithic settlement at Skara Brae, Orkney (after Childe 1931)

happened. What made Grooved Ware and other objects so attractive, but without the associated conglomerated settlements?

If we follow the argument that conglomerated settlement was the result of attempts to bring together disparate social groups in a way that was unique to Orkney, it perhaps makes sense that other communities did not need to build architecture in this way. However, broader ideas connected with the negotiation of identity may have been something that could be used in different social settings, and it was the material culture in particular that was adopted beyond Orkney. In addition to this the house as a broader structuring principle and as a social unifier was translated beyond Orkney *in monumental form*, and the various monuments of the late Neolithic can be viewed as drawing inspiration from both the houses and villages of Orkney as well as drawing on existing monumental forms such as the passage grave tradition (Bradley 2005a, 2013, Pollard 2009). In the words of Richard Bradley, 'local communities drew on distant areas as a source of ideas which they employed in idiosyncratic ways' (2007, p. 121).

In Chapter 6 the later fourth-millennium cal BC houses of Orkney were discussed, and it was noted that at this point communities on Orkney started to build houses which drew on the architecture of chambered tombs (Richards and Jones 2015a, 2015b). Specifically, the houses being built on Orkney were made to resemble monuments, thus drawing the meanings associated with the chambered tombs into the architecture of the house. The importance of the interplay and ambiguity between monuments and houses is best exemplified at one of the most recent discoveries on Orkney: the Ness of Brodgar. This is a site which reached its zenith in the late Neolithic. While the excavations at this site have only just finished, and the results are therefore not fully published,

FIGURE 7.5
Aerial view of the Ness of Brodgar, Orkney (photo by Hugo Anderson-Whymark and courtesy of Nick Card)

fieldwork has revealed the remains of multiple houses (Figure 7.5). These are mostly not comparable to the smaller houses at either nearby Barnhouse or Skara Brae, however, but can be paralleled with House 2 at Barnhouse, which was interpreted by the excavator as a ceremonial house (see previously). Like House 2 at Barnhouse, these structures at the Ness of Brodgar were occupied and have produced prolific quantities of food preparation debris and material culture. As with House 2 at Barnhouse, these structures obscure the boundaries between houses where people were living on a permanent basis and structures which were used for ceremonial purposes (which we call monuments). At this site, then, the division between house and monument, domestic and ritual, is completely blurred (cf. Bradley 2003, 2005a, Brück 1999). This theme will be picked up again in the next chapter.

For many years it was thought that the villages on Orkney may be representative of settlement in the late Neolithic throughout Britain and Ireland. They had survived in Orkney because they were built in stone and Orkney was not as intensively occupied and farmed as many parts of Britain. It was thought that similar settlements may be found, perhaps originally built in wood but nevertheless present – it was just a case of finding them. However, it now seems clear that this specific kind of conglomerated settlement did not spread beyond Orkney. There are very few late Neolithic houses known from Britain and Ireland outside of Orkney, and those that do survive are relatively small and fairly ephemeral. For example, at Trelystan, Powys, two stakehole-defined structures with central hearths were found with associated Grooved Ware. The structures produced late Neolithic radiocarbon dates, and these seem to be the remains of rather modest and flimsy structures (Gibson 1996). At Ronaldsway on the Isle of Man, a rectangular structure with a central hearth was found associated with flint waste and

Grooved Ware, as well as the carved stone plaques described subsequently (Darvill 1996). A similar structure was found at Raigmore, Inverness, where a timber structure and hearth with associated Grooved Ware were found preserved underneath a later Clava cairn (Barclay 2003). In Ireland the structures at Piperstown Hill, Co. Dublin, and possibly those at Slieve Breagh, Co. Meath, are likely to be the remains of small houses (Smyth 2014, pp. 88–91). There are clearly issues of preservation here; these examples are not substantial enough to survive ploughing and in most cases were fortuitously preserved by later activity. There remains the possibility that in many parts of both Britain and Ireland structures may simply not have been preserved in the archaeological record as they are in Orkney.

Indeed, this seemed to be reinforced by a recent discovery from southern Britain. Recent excavations at the henge monument at Durrington Walls, Wiltshire, have revealed the remains of small houses underneath the banks of the monument (Parker Pearson 2012). The houses had central hearths and packed chalk floors, and the walls would have been constructed from wattle and daub (Parker Pearson 2015). All the houses investigated were roughly square, measuring 5.25 × 5.25m, and there is evidence of slots in the ground which would have held wooden furniture much like that found in stone in the Orcadian houses (Parker Pearson 2012). The houses were also associated with middens and pit deposits (Craig *et al.* 2015). The settlement was first used between 2525 and 2470 cal BC, and it ended in 2480–2440 cal BC; this is a short-lived settlement which has been interpreted as the remains of the houses for those people involved in the construction of nearby monuments (Parker Pearson *et al.* 2024 and next chapter).

FIGURE 7.6
The remains of a late Neolithic house at Durrington Walls (photo by Adam Stanford and reproduced courtesy of Mike Parker Pearson)

That this was a short-lived settlement is further demonstrated by the fact that some of the houses have evidence of being replastered, and from this it appears that no house was occupied for more than a decade. Moreover, there is significant evidence which supports the use of this site in the winter months (Wright *et al*. 2014). All of this is highly suggestive that this was a settlement used only at particular times of the year and only for a short period of time, presumably for the duration of the construction of nearby contemporary monuments. It is also worth noting that these houses were preserved under the bank and ditch of the henge at Durrington, which effectively monumentalised this settlement but also protected the site from destruction.

Should, then, the settlement at Durrington be considered indicative of settlement more broadly? Did these houses survive only because they were covered by a substantial later monument? This is a difficult question to assess. The houses were excavated by Mike Parker Pearson and his team, who noted that under normal circumstances the houses would have been ploughed away millennia ago: all that would remain would have been lithics, hearth scoops, pits and pot sherds (Parker Pearson 2012). This may mean these small houses were used more widely than can currently be identified. However, Durrington was clearly a special place. It was the location for the bringing together of otherwise dispersed communities to be involved in monument construction. Moreover, it was a temporary settlement and one that was later turned into a monument itself. The houses at Durrington also make deliberate references to the Orcadian houses, which are far away from Wiltshire (700 miles to be precise). The knowledge of how to dwell in this fashion seems to have been understood across a wide area but could equally be something that was not considered appropriate for everyday use but reserved only for very specific and special circumstances. Again, this will be explored in more detail in the next chapter, which deals exclusively with monument construction and again will explore the significance of the house as a broader template for ritualised action.

Late Neolithic lithic scatters survive well in the archaeological record and are found in many parts of the landscape. These are a good indication of settlement, perhaps ploughed-out remains of ephemeral houses like those found at Durrington Walls. Late Neolithic lithic scatters tend to be dense, continuous spreads of material over wide areas, which implies that people returned many times to the same general area in the landscape to live (Chan 2011, Edmonds 1995, p. 80). Pits continue to be a feature of the late Neolithic and are likely to be the remains of occupation (see papers in Anderson-Whymark and Thomas 2012). Indeed, pit digging as a practice seems to have reached a zenith in the late Neolithic Britain and frequently featured the deposition of pottery (Thomas 1999, p. 69). However, there are currently smaller numbers of late Neolithic pits known in Ireland when compared with early Neolithic examples, so this may indicate an important regional difference (Smyth 2012). All late Neolithic pits demonstrate the careful selection and deposition of material, clearly relating to settlement but also indicating that specific things were appropriate to be deposited together (Barclay 1999). Moreover, in the late Neolithic, in keeping with the growing emphasis on special objects, pit deposits also contain more high-quality and exotic objects and multiple episodes of deposition (Anderson-Whymark 2012, Smyth 2012). Overall, this evidence suggests that settlement was predominantly transitory, perhaps quite dispersed, albeit focused on specific parts of the landscape. People may have built structures, but these were typically small and non-permanent, and they contrast considerably with the large timber halls found in the early Neolithic, for example. While some places drew people back many times over the centuries, many other places seem to have been sparsely populated.

DIET AND SUBSISTENCE IN THE LATE NEOLITHIC

Late Neolithic animal bone assemblages are often dominated by the remains of pig, although cattle remains are still found (Schulting 2008). This is a marked change from the dominance of cattle in the middle Neolithic and the more extensive use of sheep in the early Bronze Age (Serjeantson 2011). There is no evidence to contradict the idea that wild animals contributed little in terms of meat in the late Neolithic, although they may have played a significant role in relation to belief systems (see next chapter). There is also evidence to suggest that the way in which meat was cooked changed in some instances in the late Neolithic. There is very little evidence for roasting meat on the bone from the early Neolithic, but this method of cooking is much more common in the late Neolithic (Serjeantson 2011). For example, the pig bones from Durrington Walls indicate that entire pigs were roasted on the bone (Craig *et al*. 2015, p. 1099).

There are important issues to consider when interpreting the animal bone evidence from the late Neolithic. First, many of the large assemblages come from special, monumental sites (see next chapter). The large henge monuments of the late Neolithic were clearly places set aside from everyday activities and which were the preserve of special, ritualised activities. The animal bone assemblages from these sites, then, only indicate what was eaten on specific, probably special occasions. The vast quantities of animal bone from Durrington Walls, for example, are highly suggestive of the remains of special feasting events. There is evidence to show that the vast majority of the pigs at Durrington Walls were slaughtered during midwinter (Albarella and Payne 2005). Moreover, many of these animals were immature, slaughtered before they were one year old (Albarella and Payne 2005). This suggests the mass slaughter and consumption of animals reared for, and marking, a special occasion (Craig *et al*. 2015, Parker Pearson 2012). The more regular day-to-day consumption of meat is harder to estimate, however, due to an overall lack of settlement activity from the late Neolithic. Second, pigs produce less meat per animal than a cow, so even though pig bones may proliferate, they are not representative of meat-weight procured (Schulting 2008, p. 98). Third, animal bone does not always survive in many parts of Britain and Ireland (e.g. McCormick 2007), limiting our understanding of regionally specific animal husbandry regimes. It has been suggested, for example, that pig may not have been as important in Scotland (Schulting 2008, p. 98). Indeed, there is evidence to suggest that pig may not have been the prime source of meat in other parts of late Neolithic Britain and Ireland. The investigation of pits in the Rudston Wolds, Yorkshire, indicated that cattle remained important alongside pigs at this time (Rowley Conwy and Owen 2011). While the assemblage from Durrington Walls was dominated by pig, the lipid analysis of the pottery indicated that ruminant meat and milk were more commonly cooked in these vessels (Craig *et al*. 2015). Indeed, milk lipids are found on vessels in Ireland as much in the late Neolithic as in earlier phases (Smyth and Evershed 2015a), showing the continued importance of cattle in the economy.

There is very little evidence for the use of cereals in most parts of Britain and Ireland in the late Neolithic, a continuation of the decline of cereal use which started in the middle Neolithic (Stevens and Fuller 2012). In the case of Ireland this may be due to a lack of sites and data (McClatchie *et al*. 2014), but in much of Britain this appears to be a genuine pattern. In contrast to early Neolithic pits, cereals are rare from late Neolithic pits (Anderson-Whymark 2012, p. 192), and the absence of cereals is repeated in relation to other types of site. This would appear, therefore, to represent the genuine lack of the use of cereals in late Neolithic Britain. There are some exceptions; the Northern Isles seem to have continued to produce and use cereals, once again indicating regional differences at this time (Bishop 2015, Stevens and Fuller 2012). Instead of cereals it seems that people used wild plant resources including hazelnuts, which are commonly recovered from late Neolithic sites. The cycles of woodland clearance and regrowth recorded during the late Neolithic (Woodbridge *et al*. 2014), therefore, may not relate to the growing of cereals but the keeping of livestock and the opening up of the landscape to encourage wild plant growth. Indeed, broadly speaking there was significant woodland regeneration at this time. This evidence combines to suggest that late Neolithic people were predominantly pastoralists, relying on cattle, pig and wild plant foods. This would also suggest that people moved around the landscape with their animals, returning to particular points during the year; this can best be described as 'tethered mobility' (Whittle 1997). It has also been suggested that we may be dealing with a much lower level of population at this time, particularly when contrasted with the early Neolithic. We now turn our attention to the material culture found in the late Neolithic.

MATERIAL CULTURE: POTTERY

The late Neolithic settlement site of Barnhouse in Orkney was first discovered as a scatter of stone tools in ploughsoil. When the excavator opened up the first trench on the site to investigate what archaeology might have survived here, he very quickly came down onto a surface which had more stone tools along with a number of pot sherds. A very large sherd was found which had three lines incised on its surface. The excavator recognised this type of pottery immediately: it was Grooved Ware, a type of late Neolithic pottery that had been found at the adjacent monument of the Stones of Stenness and elsewhere such as at the famous site of Skara Brae. It was at this point that the excavator realised he had found a site that was contemporary with the Stones of Stenness stone circle, and, as we saw previously, it turned out to be one of the best-preserved late Neolithic settlements (Richards 2005). By the end of the excavations, over 6000 sherds of Grooved Ware had been recovered from the site.

The late Neolithic is characterised by this distinctive form of pottery known as Grooved Ware, so named because it has prolific decoration on its surface mainly in the form of grooves and incisions. This form of pottery was produced in a fairly restricted range of vessel forms, including tubs, buckets and barrel-shaped vessels (Gibson 2002a, p. 84). One of the most notable changes from early and middle Neolithic bowl pottery is that Grooved Ware is flat bottomed. This meant that this pottery could rest on flat surfaces,

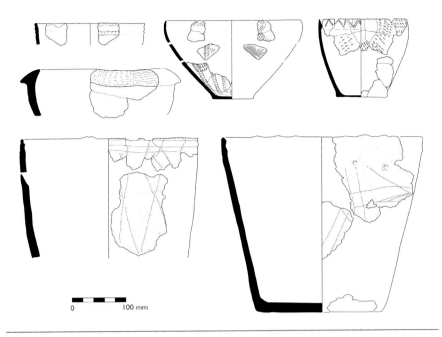

FIGURE 7.7
Grooved Ware (image by Rick Peterson)

but it also meant substantially larger vessels could be produced (Thomas 1999, p. 113). While the enormous pots found at sites such as Durrington Walls, Wiltshire, and Balfarg Riding School, Fife, are much discussed in the literature, Grooved Ware was produced in a variety of different sizes, including some quite small vessels (see Copper *et al.* 2023). Tracing the origins of early and middle Neolithic pottery has proven to be tricky, but in the case of Grooved Ware it now seems highly probable that it had originated in Orkney or northern Scotland more broadly. It has been found on Orcadian settlement sites such as Barnhouse with earlier radiocarbon dates so far than similar pottery found further south (Richards *et al.* 2016). It seems, therefore, that Grooved Ware was first made in the Orkney Isles towards the end of the fourth millennium cal BC before spreading into the rest of Britain and into Ireland from the start of the third millennium cal BC onwards.

Grooved Ware is found in both Britain and Ireland (Cleal and McSween 1999, Copper *et al.* 2023), and although there have traditionally been different sub-styles of Grooved Ware named after sites where it has been found such as Durrington Walls and Rinyo, Orkney, there are wide enough similarities to suggest it was part of a broadly understood phenomenon across Britain and Ireland (Cleal 1999, Copper and Whittle 2023). Like earlier types of Neolithic pottery, it did not instantly replace existing styles. Instead at the start of the late Neolithic, it was produced alongside the Impressed Wares which are characteristic of the middle Neolithic and, when a new style of pottery was introduced hundreds of years later, Beakers (see Chapter 9), Grooved Ware continued to be made in some areas (Sheridan 1995). This means that it is a style of pottery that was in use for many centuries (Gibson 2002a, p. 84, Müller and Peterson 2015, p. 598) but most notably and consistently used in the late Neolithic.

It is clear that Grooved Ware, like earlier types of pottery, was used for the cooking and serving of food. At Durrington Walls different sizes of vessel were used for preparing and serving different foodstuffs, notably pig meat and dairy products (Craig *et al*. 2015). This suggests that different sizes of vessel were associated with specific food types, but there are indications that this was not found consistently throughout the late Neolithic (Olet *et al*. 2023). Studies show that specific sizes and shapes of ceramics were found in the same combination in different houses, suggesting some sort of standardisation at least within individual settlements (see Jones 2002, Richards 2005). The Orcadian villages are not typical of settlement in the late Neolithic, but studies beyond Orkney suggest that Grooved Ware vessels may have been linked with specific foodstuffs. Some of the large henge sites in southern England have produced considerable quantities of pig bone alongside Grooved Ware vessels. The analysis of fatty acids in the fabric of pottery also demonstrates the cooking of pig products at these sites (Mukherjee *et al*. 2008). At Durrington Walls, however, Grooved Ware had both pig and ruminant residues as well as milk. Indeed, studies elsewhere show that Grooved Ware appears to be associated with a range of animals, with evidence for cooking both pig and ruminants (and see Rowley Conwy and Owen 2011). In Ireland, Grooved Ware, like earlier pottery, has been shown to contain lipids from milk processing (Smyth and Evershed 2015a). Therefore, the connection between Grooved Ware and pig may be less pronounced than previously thought. Instead, Grooved Ware was used to process a variety of different animal products, but which was appropriately varied from region to region. There are also suggestions that Grooved Ware, particularly the large vessels, would have been ideal for brewing beer (Dineley and Dineley 2000). At Balfarg one Grooved Ware vessel contained pollen from deadly nightshade and henbane, suggesting that people were attempting to achieve hallucinatory experiences (Barclay and Russell-White 1993).

Grooved Ware has been recovered from specific contexts in the late Neolithic. It is well known in large quantities from henge sites such as Mount Pleasant and Durrington Walls, where it has been suggested it was used in important communal events involving feasting (Parker Pearson *et al*. 2024), but this is not consistent throughout Britain and Ireland. Grooved Ware is more consistently found in pits and as surface deposits; these are likely to be the remains of occupation (Garwood 1999, Hamilton and Whittle 1999). These pits are not just the straightforward disposal of waste from settlement, however. The combinations of material deposited in pits seem to have been carefully chosen and indicate that Grooved Ware could only be deposited in the ground with certain other objects (see, for example, Barclay 1999). It has been suggested that pit deposits may represent the remains of small-scale, possibly seasonal, feasts (Rowley Conwy and Owen 2011). In the south of England Grooved Ware is also found in locations which were later used for the construction of barrows (Cleal 1999, p. 6). In Ireland Grooved Ware is found in association with enclosures and circles (Brindley 1999), and in Scotland the largest Grooved Ware assemblages are from the late Neolithic village settlements of Orkney (Cowie and McSween 1999, MacSween and Clarke 2023). This may indicate that Grooved Ware, while following a universally recognised recipe in terms of production, may have been used in different contexts in different parts of Britain and Ireland. Moreover, just as there are differences spatially, there may also be changes in the deployment of Grooved Ware over time, with settlement and occupations having Grooved Ware deposits in the earlier part of the late Neolithic and it only being deposited at henges later on (Gibson 2002a, Thomas 2010, p. 9).

One of the most intriguing aspects of Grooved Ware is that the decoration on the pottery shares similarities with designs on other forms of material culture, most notably passage tomb art, carved chalk objects, carved stone balls and maceheads (Gibson 2002a, p. 87). This may seem a rather eclectic set of material culture, but this decoration may also have been found on objects which rarely survive in the archaeological record such as on wooden objects or even houses; one of the small buildings at Wyke Down produced decorated remains of daub which suggested the house walls may have had designs on them (Thomas 2010, p. 5), and many decorated stones have been found at the Ness of Brodgar (Thomas 2020). Since this form of pottery is ostensibly associated with food processing and cooking, it could be argued that the decoration may have indicated what could have been contained within the pot and also where that material could be deposited (Thomas 1999, p. 116). However, that obviously does not translate to other objects/structures with these designs. It seems more likely, therefore, that the symbols referred to a broader system of reference concerned with containment (of food, but also other substances). Symbols and marks on material culture may have acted to contain and protect the food contained within late Neolithic pottery and may have been appropriate not just to protect food but also the occupants of houses or even the occupants of tombs (Richards 2013). Protection would have been required in relation to a whole range of different things from polluting substances (see Douglas 1966) through to misfortune or even sorcery. Indeed, wrapping appears to be a central metaphor evoked in many different spheres in the late Neolithic and will be discussed again in relation to monuments in the next chapter.

It is also worth noting here that pottery would have been used alongside a whole range of objects made from organic materials; these very rarely survive in the archaeological record but almost certainly included wooden vessels and objects, basketry and bone. The examples of Grooved Ware pots which have the impressions of basketry on them illustrate this (Figure 7.8). The use of organics in the Neolithic is discussed in more detail in Chapter 4.

MATERIAL CULTURE: OBJECTS IN STONE

In the flat landscape of what is now Norfolk, people in the late Neolithic travelled to a site which would have been known for producing flint. Here, they decided to not just collect flint from the surface but to dig into the earth to mine flint. Using only antler picks and baskets, people dug a wide and vertical shaft deep into the ground, from which they then followed seams of flint along horizontal planes. The high-quality flint was extracted and exported widely. Sometimes people left deposits such as pottery. Over time, people returned again and again, creating a remarkable pockmarked landscape where multiple shafts can, still to this day, be seen over a wider swathe of the countryside. This site is now known as Grime's Graves and is the best-known Neolithic flint mine in Britain.

Flint mining was a practice that had begun in the early Neolithic, apparently in southern England only (see Chapter 4), but it was a practice that continued in the late Neolithic. Some, but not all, of the flint mines used in the early Neolithic saw some limited use in the third millennium, including Church Hill and Blackpatch, Sussex (Russell 2000, p. 56).

FIGURE 7.8
Matting impression on the base of a Grooved Ware pot from Barnhouse, Orkney (image reproduced courtesy of Orkney Islands Council)

Grime's Graves in Norfolk, however, was used for the first time in the 27th century BC in the late Neolithic (Healy 2012). Up to 500 shafts, each around 13m deep covering an area of 7.6 hectares, were sunk into the ground in order to acquire the black flint (Edmonds 1995, p. 117). The Den of Boddam, Aberdeenshire, also probably dates to the late Neolithic and also saw the extensive extraction of flint (Saville 2005). As with early Neolithic flint mining, there is little evidence for significant or permanent occupation around Grime's Graves, and it has been suggested that people from the wider area travelled to Grime's Graves to extract flint, which was then taken away for use elsewhere (Edmonds 1995, Russell 2000), perhaps on a seasonal basis. What is clear is that Grime's Graves flint seems to have been preferentially used to make special artefacts such as knives and arrowheads (Edmonds 1995, p. 118). Furthermore, the extraction of flint was not just a practical concern; much of the quarried flint was left unused on the surface or even put back in the mine shafts (Russell 2000, p. 95). This may suggest that the act of digging into the earth was an important event (Whittle 1995), perhaps as a rite of passage, and that the flint extracted from this event was then made into special objects, perhaps regarded as markers of that rite of passage. As we saw, the series of votive deposits left in the mine shafts also indicates the importance of marking the flint extraction event.

There appears to have been a resurgence in the use of stone from quarries first used in the early Neolithic (Bradley 2007, p. 134, and see Chapter 4), alongside the opening of new quarry sites such as Creag na Caillich, Perthshire (Edmonds *et al.* 1992). This means that after a lull in production in the middle Neolithic, stone for axes was quarried

FIGURE 7.9
The visible remains of flint extraction at Grime's Graves, Norfolk (© Skyscan Balloon Photography. Historic England Archive)

and axes were made and exchanged. However, the spread of some of these items appears to be more restricted than in the early Neolithic where stone axes were found a long way from their origin (see Chapter 4). The utilisation of stone at Langdale may have decreased, for example, while it intensified at the stone axe sources in Cornwall (Edmonds 1995, p. 104); small-scale working at Creag na Caillich produced pieces that were found as far away as the Isle of Lewis (Edmonds *et al*. 1992). One of the key elements of late Neolithic material culture is the use of exotic and distinctive materials and this may explain the renewed interest in these quarries. Axes are often found as stray finds, which makes their dating problematic, but there are axes from some late Neolithic contexts. At Llandegai henge, Gwynedd, for example, a Cumbrian axe was recovered and two Cornish axes were found at Grime's Graves. Flint continued to be used to make axes as well, including the distinctive Seamer axes, and those produced from Flamborough Head flint were a distinctive colour and thus their source may have been well understood too (Edmonds 1995, p. 103).

In Chapter 4 the possible significance of polished stone axes was discussed, where it was suggested that the origin of the stone used to make each axe was an important component of these objects. Their origin from particular parts of the landscape may well have been understood by the people in possession of such items. For example the tuff axes which came from the mountains of Cumbria may well have been understood as originating from that part of the landscape, with the polish further enhancing the special quality of these objects. By the late Neolithic, however, polished stone axes were items that had been created for around a thousand years, and some early examples may well still have been in circulation. The resurgence in quarrying early Neolithic stone axe sources may be representative of a desire to make more of these important objects but perhaps also as a way of referring to ancestral practices. Moreover, the renewed quarrying of stone from these sources appears to be part of a wider set of late Neolithic practices which were about the renegotiation of social groups and the restatement of lineages of descent linked to specific parts of the country.

Maceheads first started to be made in the later part of the fourth millennium, in antler and, in some parts of the country, in stone (see Chapter 6). However, their production increased significantly in the late Neolithic, and they are often found associated with Grooved Ware (Edmonds 1995, p. 108). They are found in a variety of contexts, notably from the village settlements on Orkney (see subsequently), in henges in southern Britain and in watery contexts in Ireland (Simpson 1988). There are different styles of macehead, described as ovoid, pestle or cushion-shaped (Roe 1979), as well as miniature versions which are thought to be pendants. Maceheads are beautifully produced objects, pecked and ground into shape with a hole drilled through the middle. One of the most spectacular examples is from the passage tomb at Knowth, which has exquisite carvings on its surfaces (Eogan 1986) but there are many other fine examples (Figure 7.10–11). They were often made from distinctive raw materials such as erratics (Edmonds 1995) and are found in particular concentrations in north-east Scotland and the Orkney Isles as well as in Ireland (Simpson 1988, Simpson and Ransom 1992).

FIGURE 7.10
A finely polished macehead from the Tomb of the Eagles, Orkney

FIGURE 7.11
Two deliberately broken maceheads from Sanday, Orkney

The hole through the centre of the macehead meant that it could be mounted, and they could have been used as either a hammer or a weapon (Edmonds 1995, p. 108). However, this type of object is one of a number of special objects from the late Neolithic which would have required considerable effort to make, and it may therefore have been an ornamental object. It is interesting to note that many maceheads recovered from the archaeological record were deliberately broken in prehistory, often in two down the middle or into multiple fragments (Chris Gee *pers. comm*.). The connection between maceheads and houses in Orkney and henges in Britain may suggest that these objects were closely associated with broader social groups. Instead of being objects of individual power, as is often argued, they may instead be representative of group identity expressed in material form. The deliberate destruction of a macehead may therefore be representative of the ending of specific political allegiances.

Another kind of distinctive stone object from the late Neolithic are the carved stone balls found virtually exclusively in Scotland. Over 400 are known and 90% are from north-east Scotland, mainly as isolated finds in Aberdeenshire (Edmonds 1992). They have also been found in context at Skara Brae and the Ness of Brodgar, Orkney (Edmonds 2019 and see subsequently). They are made from locally available, but easily recognisable, stone (Edmonds 1995, p. 111, 2019). Those with six knobs are the most common, but there is considerable variation amongst these objects as a group; some have decoration which shares characteristics with the designs on passage tombs and Grooved Ware, while others are much simpler objects (Edmonds 1992). As with maceheads, their precise function is debateable. While many accounts suggest that they were weapons or symbols of individual status and power (e.g. Clarke *et al*. 1985), it seems more likely that, like maceheads, they communicated social identity, possibly to do with lines of descent (Edmonds 1992) or group affiliation. This was clearly an object which communicated allegiance in specific parts of the country, as only five examples of carved stone balls have been found outside Scotland.

It is worth considering the use of chalk in the late Neolithic. While it is clear that chalk was used to make objects in the early Neolithic, it seems to have been used more

FIGURE 7.12
The carved stone ball from Towie, Aberdeenshire (© National Museums Scotland)

extensively in the late Neolithic in Grooved Ware contexts. A whole range of different shaped objects have been found made out of chalk, including balls, axes, cups, discs and phalli (see Teather 2008). Chalk balls and a phallus were found at Mount Pleasant, and chalk axes have been recovered from Woodhenge, Wiltshire (Pollard 1995). A cup-like chalk object was found at Grime's Graves which contained vegetable fat (Russell 2000, p. 99), and decorated chalk plaques were found at Stonehenge Bottom (Clarke *et al.* 1985, p. 79). Plaques are also found in other media; for example, decorated stone plaques were found at Ronaldsway on the Isle of Man, which like their chalk counterparts have carved and incised designs (Clarke *et al.* 1985, p. 245). Perhaps the best-known, and certainly the most elaborate, chalk objects are the Folkton drums. Recovered from a barrow at Folkton, Yorkshire, these are essentially cylinders with decoration which is similar to that found on Grooved Ware (see Jones *et al.* 2015). They are not unique: there is an example recovered from a Grooved Ware pit at Lavant, Sussex (Teather 2008, p. 207), and another at Burton Agnes, the burial which accompanied the drum dating to the start of the third millennium cal BC (Garrow and Wilkin 2022). It seems, therefore, that chalk objects were just part of a whole range of special substances which were turned into ornate and spectacular things. Many of these were also inscribed with incisions and marks which made explicit links with Grooved Ware. Grooved Ware, in turn, made explicit links and connections with particular places and specific practices, particularly concerning the negotiation and admittance into corporate social groups.

Just as with the early Neolithic, stone tools dating to the late Neolithic have been found from a variety of contexts, including occupation sites, pits and monuments. Flint (both

FIGURE 7.13
One of the Folkton Drums (image by Andrew Cochrane, courtesy of the Trustees of the British Museum)

mined alongside surface-collected and beach flint) continued to be used in many parts of the Britain and Ireland alongside other types of stone including chert, quartz and pitchstone. Late Neolithic stonework is characterised by some distinctive object types. Transverse arrowheads are found in both Britain and Ireland and often found in association with Grooved Ware (Butler 2005, p. 158–160). Other distinctive late Neolithic stone tools are discoidal knives, plano-convex knives, chisels and laurel leaves (Edmonds 1995, p. 96). Scrapers continue to be made but are often made into combination tools, for example, scrapers with a notch (Butler 2005, p. 168). Scrapers would have been used for a variety of tasks, including working hides and plant materials.

It has been noted that there were some key developments in terms of stone working in the late Neolithic when compared with earlier periods. In general, there was a decline in the quality and skill exhibited. Many objects were made on flakes which had been produced using a hard hammer which resulted in short, thick and broad flakes (Butler 2005, p. 157), but there is also evidence for a Levallois-like reduction method (Ballin 2011). There is plenty of evidence for 'expedient' stone working with poor quality items made then discarded alongside large quantities of waste pieces (Chan 2010). However, alongside a general decline in flintworking there are also some exceptionally high-quality and beautifully produced objects from this period. This includes knives, some of which were also ground and polished and frequently not used (Edmonds 1995, p. 96, Loveday 2011), and the axes and maceheads already discussed. It has been suggested that these highly polished and intricate objects could be associated with the expression of personal identity (Edmonds 1995). As with the early Neolithic, some people in society may have been highly regarded as archers, with specialised arrowheads a material expression of

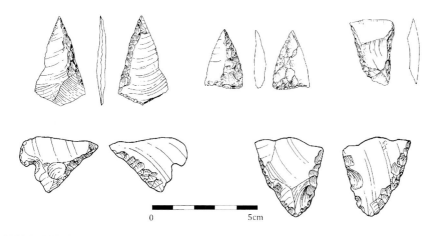

FIGURE 7.14
Late Neolithic arrowheads (after Richards 1990, Whittle *et al*. 1999)

this role. There is also evidence of regional variation in the production of tool types with some particularly distinctive flint objects found in Yorkshire. Before attention is turned to the houses where stone tools are found, it is worth considering another part of the Neolithic world which saw alteration of through incised and carved designs: rock art.

MATERIAL CULTURE: ROCK ART

Rock art is found in both Britain and Ireland and consists of geometric motifs carved on to stone (Bradley 2007, Cochrane and Jones 2012). These designs are abstract (they are non-figurative), and the most common designs are cup-and-ring marks, spirals and rosettes (Figure 7.15). They are not found everywhere in Britain and Ireland; 6500 carved panels are currently known and they are found in clusters in particular areas, notably Tayside, Dumfries and Galloway; Argyll, Northumberland; parts of upland Yorkshire; and in Ireland in Co. Kerry and Co. Wicklow (Sharpe 2012). Many of these areas have seen intensive investigation over the years, while rock art is still being located in other parts of the country so the current known distribution may not be a genuine reflection of where rock art was once carved. One of the biggest issues with the study of rock art is dating, as it is not possible to date when stone was carved. There is a general consensus that rock art dates from the Neolithic into the early Bronze (Bradley 2007, 2023, see Cummings and Richards 2021), and recent excavations around rock art panels in Kilmartin have produced associated activity which dates to the late Neolithic (Jones *et al*. 2011). It is included here because as a practice it is certainly late Neolithic in date and it fits in with broader ways of doing things, particularly relating to inscribing surfaces of things, that occurs at this time. The marking of rocks may have started earlier – incised marks are found on middle Neolithic passage graves for example (see previous chapter) – and it certainly carried on into the Bronze Age.

FIGURE 7.15
Achnabreck rock art panel, Argyll

While the designs are all abstract, there are definite regional differences in the deployment of rock art. Some appear to be located overlooking routeways through the landscape and may be related to the use and settlement of the uplands (Bradley 1997, 2023). In some areas rock art clusters around monuments (Sharpe 2012), but it also was carved onto stone where no monuments are found nearby (e.g. Bradley and Watson 2012). It has been noted that the rock art brings out the character of the stone and uses existing cracks and features of the rock (Jones 2005), and it could be interpreted as a way of animating the stone. Quartz also seems to be found in association with rock art, and it has been noted that rock art is particularly visible at certain times of the day when the sun is high or low (e.g. Jones 2012). The connection between passage tombs which also have rock art and the sun was noted in the last chapter, and this broader connection may have been drawn upon beyond that specific context.

Just as the designs on Grooved Ware may well have been found on a variety of other surfaces (see previously), the abstract designs of rock art may well have been found in other places using different materials. A few very rare examples of the use of pigment have come to light recently, found at the site of the Ness of Brodgar (Card and Thomas 2012) and on pottery from Ronaldsway on the Isle of Man (Darvill and Andrews 2014). Red, white and black pigments found on the pottery from the Isle of Man could have been used to paint designs on everything from houses through to people, and may suggest that we are seeing only a tiny portion of the decoration which seems to have been so important in the late Neolithic.

FIGURE 7.16
Rock art panel at Rydal Park, Cumbria (photo by Peter Style). This area has seen the discovery of multiple new rock art panels over the last few years (Style 2011)

CONCLUSIONS: LIFE IN THE LATE NEOLITHIC

This chapter has examined different aspects of late Neolithic life, from settlement practices and material culture through to the diets of people at the time. One of the characteristic forms of late Neolithic material culture is Grooved Ware, which is found in a variety of monumental and domestic settings. While it does not seem to be connected exclusively to the preparation or serving of only one type of food or drink, it may have been particularly apposite for use at feasting events. The importance of feasting should not be underestimated in the late Neolithic; it could have served to mark out significant events such as marriages, rites of passage and deaths, bring together otherwise quite low levels of people dispersed across the landscape and reaffirm social ties and kinship links. Moreover, the giving of feasts could have secured help with the building of the large monuments which are a feature of the late Neolithic and discussed separately in the next chapter. Grooved Ware, then, played a key role in events which may well have been focused on just on feasting but on reaffirming political alliances across large parts of the country.

Other forms of material culture from the late Neolithic such as high-quality flint knives, maceheads or carved stone balls have often been interpreted as symbols of individual power and prestige. These are not considered in isolation, but combined with the evidence for the construction of very large monument complexes they are thought to be evidence for the presence of an elite (cf. Renfrew 1973). It has been argued by some scholars in the past that only an elite could muster the effort required to build enormous monuments (see next chapter) and that the exotic material culture found in the late Neolithic was a material expression of a powerful individual's position in society. Following well-known ethnographic examples, it has been suggested that the late Neolithic elite were men, probably in the prime of their lives. Renfrew (1973) described these as 'chiefdoms', but these chiefs can also be called 'big men'. This is a seductive argument because it is easy to see how some of the exotic material culture found in the archaeological record could work in this way. Powerful men would presumably have the influence to acquire or sponsor the production of beautifully made objects which they could then carry around or display on their person as a statement of that power (see Clarke *et al*. 1985).

An alternative to this argument is that these special objects were not connected to ranked individuals but to the identity of whole groups of people, particularly kinship groups, where emphasis was placed on particular lines of descent and corporate groupings. Indeed, it can be suggested that descent was of upmost importance in late Neolithic society. By the start of the late Neolithic people had been keeping domesticated animals and following other Neolithic practices for over a thousand years: real origins may have been long forgotten or obscured or reimagined. Descent and origins in the negotiation of social groupings may well have been of uttermost importance. Therefore, perhaps the most useful way of thinking about special objects like macheads is as 'inalienable' – they could only be possessed by people who had a right to that object as a token of a connection to a specific lineage, and that significance could not be transferred (see Weiner 1992). The idea of group ownership of these objects as representative of particular lines of descent is further reinforced by the fact that stones from specific sources were used, but there is no evidence for restricted access to these sources (for example, at Grime's Graves where quarried flint was simply left lying around). This does not suggest the control of the manufacture of these objects. Instead, the use of stones from particular places in the landscape would only have significance for certain groups. Attachment to specific places is also demonstrated through the creation of panels of rock art, the beginnings of formally marking out individual group connections to particular parts of the landscape.

Connection to place and links to specific lines of descent would have been important to people who appear to have been mainly pastoralists. This chapter has discussed the issue that there is very little evidence for cereal cultivation in most of Britain and Ireland in the late Neolithic. Instead, people used wild plant resources and kept both cattle and pigs. This would have created strong connections between people and their herds in both practical terms (cattle need specific types of care) and in their belief systems (which will be discussed in more detail in the next chapter). Pastoralism also tied people and their herds via seasonal rounds to particular parts of the landscape. As we have seen, people appeared to return to the same general area of the landscape over many years. While the settlement evidence of the late Neolithic is often characterised by the extraordinary villages on Orkney, it is clear that these are not representative of the sequence in any other part of Britain or Ireland but a response to a unique set of social circumstances in that location only. The vast majority of Britain and Ireland saw occupation in the form of small and slight temporary structures, albeit ones which may have mirrored the overall form of the individual Orcadian houses. We might therefore envisage late Neolithic society as the domain of important families who were connected by wider social networks, with claims of descent from specific lineages. These lineages were themselves connected to specific parts of the landscape and were almost certainly also maintained through the creation of particular special objects. Contested identities and origins were also being played out in different spheres and arenas, for most of Britain and Ireland in the creation of monuments. It is to these monuments that we now turn.

RECOMMENDED FURTHER READING

Grooved ware pottery

Copper, M., Whittle, A., and Sheridan, A., eds., 2023. *Revisiting Grooved Ware*. Oxford: Oxbow.

Rock art

Cochrane, A. and Jones, A. M., eds., 2012. *Visualising the Neolithic*. Oxford: Oxbow.

Domesticates

Serjeantson, D., 2011. *Review of animal remains from the Neolithic and early Bronze Age of southern Britain*. Swindon: English Heritage.

Orcadian settlements

Richards, C. and Jones, R., eds., 2015b. *The development of Neolithic house societies in Orkney*. Oxford: Oxbow.

Durrington Walls settlement

Parker Pearson, M., *et al*., 2024. *Durrington Walls and Woodhenge*. Leiden: Sidestone.

CHAPTER 8

Ritual and religion in the round

Mortuary practice and monumentality in the late Neolithic of Britain and Ireland

INTRODUCTION

This chapter considers the evidence for both mortuary practice and monument construction in the late Neolithic period. This includes some of the most iconic forms of Neolithic monumentality found in Britain and Ireland, including stone circles and henges. One of the defining features of these monuments is that entire landscapes were being transformed by the construction of multiple sites including the complexes at Brodgar, Orkney; Avebury, north Wiltshire; and Durrington Walls/Stonehenge, south Wiltshire. These sets of constructions were often linked together by architecture or natural conduits such as rivers and seem to have involved the careful orchestration of movement through the landscape where monuments were located at key meeting places which already had meaning to people. However, while many of the monuments from the early and middle Neolithic seemed to have involved the burial of the dead, the builders of late Neolithic monuments appear to have been more concerned with bringing people together in the acts of building and assembly, often on an epic scale. Furthermore, following a trend started in the middle Neolithic, monuments were increasingly focused on the movements of the sun and the moon which must have played an important role in religious beliefs. As such, these creations represent a complex orchestration of people, substances and place. It will be argued here that instead of being representative of the rise of a hierarchical society, as is so often claimed for the late Neolithic, these monuments could have been the result of repeated acts of construction by otherwise dispersed communities. Equally, the episodic nature of construction, which seems to represent large groups of people coming together for short bursts of activity, particularly at the end of the late Neolithic, may well be the result of aggrandisers, individuals seeking to further their own social standing by inspiring communal projects associated with the supernatural. It will also be suggested that late Neolithic people constructed monuments as a response to a world they perceived as in flux. Through the act of

DOI: 10.4324/9781003387329-8

construction, these monuments seem to have been arenas for mediating all aspects of life, death and the cosmos, which were important for belief systems at the time.

In terms of timings, the late Neolithic in this chapter is defined as beginning around 3000 cal BC and continuing until between 2500 and 2400 cal BC, when new types of material culture, including Beakers, began to appear. It is once again worth stressing here that while new forms of material culture, including Beakers, were brought over with new people from the continent, which formally marks the end of the Neolithic, some monuments were altered and used beyond this point, which, for sake of clarity, will be included in this chapter.

FIGURE 8.1
Location of the sites mentioned in the text. For detailed maps with individual sites see: Figure 8.15 Brodgar/Steness; Figure 8.21 Calanais; Figure 8.24 Brú na Boinné; Figure 8.2 Avebury; Figure 8.26 Stonehenge/Durrington Walls

MONUMENTS ON A MASSIVE SCALE: AVEBURY, WILTSHIRE

To begin this chapter and by way of introducing the new types of monument being built at this time, we start by considering one of the largest and most impressive sets of late Neolithic sites, which are centred around Avebury in Wiltshire. At the heart of this complex is the Avebury henge, itself a monument comprising multiple separate components. Within the henge are two stone circles, the northern and southern circles, which themselves contain smaller stone settings; the northern circle has a 'cove' at its centre (a rectangular stone setting), and the southern circle contained the largest stone in the complex, the now-missing Obelisk (Gillings *et al*. 2008). There is also a possible timber circle with two concentric rings at Avebury, located just to the north-east of the northern circle (Gillings and Pollard 2004, pp. 16–17). These features pre-date the larger stone circle which encircles these smaller monuments and in doing so is the largest stone circle in Britain and Ireland; it originally comprised 98 stones and has a diameter of 335 metres (Burl 1995, Gillings and Pollard 2004, Richards and Cummings 2024). This enormous stone circle is itself surrounded by a ditch which in its final phase was 9 metres deep with an outer bank 5 metres high (Pollard 2012); this was engineering on a vast scale, and it has been estimated that it took around 1 million hours to move the 200,000 tons of chalk required to build the earthwork at Avebury (Bradley 2007, p. 128). While it seems that the two smaller stone circles were constructed at the start of the late Neolithic, it appears that other components of the site, especially the larger stone circle, were built later on in the late Neolithic. There is some evidence that activity continued on the site into the latter part of the third millennium – this makes Avebury a good example of a monument which was both being constructed and used across the Neolithic-early Bronze Age chronological divide (see Gillings *et al*. 2008). This does not just relate to the stone phases at this site; there is also evidence that the bank and ditch were reworked at different times. First, a smaller bank and ditch were constructed between 3000 and 2700 cal BC, but this appears to have been enlarged later on, perhaps at the same time as the larger stone circle was added (Gillings and Pollard 2004, p. 44).

The Avebury henge is just one of a whole series of late Neolithic monuments found in this area, two of which are actually physically linked to Avebury by virtue of avenues which lead from the henge to the south and west, respectively. The West Kennet Avenue consists of a series of paired stones and runs for 2.4km across the landscape, running within the proximity of, but not incorporating, two other monuments, the earlier West Kennet palisade enclosures and Falkner's Stone Circle. The West Kennet Avenue terminates at another monument, The Sanctuary. The Sanctuary began life as a timber monument, consisting of multiple concentric rings of timbers (see Figure 8.9); at a later date a stone element was added and it became formally attached to the terminal end of the West Kennet Avenue (Pollard 1992). Another avenue, the 1.5km long Beckhampton Avenue, runs from the west of Avebury henge to a newly found monument, the Longstones Enclosure, probably built sometime between 2800 and 2650 cal BC (Gillings *et al*. 2008, p. 201). The enclosure appears to pre-date the avenue and was later backfilled and replaced with the Beckhampton Cove (Gillings and Pollard 2004). Finally, one of the largest and most time-consuming monuments to be built in the Avebury landscape was the mound of Silbury Hill (Figure 8.4). This 30m-high

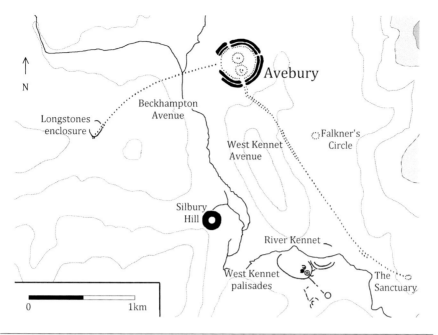

FIGURE 8.2
Plan of the henge complex at Avebury illustrating the different architectural components (after Gillings *et al*. 2008)

FIGURE 8.3
Part of the henge at Avebury

FIGURE 8.4
Silbury Hill, Wiltshire

mound stands approximately 500m from the West Kennett palisade enclosures and just under a kilometre from the West Kennet chambered tomb, the latter constructed in the early Neolithic, although unusually for this type of monument, reused in the later Neolithic (Bayliss et al. 2007). Silbury Hill was constructed right at the end of the late Neolithic and into the Beaker period (estimates suggest between 2470 and 2350 cal BC). It began life as a small mound surrounded by a ring of wooden stakes encircled by even smaller mounds; this was then capped by earth and a bank and ditch added (Leary et al. 2013). It has been argued that the growth of this monument was achieved in bursts of activity, with layers of material added over the course of several generations (Leary et al. 2013).

With this example we can see that the late Neolithic Avebury landscape saw considerable amounts of monument building, utilising timber, earth and stone. Together, these monuments created an extraordinary landscape which was completely altered by the presence of these sites; it would have been even more striking than it is today given that freshly excavated chalk is bright white. Such was the scale of construction here that it must have resembled a building site for much of the time, with piles of chalk and mud interspersed around the monuments as they were being built. In terms of scale this complex would have involved a very significant quantity of time, comparable with the other great late Neolithic complexes (see subsequently). Avebury therefore exemplifies the nature of monument building in the late Neolithic: no longer were people building and using a single site but a whole range of different monuments connected together and laid out across the landscape. Moreover, Avebury demonstrates that people came together at particular points to work together on a project, being drawn back, over the centuries, to the landscape where their forebears had also laboured on a monumental project and adding their own unique site to the complex. Circularity was a key element of these sites – at Avebury stone circles were set within stone circles, bounded by a bank and ditch and connected through avenues to other circular sites. These circular worlds must have articulated wider concepts of peoples' beliefs of the world they lived in, and perhaps other worlds (of the gods or spirits) too. With all this in mind, we will now unpick the specific types of monuments found at sites like Avebury to get a sense of the differences, and commonalities, of these late Neolithic sites.

FORMS OF MONUMENTALITY

We will now consider different types of monument one by one, covering timber circles, pit circles, stone circles and henges and all monuments allied to these broad classifications. However, this simple division of monuments into these types only gives a very broad sense of the diversity of monuments built at this time. Moreover, many sites were substantially altered over time, further confusing the use of this classification system. Indeed, as we have seen at Avebury, one of the defining features of many of these monuments was that they were part of a broader set of sites, never meant to be encountered in isolation; as such the chapter will then move on to consider other monumental complexes which represent the pinnacle of Neolithic engineering enacted on a vast scale.

Timber circles and palisade enclosures

Six miles from Belfast city centre close to the River Lagan is the monumental complex at Ballynahatty. In the late Neolithic this was the site of one of the largest timber circles in Ireland. This location had already been used in the earlier Neolithic, where a passage tomb had been constructed. In the late Neolithic an enormous timber enclosure with an elaborate entranceway was constructed alongside the remains of the passage tomb. This circle was constructed using huge and often very closely set timbers, creating a massive and impressive monument made of wood (Hartwell *et al*. 2023). It would have taken an enormous amount of effort and energy to both fell the trees and to dig the holes within which the timbers stood.

Ballynahatty is an example of a form of monument constructed in both Britain and Ireland in the late Neolithic known as a timber circle. These sites consisted of a series of upright posts set within pits which created a circle or oval-shaped monument. Some consisted of a single ring of posts, but other sites had multiple, concentric rings. There are examples of timber circles with widely spaced timbers but also monuments where the timbers are tightly clustered together such as at Ballynahatty, effectively obscuring the view into the centre of the circle. These monuments are found both in isolation as well as part of larger monumental complexes (Gibson 1998 and see subsequently). For the most part, this type of monument appears to have been constructed from 3000 cal BC onwards, and they therefore have a particular currency in the early and middle part of the third millennium BC. It is important to note, however, that this monument form persisted beyond the Neolithic and continued to be built into the later third millennium cal BC and beyond (Bradley and Nimura 2016).

There is considerable variation within this broader classification of site. Timber circles, while using large timbers, could be quite small in diameter while others were enormous constructions. The two massive timber circles at Durrington Walls, Wiltshire, are a good example of the sheer mass of timber employed at some sites. In its final phase the Southern Circle at Durrington consisted of six concentric rings of timber, the largest of which had a diameter of 39m. Some of the posts were up to a metre across and would have been enormous and heavy timbers (Parker Pearson *et al*. 2024). It has been estimated that to construct this circle, 260 tons of timber would have been required (Harding 2003, p. 75). Not all timber circles were this size, however. From the limited dating evidence from these sites, the earliest sites appear to be relatively small in size; larger circles were built towards the end of the Neolithic before they deceased in size again (see Bradley and Nimura 2016, Gibson 1998).

While it is possible to understand the layout of the timbers from surviving postholes, we do not know precisely what the timbers in these circles actually looked like. We tend to assume that the timbers were trimmed tree trunks standing like the stones in a stone circles, but equally they could have been carved, painted or with some of their branches intact, as is known from the early Bronze Age timber circle at Holme-next-the-Sea, Norfolk (Brennand and Taylor 2003). Certainly, there is no evidence of anything substantial between the vertical posts, although again wickerwork, wattle and daub, or fabric, would leave little trace and could have shielded the centre from view. It seems highly unlikely these monuments would have been roofed, contrary to older reconstructions of these sites. One of the key questions is how timber circles were used once constructed. Some excavated sites have produced very little material culture, which suggests that the bringing together of people in the act of construction was of primary concern (see subsequently). However, there are also sites which have produced a wealth of material evidence. Durrington Walls and Woodhenge are notable for the sheer amount of material culture they have produced (Parker Pearson *et al*. 2024). This material is discussed in more depth subsequently but clearly shows that feasting and depositional activity took place within some of these monuments. It also shows that while the monument form was widespread, the way in which timber circles were used was regionally specific.

It is clear that timber circles were frequently altered or reworked. At both North Mains, Perth and Kinross, and Cairnpapple Hill, West Lothian, the late Neolithic timber circles were enclosed by a bank and ditch in the early Bronze Age. A monument consisting of a bank and ditch is known as a henge (see subsequently) so the addition of these at timber circles effectively 'converted' these sites into henges (Noble 2006, pp. 146–148). A complex sequence has also been shown at Durrington Walls (and see subsequently). Some sites were also altered through the use of stone, usually with the timber component being replaced in stone, although this was not always the case; the relevant monuments are discussed in the section on stone circles subsequently.

Palisade enclosures are a variation on the late Neolithic timber structure, but instead of standing timbers closely set in a circle, these sites consisted of more tightly packed timbers encircling a wider area. There is some variation in the palisade from dense screens of timbers like a fence through to those more generously spaced (see Gibson 2002b). These were also sites that were constructed on a massive scale, frequently enclosing vast swathes of the landscape. One of the most impressive late Neolithic sites was Hindwell palisade enclosure in the Walton Basin, Powys, which had a perimeter

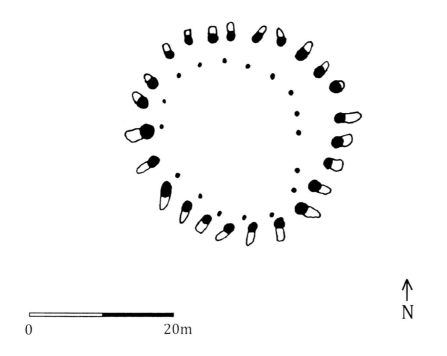

FIGURE 8.5
Plan of North Mains (Perth and Kinross) timber circle and later encircling henge in grey (after Millican 2007)

of 2.3km and could have employed 1400 oak posts, each weighing 4 tonnes (Gibson 1998). Hindwell was built sometime between 2800 and 2500 cal BC, and another recently excavated site, that of Dunragit palisade enclosure in Dumfries and Galloway, between 2900 and 2700 cal BC (Thomas 2015a). This suggests a currency for these monuments predominantly in the late Neolithic, although there are some suggestions that a few may be a little earlier, as well as a little later than this (Bayliss *et al*. 2017, Gibson 2002b). It is important to note that timber circles and palisade enclosures were not mutually exclusive; at Ballynahatty, Co. Down, timber settings and a circle were found within a larger palisade (Hartwell 1998). Indeed, some of these timber monuments saw later alteration with the addition of a bank and ditch (see subsequently).

Pit circles

A variation on the timber circle is the pit circle. These monuments consist of a circuit of pits which do not appear to have ever held posts. Without excavation it is difficult to distinguish between timber circles and pit circles, as it is not possible to identify

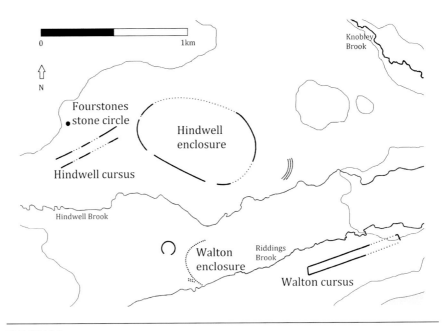

FIGURE 8.6
The monumental complex at Hindwell in the Walton Basin (after Gillings *et al*. 2008)

the presence or absence of posts, and both monuments involved the digging of pits (Millican 2007). Moreover, this type of monument is usually only identifiable as a crop mark or because it is surrounded by a bank and ditch (i.e. a henge). Nevertheless, pit circles were genuinely a distinct type of late Neolithic monument. At the site of Wyke Down, Dorset, a series of small shafts were dug into the earth (Green 2000). These shafts were filled quite quickly with the careful deposition of particular types of material culture including chalk objects and arrowheads (Thomas 1999, p. 83). A similar pattern was also found at Maumbury Rings, Dorset (Figure 8.7). Here a series of deep shafts were cut into the earth and carefully but quickly backfilled with pottery at the base of each shaft, carved chalk objects in the middle and skulls of stags and human remains towards their tops (Bradley 2000a, p. 124). Pit circles are known beyond southern England, with recorded examples from Newgrange, Co. Meath (Sweetman 1985) and Oakham, Rutland (Clay 1998).

Stone circles

On a domed hillside in what is now the Lake District, people came together in the late Neolithic to construct a circle from stone. We cannot know for certain why this particular location was chosen for the site. It overlooks a main routeway into the Lake District which is where the A66 is now found. It is also a location from where it is possible to see the encircling high mountains in every direction including the Helvellyn range as well as Blencathra and Coledale fells. This is a striking and impressive vista, one that people in the Neolithic must have noticed and selected as a special place. Today the site is known as Castlerigg stone circle, a new form of monument built in the late Neolithic.

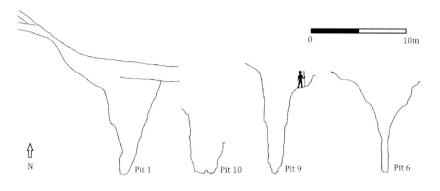

FIGURE 8.7
The excavated shafts at the Maumbury Rings, Dorset (after Harding 2003)

FIGURE 8.8
The stone circle at Castlerigg, Cumbria

Stone circles typically consist of a circle or oval of upright standing stones. Sometimes they have other features such as paired entrance stones, a cove (a smaller setting of stones) or a central hearth. They are occasionally found in multiples such as at Machrie Moor, Arran, or the Hurlers, Cornwall, but more typically they are isolated monuments. There are clusters of these sites in south-west England, particularly Cornwall, south-central England (Wessex), north-west England (Cumbria) and western Scotland (Burl 1995, Richards and Cummings 2024), but there are fewer on the east side of Britain; the recumbent stone circles of north-east Scotland are later in date and are considered briefly in the next chapter. There are numerous stone circles in Ireland, but most of these are undated, and it has been shown that this form of architecture was built from the Bronze Age into the Iron Age there (Bradley and Nimura 2016). Indeed, this highlights the fact that stone circles are difficult to date because there is often little evidence of activity associated with them. Material is best preserved in the ditches which sometimes surround these sites, yet as we will see, the bank and ditch were most likely a later addition. Moreover, material which could date their construction could potentially be recovered from the stone sockets, but logistically this is difficult to retrieve. Some stone circles have been dated, however, with early third millennium cal BC dates from the Stones of Stenness, Orkney, and Balbirnie, Fife (Gibson 2010, Schulting et al. 2010), indicating that at least some stone circles were built right at the start of the late Neolithic. There is a general sense that the large, lowland circles were late Neolithic while smaller and upland circles were probably constructed in the early Bronze Age; like other forms of late Neolithic monumentality these sites continued to have currency beyond the Neolithic (Bradley and Nimura 2016, Richards and Cummings 2024).

The relationship between stone circles and timber circles needs to be considered, since there is an obvious similarity in form, if not in building material. There is some evidence of timber circles being turned into stone circles by virtue of timbers being replaced in stone. For example at Templewood, Argyll and Bute, the northern circle had a timber component which was replaced in stone, albeit creating a monument which was never finished (Richards 2013, p. 40). At Machrie Moor, Arran, circles I and XI were originally constructed in timber but then replaced in stone (Haggarty 1991). The Sanctuary in Wiltshire also consists of both wooden and stone phases. Here, in a location which had already been used for occupation, a series of concentric timber posts were constructed somewhere around 2500 cal BC (Pollard 1992). Either while the posts were still standing, or when it was still possible to make out the posts' location, stones were added, defining one of the original timber settings, but also enclosing a larger space (see Figure 8.9). There may also have been timber components associated with stone circles. At Stanton Drew, Somerset, geophysical survey identified a series of timber rings set within the large stone circle (Oswin and Richards 2011). Only excavation could confirm whether the timber and stone components were contemporary, or probably more likely that the stone elements were added at a later date. It would be wrong, however, to assume that all timber circles were replaced in stone, or that timber always pre-dated the use of stone in monuments (see Millican 2007). It is possible that there were differences in the meanings of timber and stone which meant they stood for different sets of associations. This has been argued in relation to the complex of monuments at Stonehenge and Durrington Walls, where it is argued wood represented the living while stone stood for the dead (Parker Pearson and Ramilisonina 1998, Parker Pearson et al. 2020, 2022, 2024 and see subsequently). This may have meant that in some areas while timber and stone circles resembled one another in form, they could have been used in mutually exclusive ways.

There is surprisingly little evidence for activity from within stone circles. Occasionally, burials have been found in association with these monuments, but typically they are both later (Beaker onwards) and only ever found in small quantities (see subsequently). This has led to suggestions that these monuments were constructed primarily as

RITUAL AND RELIGION IN THE ROUND   **217**

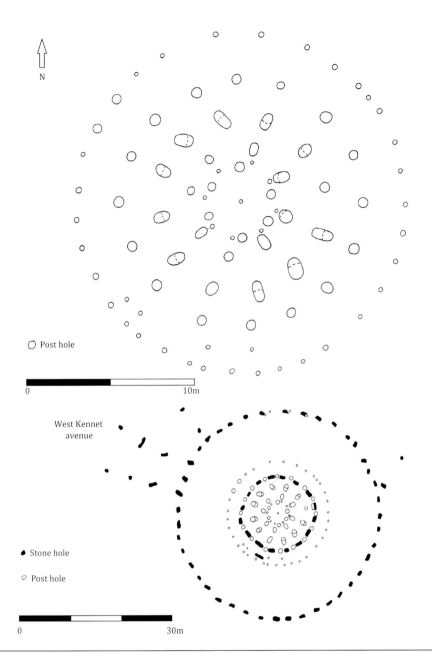

FIGURE 8.9
Plan of the stone and timber components of The Sanctuary, Wiltshire, showing the primary timber phase (top) and the secondary stone phase (bottom: after Pollard 1992)

FIGURE 8.10
The Ring of Brodgar

gathering places, designed to accommodate people for ceremonies or rituals. There is also an argument that it was the act of construction which was key (Barrett 1994 and see subsequently) and thus stone circles brought together different communities from across a wider landscape. At the Ring of Brodgar in Orkney it has been demonstrated that different stones were brought in from different parts of the landscapes, perhaps with different groups who were coming together in the act of construction (Richards 2013). Whether or not stone circles were used for deposition once completed, it is clear that they became the focus for subsequent activity, attracting further acts of construction. This is because the stone circle element is often just one component at sites which were clearly altered over a substantial period of time. This is particularly relevant in relation to stone circles in henge monuments which saw the addition of a bank and ditch around the stone circle at a later date. With this in mind it is to these monuments which we now turn.

Henges and enclosures

Over the course of between 35 and 125 years around 2500 cal BC people gathered together and constructed an enormous and complex site: the henge at Mount Pleasant, Dorset. The site consisted of a large concentric timber and stone structure, and an even larger palisade enclosure set within a vast encircling bank and ditch (Figure 8.12). Like many sites, it is located close to a river (the River Frome in this instance), one of a number of large late Neolithic sites set to the south of the river in this landscape. Due to its

FIGURE 8.11
The Rollright Stones, Oxfordshire

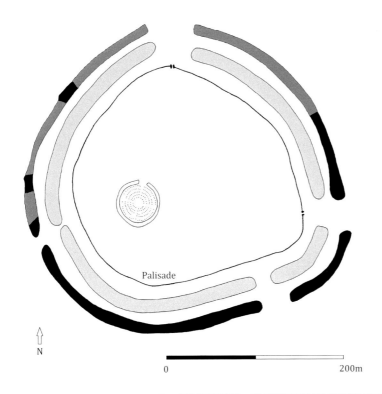

FIGURE 8.12
Plan of the henge at Mount Pleasant, Dorset, with an internal palisade and timber setting (after Gillings *et al.* 2008)

sheer size and scale (the enclosure measures 370m east-west and 320m north-south) it has been described as a 'mega-henge' (Greaney *et al*. 2020), and it represents a huge investment of time and effort by around five generations of people in the late Neolithic. It was an engineering project on a truly massive scale.

Henges more generally are monuments which usually have an external bank and internal ditch, with single or multiple causeways which acted as entrances. Henges are often associated with timber or stone circles, or both, usually found within the henge as at Mount Pleasant, but sometimes close by. An associated form of monument is described as an enclosure and does not have all the components of a henge, so it may have a ditch but no bank for example. As with other late Neolithic monuments, there is considerable variation in precise form but there seems to be broad similarity in the act of enclosure. Henges are found individually but also in clusters. One of the most exceptional clusters of sites is at Thornborough, Yorkshire. Here there are three closely spaced henges in a line along with another three separate examples, all within a 12km stretch of the River Ure (Harding 2013).

In recent years the issue of the date of construction of henges has been considered in some detail. Originally conceived as being contemporary with the timber or stone settings often found within these monuments, it now appears that in many instances the bank and ditch element was added later on (Gibson 2004). This means that existing monuments were 'henged' later in the late Neolithic, the Beaker period or even in the early Bronze Age (Bradley 2011, Pollard 2012). However, at sites such as Mount Pleasant, new dating programmes have shown that what was originally conceived as a long, drawn-out series of constructions was actually a project that was completed within a much tighter time frame (Greaney *et al*. 2020). As we will see in the next chapter, henges continued to be built as monuments in their own right in the Beaker period and early Bronze Age, making these, like stone circles, monuments which had an extended currency.

It was not just pre-existing monuments which had the bank and ditch element added; at Durrington Walls the construction of the massive bank and ditch may have been to commemorate the occupation of this site by people who built the nearby monument of Stonehenge as well as enclosing the timber circles here (Craig *et al*. 2015, Parker Pearson *et al*. 2020, 2024). Indeed, the connection between henges and settlement is significant and is discussed in more detail subsequently. While the bank and ditch component at many sites was a later addition, it is also clear that there are some examples of early henges constructed around and just after 3000 cal BC (Harding 2003, pp. 12–19). The small number of known early sites employ a bank and ditch but in quite variable ways.

Some henges are modest in size, especially the early examples, while those built post-2800 cal BC are often truly monumental in scale. At Avebury the larger stone circle, itself encircling the two inner stone circles, was surrounded by a deep ditch which would have measured 9m deep and a bank 5m high. It would have taken a massive investment of time to build the bank and ditch using only antler picks to dig out the chalk and baskets to move the spoil. Avebury is vast, but others are equally large. The bank and ditch at Durrington Walls are also very large, measuring approximately 500m in diameter. It has been estimated that the bank and ditch took close to a million hours

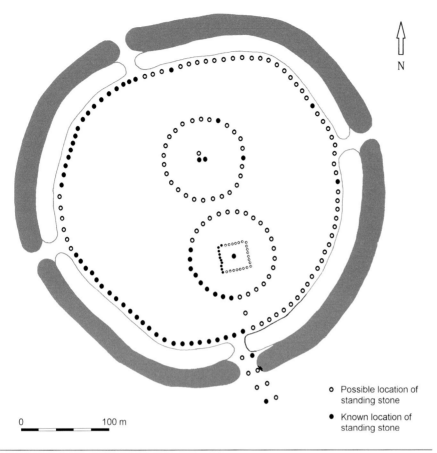

FIGURE 8.13
Plan of the stone features at henge at Avebury (after Pollard and Reynolds 2002)

to construct (Darvill 2006). In addition to this, a series of pits have been found encircling Durrington Walls, adding a further dimension to this landscape and also involving a further investment of time (Gaffney et al. 2020). Precisely what inspired people to invest so much time and energy building banks and ditches, many of which enclosed pre-existing monuments, will be discussed in more depth subsequently. Before that, however, we consider some of the great late Neolithic monumental complexes of Britain and Ireland.

MONUMENTAL COMPLEXES

So far individual monument types have been briefly considered, but as we have already seen in the case of Avebury, multiple forms of late Neolithic monumental architecture are often found in clusters within a single location, referred to as complexes. These complexes usually include more than one type of monument, and different sites within complexes were linked together either by natural features, most notably rivers, or by built features such as avenues. In some instances, pre-existing sites, especially cursus

FIGURE 8.14
The henge at Avebury

monuments, were also deliberately incorporated into these complexes. These large aggregations of monuments are both spatially and temporally complicated; different sites were constructed in episodes at different times over a period of up to a thousand years, although certainly with the intensity of construction focused in the first half of the third millennium, and in many of the very large examples were built around 2500 cal BC. It is also worth noting that some monuments were significantly altered over this time period, being remodelled or reworked several times: circuits of standing stones or timbers added, wood replaced with stone and banks and ditches added. To get a handle on these complexes is therefore quite difficult. One approach might be to consider the finished form of these complexes but this itself is problematic because first, this would have not have been achieved until the early Bronze Age and second, a final form may not have been in the minds of people building and using these sites when first started (cf. Barrett 1994). However, it is also possible that each generation of builders knew exactly what they needed to contribute to the overarching plan from the start. Bearing this in mind, the sequences at several of the best-known monumental complexes will now be considered before key themes are discussed in relation to all of these monuments.

The Brodgar-Stenness complex, Orkney

A remarkable series of monuments are found on the distinctive strip of land between the lochs of Harray and Stenness on mainland Orkney (Figure 8.15). This section of

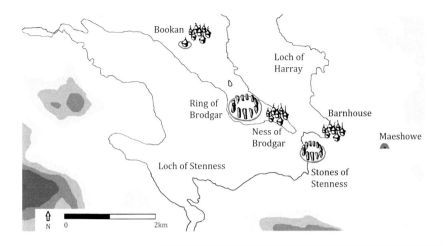

FIGURE 8.15
The late Neolithic architecture in the Brodgar-Stenness complex (after Richards 2013)

landscape is outstanding for a number of reasons. First, it is a slim boundary between two lochs, one of which contains freshwater and the other seawater. Sites located on this strip of land therefore appear to be surrounded by water on virtually all sides as well as being encircled by hills (Richards 1996), a recurring feature of late Neolithic monument complexes. Second, this is an area of landscape which saw occupation in the form of villages at the end of the fourth millennium BC and almost certainly earlier on in the Neolithic as well (Richards and Jones 2015b). The village of Barnhouse was considered in the previous chapter, where it was noted it reached its apogee in the late Neolithic. Third, there are also a range of monuments in this landscape which make it one of the most dense concentrations of late Neolithic architecture anywhere in Britain.

The first of the monuments in this complex is the Stones of Stenness (Figure 8.16), a henge monument comprising a circuit of stones surrounded by a bank and, possibly, a ditch (Richards and Cummings 2024, p. 26). This monument was constructed at the start of the third millennium cal BC (Griffiths and Richards 2013) and is located at the southern end of the complex. From the Stones of Stenness it is possible to see the earlier passage grave of Maeshowe to the east, probably constructed towards the end of the fourth millennium cal BC, although it has never been formally dated. Just over a kilometre to the north-west of Stenness stands another site, that of the Ring of Brodgar. This monument is much larger that the Stones of Stenness, roughly 104 metres in diameter, and was possibly constructed in the mid-third millennium cal BC (Griffiths and Richards 2013), making it one of the latest additions to this landscape. It currently consists of 29 standing stones and is encircled by a ditch; there is no sign of a bank, however (Richards 2013, p. 114). To the north of Brodgar is another large monument, the Ring of Bookan. This has been interpreted as both a henge monument comparable to the Stones of Stenness and also a passage grave like that at Maeshowe.

For many years this stretch of land was interpreted as a ritual landscape located in a symbolically important part of Orkney. Research over the last few decades, some of

FIGURE 8.16
The Stones of Stenness looking out towards the Loch of Stenness and the hills of Hoy

which is still ongoing, has completely changed our view of this landscape, however. First, the late Neolithic settlement of Barnhouse was discovered just a short distance away from the Stones of Stenness. Barnhouse is considered in more detail in the previous chapter, but excavations clearly demonstrated that people were living close to the monuments. Indeed, Barnhouse was occupied at the same time that people were building the Stones of Stenness (Richards 2005, Richards *et al*. 2016). Barnhouse, however, also revealed another important aspect of the sequence in this area. One of the houses at Barnhouse was much larger than the rest; House 2 was interpreted as a ceremonial or 'big house' used for restricted or special practices (Richards *et al*. 2015). Moreover, later in the sequence of occupation at Barnhouse another structure was built; while resembling the architecture of the houses at Barnhouse, Structure 8 was constructed on a monumental scale and clearly used for ritual practices (Richards 2005, p. 190, Figure 8.17).

Our understanding of this landscape was changed again with the discovery of the Ness of Brodgar. This site has seen significant excavation, but these investigations have only just finished, so more will be known once we have the final publication. However, we do know that this was a site that was clearly the location of very significant and concentrated ritualised activity in the late Neolithic. It is clear that in the early Neolithic the Ness of Brodgar was occupied in a similar way to other settlements in Orkney at this time (see Chapter 4). In the late Neolithic, however, a whole series of large ceremonial houses/monuments were constructed, similar in size and scale to House 2 at Barnhouse, which were built over the fourth millennium cal BC buildings (Card 2015). At Barnhouse there was a single large ceremonial house, but at the Ness there are

FIGURE 8.17
Barnhouse Structure 8 (Adam Stanford © Aerial-Cam Ltd)

multiple big, monumentally sized houses clustered together. For example, Structure 8 was constructed around 3100 cal BC and was designed from the outset as a large and impressive structure. Measuring 22 × 9.5m it would have been a very imposing building. Just as impressive was the interior of the building, with incised lines and decoration on the stonework, good evidence for painted surfaces as well as four hearths (Card *et al*. 2020b). The material culture from this structure suggests that it was used to host a large number of people involved in feasting. However, like many of the structures at the Ness of Brodgar, this structure was short lived, and it partly collapsed after just a hundred years of use. Only part of the original structure was then rebuilt and used at this location, and just a hundred years later, around 2900 cal BC, Structure 10 was constructed and was built over the remains of Structure 8, as well as two earlier buildings. This was a structure of a different size and order than those that had come before. With walls up to 4m thick and measuring nearly 20 × 20m, this building can be paralleled with Structure 8 at Barnhouse (see previously). The excavators have described the interior of Structure 10 as a chamber, akin to that at the nearby passage tomb of Maeshowe and demonstrating that this was a monument, not a house in the domestic sense (Card *et al*. 2020b). Although monumental in size and clearly involving large amounts of effort to construct, the structure nevertheless collapsed after only a hundred years and had to be subsequently rebuilt: it was finally fully decommissioned a few hundred years later.

Both Structure 8 and Structure 10 at the Ness of Brodgar are large and impressive buildings, but Structure 27, recently discovered at the site, is perhaps one of the most impressive structures ever built in Orkney in the Neolithic. The stonework used to build this 17 × 11m structure is exquisite, surpassing even that of Maeshowe passage tomb nearby. The masonry used to build the outer walls were chosen with such care that they fit together perfectly to create gently curving walls. On the interior, enormous thin slabs

FIGURE 8.18
The Ness of Brodgar in its wider landscape context, with the Stones of Stenness visible in the distance (photo by Hugo Anderson-Whymark and courtesy of Nick Card)

of stone seem to have been reused from a different site but carefully incorporated into this structure to create a stone-clad interior (Nick Card *pers. comm.*). This structure is likely to be contemporary with Structure 10, and like that structure it also seems to have been fairly rapidly decommissioned. Indeed, people used this location for depositing their refuse and a large midden formed over the remains of Structure 27 over time.

How might we understand the extraordinary structures found at the Ness of Brodgar? Certainly it seems that these monumental houses were set aside from everyday life for the coming together of communities perhaps on a yearly basis, or at special ceremonial or significant times such as rites of passage or religious festivals (Edmonds 2019). Clearly eating, drinking, making objects and artwork all featured in the ritual use of these structures, as evidenced by the large midden beyond the structures (Card 2015). The short-lived nature of each of the structures at the Ness of Brodgar also indicates the importance of construction, and rebuilding/reimagining these important structures every few generations. As such, it is possible to interpret this site as the ceremonial centre of all communities in this area, with each large ceremonial and monumental house the manifestation of multiple groups coming together and monumentalising their allegiance to a wider social grouping, allegiances that clearly needed renegotiating at key moments throughout the earlier part of the late Neolithic.

More recently it has been suggested that the presence of a hearth and distinctive mound at the centre of the Stones of Stenness may mean that this monument also started life as a large house which was mostly dismantled prior to the construction of the stone circle (Richards 2013, 72–4). In the light of the discoveries at both Barnhouse and the

FIGURE 8.19
Structure 27 at the Ness of Brodgar: one of the most elaborate structures at the site, which uses very large stones in its construction

FIGURE 8.20
One of the decorated stones from the Ness of Brodgar

Ness of Brodgar it now seems more likely that the Ring of Bookan is also the remains of a large ceremonial house, itself located next to another massive late Neolithic settlement (Brend *et al.* 2020). The dominant metaphor within this complex, then, is the ceremonial or monumental house – a theme returned to in more detail subsequently. It is clear, however, that this stretch of landscape from Bookan to the north to Maeshowe to the south was of considerable importance in the late Neolithic, particularly in last two centuries of the fourth millennium and the first two centuries of the third millennium, with the focus of intense construction and occupation taking a variety of forms and changing over time.

Calanais, Isle of Lewis

At Calanais (also referred to in the literature as Callanish), there is an entire landscape of stone circles and stone settings, making this another of Scotland's major late Neolithic complexes and one that is very different in nature from that at Stenness/Brodgar. Spread out across a wide landscape are a total of nine known stone circles (Figure 8.21), with Calanais I (Tursachan) the most elaborate of the circles and the focus of the other sites. Calanais I consists of a central stone circle consisting of 13 tall standing stones making a stone circle roughly 12m in diameter (Richards and Cummings 2024). At the centre of the circle is a small chambered tomb with an 5m tall standing stone as a backslab and leading away from the circle are four lines of stones including one of paired stones creating an avenue (Figure 8.22). At the southern end of this monument is a large rock

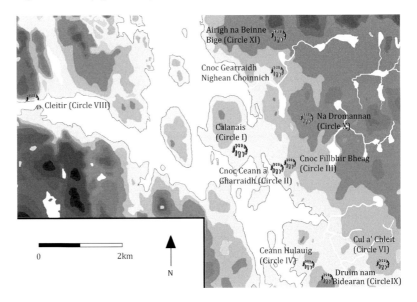

FIGURE 8.21
The location of the stone circles in the Calanais complex (after Richards 2013)

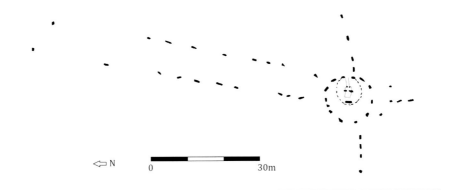

FIGURE 8.22
Plan of the main circle and avenues at Calanais (after Henley 2005)

outcrop which may have been understood as a monument in its own right (see Richards 2013). Indeed, it may be this outcrop that was the focus of the monument which was used in ongoing ritual practices. Excavations at the main circle indicate that it dates to roughly 2900 cal BC and was contemporary with the use of Grooved Ware; the lines of stone may be later, however (Ashmore 2004). The other stone circles are less elaborate than the main circle and appear to line routeways in and out of the Calanais complex; it has therefore been argued that these circles relate to the movement of people from the wider area to this central complex (Richards 2013).

The importance of movement around the landscape in relation to the Calanais sites is further illustrated by that the fact that it appears that some sites were simply designed to be seen from afar but not actively used once constructed. At the recently excavated stone circle of Na Dromannan located just under 2km to the north-east of the main circle a simple stone circle was erected with the least possible effort; large stones were propped up in place which would have appeared impressive on the skyline when approaching the main site but up close are rather shoddy (see Richards 2013, pp. 235–246). Indeed, all the stones had fallen over prior to excavation. Other sites in the complex seem to indicate that they were placed in relation to movement to the main circle, including travelling by water: the site at Cleitir (site VIII) overlooks the waterways leading to the main Calanais site (Figure 8.21).

This landscape was clearly important and saw the construction of a major ceremonial complex across a wider area. However, unlike the Stenness/Brodgar complex where intense occupation was monumentalised in stone, drawing on the architecture of the house, at Calanais occupation does not seem to have taken place on a permanent

FIGURE 8.23
The main circle at Calanais site looking down the avenue to the north

basis within this location, although there is some evidence for occupation around the main circle (Ashmore 2004). Instead the dominant metaphor here was an earlier form of architecture found in large numbers on the Outer Hebrides and beyond, that of the passage tomb (Henley 2005). With the circuits of standing stones encasing a chamber with a passage it is not hard to see how this architecture was adapted and altered in this late Neolithic complex. The avenue at the main circle at Calanais has been compared to the passage of a passage tomb and the circle of stones encasing passage tombs the stone circle itself (Henley 2005, Richards 2013). This may also explain the presence of a chambered tomb at the heart of this monument. This brings us to another important late Neolithic complex influenced by the presence of earlier passage tombs.

Brú na Boinné, Co. Meath

In Chapter 6 the large passage tombs of Knowth, Dowth and Newgrange, along with the smaller satellite tombs around these sites, were considered in detail. These architecturally sophisticated complexes of passage tombs, along with other clusters of passage tombs in Ireland, were built in the middle Neolithic. Some passage tombs show clear evidence for continuing use into the late Neolithic. For example at the Mound of the Hostages, Tara, Co. Meath, there are a number of cremation burials. It is therefore clear that passage tombs would have continued to be important places in the landscape, as is further evidenced at the Brú na Boinné complex. Here new monuments were added to the passage tomb complexes and other sites in this landscape, showing the ongoing significance of these sites but also how new forms of architecture were woven into the fabric of older monuments.

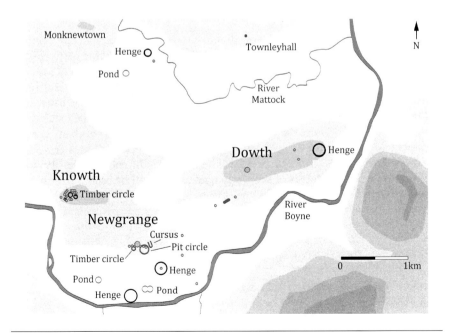

FIGURE 8.24
The Brú na Boinné landscape in the late Neolithic (after Cooney 2000)

FIGURE 8.25
Reconstruction of the timber circle at Knowth, Co. Meath

There are a number of enclosures at the Brú na Boinné complex which were positioned in relation to the earlier passage tombs and sites. They take a number of forms and include timber circles, henges and pit enclosures. Some were positioned directly next to the extant passage tombs. For example, a small timber circle was constructed just metres from the central passage tomb of Knowth (Figure 8.25). An enormous circle of pits and timbers was constructed next to Newgrange, and the presence of Grooved Ware and Beaker pottery suggest some of this monument was late Neolithic and Beaker period in date (Mount 1994). Radiocarbon dates, however, suggest a slighter later date in the early Bronze Age for this monument (Sweetman 1985). Indeed, some of these monuments are definitively later including the stone circle which surrounds Newgrange and henges such as that at Monknewtown (Sweetman 1976), illustrating the longevity of this form of architecture beyond the late Neolithic. One of the most intriguing monuments found in the Brú na Boinné landscape are the 'ponds': clay-lined pits filled with water and located a few tens of metres from henges in this landscape (Cooney 2000, p. 166). Given the ritual significance of water in the late Neolithic, particularly apposite in this complex as it is focused on the River Boyne, it can be suggested that the ponds are another variation on the circular and watery monuments of the late Neolithic. The Brú na Boinné complex, then, is different again from the complexes already considered. Here new monument types were incorporated into a complex already filled with circular architecture in the form of stone-built passage tombs, and it is interesting that the materials used to create these late Neolithic monuments avoid stone, drawing instead on the broader use of timber, earth and water.

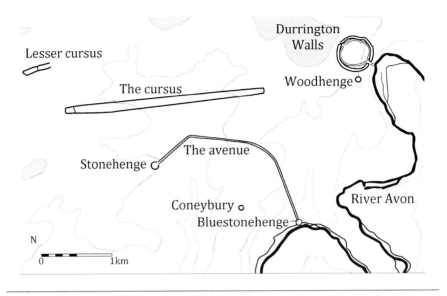

FIGURE 8.26
The Stonehenge/Durrington Walls complex, showing the main late Neolithic monuments as well as the distribution of later round barrows (after Pollard 2012)

Durrington Walls/Stonehenge, Wiltshire

The complex of monuments focused around Durrington Walls and Stonehenge is one of the best-known Neolithic landscapes in Europe. This complex has been the focus of intense investigation for many years, further enhanced by the recent Stonehenge Riverside Project (now published as a series of volumes: Parker Pearson et al. 2020, 2022, 2024) and here only the briefest of summaries of this sequence can be provided. This summary will focus on the two main monuments within this complex, Durrington Walls and Stonehenge, but will also touch upon some of the other late Neolithic and Beaker monuments found in this landscape. This section considers each of the key monuments in turn.

The first site in this complex is Stonehenge itself. At the start of the third millennium cal BC, Stonehenge phase 1 was constructed. This phase of the monument consisted of a circular enclosure consisting of a bank and a ditch and two entrances. There were timber settings at the north-east entrance and within the centre and southern portion of the enclosure (Figure 8.27) meaning this was, initially, a wooden monument. It has also been suggested that within this enclosure there may have been a series of bluestone standing stones, the stones that later became the ring of bluestones (see Parker Pearson et al. 2022, Chapter 2). These bluestones are a distinctive type of stone brought all the way from the Preseli mountains in Pembrokeshire. It has been argued that these bluestones were erected in stone holes packed with cremated human bones around the circuit of the enclosure (Parker Pearson et al. 2020, Chapter 4). These stone holes are now commonly called the Aubrey Holes, named after the seventeenth-century antiquary John Aubrey, who first noted and recorded them. In its first phase, then, Stonehenge

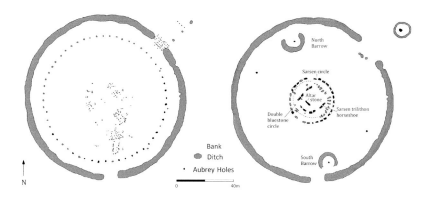

FIGURE 8.27
The first two phases at Stonehenge, phase 1 (left) and phase 2 (right)

consisted of earth, timber and perhaps stone elements with a significant quantity of human remains incorporated into the monument.

The site was completely remodelled, representing very significant levels of activity, only at the end of the late Neolithic around 2500 cal BC. This second phase saw a number of additions to the site, including the erection of a circle of sarsen stones at the centre of the monument (Parker Pearson et al. 2020, Chapter 6). The sarsen circle is unique; it is the only example of a stone circle where the stones are shaped and connected by lintels which were fixed in place by mortice and tenon joints (Bradley 2012, p. 130). The outer circle of sarsens encased a horseshoe-shaped inner setting of massive sarsen stones which consisted of five paired stones, with each pair being topped with a lintel. These inner sarsen stones are known as the trilithon horseshoe (Figure 8.27). At the very centre of the monument a central so-called Altar Stone was placed (Parker Pearson 2015, pp. 24–28), and it has recently been demonstrated that the Altar Stone originated in north-east Scotland (Clarke et al. 2024). The sarsen stones were most likely brought in from West Woods on the edge of the Marlborough Downs (Parker Pearson et al. 2020, Chapter 7). Other stones were erected within the enclosure and the bluestones from the earlier phase, along with those from a second bluestone circle (Bluestonehenge – see subsequently) were rearranged within the sarsen circle. Minor modifications to Stonehenge were then made in the Beaker period (phase 3), including the addition of an avenue, and the bluestones were rearranged again. Further pits were excavated in the early and middle Bronze Age (stages 4 and 5: Parker Pearson et al. 2022, Chapters 5 and 6) but after this date the site effectively went out of use.

Bluestonehenge is one of the new monuments revealed as part of the Stonehenge Riverside Project. Next to the River Avon where the Avenue to Stonehenge intersects the river the remains of a dismantled stone circle was found. Originally it comprised 26 standing stones and the excavators argued that the bluestones, now found as part of Stonehenge itself, had been positioned here, hence its name Bluestonehenge (Parker Pearson et al. 2020, Chapter 5). A bank and ditch encircled this stone monument, although it is unclear whether this henge component was contemporary with, or later than, the stone

FIGURE 8.28
Stonehenge (Erwin Bosman via Wikimedia Commons)

settings. The stone monument appears to have been dismantled in the mid-third millennium cal BC and the stones incorporated into the main monument at Stonehenge (Allen *et al.* 2016). This location, however, was then connected to Stonehenge by virtue of an avenue, which winds its way through the landscape up from this point towards Stonehenge, incorporating a distinctive dogleg before reaching the stone monument. New work by the Stonehenge Riverside Project has shown that the parallel bank and ditch which makes up the avenue follow a series of natural ridges in landscape. What is perhaps the most extraordinary aspect of these natural ridges is that they are aligned on the midsummer solstice (Allen *et al.* 2016, Parker Pearson *et al.* 2020, Chapter 8). It seems entirely possible, therefore, that the Avenue commemorates the route the bluestones took from their original location next to the river up into the monument at Stonehenge while also formalising an existing solar alignment (Parker Pearson 2012, p. 226). As such, it may never have been designed to be used as a processional route but was an architectural commemoration and formalisation of other events.

To the north-east of Stonehenge, connected by virtue of the River Avon, is the enormous henge of Durrington Walls. This site in itself consists of multiple components built in separate stages. Within the high bank and deep ditch are two large timber monuments, known as the Northern and Southern Circles and both were constructed here sometime around 2500 cal BC (Parker Pearson *et al.* 2024). The Northern Circle was not very well preserved when excavated and consisted of one or two rings of posts enclosing a setting of four large posts (Wainwright 1971). The Southern Circle, however, was well-preserved and appears to be a monument which was constructed in multiple phases, albeit over a relatively short period of time (Parker Pearson *et al.* 2024). First, a central setting of posts surrounded by two concentric rings of timbers was set up, after which a portal and façade were added, oriented on the midwinter sunrise (Parker Pearson 2012, pp. 84–85). Next a horseshoe arrangement of timber posts within three concentric rings of timbers was created sometime between 2485 and 2455 cal BC. Finally, a series of smaller timbers were put up both inside and outside the larger posts (Parker Pearson 2012, 86–88). At a later date a mass of material culture was deposited in pits cut into the places where posts had once stood (Darvill 2006, Parker Pearson 2012). It is worth noting that the final phase of the Southern Circle at Durrington bears a striking resemblance to the contemporary phase at Stonehenge.

There is also evidence of multiple houses at Durrington, which have been interpreted as a large settlement occupied during the construction of Stonehenge (the previous chapter details the houses found at Durrington, and see Parker Pearson *et al.* 2024, Chapter 2). This suggests contemporaneous and related activity between these two sites, with people living at Durrington while working on the stone construction at Stonehenge. Durrington was not occupied indefinitely, however. After the main phase of occupation was over at Durrington the site was transformed once again. Geophysical anomalies under the bank have been shown to be the remains of large postholes which appear to have encircled the area used for occupation. The posts in these holes were subsequently removed and the large bank and ditch constructed in their place (Parker Pearson *et al.* 2024.). The timber circles and area used for occupation were therefore commemorated by the construction of the henge which appears to have been the final act of closure at this site.

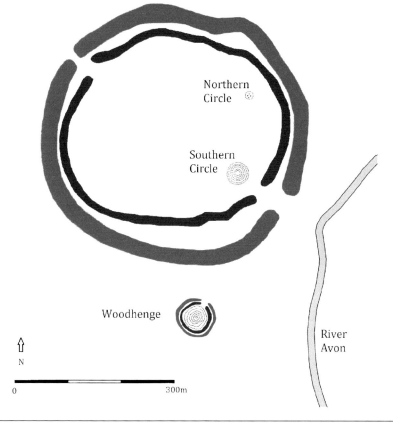

FIGURE 8.29
Plan of Durrington Walls (after Harding 2003)

FIGURE 8.30
Woodhenge – concrete bollards are positioned where timbers once stood (Midnightblueowl via Wikimedia Commons)

Only a short distance from Durrington Walls is the site of Woodhenge (Figure 8.30). Here six concentric rings of wooden posts were found creating a monument 40m long and 36m wide along with pits which once contained stones (Pollard 1995, Pollard and Robinson 2007). This circle is in alignment with the two timber circles within Durrington Walls and should be considered part of this complex. At a later date a bank and ditch were added and large quantities of material were deposited in the locations where the posts had once stood; this activity is later and included the significant deposition of human remains (see Pollard 1995).

Other complexes

Each of the complexes considered in this chapter in detail is different. Each complex emphasises a different element, architectural form or material substance so that while there are similarities between the complexes no two are the same. This means that each complex drew on a broader tradition of monument construction but was built in local settings while incorporating regionally specific traditions of practice (Bradley 2007). Moreover, only five complexes have been considered here in any detail, but there are others, including Balfarg (Fife), Kilmartin (Argyll), Machrie Moor (Arran), Dunragit (Dumfries and Galloway), Ballynahatty (Co. Down), the Milfield Basin (Northumberland), Thornborough (Yorkshire), the Priddy Circles (Somerset), Dorchester-on-Thames (Oxfordshire) and Mount Pleasant (Dorset), to name just some. Without resorting to a consideration of each complex in turn, some broader themes will now be discussed in

FIGURE 8.31
The large stone circle at Machrie Moor, Arran, part of a complex of monuments at this location

relation to these monuments and monumental complexes as a whole. However, before we do that we must first consider mortuary practice, which so far has not featured heavily in this account of the late Neolithic.

MORTUARY PRACTICE

Not far from the River Earn at Forteviot, Perth and Kinross, at some time between 3080 and 2900 cal BC people came together, bringing with them quantities of carefully collected cremated bones from funeral pyres. The remains of these individuals may well have been curated over a period of time and brought in from over a wide area. At this location people then established a cremation cemetery. Nine discrete deposits representing 18 people were deposited in pits, scoops or associated with a broken standing stone (Noble and Brophy 2015, p. 790). A number of bone pins accompanied the cremations and we know that the pins would have gone into the pyre with the bodies, perhaps on clothes or funerary garments. After the cremation cemetery was created the location then became the focus of a major late Neolithic monument complex including three henges and a timber circle (Noble et al. 2017). This cremation cemetery is not unique – over a dozen are now known from Britain including an initial phase at Stonehenge (Parker Pearson et al. 2020). However, there remains only limited evidence for mortuary practice from the late Neolithic which is in marked contrast to the early Neolithic, in particular the evidence of multiple bodies from chambered tombs and causewayed enclosures (see Chapter 5).

While cremation is found at some of the sites discussed in this chapter, it should be noted that the vast majority of monuments do not appear to have been used first and foremost as burial grounds. As we have seen, cremation burials were recovered from Stonehenge, where a total of 63 cremations were found in the Aubrey Holes; these features pre-date the construction of the stone element at this site (Craig *et al*. 2015). At other sites human remains were added during the construction phase of some monuments. At the stone circle at Balbirnie, Fife, cremated bone was found in token quantities in some of the stone sockets (Gibson 2010). In other instances, cremations were added later on in the life history of monuments. Secondary cremations, some of which dated to the late Neolithic, were found at the Site 3 post circle at Dorchester-on-Thames, Oxfordshire, and other cremations found in association with other monuments within this complex are likely to date to the same period, although it should be noted that this was a set of sites which saw use over a long period of time (Whittle *et al*. 1992). Secondary cremations were also found at Woodhenge, Wiltshire, in pits cut into the tops of postholes (Pollard 1995) and at Dunragit, Dumfries and Galloway, after the removal of a post (Thomas 2015a, p. 165). Late Neolithic inhumation burials are rather rare in the archaeological record although when they are found they are often of children (Healy 2012), suggesting that inhumation may have been reserved for the deaths of specific sectors of society.

It was not just new sites that saw burial activity, burials were added to pre-existing sites already standing in the landscape. In Chapter 6 the evidence from Duggleby Howe, Yorkshire, was considered; this site saw the digging of a deep shaft and the burial of several individuals in the early and middle Neolithic. Mortuary activity continued at this location in the late Neolithic with the construction of a round mound which contained cremations alongside the inhumation of children (Gibson 2016). The West Kennet long barrow also saw the continued deposition of human remains in the late Neolithic, including at least one child inhumation (Bayliss *et al*. 2007). Cremations dating to the very end of the fourth or start of the third millennium cal BC are found at other monuments such as Ballaharra, Isle of Man (Fowler 2004b, p. 93), Carreg Coetan, Pembrokeshire, Mound of the Hostages, Co. Meath and Carrowmore, Co. Sligo (Whittle *et al*. 2011, pp. 651–656). This suggests that the remains of the dead, usually cremations, were added to pre-existing sites, but only in small, token quantities.

Overall, then, it appears that there is very little evidence for inhumation from the late Neolithic (Bradley 2007, p. 90), with only occasional exceptions to this (for example, there is a possible burial at Radley, Oxfordshire – see Barclay and Halpin 1997, p. 279). Instead, there is much better evidence for cremation in the late Neolithic. Cremation was practised in both the early and middle Neolithic, so it does not represent a new practice. However, it does appear to be more prevalent in the late Neolithic. The transformation of the body through fire may have been considered the most appropriate way of disposing of the dead, and it is interesting that there is now evidence of plague from the middle Neolithic onwards. One cannot help but wonder if the prevalence of cremation may have been, in part, a reaction to this. We also know that human remains in cremated form were used as a substance in the creation of monuments (incorporated into stone holes for example) and also deposited in them once built. Even with the known examples of cremations it is clear that only a small portion of the population was cremated and deposited at monuments, so these may have been founders of new lineage groups or tokens of communities brought to a central place.

As such it appears that the vast majority of people in the late Neolithic were probably disposed of in other ways, perhaps with considerable continuity with earlier periods. The use of excarnation and predation as ways of dealing with the dead has been discussed in previous chapters, as has the use of waterways as places for burial, and these practices may have continued as a tradition; late Neolithic human remains from a palaeochannel at Eton Rowing Lake, Berkshire, supports this idea (Healy 2012). It is clear that rivers and water were important places in the late Neolithic world, and may well have been implicated in different types of ritual activity, including burial.

THEMES IN LATE NEOLITHIC MONUMENTALITY AND MORTUARY PRACTICE

So far this chapter has considered both individual site types and how different monuments of wood, stone and earth were organised into complexes, effectively monumentalising entire landscapes. We have also considered mortuary practice more broadly. This final section moves on to consider these sites and complexes thematically, drawing out some of the key aspects of these sites and the picture they can help us paint of society in the late Neolithic.

Monuments as places of composition

We have already seen that late Neolithic monuments are often, although not exclusively, found in clusters or complexes which means that stone circles, henges, timber settings, pits and other monuments reference one another and it is possible to suggest that these complexes accumulate significance as more and more sites were constructed. It is also worth noting that many late Neolithic monuments were themselves positioned in relation to pre-existing sites in the landscape. Late Neolithic complexes are frequently close to, or in some cases even cut across, cursus monuments. This is found at Stonehenge, Wiltshire; the Walton Basin, Powys; Thornborough, Yorkshire; and Dunragit, Dumfries and Galloway. Cursus monuments may have retained their importance for late Neolithic communities as they seem to act as the formalisation of routeways through the landscape, or restrict access to these paths (see Chapter 6). Not all late Neolithic complexes were built close to cursus monuments, however; some were built with other early Neolithic monuments close by, as demonstrated at the Avebury complex where the long barrows at South Street and West Kennet were both close to new late Neolithic monuments (see Gillings and Pollard 2004). The latter also saw renewed deposition. The location of Windmill Hill causewayed enclosure close to the Avebury complex is also significant, and Windmill Hill too saw renewed depositional activity in the late Neolithic (Whittle *et al*. 1999). It seems, then, that earlier monuments were deliberately referenced and built into the fabric of late Neolithic monuments, drawing on the significance of these earlier features (Parker Pearson *et al*. 2022, Chapter 1). Some, like chambered tombs, were over a thousand years old at this point (for example, West Kennet long barrow was probably constructed in 3670–3635 cal BC (Bayliss *et al*. 2007) and Silbury Hill just 1km away saw construction commence in the 25th century cal BC: Leary *et al*.

2013), while others may have been just a few hundred years old and tales may have been passed down about their construction.

It is not just earlier monuments that are tied into the fabric of these complexes, however. These monumental complexes also act to bring together different elements of the landscape, both natural and cultural. One of the most striking of these connections is the location of sites and complexes in relation to rivers and water more generally. This has already been noted in specific examples previously, for example with the late Neolithic complex at Brú na Boinné and the connection between Durrington Walls and Stonehenge and the River Avon. There are other examples of this. The Thornborough henges in Yorkshire are positioned close to the River Ure (Figure 8.32) and the complex

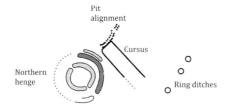

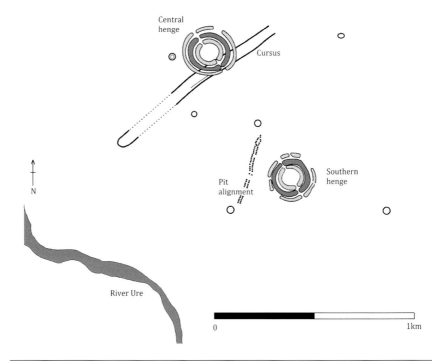

FIGURE 8.32
The location of the Thornborough henges and associated monuments in relation to the River Ure and earlier cursus monuments (after Gillings *et al.* 2008)

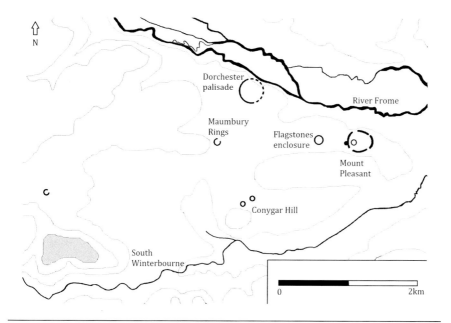

FIGURE 8.33
The location of the complex of monuments at Mount Pleasant/Maumbury Rings, Dorset (after Gillings *et al*. 2008)

of monuments around Mount Pleasant, Dorset are positioned in between the Rivers Frome and South Winterbourne (Figure 8.33). In Ireland, the Giant's Ring in Belfast is just a few hundred metres from a bend in the River Lagan. The henges at King Arthur's Round Table and Mayburgh in Cumbria are positioned between the Rivers Eamont and Lowther. This is a pattern repeated at late Neolithic complexes in Britain and Ireland (Harding 2003). It is not just rivers which are connected to these monuments; water more broadly seems to have been carefully incorporated into these complexes. A number of authors have noted how the ditches of henges seem to have regularly filled with water so that the centre of the henge was encircled by standing water (Harding 2003, p. 34–35, Richards 1996). There are also connections between late Neolithic monuments and springs (Leary and Field 2011), with the construction of Silbury Hill at the source of the River Kennet one of the most striking examples of this (Leary *et al*. 2013).

Rivers and water would have been conduits of movement throughout the Neolithic which connected different parts of the landscape. As we saw in the last chapter, people in the late Neolithic appear to have been predominantly mobile, and they may well have followed rivers through the landscape as they moved around with their animals. These would arguably have been easier to navigate along, as woodland seems to have regenerated at this time and would have made some areas more inaccessible. Rivers, then, would have structured movement and tied specific communities to particular landscapes. They would also have been important in terms of identity. It was also suggested previously that rivers may have been crucial in burial practices. Since most people were not formally buried, they may well have been disposed of in watery places (rivers or the sea; see previously). Water, then, may not just have structured movement and anchored people to landscape but may also have been a powerful symbolic substance associated with the transformation of state from living to dead (Bradley 2012) or associated with the journeys of the ancestors. Parker Pearson has made a convincing argument that the River Avon was a crucial part of the Durrington Walls-Stonehenge complex and was incorporated into rituals involving the disposal of the dead within this complex (Parker Pearson *et al*. 2020, 2022) and this may have been representative of broader practices at certain waterways across Britain and Ireland. Water, then, may have been key in ritual practice and religious beliefs as well as playing a key role in the deposition of the dead.

It is not just water that was incorporated into these complexes. The movements of the sun and the moon at key points of the year were also clearly referenced from some of these sites. In Chapter 6 we saw that some passage tombs were aligned on midwinter sunrise in particular, and celestial alignments including both midwinter and midsummer sunrise and sunset are known from a number of, although not all, late Neolithic complexes. Stonehenge has a well-known midwinter alignment (Ruggles and Chadburn 2024), but other examples include the Southern Circle at Durrington Walls, also aligned on the midwinter sunrise, and Woodhenge, aligned on midsummer sunrise/midwinter sunset (Pollard and Robinson 2007). At Long Meg and Her Daughters in Cumbria, Long Meg, a standing stone outside the main circle, is directly aligned on midwinter sunset. In some instances alignments may have fortuitous and then enhanced via architecture, as has been argued for both the Stonehenge Avenue and the location of the sites in the Stenness-Brodgar complex (Parker Pearson 2012). What is clear, however, is that an emphasis on particularly important points of the year as indicated by the movement of celestial bodies was key and being formally identified at monumental complexes suggesting an increased focus not just on marking these points but also the cosmos more widely (and see Fowler 2021). Religious practice, therefore, must have placed a considerable emphasis on watching the skies.

It was not just the movements of celestial bodies that were significant and marked out at these monuments. It appears that the movements of living communities were also as important, as it appears that many of these sites were positioned along routeways through the landscape (Noble 2006). The Dunragit complex in Dumfries and Galloway, for example, is positioned alongside natural routeways through this particular landscape (Thomas 2015a), and Forteviot, Perth and Kinross, is situated on the River Earn, potentially one of the main routes across this part of Scotland (Noble and Brophy 2011). We have already seen that Castlerigg stone circle in Cumbria is positioned on one of main routeways in and out of the central lakes which follows the River Greta. At multiple sites, then, these monumental complexes were positioned where people would have routinely moved between different landscapes. It has even been suggested that monumental complexes may have been constructed to memorialise the movement of stones in the creation of other complexes. It appears that the sarsens for Stonehenge were acquired from West Woods on the Marlborough Downs and taken to Stonehenge via a river crossing point at Marden. Here a vast henge was constructed, perhaps referencing and commemorating the movement of the sarsens (Parker Pearson 2012, Chapter 18). Likewise, the Stonehenge Avenue may have been constructed to indicate or commemorate the movement of the bluestones from Bluestonehenge.

FIGURE 8.34
The stone circle at Swinside, Cumbria

The importance of movement around these monuments and between monuments in complexes is also expressed in relation to the movement *within* monuments. It is clear that at all different forms of monument including timber circles and henges, movement was carefully channelled into the main body of the site by the provision of entrances or paired timbers or stones (Gibson 1998, p. 84). In some of the complexes discussed previously, routeways into monuments were further elaborated with the addition of formal avenues, probably as a later phase of these complexes. It is important to note here that it has been suggested that avenues could have been built to be walked alongside, not in so that the avenue at Stonehenge actually *prevented* access to a routeway that was set aside (Gillings *et al*. 2008, p. 201). Once within a site, however, the architecture operated so that movement was channelled – some routes were blocked, forcing participants to move in specific ways around the interior (Harding 2003, Pollard 1995). John Barrett (1994) has argued that the architecture at the Avebury complex makes people move around the monument in very specific and carefully orchestrated ways. First, the avenues constrict access into the outer circle; those who did not access the central area would not have been able to see over the bank into the centre of the monument. Once within the outer circle there are two inner circles, the Northern and Southern Circles, themselves acting as a further set of spaces into which an increasingly select few could enter (Barrett 1994, Pollard and Reynolds 2002). Ceremonies or rituals taking place at the very centre of these two circles could only ever have been visible to a small number of people. This is repeated at other sites such as The Sanctuary, Woodhenge and Stonehenge (Pollard 1992). This means that while these sites were constructed by large groups of people, access to central key areas may have been restricted to a limited number of people. This could indicate the presence of ritual specialists but could equally have been for those who managed to motivate construction in the first place:

aggrandisers whose force of personality inspired people to work collectively, albeit only for short periods of time (Whittle 2017 and see subsequently).

Late Neolithic monuments also acted as locations for bringing together various substances from different parts of the landscape. This has been definitively demonstrated at the Ring of Brodgar, where stones of different lithologies were brought in from different parts of the surrounding landscape (Richards 2013). This can be interpreted as indicating that these monuments were built by different groups who brought a stone from their local area and came together in one central location to build a monument. There is further evidence to support this idea. The ditch at the Ring of Brodgar was clearly built in sections, essentially dug as a series of pits, which may suggest that individual groups worked on separate sections of the monument (Richards 2013). Only at the end were the different stones and different segments of ditch combined into a single, composite site. A similar scenario could have worked in relation to timber monuments as well, although it is much harder to identify in the archaeological record. Nevertheless, at the site of Blackhouse Burn, South Lanarkshire, it has been shown that the posts were grown in different microclimates, implying that they may have been brought in from different parts of the landscape (Noble 2006, p. 194). Again, the bays in between the timber posts contained different kinds of stone, but were ultimately capped by a single, unifying layer (Lelong and Pollard 1998).

The idea that late Neolithic monuments were composed of different people and places works in a rather different way at the complex at Avebury. There is some evidence for

FIGURE 8.35
The Ring of Brodgar

exotic things being carefully incorporated into the monument, such as the fragment of a Langdale axe placed in the stone socket of Stone 40 (Gillings and Pollard 2004, p. 57). However, overall the Avebury henge saw very little material deposition, and so here it may have been the deployment of a wide range of architectural forms which referred to distant places and people. Within the henge at Avebury there are stone circles, timber circles, a row of stones (within the Southern Circle), a large standing stone (the Obelisk within the Northern Circle), a bank and ditch and avenues. Indeed, Gillings and Pollard (1999) argue that the sarsen stones deployed in both the stone circles and the avenues at Avebury were themselves important and 'known' stones in the landscape, some of them bearing axe polishing marks. Of course the most spectacular example of the incorporation of exotic stones comes from Stonehenge with the use of different stones from various places, including northern Scotland (for the altarstone: Clarke *et al*. 2024), and the Preselis, including dolerite and rhyolite (Parker Pearson 2012). Recent research has revealed that what we know as the bluestones (actually a type of rock known as spotted dolerite) came from outcrops in the Preselis, particularly the site of Carn Goedog (Parker Pearson 2015). There is also a pillar of rhyolite at Stonehenge, and this too came from Pembrokeshire from the site of Craig Rhos-y-felin. Excavations at this location have revealed the rock face from where the stone was prised. Intriguingly, the quarry at Craig Rhos-y-felin dates to around 3300 cal BC, which is 400 years earlier than the first phase at Stonehenge. Parker Pearson has suggested that these stones may have been used to build a monument in Pembrokeshire in the middle Neolithic and dismantled and taken to Stonehenge around 2900 cal BC (Parker Pearson 2015, p. 79). If this were the case, this would mean that Stonehenge is composed of different stones from different places and also is a composite site incorporating and reordering pre-existing monuments.

While the very fabric of these monuments appears to involve the coming together of different people and bits of places in the construction process, there is also important evidence that, at some of these sites, there were acts of careful structured deposition within the monuments. This is not the case at all late Neolithic monuments; some were clearly deliberately kept 'clean'. This includes some of the large sites such as Avebury and Stonehenge. At other sites, however, there are spectacular quantities of material deposited. This is notable at Durrington Walls, Woodhenge and Mount Pleasant. At these sites massive amounts of ceramics, flint and animal bones were recovered, carefully placed within the monument (see Gillings and Pollard 2004, Parker Pearson 2012, Pollard and Robinson 2007). It appears that the extensive deposition of material culture post-dates the timbers at these sites, with material being deposited in pits cut into the places where the timbers once stood. Moreover, it is not clear whether the deposited material was freshly generated or whether it was material collected from nearby middens (Thomas 2007b, p. 151). What is clear was that this was carefully structured and spatially variable, indicating the careful choice of what went where. At Woodhenge, for example, cattle bones were deposited in relation to the inner ring and pig bones with the outer ring (Pollard and Robinson 2007, p. 167).

One of the issues not considered here so far are the differences, if any, between wood and stone. Monumental complexes frequently incorporate elements of both wood and stone, and as we have seen, in some examples, timbers were replaced with stone. Parker Pearson has argued that there were fundamental differences in the use of wood and stone at late Neolithic monuments (Parker Pearson and Ramilisonina 1998, Parker Pearson et al. 2022). He noted that Stonehenge began its life as a monument predominantly composed of wood, which was later replaced entirely in stone (see previously). Once the monument was built of stone, however, it saw very little depositional activity. This is in sharp contrast to Durrington Walls at the other end of this complex of sites. At Durrington Walls, a monument constructed entirely out of wood, people were living close by, throwing lavish feasts and then depositing very significant quantities of material culture. This evidence has been used to suggest that stone was representative of the ancestors and therefore set aside from day-to-day life while monuments built of wood could be used for ritualised activities by living communities (Parker Pearson and Ramilisonina 1998). The structuring principle that stone equated to the dead and wood to the living works in contexts beyond Stonehenge. At Avebury it has already been noted that it was constructed from stone and saw very little depositional activity, while at the timber site of the Sanctuary at the other end of the West Kennet Avenue, people continued to congregate, feast and deposit material. This may not have been the case for all complexes, however, and may have had particular resonance for the two complexes at Stonehenge and Avebury. Indeed, while the broad structuring principles may have been the same, the variations between these two massive complexes may indicate two rival versions of the same overall belief systems and perhaps indicative of two competing corporate groupings.

It is important to stress here that when discussing late Neolithic monuments these are not always comparable across Britain and Ireland in terms of size, scale and the investment of time and energy. We have already discussed the large stone circle and henge at Avebury, where the outer circle is 335m in diameter, encircling the inner Northern and Southern Circles, themselves around 100m in diameter and surrounding other stone features such as the Cove. One of the stones in the Cove weighed in excess of 100 tonnes, making this one of the largest stones ever moved in Britain. It would be possible to compare the stone circles at Avebury with other examples of stone circles such as that at Gamelands, Cumbria, since these are both classed as the same form of monument. However, Gamelands is a small circle made up of knee-high stones which could have feasibly been moved by only a handful of people in a couple of days. To compare the stone circle at Avebury with Gamelands in Cumbria is therefore not comparing like with like. Likewise, the henge component at Avebury, a massive undertaking, is often discussed alongside the henge at Wyke Down, Dorset. Again, Wyke Down could have been constructed in a day or so by a couple of families (Harding 2003, p. 87). The difference here is *scale*, and it adds further difficulty in studying this diverse set of monuments. There is a tendency to discuss the biggest examples, yet these are the exceptions not the norm on a national scale. Instead, places such as Avebury have attracted particularly large bursts of activity, presumably attracting many people from a wide area. Indeed, places such as Avebury, Stonehenge and the Stenness/Brodgar complex have been described as 'luminous centres' for the very reason that they seem to have attracted high levels of activity and monumentalisation (but see Barclay 2001). We need to think about the social dynamics that drove such behaviour, however, and be wary of over-emphasising the significance of these 'mega' complexes in narratives encompassing the whole of Britain and Ireland. Instead, it seems that the investment of huge amounts of labour at places such as Stonehenge were focused on a specific part of the late Neolithic, notably in the centuries around 2500 cal BC, indicative of a specific

FIGURE 8.36
The small stone circle at Gamelands, Cumbria

set of circumstances at this particular place and time. It may well be that these people were aware of broader changes on Continental Europe (see next chapter) and were reacting by imploring higher powers to intervene. As such, they were a response to a very specific set of circumstances at a particular point in time and not representative of the late Neolithic as a whole.

Monuments as houses: ritualising the domestic sphere

We now move on to consider why the house seems to have been such a dominant metaphor in late Neolithic society. We have seen that there seems to have been an emphasis in late Neolithic monumentality on the house. In an Orcadian setting this was literally taking the architecture of the house and recreating it in monumental form. At Barnhouse, House 2 was interpreted as a ceremonial house: larger than the rest of the houses and used for restricted practices (Richards 2005). This large house may have been the material representation of a unified community with a cohesive identity (real or imagined: Richards *et al*. 2016). At the Ness of Brodgar multiple ceremonial houses were built here in the late Neolithic, possibly representing the coming together of a wider set of communities to build and conduct rituals within the ceremonial heart of Orkney. The stone circles too drew on the architecture of the house, with both having a central hearth, and possibly with the Stones of Stenness once having a large house at its centre (Richards 2013). We have also seen that houses were constructed within spaces which later became henges. At Durrington Walls a mass of late Neolithic houses were constructed which were later memorialised by the construction of a bank and ditch (see previously; Parker Pearson *et al.* 2024). At Avebury, the southern circle seems to have commemorated and enclosed an earlier house. Recent excavations at Marden also found evidence for houses under the bank (Leary *et al.* 2016). In most other parts of Britain and Ireland the evidence is rather different, however, although the house as a defining metaphor for late Neolithic society is still relevant and important.

Bradley (2012) has noted that when they survive late Neolithic houses were circular with a square central hearth or setting of four posts. He argues that this general template was used to create monuments by retaining the overall layout and form of the house but recreating it on a massive scale. There are a number of examples of the setting of four central posts, including examples at Durrington 68, Wiltshire; Wyke Down, Dorset; Knowth, Co. Meath; Ballynahatty, Co. Down; and Stanton Drew, Somerset. Bradley has argued that these structures are representative of the house and thus the ritualisation of the domestic sphere (Bradley 2003, 2012, 2013). There is additional support for this argument. The use of Grooved Ware is found in the late Neolithic in settlement contexts but also monuments, notably the large henges in Wessex (Thomas 2010). This may have been a deliberate reference and use of an essentially domestic object in a ritualised setting.

The question is: why build monuments which draw on the architecture of the house? The key issue here is what houses provided for people other than a roof over their heads and somewhere to sleep. As we saw in the previous chapter, the house was not just functional architecture but representative of family or lineage groups as well as pertaining to wider understandings of the world. Identity would have been negotiated through kinship links and social networks. In the same way that the large houses of late Neolithic Orkney appear to have stood for the wider, conglomerated community, late Neolithic monuments may have been representative of wider social groups. Bearing in mind that settlement in the late Neolithic was clearly often quite dispersed (see Chapter 7), with the suggestion that there were actually rather low levels of population, a monument in a central meeting place may well have stood for a wider corporate social group. Moreover, through the act of constructing architecture, people were able to come together to forge and create new collective identities and social units (Thomas 2015a, p. 175). In short, the interplay of ritual and domestic seems to have been a key one in late Neolithic society whereby the status and importance of the house as an entity uniting different social groups was expressed in monumental form (cf. Brück 1999), often on a massive scale.

In addition to this a number of authors have also noted that late Neolithic monuments are essentially set within circular landscapes (Bradley 1998, Richards 1996). This means that monuments were carefully situated so that the surrounding hills, water, or mountains perfectly encircled the monument and it appeared that each site was a series of circles: the stone circle, the ditch, the bank and then the hills. This careful orchestration of monument and landscape was not fortuitous and is repeated at sites across Britain and Ireland. It is argued that this is significant because it gave the impression that the monument was positioned at the very centre of the world, which was recreated at each site in miniature (Richards 1996). We can now add to that picture that it was the house that sat at the centre of many of these monuments, making the house (and, by analogy, the kinship group), the very centre of late Neolithic life. As such, monuments may well have been understood as locations where the different layers of the world came together; these would be the upper-world (sky), our realm (with the house/corporate group at the core) and the underworld (Bradley 1998, 2000a). This would mean that monuments were essentially an *axis mundi*: the centre of the world. If this was the case, these were powerful places, where interactions between the living and dead could have been mediated, as well as other beings which almost certainly were thought to inhabit the Neolithic world. Each monument complex, therefore, was the creation of a particular understanding and representation of the cosmos, drawing on important places, people and belief systems more widely, and incorporating both domestic and ritual spheres.

Monuments and the nature of society

There is evidence from the start of the Neolithic for people coming together to work on communal projects. This happened with the construction of early Neolithic causewayed enclosures, and in the middle Neolithic with passage tombs and cursus monuments. The act of construction as a mechanism for mediating social relations was thus a tradition of practice established for the best part of a thousand years in both Britain and Ireland. Why would labouring together have been so important? Quite simply, the act of construction brought dispersed communities together where they could work alongside one another (McFadyen 2006, Richards 2004). Working together would have forged new social bonds, not just through the act of building. When groups of people come together to labour, it is likely that special feasts would have been held to feed workers and celebrate the event, and there is substantial evidence for feasts from some sites such as Durrington Walls (Parker Pearson *et al.* 2024) and Newgrange (Mount 1994). In both these instances there is evidence of pigs being roasted on the bone, and the analysis of Grooved Ware from the former site indicates the use of cow meat and milk as well (Craig *et al.* 2015). Feasting and socialising, as well as negotiations of identity and status, would therefore have been powerful motivating factors for people to turn up and engage with such projects.

Because the large monumental complexes are such impressive and large sites, it has been assumed that considerable numbers of people would have been required to construct these sites. This in turn has had an effect on how we interpret the evidence. It has been suggested that an elite of some description would have been needed to inspire or coerce a workforce into undertaking such a project (see, for example, Renfrew 1973) which would then be used by the privileged few – perhaps a hereditary elite or hierarchy: chiefs in Renfrew's original interpretation. However, work in recent years has moved this debate in a different direction, and we could think of two different possibilities. Perhaps people were inspired by other events or as a reaction to things in society which needed dealing with urgently. This may have been things such as sickness (and we know that plague was present in late Neolithic society), claims of witchcraft or sorcery, animal disease or an exceptionally cold winter. There is also the possibility that knowledge of changes (new peoples and new ways of doing things: see the next chapter) on the Continent had reached the shores of Britain and Ireland. Changes there could have caused anxieties and worries on our shores. So, even with the sites that involved a massive investment of time, when we consider that these sites were probably built in bursts of activity, it may not have actually required masses of people coerced by an hereditary elite (as, for example, in Dynastic Egypt). It has been noted that the bank and ditch at Durrington Walls took nearly 1 million hours to construct. Spread that out over 50 years, and that would only involve 100 people for 200 hours per year – not a massive investment of time. This model of events would simply require people coming together at fixed times of the year to work and labour together.

However, another possibility which seems to fit the evidence best is that late Neolithic society was 'trans-egalitarian', meaning neither egalitarian nor politically stratified (Hayden 1995, 2001). Instead, it was something between, and critically, at certain points in the late Neolithic there were a series of aggrandisers – individuals who sought to further their own social standing by leading on these large monumental projects (Whittle 2017, Chapter 5). We could imagine that these were the kinds of individuals who may have been able to mobilise otherwise dispersed populations for short bursts of activity. In this scenario if we return to the 1 million hours it took to build the bank and ditch at Durrington Walls, a five-year burst of construction could still have required only 200 hours a year per person, but this time for 1000 people. In this scenario people would have wanted to see some return for their efforts and labour, and if the promises of the individual or individuals motivating this activity were not realised, people could well have shifted allegiance and loyalties elsewhere. Is it possible that this explains the presence of multiple large complexes in some parts of Britain and Ireland within close proximity to one another? That while people were invested in their religious lives and beliefs, the dispersed nature of the population at the time meant that if they did not get a good return on their spiritual investment in one place, they could, quite simply, switch allegiance to someone who offered a better and more successful version of the cosmos? The late Neolithic, then, may have been a time of competing worldviews which were expressed on a massive scale in monumental form and driven by powerful but short-lived individuals who inspired work on this epic scale.

CONCLUSIONS

In this chapter stone circles, timber circles, pit circles, henges and complexes containing some or all of these separate monument types have been considered. At the broadest level these were monuments which brought dispersed people together from across the landscape at fixed meeting places which were then formally marked by monumental construction. These monuments were sometimes built close to, or over, pre-existing monuments, and they incorporated key phenomena from the natural world, including the flow of rivers, the source of springs and light from sunrise at midwinter. All of these, it has been argued, were critical for ritual and spiritual life in the late Neolithic. Since many of these monuments involved building architecture which referenced key times of the year such as midwinter or midsummer, we might envisage dispersed and scattered communities coming together to work, feast and socialise. Political negotiations may have been held, disputes settled, ritual events conducted, powerful forces contained, the dead formally put to rest and new alliances formalised. Construction not only involved building and working together but probably incorporated other important events such as marriages, exchanges, parties and feasts. In this way monument construction fulfilled a whole variety of different roles for people in the late Neolithic, incorporating group gatherings and social negotiations while also contributing to spiritual and religious well-being. Moreover, people were drawing on the architecture of the house in these monuments as well as making reference to other key aspects of the known world, including links with material culture and passage tombs. Monuments were quite literally where all elements of the late Neolithic world came together to create an *axis mundi* – the centre of the world for those communities involved in their construction.

What is now becoming increasingly clear is that these massive monuments and complexes, often altering entire landscapes, were built in short bursts of activity, with perhaps very large numbers of people coming together to work on a communal project over just a few years. While the broad traditions of monument construction laid out in this chapter were clearly practiced over many centuries starting at the turn of the third millennium cal BC, the largest projects seem to have been focused around the last few centuries of the late Neolithic. Here it has been argued that mobile, dispersed and essentially trans-egalitarian late Neolithic societies were motivated by two different things. First, a number of aggrandisers came forward at this time to utilise elements such as feasting and knowledge of the supernatural to motivate people to come together and work on these monumental projects. Some of these aggrandisers were hugely successful and seemed to inspire competition on a monumental scale (here we might envisage the two great complexes of Avebury and Stonehenge as offering different versions of ritual and spiritual life in the centuries around 2500 cal BC). However, these aggrandisers may have also been able to draw on anxieties about changes that were afoot elsewhere in the world. For just across the English Channel there were new people with new forms of material culture, including metals. Perhaps the late burst of monument construction in Britain and Ireland was an attempt to appease supernatural forces in the face of this change. Ultimately, this was not successful, and it is this period of change to which we now turn.

RECOMMENDED READING

Stone circles

Richards, C., ed., 2013. *Building the great stone circles of the north*. Oxford: Windgather.
Richards, C. and Cummings, V., 2024. *Stone circles: A field guide*. New Haven, CT: Yale University Press.

Avebury

Gillings, M. and Pollard, M., 2004. *Avebury*. London: Duckworth.

Calanais

Ashmore, P., 2011. *Calanais: Survey and excavation 1979–88*. Edinburgh: Historic Environment Scotland.

Stenness/Brodgar

Card, N., Edmonds, M., and Mitchell, A., eds., 2020b. *The Ness of Brodgar: As it stands*. Kirkwall: The Orcadian.
Edmonds, M., 2019. *Orcadia: Land, sea and stone in Neolithic Orkney*. London: Head of Zeus.

Stonehenge/Durrington Walls

Parker Pearson, M., *et al.*, 2020. *Stonehenge for the ancestors: Part one*. Leiden: Sidestone.
Parker Pearson, M., *et al.*, 2022. *Stonehenge for the ancestors: Part two*. Leiden: Sidestone.
Parker Pearson, M., *et al.*, 2024. *Durrington Walls and Woodhenge*. Leiden: Sidestone.

Overviews

Bradley, R., 2007. *The prehistory of Britain and Ireland*. Cambridge: Cambridge University Press.
Gibson, A., 1998. *Stonehenge and timber circles*. Stroud: Tempus.
Harding, J., 2003. *Henge monuments of the British Isles*. Stroud: Tempus.

CHAPTER 9

Beakers, copper and bronze

The start of a new era in Britain and Ireland

INTRODUCTION

The end of the late Neolithic is characterised by the construction of enormous and impressive monumental complexes altering entire landscapes, while, simultaneously, there is evidence of only scattered and transient settlement. What happened next is, in many ways, as remarkable as the large monuments of the late Neolithic but in a very different way. Archaeologists have long recognised that a new suite of objects appeared in the archaeological record after the Neolithic: metals, especially bronze, but also copper and gold. A new style of pottery was made, Beakers, and new stone tools were used. Moreover, new practices including single inhumation burials appear in the record. Historically these remains were interpreted as evidence for a new group of people arriving into Britain and Ireland from the continent (the Beaker culture or folk: Childe 1925, Clarke 1970), heralding the start of a new epoch, the Bronze Age. However, as more evidence was uncovered and dated it became increasingly clear that many late Neolithic practices continued: as such subsequent interpretations suggested that there was a package of new objects which enabled a new social order via the emergence of an elite (summarised by Vander Linden 2013).

In just the last few years it has, once again, been ancient DNA that has rewritten our narratives on this period. We now know that on the continent where Beakers pre-date those in Britain and Ireland it is possible to identify two different genetic strands of Beaker-using people – those in central Europe whose DNA originated on the Eurasian Steppe and those in Iberia who used Beakers but genetically were descended from local Neolithic groups (Olalde *et al.* 2018). In Britain genetic results have indicated that people in the late Neolithic had no Steppe ancestry until around 2500 cal BC when we see the first use of Beakers and other associated material culture alongside individuals with Steppe ancestry DNA. By the end of the third millennium cal BC 93% of the gene

DOI: 10.4324/9781003387329-9

pool in Britain contained Steppe ancestry, demonstrating the near-complete turnover of population (Armit and Reich 2021).

Because of the overall lack of DNA from the late Neolithic, there is the possibility that some individuals with Steppe ancestry were in contact with communities in Britain and Ireland in the late Neolithic (Parker Pearson *et al*. 2022). At present, the evidence still supports the idea that late Neolithic Britan and Ireland were, for the most part, isolated from the continent until people in northern Europe, probably in the Low Countries, decided to expand into Britain and Ireland. It seems likely, therefore, that there was an extended period of migration of people onto our shores after 2500 cal BC. Smaller numbers of indigenous people almost certainly endured in parts of Britain and Ireland, but ultimately by the end of the third millennium cal BC the vast majority of people here were descended from populations in Europe, indicating nearly entire population replacement over this period (Armit and Reich 2021).

In the conventional three-age system the Neolithic ends when the Bronze Age begins, with the defining characteristic of this new epoch being the first use of metalwork. However, the reality is that there was a period between the end of the Neolithic and the full take-up of bronze when there were different practices. This must, in part, relate to the different genetic populations which we now know were the key actors in this period. As such, the focus of this chapter will be on aspects of this period which mark a change from pre-existing practices, so it will begin with a consideration of a new style of pottery, Beakers, and associated material culture sets. Metalworking, particularly copper mining in Ireland, will be explored alongside the broader implications of the adoption of metal for understanding this period. It will be argued that the adoption of these new forms of material culture were about the expression of new social identities, particularly the expression of links with distant places, but also relating to setting up home in a new place. Monuments and mortuary practice will then be discussed, with a particular emphasis on the new Beaker burials, as well as a brief consideration of some of regionally specific forms of monuments which emerge in the latter part of the third millennium. This chapter, then, will consider the end of the Neolithic up to the establishment of the early Bronze Age, a period covering from perhaps around 2450 cal BC to the end of the millennium (Parker Pearson *et al*. 2019). Following Needham's (2005) three-fold chronological divide of this period the emphasis here will be on phase 1 which saw the arrival of new people and new forms of material culture (Beakers and metalwork) at around 2450 cal BC, but the chapter will also consider the period which saw the wider spread of new forms of material culture and practices after 2250 cal BC or so (Needham 2005).

AMESBURY ARCHER

A few kilometres to the south-east of Stonehenge at Amesbury in Wiltshire, a single grave was uncovered in 2002 in advance of a housing development. It turned out that this is one of the richest Beaker burials ever to be found in Europe. This find became known as the 'Amesbury Archer', and it is a spectacular example of a burial dating to the Beaker period. The skeleton is the remains of an adult male, aged somewhere between 35 and 45. He was buried with an remarkable assortment of objects: five

BEAKERS, COPPER AND BRONZE 255

FIGURE 9.1
Location of the sites mentioned in this chapter

Beaker pots, a large quantity of barbed and tanged arrowheads (Figure 9.7), two archer's wristguards (see Figure 9.8), four boar's tusks, three copper knives, a shale belt ring, a pair of basket-shaped gold ornaments (perhaps hair decoration) and a cushion stone (Figure 9.2). The analysis of the skeleton revealed that he had suffered from a long-term disability in his left leg which would have affected his mobility to some extent. In addition to this he was also not of British descent but originated from somewhere in Continental

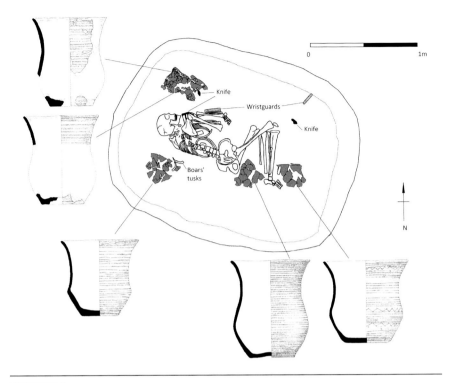

FIGURE 9.2
The Amesbury Archer Beaker burial, with the location of some of the grave goods illustrated (after Fitzpatrick 2011)

Europe (Fitzpatrick 2011). Just 3m to the east of the Amesbury Archer was another burial, named the 'Companion'. This burial was of a male aged 20–25, buried without a Beaker but with a boar's tusk, flint tools and a pair of gold basket-shaped ornaments and broadly contemporary with the Amesbury Archer (Fitzpatrick 2011).

The fact that the grave of the Amesbury Archer was found only a few kilometres to the south-east of Stonehenge led to suggestions that this man was somehow involved in the building of Stonehenge, which earned him the nickname the 'King of Stonehenge' (see Fitzpatrick 2011). We now know that the main phase of construction was complete at Stonehenge before the Amesbury Archer lived (see previous chapter), but he nevertheless remains an important discovery and one of the earliest Beaker burials in Britain. He was buried between 2480 and 2340 cal BC (Barclay and Marshall in Fitzpatrick 2011) and is an excellent exemplar of a new burial practice alongside the new material culture that was in use at this time (Figure 9.3). It is to that material culture that we now turn.

MATERIAL CULTURE

One of the key elements that we see with the start of the Beaker period was the appearance of a range of new and distinctive types of material culture. These objects have European origins and the knowledge of making such objects would have been brought

FIGURE 9.3
The material found with the Amesbury Archer when on display at the British Museum

over with the incoming new populations. Suites of this material culture are often found in assemblages in burials such as that of the Amesbury Archer and include Beakers; metalwork, notably copper and gold; archer's wristguards; barbed and tanged arrowheads; and various other objects.

As already noted, these different types of object first appeared in Britain and Ireland at different times over several hundred years as new people arrived and spread across our islands. This means that there is evidence of continuity in some areas of life, including the tail end of the use of monumental complexes, as well as a continuity in some settlement practices and types of material culture. Moreover, bronze appears to be one the last elements widely adopted in Britain, and this leaves us with a period of 300–400 years with some level of overlap of populations and before the widespread uptake of Bronze technology. Some authors have suggested this period should be called the Chalcolithic (Copper Age); this differentiates it from the preceding late Neolithic and the following fully fledged Bronze Age when the new population and all their associated practices are found across our islands (see papers in Allen *et al.* 2012, Woodward and Hunter 2015). For simplicity, this chapter will refer to this initial post-Neolithic phase as the 'Beaker period', noting that there are problems with this term too, as it prioritises one form of material culture (Beakers), and Beakers remained in use for nearly a thousand years (Needham 2005). Both new pottery styles and the first use of metal should instead be seen as part of a suite of new practices brought in by new peoples in Britain and Ireland from around 2450 cal BC, particularly after 2250 cal BC.

Pottery

Beakers are a distinctive type of pottery which first appear in the archaeological record between 2480 and 2390 cal BC in Britain (Healy 2012) and perhaps as early as 2500 cal BC in Ireland (O'Brien 2012). This form of pottery is often well made, with incised, comb or twisted cord patterns creating its characteristic form of decoration (Gibson 2002a, pp. 87–92). Early Beakers (2500–2250 cal BC) are restricted in form compared to later examples (see Figure 9.4), and three distinctive styles occur: All-Over-Cord (AOC), Finger-Nail and Incised and Maritime-Derived (see Needham 2005). Beakers are not found everywhere in Britain and Ireland initially; there are very few examples known from most of Wales, south-west England, Orkney and parts of Ireland (Parker Pearson 2012, Sheridan 2012, Vander Linden 2013). However, after around 2250 cal BC a much wider array of vessel sizes and styles are found across a much wider area. This diversification of pot styles, along with the expansion of other types of material culture, is often referred to as the 'fission horizon' (Needham 2005, 2012). This sees the proliferation of long-necked, short-necked and S-profile Beakers being produced alongside carinated forms (Figure 9.4).

Unlike Grooved Ware, the pottery style found most commonly in the late Neolithic, which arguably had its origins in the Orkney Isles, Beakers have a definite European origin (Wilkin and Vander Linden 2015). Bell Beakers are found throughout many parts

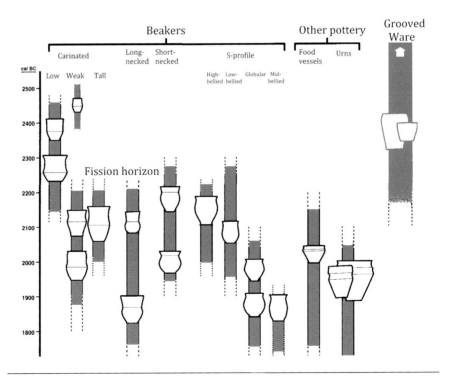

FIGURE 9.4
Schematic diagram showing different Beaker styles in relation to their appearance in Britain (after Needham 2005)

of continental Europe at an earlier date than those in Britain and Ireland and were clearly the inspiration for the Beakers found here (see Needham 2005). It has been demonstrated that British and Irish Beakers were made using locally available clays, which indicates that this new style of pottery was brought over by communities with potting experience who then sourced clay in the immediate area (Gibson 2002a, p. 88). It should be noted that Grooved Ware continued to be used in this period, both in areas where there is little Beaker and alongside Beakers for a time in other areas (Cleal and Pollard 2012). Likewise, there is variation in the contexts in which Beakers are found. Initially, they appear in both burials and settlement contexts but only in some parts of the country; subsequently a wider range of Beakers are found in more quantities in more areas (Gibson 2002a, Thomas 1999, p. 123). There is regional diversity too, as while Beakers are found in single graves in Britain, this is not the case in Ireland, where they are only found in pits and settlements and deposited in monuments (Carlin 2011, Cooney 2023, O'Brien 2004, 2012). This means that this style of pottery was appropriate for use by the living but also right from the start was designed to be deposited alongside the dead. It may also be indicative of multiple different sources of Beaker-using people arriving on our shores with varying practices.

Food Vessels first appeared in Britain sometime after 2200 cal BC and in many areas were used alongside Beakers for a time (Sheridan 2004b, 2012) but appear to replace them in northern Britain (Parker Pearson *et al*. 2016). They were also used in burials after 2200 cal BC. In Ireland Bowl Food Vessels were used from 2150 cal BC, and here they were placed in single graves where there are no Beaker burials known (O'Brien 2012). There are clear overlaps between Food Vessels and Beakers, with the

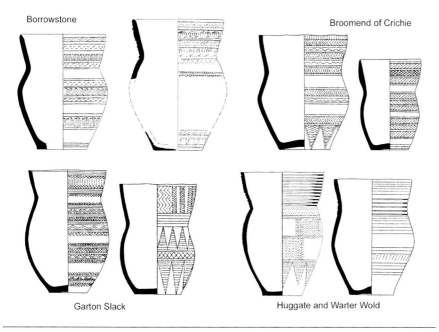

FIGURE 9.5
A selection of Beakers (after Shepherd 2012)

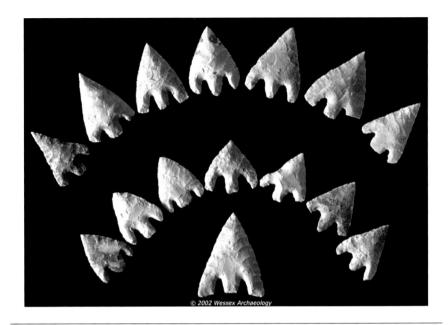

FIGURE 9.6
Distinctive barbed and tanged arrowheads found with the Amesbury Archer (© Wessex Archaeology))

two pottery types sharing similar decorative designs and the tall vase-like appearance of some Food Vessels mirroring some Beaker forms. Food Vessels are often heavier, especially around the rim, and Bowl Food Vessels are also quite squat (see Gibson 2002a, Waddell 1998, p. 141). Again, as with Beakers, there is clear evidence of some regions adopting this pottery style more extensively than others. Moreover, Chapter 4 discussed the range of objects made from organic materials, especially basketry and wood (and see Manby 2004), and these were still likely to be used extensively, especially since it seems that most people were pastoralists moving around the landscape (see subsequently). Instead, the use of distinctive designs and styles of pottery may have been a deliberate attempt to signal affiliation and ancestry with other groups of people and may only have been used at particular events such as feasts and funerals. Furthermore, the making, using and depositing these vessels contributed to the construction of particular identities at crucial times (Fokkens 2012), of particular importance at times of profound change such as this.

Material culture associated with Beakers

Beakers, in particular in burials, are found in association with a whole range of objects, each of which is considered here in turn (Beaker burial assemblages are also considered in relation to mortuary practice again subsequently). One of the most characteristic and ubiquitous finds from the Beaker period is a new style of stone tool known as the barbed and tanged arrowhead (Figure 9.7). This style of arrowhead is quite different in

FIGURE 9.7
Food Vessels from Barns Farm, Fife (after Watkins 1982)

© 2002 Wessex Archaeology

FIGURE 9.8
The two archers' wristguards found with the Amesbury Archer (© Wessex Archaeology)

design to late Neolithic transverse arrowheads. These arrowheads are found in burials but are also common finds at settlement sites in both Britain and Ireland (Harding 2013). Another new way of making a well-established tool type is represented by the thumbnail scraper. These are found in a variety of settings and are also common on settlement sites (Butler 2005, p. 168). Furthermore, they indicate the ongoing importance of making organic objects including leather. Stone axe production gradually declined as people increasingly used copper, then bronze, axes (Butler 2005, p. 175), although it seems that existing examples continued to be circulated (Carlin and Brück 2012).

Another find from the Beaker period is the archer's wristguard. Also known as bracers, over a hundred of these wristguards are known from Britain and Ireland (Woodward et al. 2006). These are thin rectangular stones with perforations at the end which would have been attached to the wrist with cord or leather (Figure 9.8). These objects are mostly found in grave contexts, but there are some examples from settlements as well (Case 2004, p. 207). Archer's wristguards were clearly finely made pieces, and few show any evidence of wear, which has led to suggestions that they were worn for display purposes on the outer side of the arm (Roe 2013, p. 111). Moreover, distinctive and exotic stones were chosen to make these objects, which further enhanced their status as special objects (Fokkens *et al.* 2008). There are 20 wristguards made from Langdale tuff (Sheridan 2012, p. 48) and several Irish examples made from porcellanite from Tievebulliagh or Rathlin Island (Roe 2013). These were sources of stone that were used extensively for stone axes in the Neolithic and offer intriguing insights into the kinds of relationships which may have been taking place in the early Beaker period. Did new people from the continent trade with indigenous people who were familiar with this type of stone, or were the raw materials extracted by the incomers? It is not beyond possibility that they reused existing stone axes which were still in circulation to make these objects.

The presence of arrowheads and wristguards could be used to suggest that archers had an important role to play in societies at this time. This is potentially problematic, however, because there is little evidence for the utilisation of wild animals in the diet, and there is also, unlike the early Neolithic period, very little evidence for interpersonal violence (Parker Pearson 2012). It may be the case that archers were valued for protecting domestic animals from predators such as wolves; if this was the case evidence of this would rarely be preserved in the archaeological record. However, since the paraphernalia of the archer rarely seems to have been used it may therefore not have been a reflection of actual function but may instead have been personal ornamentation or an expression of social identity associated with hunting. In the following, it will be argued that those buried with archer's kit were spiritual leaders or medicine men (and see Fokkens *et al.* 2008). It is also worth highlighting that other objects are found in Beaker burials including jet buttons, boars' tusks, bone pins and belt rings (see Woodward and Hunter 2015 for a full discussion). All of these objects could have been worn on the body, and this could actually indicate that another important aspect of the Beaker period was a change in clothing style and personal ornamentation. Other objects that appear to have been important for people at this time were those made of metal, and it to these that we now turn.

Metals

The Beaker period is also characterised by the first appearance of metals in Britain and Ireland. These are copper, gold and bronze. Copper objects first appear in the archaeological record around 2500 cal BC and there is a clear, albeit short, period when just copper was in use. As such, this phase is often described as the Chalcolithic or Copper Age (see papers in Allen *et al.* 2012). Copper was initially used to make only a limited range of objects, notably axeheads, daggers/knives and halberds, and occasionally smaller objects of personal ornamentation such as rings and pins (Needham 2012, O'Brien 2015). Copper objects are often found alongside other grave goods in Beaker burials and Irish Bowl burials, for example, three copper wire rings found in a Beaker grave at Barrow Hills, Radley (Barclay and Halpin 1997). Many copper objects have

BEAKERS, COPPER AND BRONZE **263**

FIGURE 9.9
Copper knife from Dorset (image courtesy of Portable Antiquities Scheme (www.finds.org.uk) DOR-FCCD7E)

been found as stray finds, and there is evidence that some were deposited as single finds in wet places like bogs and rivers (Bradley 2007, p. 147, Carlin and Brück 2012, O'Brien 2004).

The knowledge of how to make copper clearly arrived as a fully formed technology from the continent (O'Brien 2012) brought in by the incoming populations. It appears to have spread up the Atlantic façade, from northern Spain, western France and into south-west Ireland (O'Brien 2015); this may well be a good example of a pre-existing network as evidenced from the archaeology of earlier periods (see Chapter 6). The Irish origin of the first copper metallurgy in both Britain and Ireland is supported by the fact that the only known source of copper from the Beaker period in both Britain and Ireland is Ross Island in Co. Kerry (O'Brien 2004). Virtually all Irish copper from the Beaker period can be sourced to Ross Island, and it has been shown that two thirds of early copper objects in Britain also originated from this source (Bray 2012, O'Brien 2004). Thus, while this single mine was clearly the source of the most Irish and British copper, it is likely that small quantities were also imported into southern Britain from the near continent. It was only right at the end of the period being discussed here that a source of copper was exploited in Britain. This was at the site of Copa Hill, Cymystwyth, Ceredigion, where copper mining began around 2100 cal BC (O'Brien 2015, p. 138).

The Ross Island copper mine has seen extensive archaeological investigation, which has provided invaluable insights into early copper mining (O'Brien 2004). It appears that the copper ore at Ross Island was initially available on the surface, which was then mined to depths of around 10–12m (O'Brien 2015, p. 127). The rock containing the ore was broken up by setting fires which shattered the rock, which was then pounded into smaller pieces by hammerstones; many of these hammers were recovered during the excavations at Ross Island (see O'Brien 2004). The crushed ore was then removed from the mines to the adjacent miners' camp, which contained the remains of temporary shelters, food waste and Beaker pottery. The ore was then ground down using querns and smelted in furnaces, where temperatures needed to reach around 1100°C to extract the copper. Once this had been done, the copper could be collected up, remelted and made into ingots or in some cases into objects (O'Brien 2015).

Copper objects would have been distinctive objects in the Beaker repertoire and perhaps important for denoting status or power. When these objects are found in graves they are accompanied by other objects of personal ornamentation (see subsequently), and as such it could be suggested that these items were primarily designed to be attached to the human body, hanging off a belt, for example, perhaps as an object designed for display. It is clear, however, that it may not be this straightforward. Copper axes were clearly used at this time; the Corlea 6 wooden trackway in Co. Longford dating to around 2250 cal BC had the clear imprint of metal tools on the woodwork (O'Brien 2004, p. 521). Copper objects, then, had the potential to be both a practical tool as well as drawing on a wider symbolism. We have seen this before with stone axes earlier in the Neolithic (see Chapter 4), and the parallels with stone objects go further. Like Neolithic stone axes which were sourced from particular locations in the landscape such as Langdale in Cumbria or Tievebulliagh, Co. Antrim, copper was virtually entirely sourced from Ross Island in south-west Ireland. The source of the copper may well have been understood by people across Britain and Ireland and added to its exotic allure. The production of copper was, equally, not that dissimilar to making a polished stone axe (Carlin and Brück 2012). Where a polished stone axe involved the quarrying, grinding and polishing of a stone from a specific source, copper involved quarrying, crushing, smelting and casting of material from a specific source. The key difference here was the application of fire, a technology familiar to people via ceramic manufacture.

It is also worth discussing the fact that the process of mining stone was a well-established mechanism for bringing people together on communal projects. Copper mining brought people together temporarily; the very practice of mining would also have helped forge new social identities. There is no evidence for restricted access to the source of the copper at Ross Island, and it also appears that the settlement next to it was only occupied seasonally (O'Brien 2004). It may not have been access to this raw material which was restricted but knowledge of how to transform stone into metal. This may well have been understood as something of a magical process, perhaps only undertaken by particular groups or specific members of different communities. It is perhaps also fitting that many copper objects were also disposed of in very specific ways, often in watery contexts. This might imply the deliberate removal of an object from circulation so that no one individual was able to accumulate wealth. Equally, it may indicate that these were special objects intimately tied to the identity and life history of the owner which in some cases could not be passed on to another person.

Gold

Gold first appeared in the archaeological record alongside Beakers, albeit in fairly small quantities. Like copper, the knowledge of how to make gold arrived from the Continent with the new incoming people, and there is no evidence of any gold working in Britain and Ireland prior to this. Gold was used exclusively for ornamentation, and was made into flat disks, tubular beads and basket-shaped objects which were probably used as earrings or decoration in the hair or on cloth (Needham 2015). All of these objects, therefore, could be worn on the body or attached to clothing. The Amesbury Archer, for example, was buried with two gold basket-shaped objects as was the nearby 'companion' (see previously; Fitzpatrick 2011). A few hundred years later another type of gold object developed; these were 'lunulae', larger sheets of gold which could have been worn around the neck (Figure 9.11). A total of 85 lunulae are known from Ireland and date from 2200 cal BC (O'Brien 2012), and a few examples are also known from Britain and Mainland Europe. The prevalence of lunulae in Ireland has been interpreted as the result of a source of gold in Ireland, perhaps in the Mourne Mountains (Needham 2015). These gold objects are further evidence of the importance of personal ornamentation at this time.

Bronze

The use of bronze technology appeared only at the end of the period under discussion here. Bronze is an alloy – the combination of roughly nine parts copper and one part tin, which together make a much stronger metal than either of the separate metals on their own. Between 2200 and 2100 cal BC tin-bronze was widely adopted across Britain and Ireland (Needham 2012, O'Brien 2015). The copper source at Ross Island therefore continued to be utilised to provide the copper to make bronze along with tin, which was probably sourced from Cornwall. Early bronze metalwork has been found in small number of graves. For example, at Rameldry, Fife, a cist containing a crouched inhumation along with buttons and a tin-bronze dagger was found (Baker *et al*. 2003), and in Yorkshire the Gristhorpe log-coffin burial contained

FIGURE 9.10
Copper dagger from Lancashire (image courtesy of Portable Antiquities Scheme (www.finds.org.uk) LANCUM-3BEC10)

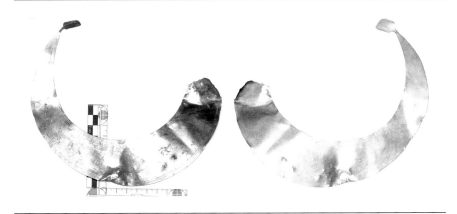

FIGURE 9.11
Gold lunula from Dorset. Part of the object is missing (image from Portable Antiquities Scheme (www.finds.org.uk) DOR-2198F8)

a male buried with various objects, including a bronze dagger (Melton *et al.* 2009). Bronze objects are also found as single finds and in small hoards; at the Hill of Finglenny, Aberdeenshire, parts of eight axeheads were recovered, some deliberately broken prior to deposition, with another well-known example at Migdale, Sutherland (Barber 2003).

FIGURE 9.12
Copper alloy flat axehead from Cumbria (image from Portable Antiquities Scheme (www.finds.org.uk) LANCUM-3324F7)

SETTLEMENT AND SUBSISTENCE

The evidence for settlement in the Beaker period for most parts of Britain and Ireland is rather similar to that from the late Neolithic in general. There are very few house structures known; instead settlement is represented in the archaeological record by the presence of stone tools, pits, hearths, stakeholes and spreads of midden material (Allen and Maltby 2012, Carlin and Brück 2012, Healy 2012, Woodward 2008). One notable exception to this are the Beaker settlements of the Western Isles, where 18 sites are known and have produced evidence of large oval buildings set amongst the machair sands (Sharples 2009). It is also interesting to note that Beaker settlement, and indeed Beakers in general, are absent from Orkney, which contrasts sharply with the late Neolithic stone villages found there (see Chapter 7). It seems, then, that for most of Britain and Ireland people may well have moved around the landscape and lived in temporary structures. However, as with late Neolithic settlement it is difficult, at present, to judge whether this picture is a genuine reflection of Beaker practices. It could, equally, be a result of preservation and that flimsy or lightly built house architecture simply does not preserve well (Parker Pearson *et al*. 2019, p. 458).

Subsistence practices in the Beaker period suggest an animal husbandry regime based on cattle and sheep/goats (Parker Pearson *et al*. 2019, Serjeantson 2011). At present there is very little animal bone from the Beaker period, but what does survive suggests the continued importance of cattle still being used for feasting events at some sites (Allen and Maltby 2012, McCormick 2007) but that sheep/goats became increasingly important throughout the early Bronze Age. It is also worth noting that the horse appears to have been introduced sometime at the end of the Neolithic or in the Beaker period (Serjeantson 2011). It has also been observed that Beakers are much less likely to contain lipids, although a few still have evidence for being used to process ruminant (cattle or sheep) meat and dairy products (Copley *et al*. 2005, Parker Pearson 2012, p. 212). This may suggest a change in the processing of animal products rather than a change in the animals being kept. Animal bone from the late Neolithic shows evidence of having been placed directly over the fire indicating meat being roasted on the bone and it is also worth noting the increased presence of burnt mounds (or *fulachtaí fia* in Ireland) where heated stones and troughs may have been used for boiling meat. Beakers in domestic settings may have been for serving drink and food rather than for cooking (Gibson 2002a, p. 88).

There is some evidence for the use of cereals, perhaps with a resurgence in cereal cultivation at this time in southern Britain (Stevens and Fuller 2012), although there is not, as yet, good evidence for widespread woodland clearance and the concomitant investment in field systems which characterise the later parts of the Bronze Age in many parts of the country (Allen and Maltby 2012). It has been suggested that the people moving into Britain and Ireland from the continent occupied areas which supported cereal agriculture first (Armit and Reich 2021) but that people may well have continued to practise pastoralism, moving around the landscape with their animals and utilising wild plant foods. The most recent isotopic evidence also indicates that there was considerable individual mobility of people at a local scale (Parker Pearson *et al*. 2016, 2019) which was fairly consistent across Britain. There is no evidence of the consumption of marine foods, even in coastal areas (Parker Pearson *et al*. 2019).

MORTUARY PRACTICE AND MONUMENTALITY

The previous chapter discussed the wide range of late Neolithic monuments found in Britain and Ireland which included stone circles, timber circles and henges. It is important to note that many of these monuments continued to be used in the Beaker period. Indeed, many saw not only continued use but also physical alteration or structural additions. For example, there was the addition of the avenues at Avebury, phase 3 at Stonehenge and the completion of Silbury Hill (Cleal and Pollard 2012, Leary *et al*. 2013, Parker Pearson *et al*. 2022). It has also been suggested that the addition of the bank and ditch at various circles may also predominantly date to this phase (Gibson 2004). Many of these monuments continued to be actively altered and used, particularly at the start of the Beaker period and this may represent the activities of the indigenous people more than the incoming Beaker people. Nevertheless, those incoming continental people would have encountered a landscape filled with monuments in active use as well as places built by previous generations, some of which were close to 1500 years old at this point. Indeed, many of these sites saw some deposition in the Beaker period by,

BEAKERS, COPPER AND BRONZE **269**

definitively, Beaker-using people. We have already seen the Amesbury Archer, who was of continental origin yet buried close to the Neolithic monumental complex at Stonehenge/Durrington Walls. We now turn to other examples of these burials.

BEAKER BURIALS AND MORTUARY PRACTICE

We have already seen one of the best-known Beaker burials in the Amesbury Archer, but there are many others known across Britain. Beaker burials are typically characterised by the presence of a body or bodies in a grave which was accompanied with a variety of objects, including at least one Beaker vessel (Figure 9.13). Other objects commonly

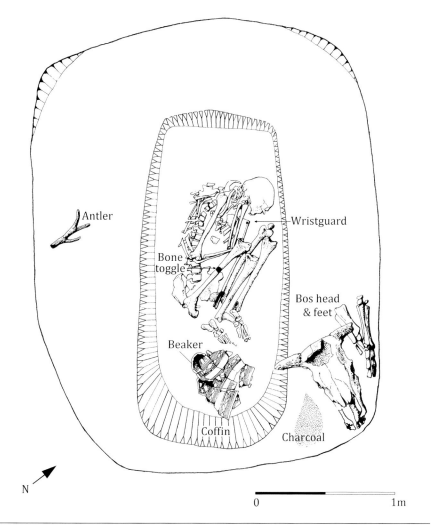

FIGURE 9.13
Hemp Knoll Beaker burial (after Fokkens *et al.* 2008)

found in Beaker burials are copper daggers and knives, archer's wristguards, simple gold objects such as flat disks and basket-shaped objects, boars' tusks, arrows, flint tools and debitage and various other assorted objects of personal decoration (Needham 2012, Parker Pearson et al. 2019, Woodward and Hunter 2015). The fact that Beaker burials have similar suites of material culture and broad similarities in the treatment of the body which was carefully placed in a grave, usually in a crouched position, shows that this was a coherent practice introduced from the Continent by incoming people. Nevertheless, there are some important regional and chronological differences (see, for example, Fowler 2013, Fowler and Wilkin 2016, Needham 2005). There is evidence for bodies being oriented so that they faced specific directions, often with differences between men and women (Shepherd 2012). However, as noted previously in relation to Beakers more broadly, Beakers and Beaker burials are not found everywhere in Britain. Instead, there are distinctive clusters in the Thames Valley and Wessex more broadly, eastern Britain including Yorkshire and Northumberland, and north-east Scotland, particularly Aberdeenshire (Garwood 2012, Vander Linden 2013); very few are known from the west of Britain, and no Beaker inhumation burials are known from Ireland, although there were equivalent practices (see subsequently). From the evidence we now have it appears that Beaker burials first appeared in Britain between 2450 and 2390 cal BC and they continued into the early Bronze Age and the second millennium cal BC (Healy 2012, Parker Pearson et al. 2016). These Beaker burials represent a step change from late Neolithic burial traditions, perhaps not unsurprising since they represent the burial practices of an incoming population. Indeed, these Beaker burial practices are paralleled on the Continent, where we also find the burial of individuals accompanied with lavish and exotic grave goods (Vander Linden 2013).

There is some interesting evidence from these burials which indicate practices which are slightly more complex than they may first seem. Both the Amesbury Archer and the Companion were not complete burials; both had skeletal parts missing. The Amesbury Archer had one rib missing, and the Companion had several ribs missing. The Companion also had the addition of a child's tooth in the grave. These ribs must have been removed once the bodies had decayed and indicate that these burials were not single events where the dead were laid to rest permanently, but, just as with preceding periods, bodies were revisited, manipulated and reordered, including the removal of some bones and the addition of others. There are other examples of this practice. At Chilbolton, Hampshire, the primary burial has ribs removed, and the vertebrae were jumbled; the arms moved; the tibia, fibia and a femur reversed; and the head turned upside down (Fitzpatrick 2011, p. 200). At Manston, Kent, the bones in the burial were arranged to look like a standard inhumation, but vertebrae, the pelvis, the upper arms and the mandible were all missing, clearly through human agency (Gibson 2007).

One of the best examples of this practice are the remains of the 'Boscombe Bowmen'. Located 600m to the north of the Amesbury Archer, the Boscombe Bowmen are the remains of nine or ten Beaker burials in a single grave (Fitzpatrick 2011). Some bodies were articulated inhumations, some are disarticulated remains and there is also a cremation. The grave goods include at least eight Beakers, antler pendants, a boar's tusk and barbed and tanged arrowheads. It seems that not all the burials were contemporary, suggesting the addition (and removal) of bodies and body parts over an extended period between 2510 and 2300 cal BC (Fitzpatrick 2011). All of this evidence indicates that the disarticulation of the human body, and the manipulation of those remains interred in the ground, was an important practice in the Beaker period (Gibson 2007). This means that while Beaker burials are often portrayed as the internment of an individual, they are much more variable than this (Fowler 2013, Wilkin and Vander Linden 2015).

Another key aspect of these burials is that they do not always just involve the placing of a body in the ground. There is clear evidence for the creation of grave furniture in the form of wooden coffins (see Jones *et al*. 2023), wooden chambers and stone cists (Cooney 2023, Downes and Richards 2025). The presence of this architecture at some sites would not only have facilitated repeat access to the body or bodies but would have also drawn parallels with existing architecture, particularly that of chambered tombs: the Beaker period saw a renewed interest in this form of architecture, interesting since these monuments were over 1000 years old at this point. There is also evidence that some Beaker burials at least were covered with a small mound. This appears to be part of a growing tradition of erecting round mounds from this point onwards and which reached an apogee in the early Bronze Age after about 2000 cal BC (Garwood 2007). The marking of Beaker burials above ground is perhaps not surprising if people were planning on returning to a grave in order to remove or add bones. Furthermore, there are examples of Beaker burials in sequential lines or clusters, probably deposited over an extended period (see Johnston 2021). This has led to suggestions that the dead were buried alongside routeways (Garwood 2012), so that these burials were meant to be repeatedly visited and accessed as people moved around the landscape with their animals.

There have also been suggestions that Beaker burials emphasised feasting and drinking. This is partly because Beakers have often been thought of as drinking vessels (Brodie 1997), in particular associated with men and the consumption of alcohol. The placing of the Beaker or Beakers in the grave therefore furnished the deceased for the afterlife. The most extraordinary example of the potential role of feasting at Beaker burials comes from the site of Irthlingborough, Northamptonshire. Here a male was found in a pit along with a Beaker, a flint dagger, five jet buttons, an archer's wristguard and a boar's tusk. On top of the burial and barrow covering it were 184 domestic cattle skulls and one skull from an aurochs (Davis and Payne 1993). If these were simply the remains of a feast, they would have produced 40 tons of meat, enough for a feast for 40,000 people (Davis and Payne 1993), an unfeasibly large gathering. It seems more likely that these cattle skulls were brought in from elsewhere as tokens of other events or that this was the deliberate destruction of material wealth in the same way that depositing metalwork took an object out of circulation (see previously).

How should we interpret the evidence provided by the Beaker burials? The presence of prestige goods in Beaker burials, including gold, has led to interpretations that the people being buried were part of a social elite (Burgess and Shennan 1976). Authors have noted that many of the grave goods would actually have been worn on the body, including the gold objects, boars' tusks, and archer's wristguards. Copper objects could have effective for display, hanging off a belt as a visible sign of access to a rare resource. This could mean that these were the burials of people who, in life, wore highly elaborated clothes befitting of high status. In death, they were buried in their finery. It has been noted that there is a preponderance of male Beaker burials, leading to the suggestion that this was a male-dominated society (but see Brodie 1997). Precisely why these individuals may have had such a high status varies, from the idea that they controlled the production of prestigious objects such as copper and gold to the idea of big men with considerable political power or a warrior elite (Case 2004). We could well envisage them as being the heads of new lineages of families establishing themselves on our shores.

FIGURE 9.14
The grave goods found in the Ferry Fryston Beaker burial, Yorkshire (© Oxford Archaeology Ltd)

In taking the evidence of Beaker burials alongside other evidence for the period, notably that people continued to practise pastoralism, therefore moving around the landscape, Beaker burials seem most likely to fill a niche in terms of the creation and negotiation of identity and descent at particular points in the landscape. This may have been a deep concern with the forging and recreation of specific networks and identities. These were not necessarily hierarchical, although in some cases they may have been. Instead, they were concerned with origin, descent and belief in a new ritual order. Beakers, objects associated with Beakers and broader practices involving the burial of the dead, then, were statements by groups of people attempting to negotiate and reformulate their identity in a new location (cf. Brück 2004). They were emphasising materials which ostensibly demonstrated networks of contacts with people far distant (Fokkens 2012, Garwood 2012, Thomas 1999): continental origins of the people themselves but also objects whereby the biographies of the source may well have been known and celebrated.

In previous chapters it has been argued that the primary way of disposing of the dead throughout the Neolithic was through excarnation and leaving bodies out for scavengers. This would suggest a strong link between wild animals and the dead, with the notion that the souls of the deceased were taken to the otherworld through this process (see Chapters 4 and 8). While Beaker burials clearly represent a new practice which gathered pace throughout the Beaker period, it is important to note that the vast majority of people were still not being formally buried (Garwood 2012). Indeed, the dominant practice may still have involved disarticulation, perhaps via excarnation and predation, and/or disposal in places such as rivers or the sea. The presence of equipment associated with hunting animals in some Beaker burials may therefore have been associated with ritual specialists during life (see previously), and thus may have taken on a special significance for people who mediated between the world of the living and that of the dead if wild animals were a key part of the transformation from the living to the dead. The presence of hunting equipment in some Beaker burials, therefore, may have been used not by those with a warrior status or male-dominated elite, but ritual specialists who had to deal with the realms of the living and the dead.

In marked contrast to the British sequence, Beaker burials are not found in Ireland. There are a few examples of Beaker pottery associated with cremated human remains (Carlin and Brück 2012, Waddell 1998, p. 118), in some instances placed in existing monuments or put into wedge tombs (see subsequently). Instead, when found, inhumations in Ireland were buried with Bowl Food Vessels in single graves, along with the kind of material culture associated with Beakers such as boars' tusks, metal knives and objects of personal adornment. However, these are later than the British Beaker burials, dating to after 2200 cal BC (O'Brien 2012). It is also worth noting here that in both Ireland and Britain the Beaker phase saw the reuse of existing monuments and places previously associated with burial. There are Beakers found in court cairns in Ireland, and Beaker burials were added to the long barrow at Thickthorn Down, Dorset, for example (Drew and Piggott 1936). There was even renewed Beaker activity in caves which had previously been associated with human remains in the early Neolithic in particular (Dowd 2015, pp. 125–130, Thomas 1999, p. 160). This may be indicative of a different history of Beaker-using people coming into Ireland compared to the sequence in Britain and will benefit from detailed aDNA analysis in due course.

MONUMENTALITY

The Beaker period also saw the construction of some new monumental forms; some of these had antecedents in the Neolithic period such as round mounds and henge monuments, while others appear to be new architectural forms such as wedge tombs. This final section will highlight some of the main forms of monumental architecture constructed during the latter part of the third millennium cal BC. It is worth noting that some of these monuments are found more widely than others, which suggests that, just as with Beaker burials, these practices were adopted piecemeal. Monuments more broadly at this time utilised similar features which transcend the different monument types: as such people seem to have been drawing from a broader repertoire of monumentality. With the exception of wedge tombs, Beaker monuments are relatively small and circular.

Wedge tombs

A new form of chambered tomb was constructed in Ireland after 2500 cal BC. This is the wedge tomb, so called because the chamber narrows towards the terminal end, making it wedge shaped. There are over 500 known examples in Ireland, with a distinctive western distribution (O'Brien 1999). Large numbers are found in the south-west, particularly Co. Cork and Co. Clare (Shee Twohig 1990). These are monuments constructed from stone and usually set within a stone cairn. Some of the stones in these monuments have rock art in the form of cupmarks on them (Figure 9.15). When excavated these monuments do not typically produce much material culture, although both inhumations and cremations have been found within the chambers (Jones 2007). There is evidence for the careful manipulation of human bones as seen at other Beaker sites (see previously). For example, at Labbacallee, Co. Cork, the remains of a woman were

FIGURE 9.15
The Giant's Leap wedge tomb, Co. Cavan, with the cupmarks on the front capstone illustrated

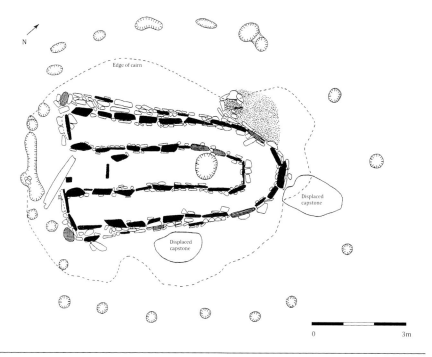

FIGURE 9.16
Plan of Island wedge tomb, Co. Cork (after Jones 2007)

recovered from the eastern chamber; the bones from her arm were in incorrect anatomical positions, and her skull and neck bones were missing (Leask and Price 1936). Beaker pottery has been recovered from some sites, along with barbed and tanged arrowheads (Waddell 1998, p. 98). One of the most striking features of these monuments is that they are consistently oriented towards the west and south-west, which may suggest an interest in the setting sun (Fowler 2013, p. 179, Jones 2007, O'Brien 1999, p. 217).

Round mounds and cairns

It has already been noted that some Beaker burials had small mounds constructed over them (see previously), but round mounds and cairns more generally were built in the second half of the third millennium. It is difficult precisely to track the genealogy of round mounds because there are previous examples found in the early Neolithic (see Chapter 4), and there are middle Neolithic round mounds too (see Chapter 6). There are also an enormous number of round barrows and cairns which were built after 2000 cal BC; without excavation it can be impossible to date these monuments. From those examples with clear dating evidence it seems that round mounds and cairns from the second half of the third millennium cal BC are usually small in size with single inhumations, often, although not always, with Beaker pottery (Garwood 2007). This became a much wider tradition after 2000 cal BC when larger and more elaborate forms of round mound, sometimes in association with more abundant quantities of grave goods, are found across many parts of Britain and Ireland. There are a few examples of known clusters of round mounds from the Beaker period, for example, around Stonehenge as well as at Radley in Oxfordshire (Barclay and Halpin 1997, Garwood 2012), but most of the large-scale concentrations of round mounds were constructed after about 2100 cal BC (Cleal and Pollard 2012). It is also worth noting that ring barrows and ring cairns were sometimes built in this phase but were not associated with burials (Garwood 2007). Instead these can be linked to another type of site, the hengiform, to which we now turn.

Hengiform monuments

The previous chapter considered henges in depth, and it was noted that the addition of a bank and ditch may have been the final phase in the sequence at a number of sites (Gibson 2004), acting to seal off the interiors of sites from further use (Bradley 2011). While some henges were constructed in the late Neolithic, others appear to be later in date (see previous chapter). In particular, smaller banked and ditched monuments, often referred to as 'hengiforms', were built in the Beaker period. Richard Bradley's work in northern Scotland has been particularly informative in understanding these monuments. At the Broomend of Crichie, Aberdeenshire, the small henge was constructed around a pre-existing Beaker cist and incorporated into a linear set of monuments and burials (Bradley 2011, p. 85). It is likely that the henge dates towards the end of the third millennium cal BC, but it is also clear that this was a landscape which saw activity over a long period of time and into the second millennium (Bradley 2011). The henge at Broomend of Crichie can be paralleled with other small henges in both Britain and Ireland, including

FIGURE 9.17
Broomend of Crichie

Cairnpapple, West Lothian; Dun Ruadh, Co. Tyrone; Arbour Low, Derbyshire; and Fargo Plantation, Wiltshire (Bradley 2011). It is worth noting here that enclosures of this form continued to be constructed after the period under consideration here, continuing in some instances, for example in Ireland, to be built into the first millennium cal BC (Carlin and Brück 2012, Waddell 1998).

Recumbent stone circles

Recumbent stone circles are a distinctive type of stone circle predominantly found in north-east Scotland (Bradley 2005b, Bradley and Nimura 2016, Welfare 2011). They differ from the stone circles discussed in the previous chapter in several key ways. First, like stone circles they comprise a ring of upright stones, but between the two tallest stones is a stone lying on its side: the recumbent. Second, there is evidence that many sites were constructed around pre-existing monuments, including cairns; this has implications for how they were used once constructed. Finally, this type of monument dates to the Beaker period. The excavations at Tomnaverie, Aberdeenshire, revealed an interesting sequence of events. The first activity on site was the creation of a low mound containing cremated human bone, possibly the site of a cremation pyre (Bradley 2005b, p. 105). This was then subsumed by a platform cairn, which was, in turn, remodelled when the recumbent stone circle was added (Bradley 2005b). Beaker pottery was found at the site, and while it is clear that this site saw activity over an extended period of time, it is likely that the recumbent stone circle was constructed sometime in the second half of the third millennium cal BC (Bradley 2005b, pp. 48–51). Tomnaverie also highlights the wider pattern of the use of distinctive coloured stones in recumbent stone circle architecture, particularly those which are red, grey and white, which included the

FIGURE 9.18
The recumbent stone circle at Easter Aquhorthies, Aberdeenshire

use of quartz. This makes these very visually striking monuments. Recumbent stone circles may also be aligned on the moon, again a shift from earlier stone circles which were concerned with the movements of the sun (see previous chapter).

While some stone circles are definitively late Neolithic in date, it is clear that this form of architecture was also constructed in the Beaker period and beyond, although perhaps on a smaller scale than the great stone circles of the late Neolithic. Bradley (2005b, pp. 102–103) suggests that the stone circles at Machrie Moor, Arran; Oddendale, Cumbria; and Balfarg, Fife, date to the Beaker period, and we could suggest that many other smaller stone circles in both Britain and Ireland date to this period as well (see Burl 1995). What is unclear at present is whether these monuments were constructed by the surviving descendants of Neolithic populations, or whether the new communities using Beakers were inspired by the monuments they encountered in the landscape and started building their own, albeit, smaller versions.

Clava cairns

The continued importance of circles of stone is highlighted in another regionally distinctive set of monuments also in Scotland: the Clava cairns, Highland. Some of these monuments consist of a central open chamber area entirely surrounded by a cairn which itself is enclosed by a free-standing stone circle, while others have a small passage leading from the chamber through the cairn (Bradley 2000b). These did not act as places for the deposition of quantities of human remains as early Neolithic chambered tombs did, although token burials were added to some sites (Bradley 2000b, p. 224). Instead, they were built close to settlements and in some cases on abandoned habitation sites. Moreover, these are monuments which are sometimes found in clusters, as is the case at the best-known site at Balnuaran of Clava which consists of seven separate monuments. Just like the recumbent stone circles, some of the Clava cairns use distinctive coloured stones in their architecture, and this may have enhanced connections with both the moon and the setting sun. It is likely that these monuments began to

FIGURE 9.19
Balnuaran of Clava

be constructed towards the end of the third millennium cal BC and continued into the second millennium cal BC (Bradley 2000b, p. 160), and they appear to be a localised architectural form based on wider understandings of the world and the cosmos.

CONCLUSIONS: LIFE AND DEATH AT THE TIME OF BEAKERS

This chapter has considered the evidence from the second half of the third millennium cal BC in Britain and Ireland, with a particular emphasis on new materials and practices which emerged at this time. It is clear that some distinctive forms of material culture were introduced by people from the continent, which included a new style of pottery, Beakers, along with barbed and tanged arrowheads, archer's wristguards and other objects of personal decoration. In addition to this, metal objects were produced, first copper and gold and later on, tin-bronze. These Beaker-associated objects are most clearly identified in the burial record along with a new burial practice, and in association with monuments. This new material culture is informative about certain aspects of life at this time. First, this is evidence of new incoming people who originated in mainland Europe; Beakers, Beaker-associated objects and metalworking have clear European origins and are found in many parts of Europe at this time, and the ancient DNA demonstrates the extensive movement of people in the second half of the third millennium cal BC. In the previous chapter it was argued that people in Britain and Ireland and those on mainland Europe may have not been in regular contact in the late Neolithic. In such a scenario the appearance of new people and new traditions of practice marks a major change and potentially indicates, although at present not definitively, a significant migration of people from the continent. Secondly, this Beaker phase involved considerable emphasis on personal ornamentation and objects used to decorate the body. Some interpretations would suggest that this was a reflection of the enhanced status of certain individuals at this time: elites who gained prestige through the control of the production of certain objects. It may have been more to do with the creation of a new social identity (Brück 2004) or even the establishment, once again, of new kinship networks.

It remains important to emphasise that Beaker material culture and burial practices were not found everywhere in Britain and Ireland after around 2450 cal BC. Instead, there were distinctive trajectories for Britain and Ireland, with further and considerable variations within those islands, which must represent the different histories and movements of people, both from the continent but also once they were resident on our islands. It has been noted that there were essentially Beaker enclaves or heartlands: in Britain these were eastern England, Wessex, the East Midlands, Yorkshire, the Peak District and eastern Scotland (Parker Pearson *et al*. 2019, p. 457). Other parts of Britain remained, at least at first, devoid of Beaker activities. In Ireland the early extraction and use of copper from the south-west of the island indicate one possible motivation for people to move there. However, there are no single inhumation Beaker burials from Ireland, perhaps indicative of a different source of people in this area, at least initially. The construction of wedge tombs and later on, Bowl burials, indicated a different trajectory of social expression in Ireland, but again with specific areas only seeing this activity (the west coast of Ireland predominantly). Much of western Britain, too, did not adopt the Beaker burial tradition, continuing instead to use monuments as locations for the negotiation of group affiliation and identity.

What does seem clear is that over this period the burial of the dead and new, smaller forms of monument replaced the use of the complexes used for the gathering of people and concomitant social negotiations in the late Neolithic. Nevertheless, the Beaker period in general saw the tail end of the use of the large monumental complexes and it seems likely that this may well represent the last big, public acts of the indigenous people. The new Beaker-era monuments varied from area to area and it is interesting that one of the most vibrant areas of monument construction was north-eastern Scotland, where recumbent stone circles, hengiforms and Clava cairns were all built between 2500 and 2000 cal BC. We might interpret this as an area of intense political negotiations at this time, and monument construction was the medium through which these negotiations took place. Although these monuments were smaller in scale than the largest monuments in the complexes from the late Neolithic many were also connected with burial. This may indicate an increased emphasis on the use of the dead in monumental spheres and may suggest that the dead were perceived to have a powerful role to play in the lives of the living. Monuments were not solely concerned with the burial of the dead, however, as celestial alignments and orientations within the landscape seem to have been important and may hint at the types of belief system in place at this time.

It has been argued, then, that Beakers and associated material culture including metalwork were employed at this time as a social strategy for creating new lines of descent and recreating new group identities in a new land. Lineages and descent also seem to have been played out in monumental form. Beaker burials, round mounds, even small hengiforms, were not just one-off events where the dead were buried and monuments were constructed commemorating them. Instead, they looked back to previous generations and earlier locations in the landscape, but with a firm focus on the creation, and recreation of their own, new identities (see Barrett 1994). This was not the rise of the individual or the emergence of social elites but the appearance and consolidation of groups concerned with their broader place in wide-ranging networks of early Bronze Age northern Europe and also the wider cosmos. It truly was the start of a new era for Britain and Ireland.

RECOMMENDED FURTHER READING

Ancient DNA evidence is neatly summarised in

Armit, I. and Reich, D., 2021. The return of the Beaker folk? Rethinking migration and population change in British prehistory. *Antiquity*, 95, 1464–1477.

Amesbury Archer and Boscombe Bowmen

Fitzpatrick, A., 2011. *The Amesbury Archer and the Boscombe Bowmen*. Salisbury: Wessex Archaeology.

Material culture

O'Brien, W., 2015. *Prehistoric copper mining in Europe*. Oxford: Oxford University Press.

Diet and mobility

Mike Parker Pearson, *et al.*, 2019. *The Beaker people: Isotopes, mobility and diet in prehistoric Britain*. Oxford: Oxbow.
Woodward, A. and Hunter, J., 2015. *Ritual in early Bronze Age grave goods*. Oxford: Oxbow.

Introduction to metalworking and the Irish Beaker period:

Monuments

Bradley, R., 2000b. *The good stones: A new investigation of the Clava cairns*. Edinburgh: Society of Antiquaries of Scotland.
Bradley, R., 2005b. *The moon and the bonfire: An investigation of three stone circles in north-east Scotland*. Edinburgh: Society of Antiquaries of Scotland.
Bradley, R., 2011. *Stages and screens. An investigation of four henges in northern and north-eastern Scotland*. Edinburgh: Society of Antiquaries of Scotland.
O'Brien, W., 1999. *Sacred ground. Megalithic tombs in coastal south-west Ireland*. Galway: Galway University Press.
Parker Pearson, M., *et al.*, 2022. *Stonehenge for the ancestors: Part two*. Leiden: Sidestone.

CHAPTER 10

The Neolithic of Britain and Ireland

Overview and future directions

INTRODUCTION

This final chapter presents a wider view on the material discussed within the previous chapters, beginning with a reflection on the changes made to the book since the first edition as well as a consideration of the broad picture and narrative. The chapter then goes on to pick up some of the key themes which have been discussed in a number of the chapters. For me, much of the most archaeologically visible remnants of the Neolithic were a product of social negotiations, and I am particularly keen on the idea that both architecture and material culture were often concerned about identity and kinship, in a number of cases connecting lineages of people with the broader cosmological sphere. Finally the chapter looks forward to highlight some of key research aims for future studies of this period. As such, this chapter is something of a personal reflection on the Neolithic period and the themes and issues which I have identified as important when writing the second edition of this book.

THE BIG PICTURE AS PRESENTED IN THE SECOND EDITION

Much of the detail in the first edition remains the same in this second edition: the form of the magnificent monuments we find in many parts of Britain and Ireland. Some of the most spectacular examples of early Neolithic monuments, such as the West Kennet long barrow in Wiltshire, Midhowe in Orkney and Brownshill in Ireland, from the middle Neolithic the passage tombs of Newgrange and Knowth in Co Meath, and from the late Neolithic Stonehenge, Avebury and the Ring of Brodgar, are some of the best-known sites which continue to dominate our narratives. This is because these monuments are the pinnacle of building in their respective time frames. Moreover, the objects that characterise the Neolithic and found in quantity in our museums continue to attract deserved emphasis due to their distinctive qualities: colour, polish and decoration in the case of stone axes, maceheads and carved stone balls.

While the sites and objects discussed in the first edition remain the same (with the addition of new sites discovered over the last decade) the narratives of this period are, in many instances in this second edition, radically different from those presented in the first edition. It is now clear that the Neolithic arrived into Britain and Ireland primarily through the arrival of people from continental Europe. This results in a very different interpretation of the earliest Neolithic practices on these islands, which, broadly speaking, can now be understood as making distinctive statements about being in a new place and creating new communities and social groupings in these new places.

This new perspective on the start and spread of the Neolithic has been brought about by the advent and wide application of the analysis of ancient DNA. These results have not just had an impact on the big picture. In Chapter 1 I introduced and discussed the results of the analysis of individuals from Hazleton North long cairn, where the genetic analysis of the people interred here in the early Neolithic have been interpreted as the remains of a new kinship group establishing a line of descent in this particular location. This feeds into wider debates on the nature of early Neolithic society. It now seems that the early Neolithic, once interpreted as a time of either egalitarianism or limited social hierarchies, may actually have been a period of considerable conflict and dissent. The numerous chambered tombs and causewayed enclosures found in some, if not all, parts of Britain and Ireland can be interpreted as the remains of groups being established at specific places in the landscape and marked out by monumental construction. However, these social statements appear to have been in need of constant renegotiation, and some of these ended in conflict and violence. The first 500 years of the establishment of Neolithic communities in Britain and Ireland may have been, socially at least, some of the most chaotic and dynamic.

Early Neolithic people excelled in their new home, spreading across our islands as far north as Shetland. They took domesticated animals and successfully grew cereals even in the Northern Isles. They did not rely on marine resources only using these in times of dire need. They quarried distinctive coloured stone from remote places and mined for flint, traditions which their forebears had practiced in continental Europe. Yet, by the middle part of the fourth millennium cal BC (the rather amorphous middle Neolithic), things had changed again. Archaeologically we can observe the decline in cereals and the cessation of monument construction throughout much of Britain. Conversely, some parts of Ireland and northern Scotland saw a new form of monument being built: the passage tomb. The genetic data are now being used to indicate a possible cause of this broad and rather mixed picture: the potential introduction of plague from Europe combined with an environmental downturn. This may, in turn, have had a knock-on effect of changing population numbers and perhaps the ways in which groups responded to illness and social interaction. This may have differed from region to region: in Ireland there is evidence of much wider connections at this time, with genetically related individuals being deposited at both Newgrange, Co. Meath, and Carrowkeel, Co. Sligo, sites found on the opposite sides of the island of Ireland. Similarities along the Atlantic façade more widely indicate ongoing, predominately seaborne connections.

The late Neolithic was once considered a time which saw the emergence of chiefdoms, 'big men' or an hereditary elite who were responsible for orchestrating huge numbers of people to build the vast monumental landscapes of the time, but this may now no longer be the preferred interpretation of this evidence. Instead, it may now be the case that this was actually a period of low population levels, widely dispersed in the landscape and relying more on pig than cattle, wild foods than cereals. Instead, people may only have come together at particular times of the year to labour and feast and socialise, although potentially in short bursts of activity, especially towards the end of the late Neolithic. Instead of an hereditary elite, it may have been short-lived aggrandisers motivating the bursts of monument construction set against a wider backdrop of change on the near continent. Finally, we now know that the onset of new practices which heralded the start of a new archaeological age, the Bronze Age, was also a result of incoming peoples, again confirmed through the genetic analyses of individuals in Britain, Ireland and the continent. The end of one era, the Neolithic, was therefore marked by exciting and dynamic changes in of both people and practices.

KEY THEMES

Identity and lineage

One of the key themes discussed repeatedly throughout the various chapters in this book is the construction of identity. It has been suggested that people came together, built monuments, used material culture and buried the dead all as part of the negotiation of identity, in particular in relation to lines of descent and wider sets of connections. This, it has been suggested throughout the book, is a more apposite way of understanding Neolithic social relations than the emergence of chiefdoms and the elite which has been dominant in discussions since Colin Renfrew's highly influential 1973 paper, 'Monuments, Mobilisation and Social Organisation'. While the construction of large passage graves like Newgrange, the building of monuments such as Stonehenge and the burial of individuals with lavish and exotic grave goods is most easily interpreted as the presence of influential leaders or chiefdoms, there is little evidence in other forms of life for this. There is very little sign of high levels of violence outside the early Neolithic of southern Britain, little evidence of different dwelling sizes (big houses for big men), no defensive structures of any kind and no evidence for restricted access to key resources. Compare the evidence from Neolithic Britain and Ireland to the Iron Age, and a very distinct set of differences is immediately obvious. Indeed, there is evidence that some parts of Britain and Ireland were only thinly or temporally occupied, meaning if people were unhappy, they could simply up and leave.

So why was identity so important to people? Why did it need to be constantly renegotiated?

It some ways it did not. The simple fact is that for most areas for most of the Neolithic, people seemed to have been living their lives without investing vast amounts of time in monuments or material culture that was time consuming to make. But, at certain key points it seems to have been contested, and we might look to how people conceptualised their origins from mainland Europe as one source of contention. However, other causes could have been catalysts, and these could have been anything from crop failure, illness and disease, all of which we have evidence for, to claims of witchcraft, sorcery or misfortune, which we might suggest would have been present at the time. Influential individuals such as aggrandisers at certain points may well have been involved, not necessarily holding positions of power but perhaps claiming divine knowledge or spiritual guidance. Various things may have been contested, from ownership of property through to resources or even people. These were all matters that could be resolved through groups being involved in particular activities, like building monuments or making material culture, and identities renegotiated. The small early Neolithic monuments (chambered tombs), perhaps representing specific kinship groups, were rapidly accompanied by larger group projects (e.g. causewayed enclosures and later on stone circles), indicative perhaps of larger corporate groups, and it is easy to see how the practice of building, with all the accompanying social dimensions, would have become the norm, embedded into yearly rounds and social routines. They would also have needed constant renegotiation.

Ongoing maritime connections

Throughout this book it has been argued that people were enmeshed in broader networks, specifically between Britain and Ireland but also further afield to mainland Europe. This was argued for the fifth millennium, at key points in the Neolithic and was certainly present with the start of the early Beaker period. The exact nature of these contacts probably varied over time. In some instances they may be best characterised as kin networks involving the exchange of marriage partners and maintaining ties with extended family groups. In some instances contact may have involved the exchange of various goods and relations were embedded in subsistence economies or trade networks. We should also not underestimate the importance of social engagements, parties, feasts, weddings and funerals alongside gossip and knowledge of the wider world as motives for people to maintain long-distant contacts in various ways.

Quite simply, moving around by boat would have been one of the easiest ways of maintaining contact in the Neolithic. The use of boats is most obvious in some areas such as the Scottish islands, where boat travel would have been a necessity, but it may well have been used by people throughout Britain and Ireland on rivers as much as the sea. In this regard it is interesting that people do not seem to have eaten foods from the sea, and it has been suggested that water was a crucial part of a sacred geography, which may also have involved the disposal of the dead.

As the Neolithic progressed, certain luminous centres seem to have developed which attracted people from a wider area. An early example is the complex of monuments at the Bru na Boinne, Co. Meath, which in the latter part of the fourth millennium cal BC saw intensive monument construction clearly involving people and materials from a wider area (see Chapter 6). This alteration of an entire landscape through monument construction was subsequently adopted more widely with the late Neolithic monumental complexes being constructed in the third millennium cal BC, and again some of these attracted people from a broad area. This has been most clearly demonstrated at

Stonehenge/Durrington Walls, where stones for the monuments came from south-west Wales and Scotland along with other people and things (see Parker Pearson 2012), but the location of monument complexes along axes of movement seems to have occurred at most sites. The interplay and similarities of architecture across a wide area in the late Neolithic indicates broad connections from the Northern Isles all the way down to southern England and across to Ireland but interestingly may not have regularly included continental Europe. Connectivity with Europe comes sharply into focus once more in the latter two centuries of the late Neolithic and then with the arrival of new peoples, marking the start of a new epoch in Britain and Ireland. Again, only sea travel and broad connections across north-west Europe can adequately explain the evidence from this period.

While there is evidence for connectivity between communities across Britain and Ireland, we should also note how different regions and areas had quite distinctive trajectories: in terms of monument forms, burial practices and material culture. These regional differences would have been clearly visible when people were engaging with others from the wider world and may well have been expressed in other ways too: clothing and hairstyles perhaps. It is also tempting to homogenise belief systems at different points in the Neolithic – but there is the genuine possibility that different sequences of monument construction, or even monument presences and absences (such as passage tombs), reflect differing belief systems in different parts of Britain and Ireland. Since we know the central importance and significance of belief for people, this may have meant that day-to-day practices, as well as ritual practice, varied quite considerably for people in different regions.

Here, then, it is worth noting that while this volume has separate chapters on life and monuments and mortuary practice, this was simply an organisational device and does not imply that monuments or mortuary practice had no bearing on everyday life. Indeed, several authors have been at pains to stress that there was no meaningful divide between ritual and domestic spheres in prehistory (see, for example, Bradley 2007, Brück 1999). This issue is worth reiterating again here. Monuments often discussed to in relation to belief systems and ritual practices would nevertheless have figured in people's everyday lives, at certain points quite prominently. In the same way, mortuary practices, now very much on the periphery of day-to-day life, may have figured much more in day-to-day life, with the human body itself a material substance that could be used by the living alongside stone, wood and clay. We have also seen in this book the interplay between the architecture of houses and monuments and how the two influenced one another.

LOOKING FORWARD: THE FUTURE OF NEOLITHIC STUDIES

I have painted a picture of life and death in the Neolithic, drawing on the data and different interpretations of the evidence; however, there is still much we do not know. Here are some of the areas which I hope we will have further insight into over the coming years.

Questions still to resolve:

- What were the push and pull factors for people on continental Europe in choosing to move to Britain and Ireland at the start of the fourth millennium? Was it a pioneering spirit and a sense of adventure? Was something on these islands particularly attractive to people? Was it the desire to start new lineages and kinship groups? It could easily be all of these and more, and we should not seek to reduce a long and complex process to a single causal event or factor.

- What precisely happened to the native hunter-gatherers of Britain and Ireland? There is limited and variable evidence of them having offspring with incoming Neolithic people, and they are therefore not hugely visible in the generic signature of subsequent Neolithic populations. Did they die out? Did they move to areas with other hunter-gatherer populations? Did they succumb to disease?

- What is the scale of contact within Britain and Ireland and over to the continent once the Neolithic was fully established? Did high levels of contact continue or were contacts more sporadic? This question is relevant for the early, middle and late Neolithic.

- What was the motivation for the construction of passage tombs in the middle Neolithic? Does this represent another influx of people from elsewhere or simply new practices, albeit ones with continental origins?

- What was the fate of the late Neolithic people of Britain and Ireland? Like the Mesolithic people before them, did they die out, move away or succumb to disease?

How might we answer these questions? Excavation will continue to provide important detail on the bigger picture. For me, excavation priorities are:

- Targeting sites with organic preservation. Chapter 4 in particular outlined what evidence we have for the use of organic materials, and more examples of these have the potential to make a critical comparison to durables such as stone tools.

- Large-scale projects which investigate entire landscapes, in particular in those areas which appear to be 'blank' or devoid of the classic Neolithic monuments. These areas are likely to be able to tell an interesting story and make a clear contrast to better-known sequences.

- Targeting sites dating to the middle Neolithic to fill in the gap between the early and late Neolithic monumental sequences.

It is not just excavation projects that have changed our understanding of the Neolithic. Extensive survey work, particularly aerial photography, has greatly enhanced our understanding of the use of landscapes and made visible entire types of monument especially those once constructed in wood. This has been successfully deployed in lowland Scotland where hitherto 'blank' areas are now filled with monuments and, in some cases, settlement. Geophysical survey is an important tool and is often used alongside excavation to investigate landscapes. Priorities now are:

- Expanding surveys to other, less-explored parts of Britain and Ireland, specifically western Ireland and upland Britain.

- The use of LiDAR to identify new sites.

The last 20 years have also been important in terms of scientific advances. The Bayesian modelling of the dates for the start and development of the early Neolithic have given us a new chronological framework through which to explore the arrival and spread of Neolithic people and things into Britain and Ireland. Stable isotope analysis and the analysis of lipids from ceramic vessels is much more commonplace and gives us new insights into the diets of people. Strontium isotope analysis is increasingly being deployed, and as this technique expands, further insights will be gained into the movements of people in the Neolithic. The study of ancient DNA will also continue to produce exciting results, and as we are currently seeing, results will expand out not just to explore broad patterns but details of relatedness at specific sites and relating to specific issues such as disease.

A continued engagement with archaeological theory remains critical for understanding and critiquing how we interpret the archaeological evidence. Insights gained from subject areas outside of archaeology are important for thinking critically about otherness and imagining other ways of being that may share some, if not all, similarities with life in the Neolithic. Clearly, then, there is still much to do in our attempts to understand this long and regionally diverse period of time. It is therefore exciting to think how the next phase of archaeological research will change our understanding of the Neolithic of Britain and Ireland. I have suggested some research priorities, and almost certainly new discoveries alongside refined scientific techniques and interpretations will provide more for us to consider. This will enable new interpretations and narratives to be written about this distinctive period of prehistory.

Bibliography

Affleck, T., 1983. Smitton (Carsphairn p), enclosure, Mesolithic flints. *Discovery and Excavation Scotland*, 5–6.

Albarella, U. and Payne, S., 2005. Neolithic pigs from Durrington Walls, Wiltshire, England: A biometrical database. *Journal of Archaeological Science*, 32, 589–599.

Albert, B. and Innes, J., 2020. On the distinction of pollen grains of early varieties of hordeum from glyceria species: Addressing the early cereal cultivation problem in palynology. *Palynology*, 44, 369–381.

Allen, M., Barclay, A., Cromarty, A. M., Anderson-Whymark, H., Parker, A., Robinson, M., and Jones, G., 2013. *Opening the wood, making the land*. Oxford: Oxford Archaeology.

Allen, M., Chan, B., Cleal, R., French, C., Marshall, P., Pollard, J., Pullen, R., Richards, C., Ruggles, C., Robinson, D., Rylatt, J., Thomas, J., Welham, K., and Parker Pearson, M., 2016. Stonehenge's avenue and 'Bluestonehenge'. *Antiquity*, 352, 991–1008.

Allen, M., Gardiner, J., and Sheridan, A., eds., 2012. *Is there a British chalcolithic? People, place and polity in the late 3rd millennium*. Oxford: Oxbow.

Allen, M. and Maltby, M., 2012. Chalcolithic land-use, animals and economy – a chronological changing point. *In*: M. Allen, J. Gardiner, and A. Sheridan, eds. *Is there a British chalcolithic? People, place and polity in the late 3rd millennium*. Oxford: Oxbow, 281–297.

Allentoft, M., Sikora, M., Refoyo-Martinez, A., et al., 2022. Population genomics of Stone Age Eurasia. *BioRXrv*. https://doi.org/10.1101/2022.05.04.490594

Ammerman, A. and Cavalli-Sforza, L., 1984. *The Neolithic transition and the genetics of populations in Europe*. Princeton, NJ: Princeton University Press.

Anderson-Whymark, H., 2012. Neolithic to early Bronze Age pit deposition practices and the temporality of occupation in the Thames Valley. *In*: H. Anderson-Whymark and J. Thomas, eds. *Regional perspectives on Neolithic pit deposition*. Oxford: Oxbow, 171–186.

Anderson-Whymark, H., Garrow, D., and Sturt, F., 2015. Microliths and maritime mobility: A continental European-style late Mesolithic flint assemblage from the Isles of Scilly. *Antiquity*, 89, 954–971.

Anderson-Whymark, H. and Thomas, J., eds., 2012. *Regional perspectives on Neolithic pit deposition*. Oxford: Oxbow.

Armit, I., 2003. The drowners: Permanence and transience in the Hebridean Neolithic. *In:* I. Armit, E. Murphy, E. Nelis, and D. Simpson, eds. *Neolithic settlement in Ireland and western Britain.* Oxford: Oxbow, 93–100.

Armit, I. and Reich, D., 2021. The return of the Beaker folk? Rethinking migration and population change in British prehistory. *Antiquity*, 95, 1464–1477.

Ashmore, P., 2004. Time, space and the standing stones round Calanais. *In:* A. Gibson and A. Sheridan, eds. *From sickles to circles.* Stroud: Tempus, 64–77.

Ashmore, P., 2011. *Calanais: Survey and excavation 1979–88.* Edinburgh: Historic Environment Scotland.

Baczkowski, J., 2019. Coming and goings. The wider landscape of early Neolithic flint mining in Sussex. *In:* A. Teather, P. Topping, and J. Baczkowski, eds. *Mining and quarrying in Neolithic Europe: A social perspective.* Oxford: Oxbow, 21–36.

Bailey, G. and Spikins, P., eds., 2008. *Mesolithic Europe.* Cambridge: Cambridge University Press.

Baker, L., Sheridan, A., and Cowie, T., 2003. An early Bronze Age 'dagger grave' from Rameldry farm, near Kingskettle, Fife. *Proceedings of the Society of Antiquaries of Scotland*, 133, 85–123.

Ballin, T. B., 2011. The Levallois-like approach of late Neolithic Britain. *In:* A. Saville, ed. *Flint and stone in the Neolithic period.* Oxford: Oxbow, 37–61.

Barber, J., 1997. *The excavation of a stalled cairn at the Point of Cott, Westray, Orkney.* Edinburgh: Scottish Trust for Archaeological Research.

Barber, M., 2003. *Bronze and the Bronze Age.* Stroud: Tempus.

Barber, M., Field, D., and Topping, P., 1999. *The Neolithic flint mines of England.* Swindon: English Heritage.

Barclay, A., 1999. Grooved Ware from the upper Thames region. *In:* R. Cleal and A. McSween, eds. *Grooved Ware in Britain and Ireland.* Oxford: Oxbow, 9–22.

Barclay, G., 2001. 'Metropolitan' and 'parochial'/'core' and 'periphery' a historiography of the Neolithic of Scotland. *Proceedings of the Prehistoric Society*, 67, 1–18.

Barclay, G., 2003. Neolithic settlement in the lowlands of Scotland. *In:* I. Armit, E. Murphy, E. Nelis, and D. Simpson, eds. *Neolithic settlement in Ireland and western Britain.* Oxford: Oxbow, 71–83.

Barclay, A., 2014. Horton's Neolithic houses. *Current Archaeology*, 292.

Barclay, A. and Bayliss, A., 1999. Cursus monuments and the radiocarbon problem. *In:* A. Barclay and J. Harding, eds. *Pathways and ceremonies: The cursus monuments of Britain and Ireland.* Oxford: Oxbow, 11–29.

Barclay, A., Field, D., and Leary, J., eds., 2020. *Houses of the dead?* Oxford: Oxbow.

Barclay, A. and Halpin, C., 1997. *Excavations at Barrow Hills, Radley, Oxfordshire. Volume 1: The Neolithic and Bronze Age complex.* Oxford: Oxbow.

Barclay, A. and Harding, J., eds., 1999. *Pathways and ceremonies: The cursus monuments of Britain and Ireland.* Oxford: Oxbow.

Barclay, G. and Maxwell, G., 1999. The Cleaven Dyke: A summary account of survey and excavation 1993–96. *In:* A. Barclay and J. Harding, eds. *Pathways and ceremonies: The cursus monuments of Britain and Ireland.* Oxford: Oxbow, 98–106.

Barclay, G. and Russell-White, C., eds., 1993. Excavations in the ceremonial complex of the fourth to second millennium at Balfarg/Balbirnie, Glenrothes, Fife. *Proceedings of the Society of Antiquaries of Scotland*, 123, 43–210.

Barker, C., 1992. *The chambered tombs of south-west Wales: A reassessment of the Neolithic burial monuments of Carmarthenshire and Pembrokeshire.* Oxford: Oxbow.

Barker, G., 2004. *The agricultural revolution in prehistory: Why did foragers become farmers?* Oxford: Oxford University Press.

Barnatt, J. and Edmonds, M., 2002. Places apart? Caves and monuments in Neolithic and earlier Bronze Age Britain. *Cambridge Archaeological Journal*, 12, 113–129.

Barrett, J., 1994. *Fragments from antiquity*. Oxford: Blackwell.

Barton, H., 2014. The persistence of hunting and gathering amongst farmers in south-east Asian in prehistory and beyond. *In:* V. Cummings, P. Jordan, and M. Zvelebil, eds. *The Oxford handbook of the archaeology and anthropology of hunter-gatherers*. Oxford: Oxford University Press, 857–880.

Barton, R., Berridge, P., Walker, M., and Bevins, R., 1995. Persistent places in the Mesolithic landscape: An example from the Black Mountain uplands of South Wales. *Proceedings of the Prehistoric Society*, 61, 81–116.

Barton, N. and Roberts, A., 2004. The Mesolithic period in England. *In:* A. Saville, ed. *Mesolithic Scotland and its neighbours*. Edinburgh: Society of Antiquaries of Scotland, 339–358.

Batchelor, C. R., Branch, N. P., Allison, E. A., *et al*., 2014. The timing and causes of the Neolithic elm decline: New evidence from the lower Thames Valley (London, UK). *Environmental Archaeology: The Journal of Human Palaeoecology*, 19 (3), 263–290.

Bayliss, A., Cartwright, C., Cook, G., Griffiths, G., Madgwick, R., Marshall, P., and Reimer, P., 2017. Rings of fire and Grooved Ware settlement at west Kennet, Wiltshire. *In:* P. Bickle, V. Cummings, D. Hoffman, and J. Pollard, eds. *The Neolithic of Europe*. Oxford: Oxbow.

Bayliss, A. and Whittle, A., 2007. Histories of the dead: Building chronologies for five southern British long barrows. *Cambridge Archaeological Journal*, 17 (1).

Bayliss, A., Whittle, A., and Wysocki, M., 2007. Talking about my generation: The date of the west Kennet long barrow. *Cambridge Archaeological Journal*, 17 (1), 85–101.

Bell, J. and Foley, C., 2005. *Excavations at Creggandevesky, Co. Tyrone*. Belfast: Queen's University Belfast.

Bell, M., 2007. *Prehistoric coastal communities: The Mesolithic of western Britain*. New York, NY: CBA.

Bender, B., ed., 1993. *Landscape: Politics and perspectives*. Oxford: Berg.

Benson, D. and Whittle, A., 2007. *Building memories: The Neolithic Cotswold long barrow at Ascott-under-Wychwood, Oxfordshire*. Oxford: Oxbow.

Bergh, S., 1995. *Landscape of the monuments: A study of the passage tombs in the Cúil Irra region, Co. Sligo*. Stockholm: Riksantikvarieämbet Arkeologska Undersöknigar.

Bergh, S. and Hensey, R., 2013. Unpicking the chronology of Carrowmore. *Oxford Journal of Archaeology*, 32, 343–366.

Bird-David, N., 1990. The giving environment: Another perspective on the economic system of gatherer-hunters. *Current Anthropology*, 31, 189–196.

Bishop, R., 2015. Did late Neolithic farming fail or flourish? *World Archaeology*, 47, 1–22.

Bishop, R., Church, M., and Rowley-Conwy, P., 2009. Cereals, fruits and nuts in the Scottish Neolithic. *Proceedings of the Society of Antiquaries of Scotland*, 139, 47–103.

Bishop, R., Grocke, D., Ralston, I., *et al*., 2022. Scotland's first farmers: New insights into early farming practices in north-west Europe. *Antiquity*, 96, 1087–1104.

Bogaard, A. and Jones, G., 2007. Neolithic farming in Britain and central Europe: Contrast or continuity? *In:* A. Whittle and V. Cummings, eds. *Going over: The Mesolithic-Neolithic transition in north-west Europe*. London: British Academy, 357–376.

Bollongino, R. and Burger, J., 2007. Neolithic cattle domestication as seen from ancient DNA. *In:* A. Whittle and V. Cummings, eds. *Going over*. London: British Academy, 165–187.

Bonsall, C., Sutherland, D., Tipping, R., and Cherry, J., 1990. The Eskmeals project. Late Mesolithic settlement and environment in north-west England. *In:* C. Bonsall, ed. *The Mesolithic in Europe*. Edinburgh: John Donald, 175–205.

Bostyn, F., Monchablon, C., Praud, I., and Vanmortfort, B., 2011. Le Néolithique Moyen II dans le sud-ouest du Bassin de I-Escault. *Revue archéologique de Picardie*, S28, 55–76.

Brace, S. and Booth, T. J., 2022. The genetics of the inhabitants of Neolithic Britain: A review. *In:* A. Whittle, J. Pollard, and S. Greaney, eds. *Ancient DNA and the European Neolithic*. Oxford: Oxbow, 123–146.

Brace, S., Diekmann, Y., Booth, T. J., *et al*., 2019. Ancient genomes indicate population replacement in early Neolithic Britain. *Nature Ecology & Evolution*, 3, 765–771. https://doi.org/10.1038/s41559-019-0871-9

Bradley, J., 1991. Excavations at Moynagh Lough, Co. Meath. *Journal of the Royal Society of Antiquaries of Ireland*, 121, 5–26.

Bradley, R., 1993. *Altering the earth*. Edinburgh: Society of Antiquaries of Scotland.

Bradley, R., 1997. *Rock art and the prehistory of Atlantic Europe*. London: Routledge.

Bradley, R., 1998. *The significance of monuments*. London: Routledge.

Bradley, R., 2000a. *The archaeology of natural places*. London: Routledge.

Bradley, R., 2000b. *The good stones: A new investigation of the Clava cairns*. Edinburgh: Society of Antiquaries of Scotland.

Bradley, R., 2003. A life less ordinary: The ritualization of the domestic sphere in later prehistoric Europe. *Cambridge Archaeological Journal*, 13, 5–23.

Bradley, R., 2005a. *Ritual and domestic life in prehistoric Europe*. London: Routledge.

Bradley, R., 2005b. *The moon and the bonfire: An investigation of three stone circles in north-east Scotland*. Edinburgh: Society of Antiquaries of Scotland.

Bradley, R., 2007. *The prehistory of Britain and Ireland*. Cambridge: Cambridge University Press.

Bradley, R., 2011. *Stages and screens. An investigation of four henges in northern and north-eastern Scotland*. Edinburgh: Society of Antiquaries of Scotland.

Bradley, R., 2012. *The idea of order*. Oxford: Oxford University Press.

Bradley, R., 2013. Houses of commons, houses of lords: Domestic dwellings and monumental architecture in prehistoric Europe. *Proceedings of the Prehistoric Society*, 79, 1–17.

Bradley, R., 2023. Long distance connections within Britain and Ireland: The evidence of insular rock art. *Proceedings of the Prehistoric Society*, 79, 1–17.

Bradley, R. and Edmonds, M., 1993. *Interpreting the axe trade: Production and exchange in Neolithic Britain*. Cambridge: Cambridge University Press.

Bradley, R. and Gordon, K., 1988. Human skulls from the River Thames, their dating and significance. *Antiquity*, 62, 503–509.

Bradley, R. and Nimura, C., 2016. *The use and reuse of stone circles*. Oxford: Oxbow.

Bradley, R. and Sanjuán, L., 2017. Sudden time. Natural disasters as a stimulus to monument building. *In:* P. Bickle, V. Cummings, D. Hofmann, and J. Pollard, eds. *Europe in the Neolithic*. Oxford: Oxbow.

Bradley, R., Cleal, R., Cook, M., Levitan, B., Mead, B., and Harman, M., 1992. The excavation of an oval barrow beside the Abingdon causewayed enclosure, Oxfordshire. *Proceedings of the Prehistoric Society*, 58, 127–142.

Bradley, R., Phillips, T., Richards, C., and Webb, M., 2001. Decorating the houses of the dead: Incised and pecked motifs in Orkney chambered tombs. *Cambridge Archaeological Journal*, 11, 45–67.

Bradley, R. and Watson, A., 2012. Ben Lawers: Carved rocks on a loud mountain. *In:* A. Cochrane and A. M. Jones, eds. *Visualising the Neolithic*. Oxford: Oxbow, 64–78.

Bray, P., 2012. Before 29Cu became copper. *In:* M. Allen, J. Gardiner, and A. Sheridan, eds. *Is there a British chalcolithic? People, place and polity in the late 3rd millennium*. Oxford: Oxbow, 56–70.

Brend, A., Card, N., Downes, J., Edmonds, M., and Moore, J., eds., 2020. *Landscapes revealed: Geophysical survey in the hearth of Neolithic Orkney world heritage area 2002–2011*. Oxford: Oxbow.

Brennand, M. and Taylor, M., 2003. The survey and excavation of a Bronze Age timber circle at Holme-next-the-Sea, Norfolk, 1998–9. *Proceedings of the Prehistoric Society*, 69, 1–84.

Brindley, A., 1999. Irish Grooved Ware. *In:* R. Cleal and A. McSween, eds. *Grooved Ware in Britain and Ireland*. Oxford: Oxbow, 23–35.

Britness, W., 2022. Gwernvale Neolithic long cairn reconsidered. *In:* W. Britnell and A. Whittle, eds. *The first stones: Penywyrlod, Gwernvale and the Black Mountains Neolithic long cairns of south-east Wales*. Oxford: Oxbow, 53–78.

Britnell, W. and Whittle, A., eds., 2022. *The first stones: Penywyrlod, Gwernvale and the Black Mountains Neolithic long cairns of south-east Wales*. Oxford: Oxbow.

Brodie, N., 1997. New perspectives on the Bell Beaker culture. *Oxford Journal of Archaeology*, 16, 297–314.

Brophy, K., 2000. Water coincidence? Cursus monuments and water. *In:* A. Ritchie, ed. *Neolithic Orkney in its European context*. Cambridge: McDonald Institute for Archaeological Research, 59–70.

Brophy, K., 2007. From big houses to cult houses: Early Neolithic timber halls in Scotland. *Proceedings of the Prehistoric Society*, 73, 75–96.

Brophy, K., 2016a. On ancient farms. *In:* K. Brophy, G. McGregor, and I. Ralston, eds. *The Neolithic of mainland Scotland*. Edinburgh: Edinburgh University Press, 200–235.

Brophy, K., 2016b. *Reading between the lines. The Neolithic cursus monuments of Scotland*. London: Routledge.

Brophy, K. and McGregor, G., 2016. *The Neolithic of mainland Scotland*. Edinburgh: Edinburgh University Press.

Brophy, K. and Millican, K., 2015. Wood and fire: Scotland's timber cursus monuments. *Archaeological Journal*, 172, 287–324.

Brophy, K. and Noble, G., 2012. Within and beyond pits. *In:* H. Anderson-Whymark and J. Thomas, eds. *Regional perspectives on Neolithic pit deposition*. Oxford: Oxbow, 63–76.

Brown, A., 2007. Dating the onset of cereal cultivation in Britain and Ireland: The evidence from charred cereal grains. *Antiquity*, 81, 1042–1052.

Brück, J., 1999. Ritual and rationality: Some problems of interpretation in European archaeology. *European Journal of Archaeology*, 2, 313–344.

Brück, J., 2004. Material metaphors. The relational construction of identity in early Bronze Age burials in Ireland and Britain. *Journal of Social Archaeology*, 4, 307–333.

Burgess, C. and Shennan, S., 1976. The Beaker phenomenon: Some suggestions. *In:* C. Burgess and R. Miket, eds. *Settlement and economy in the third and second millennia BC*. Oxford: BAR.

Burl, A., 1995. *A guide to the stone circles of Britain, Ireland and Brittany*. New Haven, CT: Yale University Press.

Butler, C., 2005. *Prehistoric flintwork*. Stroud: History Press.

Byrne, G., Warren, G., Rathbone, S., McIlreavy, D., and Walsh, P., 2009. *Archaeological excavations at Racklackan*. Dublin: UCD.

Callaghan, R. and Scarre, C., 2009. Simulating the western seaways. *Oxford Journal of Archaeology*, 28, 357–372.

Cannon, A., 2011. Cosmology and everyday perception in northwest coast production, reproduction and settlement. *In:* A. Cannon, ed. *Structured worlds: The archaeology of hunter-gatherer thought and action*. Oakville: Equinox, 54–68.

Card, N., 2015. *The Ness of Brodgar*. Kirkwall: Ness of Brodgar Trust.

Card, N., Edmonds, M., and Mitchell, A., 2020a. As it stands. *In:* N. Card, M. Edmonds, and A. Mitchell, eds. *The ness of Brodgar: As it stands*. Kirkwall: The Orcadian, 334–347.

Card, N., Edmonds, M., and Mitchell, A., eds., 2020b. *The ness of Brodgar: As it stands*. Kirkwall: The Orcadian.

Card, N. and Thomas, A., 2012. Painting a picture of Neolithic Orkney: Decorated stonework from the Ness of Brodgar. *In:* A. Cochrane and A. M. Jones, eds. *Visualising the Neolithic*. Oxford: Oxbow, 111–124.

Carlin, N., 2011. Into the west: Placing Beakers within their Irish contexts. *In:* A. Jones and G. Kirkham, eds. *Beyond the core*. Oxford: Oxbow, 87–100.

Carlin, N. and Brück, J., 2012. Searching for the Chalcolithic: Continuity and change in the Irish final Neolithic. *In:* M. Allen, J. Gardiner, and A. Sheridan, eds. *Is there a British chalcolithic? People, place and polity in the late 3rd millennium*. Oxford: Oxbow, 193–210.

Carlin, N. and Cooney, G., 2020. On the sea roads: The ebb and flow of links with a wider world. *In:* N. Card, M. Edmonds, and A. Mitchell, eds. *The Ness of Brodgar: As it stands*. Kirkwall: The Orcadian, 320–333.

Case, H., 2004. Bell Beaker and Corded Ware culture burial associations. *In:* A. Gibson and A. Sheridan, eds. *From sickles to circles*. Stroud: Tempus, 201–214.

Cassen, S., ed., 2009. *Autour de la Table: Explorations archéologiques et discours savants sur des architectures néolithiques à Locmariaquer, Morbihan (Table des Marchands et Grand Menhir)*. Nantes: Laboratoire de recherches archeologiques, CNRS & Universitaires de Nantes.

Cassen, S., Audren, C., Hinguant, S., Lannuzel, G., and Marchand, G., 1998. L'habitat Villeneuve-Saint-Germain du Haut-Mée (Saint-Étienne-en-Coglès, Ille-et-Vilaine). *Bulletin de la Société préhistorique française*, 95, 41–75.

Cassidy, L., Martiniano, R., Murphy, E., Teasdale, M., Mallory, J., Hartwell, B., and Bradley, D., 2016. Neolithic and Bronze Age migration to Ireland and establishment of the insular Atlantic genome. *Proceedings of the National Academy of Sciences*, 113, 368–373.

Cassidy, L. M., Maoldúin, R. Ó., Kador, T., *et al*., 2020. A dynastic elite in monumental Neolithic society. *Nature*, 582, 384–388. https://doi.org/10.1038/s41586-020-2378-6

Caulfield, S., 1988. *Ceide fields and Belderrig guide*. Killala: Morrigan.

Chambon, P. and Thomas, A., 2010. The first monumental cemeteries of western Europe: The 'Passy type' necropolis in the Paris Basin around 4500 BC. *Journal of Neolithic Archaeology*, 37.

Chan, B., 2010. Durrington Walls then and now. *Lithics*, 31, 44–54.

Chan, B., 2011. Stonehenge, looking from the inside out. *In:* A. Saville, ed. *Flint and stone in the Neolithic period*. Oxford: Oxbow, 116–138.

Chatterton, R., 2003. South Haw, northern England. An upland Mesolithic site in context. *In:* C. Waddington and K. Pedersen, eds. *Mesolithic studies in the north sea Basin and beyond*. Oxford: Oxbow, 69–80.

Chatterton, R., 2006. Ritual. *In:* C. Conneller and G. Warren, eds. *Mesolithic Britain and Ireland. New approaches*. Stroud: Tempus, 101–120.

Childe, V. G., 1925. *The dawn of European civilisation*. London: Kegan Paul.

Childe, V. G., 1931. *Skara brae*. London: Kegan Paul.

Clarke, A., Kirkland, C., Bevins, R., Pearce, N., Glorie, S., and Ixer, R., 2024. A Scottish provenance for the Altar Stone of Stonehenge. *Nature*, 632, 570–575.

Clarke, D., 1970. *Beaker pottery of Great Britain and Ireland*. Cambridge: Cambridge University Press.

Clarke, D., Cowie, T., and Foxon, A., 1985. *Symbols of power at the time of Stonehenge*. Edinburgh: HMSO.

Clay, P., 1998. Neolithic/early Bronze Age pit circles and their environs at Oakham, Rutland. *Proceedings of the Prehistoric Society*, 64, 293–330.

Clay, P. and Salisbury, C. R., 1990. Norman mill dam and other sites at Hemington fields, Castle Donington, Leicestershire. *Archaeological Journal*, 147, 276–307.

Cleal, R., 1999. Introduction. *In:* R. Cleal and A. McSween, eds. *Grooved Ware in Britain and Ireland*. Oxford: Oxbow, 1–8.

Cleal, R., 2004. The dating and diversity of the earliest ceramics of Wessex and south-west England. *In:* R. Cleal and J. Pollard, eds. *Monuments and material culture*. East Knoyle: Hobnob, 164–192.

Cleal, R. and McSween, A., 1999. *Grooved Ware in Britain and Ireland*. Oxford: Oxbow.

Cleal, R. and Pollard, J., 2012. The revenge of the native. *In:* M. Allen, J. Gardiner, and A. Sheridan, eds. *Is there a British chalcolithic? People, place and polity in the late 3rd millennium*. Oxford: Oxbow, 317–332.

Cleary, R. and Kelleher, H., 2011. *Archaeological excavations at Tullahedy, County Tipperary: Neolithic settlement in north Munster*. Cork: Collins.

Clough, T. and Cummins, W., eds., 1988. *Stone axe studies: Volume two*. London: Council for British Archaeology.

Cochrane, A. and Jones, A. M., eds., 2012. *Visualising the Neolithic*. Oxford: Oxbow.

Coles, J., 1971. The early settlement of Scotland: Excavations at Morton, Fife. *Proceedings of the Prehistoric Society*, 37, 284–366.

Coles, B. and Coles, J., 1986. *From sweet track to Glastonbury*. London: Thames and Hudson.

Coles, S., Ford, S., and Taylor, A., 2008. An early Neolithic grave and occupation, and an early Bronze Age hearth on the Thames foreshore at Yabsley Street, Blackwall, London. *Proceedings of the Prehistoric Society*, 74, 215–233.

Collins, A. E. P., 1954. The excavation of a double horned cairn at Audleystown, Co. Down. *Ulster Journal of Archaeology*, 17, 7–56.

Conneller, C., 2006. Death. *In:* C. Conneller and G. Warren, eds. *Mesolithic Britain and Ireland. New approaches*. Stroud: Tempus, 139–164.

Conneller, C., 2022. *The Mesolithic in Britain*. London: Routledge.

Conneller, C. and Warren, G., eds., 2006. *Mesolithic Britain and Ireland. New approaches*. Stroud: Tempus.

Connock, D., Finlayson, B., and Mills, K., 1993. The excavation of a shell midden site at Carding Mill Bay, near Oban, Scotland. *Glasgow Archaeological Journal*, 17, 25–38.

Cooney, G., 2000. *Landscapes of Neolithic Ireland*. London: Routledge.

Cooney, G., 2023. *Death in Irish prehistory*. Dublin: Royal Irish Academy.

Cooney, G., Megarry, W., Markham, M., *et al.*, 2019. Tangled up in blue. The role of riebeckite felsite in Neolithic Shetland. *In:* A. Teather, P. Topping, and J. Baczkowski, eds. *Mining and quarrying in Neolithic Europe: A social perspective*. Oxford: Oxbow, 49–66.

Cooper, A., Garrow, D., Gibson, C., Giles, M., and Wilkin, N., 2022. *Grave goods: Objects and death in later prehistoric Britain*. Oxford: Oxbow.

Copley, M. S., Berstan, R., Dudd, S. N., Mukherjee, A. J., Straker, V., Payne, S., and Evershed, R. P., 2005. Dairying in antiquity. III. Evidence from absorbed lipid residues dating to the British Neolithic. *Journal of Archaeological Science*, 32, 523–546.

Copper, A. and Armit, I., 2018. A conservative party? Pots and people in the Hebridean Neolithic. *Proceedings of the Prehistoric Society*, 84.

Copper, M. and Whittle, A., 2023. Introduction. *In:* M. Copper, A. Whittle, and A. Sheridan, eds. *Revisiting Grooved Ware*. Oxford: Oxbow, 1–18.

Copper, M., Whittle, A., and Sheridan, A., eds., 2023. *Revisiting Grooved Ware*. Oxford: Oxbow.

Corcoran, J. X. W. P., 1969a. The Cotswold-severn group. *In:* T. G. E. Powell, J. X. W. P. Corcoran, F. Lynch, and J. G. Scott, eds. *Megalithic enquiries in the west of Britain*. Liverpool: Liverpool University Press, 13–72.

Corcoran, J. X. W. P., 1969b. Excavation of two chambered tombs at mid Gleniron farm, Glenluce. *Transactions of the Dumfries and Galloway Natural History and Antiquarian Society*, 46, 29–90.

Counihan, C., ed., 1999. *Anthropology of food and gender*. London: Routledge.

Cowie, T. and McSween, A., 1999. Grooved Ware from Scotland: A review. *In:* R. Cleal and A. McSween, eds. *Grooved Ware in Britain and Ireland*. Oxford: Oxbow, 48–56.

Craig, O., Shillito, L. M., Albarella, U., *et al.*, 2015. Feeding Stonehenge: Cuisine and consumption at the late Neolithic site of Durrington Walls. *Antiquity*, 89, 1096–1109.

Crockett, A., Allen, M., and Scaife, R., 2002. A Neolithic trackway within peat deposits at Silvertown, London. *Proceedings of the Prehistoric Society*, 68, 185–214.

Crombé, P. and Vanmortfort, B., 2007. The Neolithisation of the Scheldt basin in western Belgium. *In:* A. Whittle and V. Cummings, eds. *Going over: The Mesolithic-Neolithic transition in north-west Europe*. London: British Academy, 263–285.

Cross, S., 2003. Irish Neolithic settlement architecture – a reappraisal. *In:* I. Armit, E. Murphy, E. Nelis, and D. Simpson, eds. *Neolithic settlement in Ireland and western Britain*. Oxford: Oxbow, 195–202.

Crown, P. and Wills, W., 1995. Economic intensification and the origins of ceramic containers in the American southwest. *In:* W. Barnett and J. Hoopes, eds. *The emergence of pottery*. Washington, DC: Smithsonian, 241–254.

Crozier, R., Richards, C., Robertson, J., and Challands, A., 2016. Re-orientating the dead of Crossiecrown: Quanterness & Ramberry Head. *In:* C. Richards and R. Jones, eds. *The development of Neolithic house societies in Orkney*. Oxford: Windgather, 196–223.

Cummings, V., 2007. *The anthropology of hunter-gatherers: Key themes for archaeologists*. London: Duckworth.

Cummings, V., 2009. *A view from the west: The Neolithic of the Irish Sea zone*. Oxford: Oxbow.

Cummings, V., 2014. Hunting and gathering in a farmers' world. *In:* V. Cummings, P. Jordan, and M. Zvelebil, eds. *The Oxford handbook of the archaeology and anthropology of hunter-gatherers*. Oxford: Oxford University Press, 767–786.

Cummings, V., Barton, R., Brend, A., and Reay, D., Forthcoming. The excavation of a Neolithic and Bronze Age domestic and funerary complex on the Hill of Crooksetter, Delting, Shetland. *In:* V. Cummings, J. Downes, and C. Richards, eds., *Neolithic occupation in Orkney and Shetland: New research*.

Cummings, V., Downes, J., and Richards, C., eds., Forthcoming. *Neolithic occupation in Orkney and Shetland: New research*.

Cummings, V. and Fowler, C., 2023. Materialising descent: Lineage formation and transformation in early Neolithic southern Britain. *Proceedings of the Prehistoric Society*, 89, 1–21.

Cummings, V. and Harris, O., 2011. Animals, people and places: The continuity of hunting and gathering practices across the Mesolithic-Neolithic transition in Britain. *European Journal of Archaeology*, 14 (3), 361–382.

Cummings, V. and Harris, O., 2014. The continuity of hunting and gathering in a farmer's world in Britain and Ireland. *In:* V. Cummings, P. Jordan, and M. Zvelebil, eds. *Oxford handbook of the archaeology and anthropology of hunter gatherers*. Oxford: Oxford University Press.

Cummings, V., Hoffman, D., Bjornevad-Ahlqvist, M., and Iversen, R., 2022. Muddying the waters: Reconsidering migration in the Neolithic of Britain, Ireland and Denmark. *Danish Journal of Archaeology*, 11, 1–25.

Cummings, V. and Morris, J., 2022. Neolithic explanations revisited: Modelling the arrival and spread of domesticated animals into Neolithic Britain and Ireland. *Environmental Archaeology*, 27.

Cummings, V. and Richards, C., 2013. The peristalith and the context of Calanais: Transformational architecture in the Hebridean early Neolithic. *In:* C. Richards, ed. *Building the great stone circles of the north*. Oxford: Windgather, 186–200.

Cummings, V. and Richards, C., 2017. Passage graves as material technologies of wrapping. *In:* P. Bickle, V. Cummings, D. Hoffman, and J. Pollard, eds. *The Neolithic of Europe*. Oxford: Oxbow.

Cummings, V. and Richards, C., 2021. *Monuments in the making. Building the great dolmens of early Neolithic northern Europe*. Oxford: Oxbow.

Cummings, V. and Robinson, G., 2015. *The Southern Kintyre project: Exploring social interactions across the Irish Sea from the Mesolithic to the Bronze Age*. Oxford: British Archaeological Reports, 618.

Cummings, V. and Whittle, A., 2004. *Places of special virtue: Megaliths in the Neolithic landscapes of Wales*. Oxford: Oxbow.

Damm, C. and Forsberg, L., 2014. Forager-farmer contacts in northern Fennoscandia. *In:* V. Cummings, P. Jordan, and M. Zvelebil, eds. *The Oxford handbook of the archaeology and anthropology of hunter-gatherers*. Oxford: Oxford University Press, 838–856.

Darvill, T., 1996. Neolithic buildings in England, Wales and the Isle of Man. *In:* T. Darvill and J. Thomas, eds. *Neolithic houses in north-west Europe and beyond*. Oxford: Oxbow, 77–112.

Darvill, T., 2004. *Long barrows of the Cotswolds and surrounding areas*. Stroud: Tempus.

Darvill, T., 2006. *Stonehenge: The biography of a landscape*. Stroud: Tempus.

Darvill, T. and Andrews, K., 2014. Polychrome pottery from the later Neolithic of the Isle of Man. *Cambridge Archaeological Journal*, 24 (3), 531–541.

David, A., 2007. *Palaeolithic and Mesolithic settlement in Wales: With special reference to Dyfed*. Oxford: British Archaeological Report.

Davies, O., 1949. Excavations at the horned cairn of Ballymarlagh, Co. Antrim. *Ulster Journal of Archaeology*, 12, 26–42.

Davis, S. and Payne, S., 1993. A barrow full of cattle skulls. *Antiquity*, 67, 12–22.

De Valera, D., 1960. The court cairns of Ireland. *Proceedings of the Royal Irish Academy*, 60, 1–139.

Dietrich, O., Heun, M., Notroff, J., Schmidt, K., and Zarnkow, M., 2012. The role of cult and feasting in the emergence of Neolithic communities. New evidence from Gobekli Tepe, south-eastern Turkey. *Antiquity*, 86, 674–695.

Dineley, M. and Dineley, G., 2000. Neolithic ale: Barley as a source of malt sugars for fermentation. *In:* A. Fairbairn, ed. *Plants in Neolithic Britain and beyond*. Oxford: Oxbow, 137–153.

Douglas, M., 1966. *Purity and danger: An analysis of the concepts of pollution and taboo*. London: Routledge and Kegan Paul.

Dowd, M., 2015. *The archaeology of caves in Ireland*. Oxford: Oxbow.

Downes, J. and Richards, C., 2025. *Animating the dead: An archaeology of Bronze Age burial practices in Orkney*. Oxford: Oxbow.

Drew, C. and Piggott, S., 1936. The excavation of long barrow 163a on Thickthorn Down, Dorset. *Proceedings of the Prehistoric Society*, 2, 77–96.

Drewett, P., 1977. The excavation of a Neolithic causewayed enclosure at Offham Hill, East Sussex. *Proceedings of the Prehistoric Society*, 42, 201–241.

Driscoll, K., 2009. Constructing later Mesolithic landscapes. *In:* N. Finlay, S. McCartan, N. Milner, and C. Wickham Jones, eds. *From Bann Flakes to Bushmills*. Oxford: Oxbow, 101–112.

Dronfield, J., 1996. Entering alternative realities: Cognition, art and architecture in Irish passage tombs. *Cambridge Archaeological Journal*, 6 (1), 37–72.

Eadie, G. and Waddington, C., 2013. *Rescue recording of an eroding inter-tidal peat bed at Low Hauxley, Northumberland*. Gateshead: Archaeological Research Services.

Edinborough, K., Shennan, S., Teather, A., *et al*., 2020. New radiocarbon dates show early Neolithic date of flint-mining and stone quarrying in Britain. *Radiocarbon*, 62 (1), 1–31.

Edmonds, M., 1992. Their use is wholly unknown. *In:* N. Sharples and A. Sheridan, eds. *Vessels for the ancestors: Essays on the Neolithic of Britain and Ireland*. Edinburgh: Edinburgh University Press, 179–193.

Edmonds, M., 1995. *Stone tools and society*. London: Batsford.

Edmonds, M., 1998. *Ancestral geographies of the Neolithic*. London: Routledge.

Edmonds, M., 2019. *Orcadia: Land, sea and stone in Neolithic Orkney*. London: Head of Zeus.

Edmonds, M., Sheridan, A., and Tipping, R., 1992. Survey and excavation at Creag na Caillich, Killin, Perthshire. *Proceedings of the Society of Antiquaries of Scotland*, 122, 77–112.

Edwards, K., 1996. The contribution of Tom Affleck to the study of the Mesolithic of southwest Scotland. *In:* T. Pollard and A. Morrison, eds. *The early prehistory of Scotland*. Edinburgh: Edinburgh University Press, 108–222.

Elliott, B., 2015. Facing the chop: Redefining British antler mattocks to consider larger-scale maritime networks in the early fifth millennium cal BC. *European Journal of Archaeology*, 18, 222–244.

Ellis, C., Crone, A., Reilley, E., and Hughes, P., 2002. Excavation of a Neolithic wooden platform, Stirlingshire. *Proceedings of the Prehistoric Society*, 68, 247–256.

Eogan, G., 1986. *Knowth and the passage tombs of Ireland*. London: Thames and Hudson.

Eogan, G. and Cleary, K., 2017. *Excavations at Knowth 6. The passage tomb archaeology of the great mound at Knowth*. Dublin: Royal Irish Academy.

Eogan, G. and Richardson, H., 1982. Two maceheads from Knowth, County Meath. *The Journal of the Royal Society of Antiquaries of Ireland*, 112, 123–138.

Evans, C. and Hodder, I., 2006. *A woodland archaeology: Neolithic sites at Haddenham: The Haddenham project volume 1*. Cambridge: McDonald Institute for Archaeological Research.

Evans, E. E., 1938. Dooey's cairn, Dunloy, County Antrim. *Ulster Journal of Archaeology*, 1, 59–78.

Evans, E. E., 1973. *The personality of Ireland*. Cambridge: Cambridge University Press.

Evans, H., 2008. *Neolithic and Bronze Age landscapes of Cumbria*. Oxford: British Archaeological Reports.

Evans, N., Montgomery, J., and Scarre, C., 2016. Isotopic evidence for residential mobility of farming communities during the transition to agriculture in Britain. *Royal Society Open Science*, 3, 150522.

Fairbairn, A., 2000. On the spread of crops across Neolithic Britain, with special reference to southern England. *In:* A. Fairnbairn, ed. *Plants in Neolithic Britain and beyond*. Oxford: Oxbow, 107–121.

Fairweather, A. and Ralston, I., 1993. The Neolithic timber hall at Balbridie, Grampion region, Scotland: The building, the date, the plant macrofossils. *Antiquity*, 67, 313–323.

Farrell, M., Bunting, M. J., Lee, D., and Thomas, A., 2014. Neolithic settlement at the woodland's edge: Palynological data and timber architecture in Orkney, Scotland. *Journal of Archaeological Science*, 51, 225–236.

Fernandes, D. M., Strapagiel, D., Borówka, P., *et al*., 2018. Genomic Neolithic time transect of hunter-farmer admixture in central Poland. *Nature Scientific Reports*, 8, 14879.

Fernandez, E., and Reynolds, L., 2019. The Mesolithic-Neolithic transition in Europe: A perspective from ancient human DNA. *In*: O. Garcia Puchol and D. Salazr-Garcia, eds., *Times of Neolithic transition along the western Mediterranean*. Springer, 311–338.

Fernández-Dominguez, E., 2022. Ancient DNA of near eastern populations: The knowns and unknowns. *In:* A. Whittle, J. Pollard, and S. Greaney, eds. *Ancient DNA and the European Neolithic*. Oxford: Oxbow, 63–77.

Field, D., 2006. *Earthen long barrows*. Stroud: Tempus.

Finlay, N., Cerón-Carrasco, R., Housley, R., *et al*., 2019. Calling time on Oronsay: Revising settlement models around the Mesolithic – Neolithic transition in western Scotland, new evidence from Port Lobh, Colonsay. *Proceedings of the Prehistoric Society*, 85, 83–114.

Fitzpatrick, A., 2011. *The Amesbury Archer and the Boscombe Bowmen*. Salisbury: Wessex Archaeology.

Fokkens, H., 2012. Dutchmen on the move? *In:* M. Allen, J. Gardiner, and A. Sheridan, eds. *Is there a British chalcolithic? People, place and polity in the late 3rd millennium*. Oxford: Oxbow, 115–125.

Fokkens, H., Achterkamp, Y., and Kuijpers, M., 2008. Bracers or bracelets? About the functionality and meaning of Bell Beaker wrist-guards. *Proceedings of the Prehistoric Society*, 74, 109–140.

Forsythe, W. and Gregory, N., 2007. A Neolithic logboat from Greyabbey Bay, Co. Down. *Ulster Journal of Archaeology*, 66, 6–13.

Fowler, C., 2004a. In touch with the past? *In:* V. Cummings and C. Fowler, eds. *The Neolithic of the Irish sea: Materiality and traditions of practice*. Oxford: Oxbow, 91–102.

Fowler, C., 2004b. *The archaeology of personhood*. London: Routledge.

Fowler, C., 2010. Pattern and diversity in the early Neolithic mortuary practices of Britain and Ireland: Contextualising the treatment of the dead. *Documenta Praehistorica*, 37, 1–22.

Fowler, C., 2013. *The emergent past: A relational realist archaeology of early Bronze Age mortuary practice*. Oxford: Oxford University Press.

Fowler, C., 2021. Ontology in Neolithic Britain and Ireland: Beyond animism. *Religions*, 12. https://doi.org/10.3390/rel12040249

Fowler, C., 2022. Social arrangements. Kinship, descent and affinity in the mortuary architecture of early Neolithic Britain and Ireland. *Archaeological Dialogues*, 29, 67–88.

Fowler, C., Harding, J., and Hofmann, D., eds., 2015. *The Oxford handbook of Neolithic Europe*. Oxford: Oxford University Press.

Fowler, C., Olalde, I., Cummings, V., *et al*., 2021. Complex kinship practices revealed in a five-generation family from Neolithic Britain. *Nature*, 601, 584–587.

Fowler, C. and Wilkin, N., 2016. Early Bronze Age mortuary practices in north-east England and south-east Scotland. *In:* R. Crellin, C. Fowler, and R. Tipping, eds. *Prehistory without borders*. Oxford: Oxbow, 112–135.

Fox, C., 1932. *The personality of Britain*. Cardiff: National Museum of Wales.

Framework Archaeology, 2011. *Landscape evolution in the middle Thames Valley*. Salisbury: Wessex Archaeology.

Fraser, M., Sanchez-Quinto, F., Evans, J., *et al*., 2018. New insights on cultural dualism and population structure in the middle Neolithic Funnel Beaker culture on the island of Gotland. *Journal of Archaeological Science: Reports*, 17, 325–334.

Fredengren, C., 2002. *Crannogs*. Dublin: Wordwell.

Fredengren, C., 2009. Lake platforms at Lough Kinale – memory, reach and place: A discovery programme project in the Irish Midlands. *In:* S. McCartan, R. Schulting, G. Warren, and P. Woodman, eds. *Mesolithic horizons*. Oxford: Oxbow, 882–886.

Gaffney, V., Baldwin, E., Bates, M., et al., 2020. A massive late Neolithic pit structure associated with Durrington Walls henge. *Internet Archaeology*, 55. https://doi.org/10.11141/ia.55.4

Garrow, D., 2007. Placing pits: Landscape occupation and depositional practice during the Neolithic in east Anglia. *Proceedings of the Prehistoric Society*, 73, 1–24.

Garrow, D. and Sturt, F., 2011. Grey waters bright with Neolithic argonauts? Maritime connections and the Mesolithic-Neolithic transition within the 'western seaways' of Britain, c. 5000–3500 BC. *Antiquity*, 85, 59–72.

Garrow, D. and Sturt, F., 2019. Neolithic crannogs: Rethinking settlement, monumentality and deposition in the Outer Hebrides and beyond. *Antiquity*, 93.

Garrow, D. and Wilkin, M., 2022. *The world of Stonehenge*. London: British Museum Press.

Garwood, P., 1999. Grooved Ware in Southern Britain: Chronology and interpretation. *In:* R. Cleal and A. McSween, eds. *Grooved Ware in Britain and Ireland*. Oxford: Oxbow, 145–176.

Garwood, P., 2007. Before the hills in order stood: Chronology, time and history in the interpretation of early Bronze Age round barrows. *In:* J. Last, ed. *Beyond the grave*. Oxford: Oxbow, 30–52.

Garwood, P., 2012. The present dead. *In:* M. Allen, J. Gardiner, and A. Sheridan, eds. *Is there a British chalcolithic? People, place and polity in the late 3rd millennium*. Oxford: Oxbow, 298–316.

Geber, J., Hensey, R., Meehan, P., Moore, S., and Kador, T., 2017. Facilitating transitions: Post-mortem processing of the dead at the Carrowkeel passage tomb complex, Ireland (3500–3000 cal. B.C.). *Bioarchaeology International*, 1, 35–51.

Gibson, A., 1996. The later Neolithic structures at Trelystan, Poweys, Wales: Ten years on. *In:* T. Darvill and J. Thomas, eds. *Neolithic houses in north-west Europe and beyond*. Oxford: Oxbow, 133–141.

Gibson, A., 1998. *Stonehenge and timber circles*. Stroud: Tempus.

Gibson, A., 1999. *The Walton Basin project: Excavation and survey in a prehistoric landscape 1993–7*. London: CBA.

Gibson, A., 2002a. *Prehistoric pottery in Britain and Ireland*. Stroud: Tempus.

Gibson, A., 2002b. The later Neolithic palisaded sites of Britain. *In:* A. Gibson, ed. *Behind wooden walls*. Oxford: British Archaeological Reports, 5–23.

Gibson, A., 2003. What do we mean by Neolithic settlement? Some approaches, 10 years on. *In:* I. Armit, E. Murphy, E. Nelis, and D. Simpson, eds. *Neolithic settlement in Ireland and western Britain*. Oxford: Oxbow, 136–145.

Gibson, A., 2004. Round in circles: Timber circles, henges and stone circles. *In:* R. Cleal and J. Pollard, eds. *Monuments and material culture*. East Knoyle: Hobnob, 70–82.

Gibson, A., 2007. A Beaker veneer? Some evidence from the burial record. *In:* M. Larsson and M. Parker Pearson, eds. *From Stonehenge to the Baltic*. Oxford: BAR, 47–64.

Gibson, A., 2010. Dating Balbirnie. *Proceedings of the Society of Antiquaries of Scotland*, 140, 51–77.

Gibson, A., 2016. Space and episodic ritual at the monumental Neolithic round mound at Duggleby Howe, north Yorkshire, England. *In:* G. Robin, A. D'Anna, A. Schmitt, and M. Bailly, eds. *Fonctions, utilisations et représentatations de l'espace dans les sépultures monumentales du Néolithique européen*. Aix: Presses Universitaires de Provence, 117–130.

Gibson, A. and Bayliss, A., 2010. Recent work on the Neolithic round barrows of the upper Great Wold Valley, Yorkshire. *In:* J. Leary, T. Darvill, and D. Field, eds. *Round mounds and monumentality*. Oxford: Oxbow, 72–107.

Gillings, M. and Pollard, J., 1999. Non-portable stone artefacts and contexts of meaning: The tale of Grey Wether (museums.ncl.ac.uk/Avebury/stone4.htm). *World Archaeology*, 31 (2), 179–193.

Gillings, M., Pollard, J., Wheatley, D., and Peterson, R., 2008. *Landscape of the megaliths*. Oxford: Oxbow.

Gillings, M. and Pollard, M., 2004. *Avebury*. London: Duckworth.

Gosden, C., 1999. *Anthropology and archaeology: A changing relationship*. London: Routledge.

Greaney, S., Hazell, Z., Baclay, A., et al., 2020. Tempo of a mega-henge: A new chronology for Mount Pleasant, Dorchester, Dorset. *Proceedings of the Prehistoric Society*, 86, 199–236.

Greaney, S. and Whittle, A., Forthcoming. The middle and late Neolithic. *In:* V. Cummings and S. Driscoll, eds. *The archaeology of Britain*. 3rd ed. London: Routledge.

Green, M., 2000. *A landscape revealed. 10,000 years on a chalkland farm*. Stroud: History Press.

Griffiths, S., 2014. Points in time. The Mesolithic-Neolithic transition and the chronology of late rod microliths in Britain. *Oxford Journal of Archaeology*, 33, 221–243.

Griffiths, S., 2016. Beside the ocean of time: A chronology of early Neolithic burial monuments. *In:* C. Richards and R. Jones, eds. *The development of Neolithic house societies in Orkney*, 254–302. Oxford: Windgather.

Griffiths, S. and Richards, C., 2013. *In:* C. Richards, ed. *Building the great stone circles of the north*. Oxford: Windgather, 281–291.

Grimes, W., 1948. Pentre Ifan burial chamber, Pembrokeshire. *Archaeologia Cambrensis*, 100, 3–23.

Gron, K., Rowley-Conwy, P., Fernandez-Dominguez, E., et al., 2018. A meeting in the forest: Hunters and farmers at the Coneybury 'Anomaly', Wiltshire. *Proceedings of the Prehistoric Society*, 84, 111–144.

Habu, J., 2014. Post-pleistocene transformations of hunter-gatherers in east Asia: The Jomon and Chulmun. *In:* V. Cummings, P. Jordan, and M. Zvelebil, eds. *The Oxford handbook of the archaeology and anthropology of hunter-gatherers*. Oxford: Oxford University Press, 507–520.

Haggarty, A., 1991. Machrie Moor, Arran: Recent excavations at two stone circles. *Proceedings of the Society of Antiquaries of Scotland*, 121, 51–94.

Hamilton, J. and Hedges, R., 2011. Carbon and nitrogen stable isotope values of animals and humans from causewayed enclosures. *In:* A. Whittle, F. Healy, and A. Bayliss, eds. *Gathering time*. Oxford: Oxbow, 670–681.

Hamilton, M. and Whittle, A., 1999. Grooved Ware of the Avebury area. *In:* R. Cleal and A. McSween, eds. *Grooved Ware in Britain and Ireland*. Oxford: Oxbow, 36–47.

Hammann, S., Bishop, R. R., Copper, M., et al., 2022. Neolithic culinary traditions revealed by cereal, milk and meat lipids in pottery from Scottish crannogs. *Nature Communications*, 13, 5045.

Harding, J., 2003. *Henge monuments of the British Isles*. Stroud: Tempus.

Harding, J., 2013. *Cult, religion and pilgrimage: Archaeological investigations at the Neolithic and Bronze Age monument complex of Thornborough, North Yorkshire*. New York, NY: CBA.

Harding, J. and Healy, F., 2011. *The Raunds area project: A Neolithic and Bronze Age landscape in Northamptonshire*. Swindon: English Heritage.

Harding, P., 2013. Flint finds from the grave of the Amesbury Archer. *In:* A. Fitzpatrick, ed. *The Amesbury Archer and the Boscombe Bowmen*. Salisbury: Wessex Archaeology.

Harris, O., 2010. Emotional and mnemonic gatherings at Hambledon Hill: Texturing Neolithic places with bodies and bones. *Cambridge Archaeological Journal*, 20, 357–371.

Harris, O., 2021. *Assembling past worlds: Materials, bodies and architecture in Neolithic Britain*. London: Routledge.

Harris, S., 2014. Flax fibre: Innovation and change in the early Neolithic. *Textile Society of America Symposium Proceedings*, 2014.

Hart, D., 2015. Early Neolithic trackways in the Thames floodplain at Belmarsh, London Borough of Greenwich. *Proceedings of the Prehistoric Society*, 81, 215–237.

Hartwell, B., 1998. The Ballynahatty complex. *In:* A. Gibson and D. Simpson, eds. *Prehistoric ritual and religion*. Stroud: Sutton, 32–44.

Hartwell, B., Gormley, S., Brogan, S., and Malone, C., eds., 2023. *Ballynahatty: Excavations in a Neolithic monumental landscape*. Oxford: Oxbow.

Hartz, S., Lübke, H., and Terberger, T., 2007. From fish and seal to sheep and cattle: New research into the process of Neolithisation in northern Germany. *In:* A. Whittle and V. Cummings, eds. *Going over: The Mesolithic-Neolithic transition in north-west Europe*. London: British Academy, 567–594.

Hayden, B., 1995. Pathways to power: Principles for creating socioeconomic inequalities. *In:* T. D. Price and G. M. Feinman, eds. *Foundations of social inequality*. New York, NY and London: Plenum Press, 15–86.

Hayden, B., 2001. Richman, poorman, beggarman, chief: The dynamics of social inequality. *In:* G. M. Feinman and T. D. Price, eds. *Archaeology at the millennium: A sourcebook*. New York, NY: Kluwer Academic/Plenum Publishers, 231–272.

Hayden, B., 2014. *The power of feasts: From prehistory to the present*. Cambridge: Cambridge University Press.

Hayden, C., 2007. *White Horse Stone and the earliest Neolithic in the south east* [Online publication]. Available from: www.kent.gov.uk/__data/assets/pdf_file/0005/55697/SERF-chris-hayden.pdf

Healy, F., 2012. Chronology, corpses, ceramics, copper and lithics. *In:* M. Allen, J. Gardiner, and A. Sheridan, eds. *Is there a British chalcolithic?* Oxford: Oxbow, 144–163.

Hedges, R., Saville, A., and O'Connell, T., 2008. Characterizing the diet of individuals at the Neolithic chambered tomb of Hazleton north, Gloucestershire, England, using stable isotope analysis. *Archaeometry*, 50, 114–128.

Helbaek, H., 1960. (The pottery. *In:* J. D. Clarke) The excavations at the Neolithic site at Hurst Fen, Mildenhall, Suffolk. *Proceedings of the Prehistoric Society*, 28, 220–248.

Henley, C., 2005. Choreographed monumentality: Recreating the centre of other worlds at the monument complex of Callanish, western Lewis. *In:* V. Cummings and A. Pannett, eds. *Set in stone*. Oxford: Oxbow, 95–106.

Hensey, R., 2015. *First light: The origins of Newgrange*. Oxford: Oxbow.

Hensey, R., Meehan, P., Dowd, M., and Moore, S., 2014. A century of archaeology – historical excavation and modern research at the Carrowkeel passage tombs, County Sligo. *Proceedings of the Royal Irish Academy*, 114C, 1–31.

Henshall, A., 1963. *The chambered tombs of Scotland volume one*. Edinburgh: Edinburgh University Press.

Henshall, A., 1972. *The chambered tombs of Scotland volume two*. Edinburgh: Edinburgh University Press.

Herity, M., 1974. *Irish passage graves: Neolithic tomb builders in Ireland and Britain 2500 BC*. Dublin: Irish University Press.

Hey, G. and Barclay, A., 2007. The Thames Valley in the late fifth and early fourth millennium cal BC. *In:* A. Whittle and V. Cummings, eds. *Going over: The Mesolithic-Neolithic transition in north-west Europe*. London: British Academy, 399–422.

Hey, G., Bell, C., Dennis, C., and Robinson, M., 2016. *Yarnton: Neolithic and Bronze settlement and landscape*. Oxford: Oxbow.

Hodder, I., 1990. *The domestication of Europe*. Oxford: Blackwell.

Holgate, R., 2019. Flint working areas and bifacial implement production at the Neolithic flint-mining sites in southern and eastern England. *In:* A. Teather, P. Topping, and J. Baczkowski, eds. *Mining and quarrying in Neolithic Europe: A social perspective*. Oxford: Oxbow, 1–20.

Hoskins, J., 1986. So my name shall live: Stone dragging and grave-building in Kodi, West Sumba. *Bijdragen tot de Taal-Land-en Volkenkunde*, 142, 31–51.

Hunter, J., 2000. Pool, Sanday and a sequence for the Orcadian Neolithic. *In:* A. Ritchie, ed. *Neolithic Orkney in its European context*. Cambridge: McDonald Institute for Archaeological Research, 117–125.

Hurcombe, L., 2014. *Perishable material culture in prehistory*. London: Routledge.

Ingold, T., 2000. *The perception of the environment: Essays on livelihood, dwelling and skill*. London: Routledge.

Johnston, R., 1999. An empty path? Processions, memories and the Dorset cursus. *In:* A. Barclay and J. Harding, eds. *Pathways and ceremonies: The cursus monuments of Britain and Ireland*. Oxford: Oxbow, 39–48.

Johnston, R., 2021. *Bronze Age worlds*. Cambridge: Cambridge University Press.

Jones, A. M., 2002. *Archaeological theory and scientific practice*. Cambridge: Cambridge University Press.

Jones, A. M., 2005. Between a rock and a hard place. *In:* V. Cummings and A. Pannett, eds. *Set in stone*. Oxford: Oxbow, 107–117.

Jones, A. M., 2012. Living rocks. *In:* A. Cochrane and A. M. Jones, eds. *Visualising the Neolithic*. Oxford: Oxbow, 79–88.

Jones, A. M., Cochrane, A., Carter, C., Dawson, I., Díaz-Guardamino, M., Kotoula, E., and Minkin, L., 2015. Digital imaging and prehistoric imagery: A new analysis of the Folkton Drums. *Antiquity*, 89, 1083–1095.

Jones, A. M., Freedman, D., O'Connor, B., Lamdin-Whywark, H., Tipping, R., and Watson, A., 2011. *An animate landscape*. Oxford: Windgather.

Jones, A. M., Griffiths, S., and Brunning, R., 2023. The Early Bronze Age log coffin burials of Britain: The origins and development of a burial rite(s). *Proceedings of the Prehistoric Society*, 89, 51–81.

Jones, C., 2007. *Temples of stone*. Cork: Collins.

Jones, G., 2000. Evaluating the importance of cultivation and collecting in Neolithic Britain. *In:* A. Fairbairn, ed. *Plants in Neolithic Britain and beyond*. Oxford: Oxbow, 79–90.

Jones, G. and Rowley-Conwy, P., 2007. On the importance of cereal cultivation in the British Neolithic. *In:* S. Colledge and J. Connelly, eds. *The origins and spread of domestic plants in southwest Asia and Europe*. London: Routledge.

Jones, P., 2013. *A Mesolithic persistent place at north Park Farm, Bletchingley, Surrey*. Norwich: Spoilheap Publications.

Jordan, P. and Zvelebil, M., 2009. *Ex Oriente Lux*: The prehistory of hunter-gatherer ceramic dispersals. *In:* P. Jordan and M. Zvelebil, eds. *Ceramics before farming*. London: Taylor and Francis, 33–89.

Kador, T., 2007. Stone Age motion pictures: An object's perspective. *In:* V. Cummings and R. Johnston, eds. *Prehistoric journeys*. Oxford: Oxbow, 32–44.

Kador, T., 2010. The last of the old: A homogenous later Mesolithic Ireland? *In:* B. Finlayson and G. Warren, eds. *Landscapes in transition*. Oxford: Oxbow, 147–157.

Kador, T., Gerber, J., Hensey, R., Meehan, P., and Moore, S., 2015. New dates from Carrowkeel. *PAST*, 79, 12–14.

Keiller, A., 1965. *Windmill Hill and Avebury*. Oxford: Clarendon Press.
Kenney, J., 2008. Recent excavations at Parc Bryn Cegin Llandygai near Bangor. *Archaeologia Cambrensis*, 157, 9–142.
Kent, S., ed., 1989. *The implications of sedentism*. Cambridge: Cambridge University Press.
Kimball, M., 2006. Common pools and private tools? Mobility and economy during Ireland's later Mesolithic. *Journal of Anthropological Archaeology*, 25, 239–247.
Kytmannow, T., 2008. *Portal tombs in the landscape: The chronology, morphology and landscape setting of the portal tombs of Ireland, Wales and Cornwall*. Oxford: British Archaeological Reports.
Laporte, L., Joussaume, R., and Scarre, C., 2001. The perception of space and geometry: Megalithic monuments of west-central France in their relationship to the landscape. *In:* C. Scarre, ed. *Monuments and landscape*. London: Routledge, 73–83.
Larson, G. and Burger, J., 2013. A population genetics view of animal domestication. *Trends in Genetics*, 29, 197–205.
Larsson, L. B., 2007. Mistrust traditions, consider innovations? The Mesolithic-Neolithic transition in southern Scandinavia. *In:* A. Whittle and V. Cummings, eds., *Going over: The Mesolithic-Neolithic transition in north-west Europe*. London: British Academy, 595–616.
Last, J., ed., 2022. *Marking place: New perspectives on early Neolithic enclosures*. Oxford: Oxbow.
Lawrence, T., Donnelly, M., Kennard, L., Souday, C., and Grant, R., 2022. Britain in or out of Europe during the late Mesolithic? A new perspective of the Mesolithic-Neolithic transition. *Open Archaeology*. https://doi.org/10.1515/opar-2022-0249
Leary, J., Clark, A., and Bell, M., 2016. Valley of the henges. *Current Archaeology*, 316, 28–34.
Leary, J. and Field, D., 2011. Great monuments, great rivers. *British Archaeology*, 120.
Leary, J., Field, D., and Campbell, G., 2013. *Silbury Hill*. Swindon: English Heritage.
Leask, H. and Price, L., 1936. The Labbacallee megalith. *Proceedings of the Royal Irish Academy*, 43, 77–101.
Lee, D. and Reay, D., Forthcoming. A middle Neolithic house with evidence of felsite axe reworking at Firths Voe, Delting, Shetland. *In:* V. Cummings, J. Downes, and C. Richards, eds. *Neolithic occupation in Orkney and Shetland: New research*.
Lee, D. and Thomas, A., 2012. Orkney's first farmers. *Current Archaeology*, 268, 5–10.
Lelong, O. and Pollard, T., 1998. The excavation and survey of prehistoric enclosures at Blackhouse Burn, Lanarkshire. *Proceedings of the Society of Antiquaries of Scotland*, 128, 13–53.
Lewis, J., 2000. The Neolithic period. *In:* MoLAS, *the archaeology of greater London*, 63–80. London: MoLAS.
Little, A., 2009. Fishy settlement patterns and their social significance: A case study from the northern Midlands of Ireland. *In:* S. McCartan, R. Schulting, G. Warren, and P. Woodman, eds. *Mesolithic horizons*. Oxford: Oxbow, 882–886.
Loader, R., 2007. The Wootton-Quarr archaeological survey, Isle of Wight. *In:* J. Siddell and F. Haughey, eds. *Neolithic archaeology in the intertidal zone*. Oxford: Oxbow.
Louwe Koojimans, L., 2007. The gradual transition to farming in the lower Rhine Basin. *In:* A. Whittle and V. Cummings, eds. *Going over: The Mesolithic-Neolithic transition in north-west Europe*. London: British Academy, 287–310.
Loveday, R., 2009. From ritual to riches – the route to individual power in later Neolithic eastern Yorkshire. *In:* K. Brophy and G. Barclay, eds. *Defining a regional Neolithic*. Oxford: Oxbow, 35–52.
Loveday, R., 2011. Polished rectangular flint knives – elaboration or replication? *In:* A. Saville, ed. *Flint and stone in the Neolithic period*. Oxford: Oxbow, 234–246.

Loveday, R. and Barclay, A., 2010. "One of the most interesting barrows ever examined" – Liffs low revisited. *In:* J. Leary, T. Darvill, and D. Field, eds. *Round mounds and monumentality*. Oxford: Oxbow, 108–129.

Loveday, R., Gibson, A., Marshall, P., Bayliss, A., Bronk Ramsey, C., and van der Plicht, H., 2007. The antler maceheads dating project. *Proceedings of the Prehistoric Society*, 73, 381–392.

Lynch, A., 2014. *Poulnabrone: An early Neolithic portal tomb in Ireland*. Dublin: Wordwell.

Lynch, F., 1973. The use of the passage in certain passage graves as a means of communication rather than access. *In:* G. Daniel and P. Kjaerum, eds. *Megalithic graves and ritual*. Copenhagen: Jutland Archaeological Society, 147–162.

Lysaght, P., ed. 2002. *Food and celebration: From fasting to feasting*. Ljubljana: ZRC.

MacSween, A. and Clarke, D., 2023. Skara Brae: The significance of the Grooved Ware assemblages. *In:* M. Copper, A. Whittle, and A. Sheridan, eds. *Revisiting Grooved Ware*. Oxford: Oxbow, 31–45.

Mallory, J., Nelis, E., and Hartwell, B., 2011. *Excavations on Donegore Hill, Co. Antrim*. Dublin: Wordwell.

Malloy, K. and O'Connell, M., 1995. Palaeoecological investigations towards the reconstruction of environment and land-use changes during prehistory at Céide Fields, western Ireland. *Probleme der Küstenforschung im Südlichen Nordseegebiet*, 23, 187–225.

Manby, T. G., 2004. Food vessels with handles. *In:* A. Gibson and A. Sheridan, eds. *From sickles to circles*. Stroud: Tempus, 215–242.

Masters, L., 1973. The Lochhill long cairn. *Antiquity*, 47, 96–100.

McCartan, S., 2004. The Mesolithic of the Isle of Man. *In:* A. Saville, ed. *Mesolithic Scotland and its neighbours*. Edinburgh: Society of Antiquaries of Scotland, 271–283.

McClatchie, M., Bogaard, A., Whitehouse, N., Schulting, R., Barratt, P., and McLaughlin, T., 2014. Neolithic farming in north-western Europe: Archaeo-botanical evidence from Ireland. *Journal of Archaeological Science*, 51, 206–215.

McClatchie, M., Schulting, R., McLaughlin, R., *et al.*, 2022. Food production, processing and foodways in Neolithic Ireland. *Environmental Archaeology*, 27, 80–92.

McCormick, F., 2007. Mammal bone studies from prehistoric Irish sites. *In:* E. Murphy and N. Whitehouse, eds. *Environmental archaeology in Ireland*. Oxford: Oxbow, 77–101.

McFadyen, L., 2006. Building technologies, quick and slow architectures and early Neolithic long barrow sites in southern Britain. *Archaeological Review from Cambridge*, 21, 70–81.

McKinley, J., 2008. Human remains. *In:* F. Healy and R. Mercer, *Hambledon Hill, Dorset, England*. Swindon: English Heritage.

McMann, J., 1993. *Loughcrew: The cairns*. Dublin: Gallery Press.

Meadows, J., Barclay, A., and Bayliss, A., 2007. A short passage of time: The dating of the Hazleton long cairn revisited. *Cambridge Archaeological Journal*, 17 (1), 45–64.

Meiklejohn, C. and Woodman, P., 2012. Radiocarbon dating of Mesolithic human remains in Ireland. *Mesolithic Miscellany*, 22, 22–41.

Mellars, P., 1987. *Excavations on Oronsay*. Edinburgh: Edinburgh University Press.

Melton, N., Montgomery, J., Knüsel, C. J., Batt, C., Needham, S., Pearson, M. P., Sheridan, A., Heron, C., Horsley, T., Schmidt, A., Evans, A., *et al.*, 2009. Gristhorpe man: An early Bronze Age log-coffin burial scientifically dated. *Antiquity*, 84, 796–815.

Mercer, R., 2003. The early farming settlement of south Western England in the Neolithic. *In:* I. Armit, E. Murphy, E. Nelis, and D. Simpson, eds. *Neolithic settlement in Ireland and western Britain*. Oxford: Oxbow, 56–70.

Mercer, R. and Healy, F., 2008. *Hambledon Hill, Dorset, England: Excavation and survey of a Neolithic monument complex and its surrounding landscape*. Swindon: English Heritage.

Metcalf, P. and Huntington, P., 1991. *Celebrations of death: The anthropology of mortuary ritual*. Cambridge: Cambridge University Press.

Midgley, M., 2005. *The monumental cemeteries of prehistoric Europe*. Stroud: Tempus.

Millican, K., 2007. Turning in circles: A new assessment of the Neolithic timber circles of Scotland. *Proceedings of the Society of Antiquaries of Scotland*, 137, 5–34.

Milne, G., Cohen, N., and Cotton, J., 2010. London's top secret. *London Archaeologist*, 10/11, 287–289.

Milner, N., 2010. Subsistence at 4000–3700 cal BC: Landscapes of change or continuity? *In:* B. Finlayson and G. Warren, eds. *Landscapes in transition*. Oxford: Oxbow, 46–54.

Mithen, S., 2022. How long was the Mesolithic-Neolithic overlap in Scotland? Evidence from the fourth millennium BC on the Isle of Islay and the evaluation of three scenarios for Mesolithic-Neolithic interaction. *Proceedings of the Prehistoric Society*, 88, 53–77.

Mithen, S. and Finlayson, B., 1991. Red deer hunters on Colonsay? The implications of Staosnaig for the interpretation of the Oronsay middens. *Proceedings of the Prehistoric Society*, 57, 1–8.

Molloy, K. and O'Connell, M., 1995. Palaeoecological investigations towards the reconstruction of environment and land-use changes during prehistory at Céide Fields, western Ireland. *Probleme der Küstenforschung im südlichen Nordseegebiet*, 23, 187–225.

Montgomery, J., Beaumont, J., Jay, A., Keefe, K., Gledhill, A., Cook, G., Dockrill, S. J., and Melton, N. D., 2013. Strategic and sporadic marine consumption at the onset of the Neolithic: Increasing temporal resolution in the isotope evidence. *Antiquity*, 87 (338), 1060–1072.

Moore, S., 2012. *The archaeology of Slieve Donard*. Downpatrick: Down County Museum.

Moore, S., 2016. Movement and thresholds: Architecture and landscape at the Carrowkeel-Keshcorran passage tomb complex, Co. Sligo, Ireland. *In:* J. Leary and T. Kador, eds. *Moving on in Neolithic studies: Understanding mobile lives*. Oxford: Oxbow, 45–66.

Mossop, M., 2009. Lakeside developments in County Meath, Ireland: A late Mesolithic fishing platform and possible mooring at Clowanstown. *In:* S. McCartan, R. Schulting, G. Warren, and P. Woodman, eds. *Mesolithic horizons*. Oxford: Oxbow, 895–899.

Mount, C., 1994. Aspects of ritual deposition in the late Neolithic and Beaker periods at Newgrange, Co. Meath. *Proceedings of the Prehistoric Society*, 60, 433–443.

Mukherjee, A., Gibson, A., and Evershed, R., 2008. Trends in pig product processing at British Neolithic Grooved Ware sites traced through organic residues in potsherds. *Journal of Archaeological Science*, 35, 2059–2073.

Müller, J., 2015. Movement of plants, animals, ideas and people in south-east Europe. *In:* C. Fowler, J. Harding, and D. Hofmann, eds. *The Oxford handbook of Neolithic Europe*. Oxford: Oxford University Press, 63–80.

Müller, J. and Peterson, R., 2015. Ceramics and society in northern Europe. *In:* C. Fowler, J. Harding, and D. Hofmann, eds. *The Oxford handbook of Neolithic Europe*. Oxford: Oxford University Press, 573–604.

Murray, H., Murray, J., and Fraser, S., 2009. *A tale of unknown unknowns: A Mesolithic pit alignment and a Neolithic timber hall at Warren fields, Crathes, Aberdeenshire*. Oxford: Oxbow.

Needham, S., 2005. Transforming Beaker culture in north-west Europe. *Proceedings of the Prehistoric Society*, 71, 171–217.

Needham, S., 2012. Case and place for the British chalcolithic. *In:* M. Allen, J. Gardiner, and A. Sheridan, eds. *Is there a British chalcolithic? People, place and polity in the late 3rd millennium*. Oxford: Oxbow, 1–26.

Needham, S., 2015. Discussion: Reappraising Wessex goldwork. *In:* A. Woodward and J. Hunter, eds. *Ritual in early Bronze Age grave goods*. Oxford: Oxbow, 235–260.

Neil, S., Evans, J., Montgomery, J., and Scarre, C., 2016. Isotopic evidence for residential mobility of farming communities during the transition to agriculture in Britain. *Royal Society Open Science*, 3, 1–14.

Nelis, E., 2004. Neolithic flintwork from the north of Ireland. *In:* A. Gibson and A. Sheridan, eds. *From sickles to circles*. Stroud: Tempus, 155–175.

NMS, 1992. Rotten Bottom, Tweedsmuir Hills (Moffat parish): Neolithic longbow. *Discovery and Excavation Scotland*, 21.

Noble, G., 2006. *Neolithic Scotland: Timber, stone, earth and fire*. Edinburgh: Edinburgh University Press.

Noble, G. and Brophy, K., 2011. Big enclosures: The later Neolithic palisaded enclosures of Scotland in their northwestern European context. *European Journal of Archaeology*, 14, 60–87.

Noble, G. and Brophy, K., 2015. Ritual and remembrance at a prehistoric ceremonial complex in central Scotland: Excavations at Forteviot, Perth and Kinross. *Antiquity*, 85, 787–804.

Noble, G. and Brophy, K., 2017. Cremation practices and the creation of monument complexes: The Neolithic cremation cemetery at Forteviot, Strathearn, Perth and Kinross, Scotland, and its comparanda. *Proceedings of the Prehistoric Society*, 83, 213–245.

Noble, G., Brophy, K., Hamilton, D., Leach, S., and Sheridan, A., 2017. Cremation practices and the creation of monument complexes: The Neolithic cremation cemetery at Forteviot, Strathearn, Perth and Kinross, Scotland, and its comparanda. *Proceedings of the Prehistoric Society*, 83, 213–245.

O'Brien, W., 1999. *Sacred ground. Megalithic tombs in coastal south-west Ireland*. Galway: Galway University Press.

O'Brien, W., 2004. *Ross Island: Mining, metal and society in early Ireland*. Galway: NUI Galway Press.

O'Brien, W., 2012. The Chalcolithic of Ireland. *In:* M. Allen, J. Gardiner, and A. Sheridan, eds. *Is there a British chalcolithic? People, place and polity in the late 3rd millennium*. Oxford: Oxbow, 211–225.

O'Brien, W., 2015. *Prehistoric copper mining in Europe*. Oxford: Oxford University Press.

O'Kelly, M., 1982. *Newgrange*. London: Thames and Hudson.

Olalde, I., Brace, S., Allentoft, M., *et al.*, 2018. The Beaker phenomenon and the genomic transformation of northwest Europe. *Nature*, 555, 190–196. https://doi.org/10.1038/nature25738

Olet, M., Evershed, R., and Smyth, J., 2023. Land of milk and honey? *In:* M. Copper, A. Whittle, and A. Sheridan, eds. *Revisiting Grooved Ware*. Oxford: Oxbow, 45–68.

Olliver, M., Tresset, A., Frantz, L., *et al.*, 2018. Dogs accompanied humans during the Neolithic expansion into Europe. *Biology Letters*, 14.

Oswald, A., Dyer, C., and Barber, M., 2001. *The creation of monuments. Neolithic causewayed enclosures in the British Isles*. Swindon: English Heritage.

Oswin, J. and Richards, J., 2011. *Stanton Drew 2010: Geophysical survey and other archaeological investigations*. Bath: Bath and Camerton Archaeological Society.

Ottoni, C., Girdland Flink, L., Evin, A., *et al.*, 2013. Pig domestication and human-mediated dispersal in western Eurasia revealed through ancient DNA and geometric morphometrics. *Molecular Biology and Evolution*, 30, 824–832.

Palmer, S., 1999. *Culverwell Mesolithic habitation site, Isle of Portland, Dorset*. Oxford: British Archaeological Reports.

Parker Pearson, M., 2012. *Stonehenge: Exploring the greatest Stone Age mystery*. London: Simon and Schuster.

Parker Pearson, M., 2015. *Stonehenge: Making sense of a prehistoric mystery*. New York, NY: CBA.

Parker Pearson, M., Chamberlain, A., Jay, M., et al., 2016. Beaker people in Britain: Migration, mobility and diet. *Antiquity*, 90, 620–637.

Parker Pearson, M., Chamberlain, A., Jay, M., Richards, M., Evans, J., and Sheridan, A., eds., 2019. *The Beaker people: Isotopes, mobility and diet in prehistoric Britain*. Oxford: Oxbow.

Parker Pearson, M. and Ramilisonina, 1998. Stonehenge for the ancestors: The stones pass on the message. *Antiquity*, 72, 308–326.

Parker Pearson, M., Joshua, P., Colin, R., Julian, T., Chris, T., and Kate, W., 2020. *Stonehenge for the ancestors: Part one*. Leiden: Sidestone.

Parker Pearson, M., Joshua, P., Colin, R., Julian, T., Chris, T., and Kate, W., 2022. *Stonehenge for the ancestors: Part two*. Leiden: Sidestone.

Parker Pearson, M., Joshua, P., Colin, R., Julian, T., Chris, T., and Kate, W., 2024. *Durrington Walls and Woodhenge*. Leiden: Sidestone.

Pedrosa, S., Uzan, M., Arranz, J.-J., Gutiérrez-Gil, B., San Primitivo, F., and Bayón, Y., 2005. Evidence of three maternal lineages in near eastern sheep supporting multiple domestication events. *Proceedings of the Royal Society B*. https://doi.org/10.1098/rspb.2005.3204

Péquart, M. and Péquart, S., 1954. *Hoëdic, deuxiéme station-nécropole du Mésolithique côtier Armoricain*. Anvers: De Sikkel.

Perry I. and Moore, P., 1987. Dutch elm disease as an analogue of Neolithic elm decline. *Nature*, 326, 72–73.

Peterson, R., 2003. *Neolithic pottery from Wales: Traditions of construction and use*. Oxford: British Archaeological Report.

Peterson, R., 2012. Social memory and ritual performance. *Journal of Social Archaeology*, 13, 266–283.

Peterson, R., 2019. *Neolithic cave burials of Britain*. Manchester: Manchester University Press.

Pétrequin, P., Pétrequin, A.-M., Jeudy, F., Jeunesse, C., Monnier, J.-L., Pelegrin, J., and Praud, I., 1998. From raw material to the Neolithic stone axe. Production processes and social context. *In*: M. Edmonds and C. Richards, eds. *Understanding the Neolithic of north-western Europe*. Glasgow: Cruithne Press, 278–311.

Piggott, S., 1954. *The Neolithic cultures of the British Isles*. Cambridge: Cambridge University Press.

Piggott, S. and Powell, T. G. E., 1949. The excavation of three Neolithic chambered tombs in Galloway. *Proceedings of the Society of Antiquaries of Scotland*, 83, 103–161.

Pigiére, F. and Smyth, J., 2022. First evidence for cattle traction in middle Neolithic Ireland: A pivotal element for resource exploitation. *PLoS One*. https://doi.org/10.1371/journal.pone.0279556

Pollard, J., 1992. The Sanctuary, Overton Hill, Wiltshire: A re-examination. *Proceedings of the Prehistoric Society*, 58, 213–226.

Pollard, J., 1995. Inscribing space: Formal deposition at the later Neolithic monument of Woodhenge, Wiltshire. *Proceedings of the Prehistoric Society*, 61, 137–156.

Pollard, J., 2000. Ancestral places in the Mesolithic landscape. *Archaeological Review from Cambridge*, 17, 123–138.

Pollard, J., 2009. The materialization of religious structures in the time of Stonehenge. *Material Religion*, 5, 332–353.

Pollard, J., 2012. Living with scared spaces: The henge monuments of Wessex. *In*: A. Gibson, ed. *Enclosing the Neolithic*. Oxford: British Archaeological Reports, 93–107.

Pollard, J. and Reynolds, A., 2002. *Avebury: Biography of a landscape*. Stroud: Tempus.

Pollard, J. and Robinson, D., 2007. A return to Woodhenge. *In*: M. Larsson and M. Parker Pearson, eds. *From Stonehenge to the Baltic*. Oxford: BAR, 159–168.

Pollard, T., 1996. Time and tide: Coastal environments, cosmology and ritual practice in early prehistoric Scotland. *In:* T. Pollard and A. Morrison, eds. *The early prehistory of Scotland*. Edinburgh: Edinburgh University Press, 198–210.

Powell, A., 2016. Corporate identity and clan affiliation: An explanation of form in Irish Megalithic tomb construction. *In:* G. Robin, A. D'Anna, A. Schmitt, and M. Bailly, eds. *Fonctions, utilisations et représentatations de l'espace dans les sépultures monumentales du Néolithique européen*. Aix: Presses Universitaires de Provence, 81–95.

Powell, T. G. E., 1973. Excavations at the Megalithic chambered cairn at Dyffryn Ardudwy, Merioneth, Wales. *Archaeologia*, 104, 1–50.

Powell, T. G. E. and Daniel, G., 1956. *Barclodiad y Gawres*. Liverpool: Liverpool University Press.

Powell, T. G. E., Oldfield, F., and Corcoran, J. X. W. P., 1971. Excavations in zone VII peat at Storrs Moss, Lancashire, England, 1965–67. *Proceedings of the Prehistoric Society*, 37, 112–137.

Pryor, F., 1999. *Etton. Excavations at a Neolithic causewayed enclosure near Maxey, Cambridge, 1982–7*. London: English Heritage.

Raemaekers, D., Demirci, Ö., Kamjan, S., *et al.*, 2021. Timing and pace of Neolithisation in the Dutch wetlands (c. 5000–3500 cal. BC). *Open Archaeology*, 7 (1), 658–670.

Raftery, B., ed., 1996. *Trackway excavations in the Mountdillon Bogs, Co. Longford, 1985–1991*. Dublin: Crannog.

Ray, K. and Thomas, J., 2003. The kinship of cows: The social centrality of cattle in the earlier Neolithic of southern Britain. *In:* M. Parker Pearson, ed. *Food, culture and identity in the Neolithic and early Bronze Age*. Oxford: British Archaeological Reports, 37–44.

Ray, K., Thomas, J., Overton, N., *et al.*, 2023. Dorstone Hill: A Neolithic timescape. *Antiquity*, 1–18. https://doi.org/10.15184/aqy.2023.93

Rees, C. and Jones, C., 2015. Neolithic houses from Llanfaethlu, Anglesey. *PAST*, 81, 1–3.

Renfrew, C., 1973. Monuments, mobilisation and social organisation in Neolithic Wessex. *In:* C. Renfrew, ed. *The explanation of culture change*. Pittsburgh, PA: University of Pittsburgh Press, 539–558.

Renfrew, C., 1976. *Before civilisation*. London: Penguin.

Richards, C., 1988. Altered images: A re-examination of Neolithic mortuary practices in Orkney. *In:* J. Barrett and I. Kinnes, eds. *The archaeology of context in the Neolithic and Bronze Age: Recent trends*. Sheffield: Department of Archaeology and Prehistory, 42–56.

Richards, C., 1992. Doorways into another world: The Orkney-Cromarty chambered tombs. *In:* N. Sharples and A. Sheridan, eds. *Vessels for the ancestors: Essays on the Neolithic of Britain and Ireland*. Edinburgh: Edinburgh University Press, 62–76.

Richards, C., 1996. Henges and water. *Journal of Material Culture*, 1, 313–336.

Richards, C., 2004. Labouring with monuments: Constructing the dolmen at Carreg Samson, south-west Wales. *In:* V. Cummings and C. Fowler, eds. *The Neolithic of the Irish Sea: Materiality and traditions of practice*. Oxford: Oxbow, 72–80.

Richards, C., 2005. *Dwelling among the monuments: The Neolithic village of Barnhouse, Maeshowe passage grave and surrounding monuments at Stenness, Orkney*. Cambridge: McDonald Institute.

Richards, C., ed., 2013. *Building the great stone circles of the north*. Oxford: Windgather.

Richards, C. and Cummings, V., 2024. *Stone circles: A field guide*. New Haven, CT: Yale University Press.

Richards, C. and Jones, A., 2015a. Houses of the dead: The transition of wood to stone architecture at Wideford Hill. *In:* C. Richards and A. Jones, eds. *The development of Neolithic house societies in Orkney*. Oxford: Oxbow.

Richards, C. and Jones, R., eds., 2015b. *The development of Neolithic house societies in Orkney*. Oxford: Oxbow.

Richards, C., Downes, J., Gee, C., and Carter, S., 2015. Materializing Neolithic house societies in Orkney: Introducing Varme Dale and Muckquoy. *In:* C. Richards and A. Jones, eds. *The development of Neolithic house societies in Orkney*. Oxford: Oxbow, 224–253.

Richards, C., Jones, A., McSween, A., Sheridan, A., *et al*., 2016. Settlement duration and materiality: A formal chronological model for the development of Barnhouse, a Grooved Ware settlement in Orkney. *Proceedings of the Prehistoric Society*, 82.

Richards, J., 1990. *The Stonehenge environs project*. Swindon: English Heritage.

Richards, M., 2003. Explaining the dietary isotope evidence for the rapid adoption of the Neolithic in Britain. *In:* M. Parker Pearson, ed. *Food, culture and identity in the Neolithic and early Bronze Age*. Oxford: BAR, 31–36.

Richards, M. and Mellars, P., 1998. Stable isotopes and the seasonality of the Oronsay middens. *Antiquity*, 72, 178–184.

Ritchie, A., 1984. Excavation of a Neolithic farmstead at Knap of Howar, Papa Westray, Orkney. *Proceedings of the Society of Antiquaries of Scotland*, 113, 40–121.

Ritchie, A., 2009. *On the fringe of Neolithic Europe: Excavation of a chambered cairn on the Holm of Papa Westray, Orkney*. Edinburgh: RCAHMS.

Rivollat, M., Jeong, C., Schiffels, S., *et al*., 2020. Ancient genome-wide DNA from France highlights the complexity of interactions between Mesolithic hunter-gatherers and Neolithic farmers. *Science Advances*, 6. https://doi.org/10.1126/sciadv.aaz5344

Rivollat, M., Thomas, A., Ghesquière, E., *et al*., 2022. Ancient DNA gives new insights into a Norman Neolithic monumental cemetery dedicated to male elites. *Proceedings of the National Academy of Sciences*, 119(18). https://doi.org/10.1073/pnas.2120786119

Robb, J. and Michelaki, K., 2009. In small things remembered: Pottery decoration in Neolithic southern Italy. *In:* M. Jessen, N. Johannsen, and H. J. Jensen, eds. *Excavating the mind: Cross-sections through culture, cognition and materiality*. Aarhus: University of Aarhus Press, 161–181.

Robin, G., 2010. Spatial structures and symbolic systems in Irish and British passage tombs: The organization of architectural elements, parietal carved signs and funerary deposits. *Cambridge Archaeological Journal*, 20, 373–418.

Robinson, G., 2013. 'A sea of small boats': Places and practices on the prehistoric seascape of western Britain. *Internet Archaeology*, 34.

Robinson, G., Town, M., Ballin, T., *et al*., 2020. Furness' first farmers: Evidence of early Neolithic settlement and dairying in Cumbria. *Proceedings of the Prehistoric Society*, 86, 165–198.

Robinson, M., 2000. Further considerations of Neolithic charred cereals, fruit and nuts. *In:* A. Fairnbairn, ed. *Plants in Neolithic Britain and beyond*. Oxford: Oxbow, 85–90.

Roe, F., 1979. Typology of stone implements with shaftholes. *In:* T. Clough and W. Cummins, eds. *Stone axe studies: Volume two*. London: Council for British Archaeology, 23–48.

Roe, F., 2013. Bracers from the grave of the Amesbury Archer. *In:* A. Fitzpatrick, ed. *The Amesbury Archer and the Boscombe Bowmen*. Salisbury: Wessex Archaeology.

Rowley Conwy, P., 2004. How the west was lost: A reconsideration of agricultural origins in Britain, Ireland and southern Scandinavia. *Current Anthropology*, 45, 83–114.

Rowley Conwy, P. and Owen, A., 2011. Grooved Ware feasting in Yorkshire: Late Neolithic animal consumption at Rudston Wold. *Oxford Journal of Archaeology*, 30, 325–367.

Roy, A., Crellin, R., and Harris, O., 2023. Use wear analysis reveals the first direct evidence for the use of Neolithic polished stone axes in Britain. *Journal of Archaeological Science Reports*. https://doi.org/10.1016/j.jasrep.2023.103882

Ruggles, C. and Chadburn, A., 2024. *Stonehenge: Sighting the sun*. Swindon: Historic England.
Russell, M., 2000. *Flint mines in Neolithic Britain*. Stroud: Tempus.
Salamini, F., Özkan, H., Brandolini, A., *et al*., 2002. Genetics and geography of wild cereal domestication in the near east. *Nature Reviews Genetics*, 3, 429–441.
Saville, A., 1990. *Hazelton north: The excavation of a Neolithic long cairn of the Cotswold-Severn group*. London: English Heritage.
Saville, A., 2004. The material culture of Mesolithic Scotland. *In:* A. Saville, ed. *Mesolithic Scotland and its neighbours*. Edinburgh: Society of Antiquaries of Scotland, 185–220.
Saville, A., 2005. Prehistoric quarrying of a secondary flint source: Evidence from north-east Scotland. *In:* P. Topping and M. Lynott, eds. *The cultural landscape of prehistoric mines*. Oxford: Oxbow, 1–13.
Saville, A., 2009. Speculating on the significance of an axehead and a bead from Luce Sands, Dumfries and Galloway, south-west Scotland. *In:* N. Finlay, S. McCartan, N. Milner, and C. Wickham Jones, eds. *From Bann Flakes to Bushmills*. Oxford: Oxbow, 50–58.
Scarre, C., 2011. *Landscapes of Neolithic Brittany*. Oxford: Oxford University Press.
Scheib, C., Hui, R., D'Atanasio, E., *et al*., 2019. East Anglian early Neolithic monument burial linked to contemporary megaliths. *Annals of Human Biology*, 46, 145–149.
Schulting, R., 1996. Antlers, bone pins and flint blades: The Mesolithic cemeteries of Téviec and Hoëdic, Brittany. *Antiquity*, 70, 335–350.
Schulting, R., 2007. Non-monumental burial in Britain: A (largely) cavernous view. *In:* L. Larsson, F. Lüth, and T. Terberger, eds. *Non-megalithic mortuary practices in the Baltic – new methods and research into the development of Stone Age society*. Schwerin: Bericht der Römisch-Germanischen Kommission, 581–603.
Schulting, R., 2008. Foodways and social ecologies from the early Mesolithic to the early Bronze Age. *In:* J. Pollard, ed. *Prehistoric Britain*. Oxford: Blackwell, 90–120.
Schulting, R., 2012. Skeletal evidence for interpersonal violence: Beyond mortuary monuments in southern Britain. *In:* R. Schulting and L. Fibiger, eds. *Sticks, stones and broken bones*. Oxford: Oxford University Press, 223–248.
Schulting, R., Gardiner, P., Hawkes, C., and Murray, E., 2010. The Mesolithic and Neolithic human bone assemblage from Totty Pot, Cheddar, Somerset. *Proceedings of the University of Bristol Spelaeological Society*, 25, 75–95.
Schulting, R., Murphy, E., Jones, C., and Warren, G., 2011. New dates from the north and a proposed chronology for Irish court tombs. *Proceedings of the Royal Irish Academy*, 112C, 1–60.
Schulting, R. J. and Richards, M. P., 2001. Dating women and becoming farmers: New palaeodietary and AMS data from the Breton Mesolithic cemeteries of Téviec and Hoëdic. *Journal of Anthropological Archaeology*, 20, 314–344.
Schulting, R. J. and Richards, M. P., 2002. The wet, the wild and the domesticated: The Mesolithic-Neolithic transition on the west coast of Scotland. *European Journal of Archaeology*, 5, 147–89.
Schulting, R., Sheridan, A., Crozier, R., and Murphy, E., 2010. Revisiting Quanterness: New AMS dates and stable isotope data from an Orcadian chamber tomb. *Proceedings of the Society of Antiquaries of Scotland*, 140, 1–50.
Schulting, R. and Wysocki, M., 2005. 'In this chambered tumulus were found cleft skulls . . .': An assessment of the evidence for cranial trauma in the British Neolithic. *Proceedings of the Prehistoric Society*, 107–138.
Schutz Paulsson, B., 2017. *Time and stone: The emergence and development of megaliths and megalithic societies in Europe*. Oxford: Archaeopress.

Scott, J., 1969. The Clyde cairns of Scotland. *In:* T. G. E. Powell, J. X. W. P. Corcoran, F. Lynch, and J. G. Scott, eds. *Megalithic enquiries in the west of Britain*. Liverpool: Liverpool University Press, 175–222.

Scott, J., 1992. Mortuary structures and megaliths. *In:* N. Sharples and A. Sheridan, eds. *Vessels for the ancestors*. Edinburgh: Edinburgh University Press, 104–119.

Seersholm, F., Sjögren, K. G., Koelman, J., *et al.*, 2024. Repeated plague infections cross six generations of Neolithic farmers. *Nature*. https://doi.org/10.1038/s41586-024-07651-2

Serjeantson, D., 2011. *Review of animal remains from the Neolithic and early Bronze Age of southern Britain*. Swindon: English Heritage.

Shanks, M. and Tilley, C., 1987a. *Reconstructing archaeology: Theory and practice*. London: Routledge.

Shanks, M. and Tilley, C., 1987b. *Social theory and archaeology*. Cambridge: Polity.

Sharpe, K., 2012. Reading between the grooves. *In:* A. Cochrane and A. M. Jones, eds. *Visualising the Neolithic*. Oxford: Oxbow, 47–63.

Sharples, N., 2000. Antlers and Orcadian rituals: An ambiguous role for red deer in the Neolithic. *In:* A. Ritchie, ed. *Neolithic Orkney in its European context*. Oxford: Oxbow, 107–116.

Sharples, N., 2009. Beaker settlement in the western Isles. *In:* M. Allen, N. Sharples, and T. O'Connor, eds. *Land and people: Papers in memory of John G. Evans*. Oxford: Oxbow, 147–158.

Shee Twohig, E., 1990. *Irish megalithic tombs*. Princes Risborough: Shire.

Shennan, S., 2018. *The first farmers of Europe: An evolutionary perspective*. Cambridge: Cambridge University Press.

Shennan, S., Downey, S., Timpson, A., *et al.,* 2013. Regional population collapse followed initial agriculture booms in mid-Holocene Europe. *Nature Communications*, 4, 2486. https://doi.org/10.1038/ncomms3486

Shepherd, A., 2012. Stepping out together. *In:* M. Allen, J. Gardiner, and A. Sheridan, eds. *Is there a British chalcolithic? People, place and polity in the late 3rd millennium*. Oxford: Oxbow, 257–280.

Sheridan, A., 1995. Irish Neolithic pottery: The story in 1995. *In:* I. Kinnes and G. Varndell, eds. *'Unbaked urns of rudely shape': Essays on British and Irish pottery*. Oxford: Oxbow, 3–22.

Sheridan, A., 2004a. Neolithic connections along and across the Irish sea. *In:* V. Cummings and C. Fowler, eds. *The Neolithic of the Irish sea: Materiality and traditions of practice*. Oxford: Oxbow, 9–21.

Sheridan, A., 2004b. Scottish food vessel chronology revisited. *In:* A. Gibson and A. Sheridan, eds. *From sickles to circles*. Stroud: Tempus, 243–267.

Sheridan, A., 2007. From Picardie to Pickering and Pencraig Hill? New information on the 'Carinated Bowl Neolithic' in northern Britain. *In:* A. Whittle and V. Cummings, eds. *Going over*. London: British Academy, 441–492.

Sheridan, A., 2010a. Scotland's Neolithic non-megalithic round mounds; New dates, problems and potential. *In:* J. Leary, T. Darvill, and D. Field, eds. *Round mounds and monumentality*. Oxford: Oxbow, 28–52.

Sheridan, A., 2010b. The Neolithization of Britain and Ireland: The 'big picture'. *In:* B. Finlayson and G. Warren, eds. *Landscapes in transition*. Oxford: Oxbow, 89–105.

Sheridan, A., 2012. A Rumsfeld reality check. *In:* M. Allen, J. Gardiner, and A. Sheridan, eds. *Is there a British chalcolithic?* Oxford: Oxbow, 40–55.

Sheridan, A., 2016a. Scottish Neolithic pottery in 2016: The big picture and some details of the narrative. *In:* F. Hunter and A. Sheridan, eds. *Ancient lives: Objects, people and place in early Scotland. Essays for David V. Clarke on his 70th birthday*. Leiden: Sidestone, 189–212.

Sheridan, A., 2016b. The Neolithisation of Britain and Ireland: The arrival of immigrant farmers from continental Europe and its impact on pre-existing lifeways. *In:* N. Sanz, ed. *The origins of food production*. Mexico City: UNESCO, 226–245.

Sheridan, A. and Pailler, Y., 2012. Les haches alpines et leurs imitations en Grande-Bretagne, dans l'île de Man, en Irlande et dans les île Anglo-Normandes. *In:* P. Pétrequin, S. Cassen, M. Errera, L. Klassen, A. Sheridan, and A.-M. Pétrequin, eds. *JADE. Grandes haches alpines du Néolithique européen, Ve au IVe millénaires av*. J.-C. Besançon: Presses universitaires de Franche-Comté.

Sheridan, A., Pétrequin, P., Pétrequin, A.-M., *et al*., 2019. Fifty shades of green. *In:* C. Rodriguez-Reillan, B. Nelson, and R. Fábregas Valcarce, eds. *A taste for green. A global perspective on ancient jade, turquoise and variscite exchange*. Oxford: Oxbow, 97–120.

Sheridan, A., Schulting, R., Quinnell, H., and Taylor, R., 2008. Revisiting a small passage tomb at Broadsands, Devon. *Proceedings of the Devon Archaeological Society*, 66, 1–26.

Simpson, D., 1988. The stone maceheads of Ireland. *Proceedings of the Royal Society of the Antiquaries of Ireland*, 118, 27–52.

Simpson, D., 1996. The Ballygalley house, Co. Antrim, Ireland. *In:* T. Darvill and J. Thomas, eds. *Neolithic houses in north-west Europe and beyond*. Oxford: Oxbow, 123–132.

Simpson, D. and Ransom, R., 1992. Maceheads and the Orcadian Neolithic. *In:* N. Sharples and A. Sheridan, eds. *Vessels for the ancestors: Essays on the Neolithic of Britain and Ireland*. Edinburgh: Edinburgh University Press, 221–243.

Smith, M. and Brickley, M., 2009. *People of the long barrows*. The History Press.

Smith, R., Healy, F., Allen, M., Morris, E., Barnes, I., and Woodward, P., 1997. *Excavations along the route of the Dorchester By-pass, Dorset, 1986–88*. Salisbury: Wessex Archaeology.

Smyth, J., 2012. Breaking ground: An overview of pits and pit-digging in Neolithic Ireland. *In:* H. Anderson-Whymark and J. Thomas, eds. *Regional perspectives on Neolithic pit deposition*. Oxford: Oxbow, 13–29.

Smyth, J., 2014. *Settlement in the Irish Neolithic*. Oxford: Oxbow.

Smyth, J., 2020. House of the living, house of the dead. An open and shut case from Ballyglass, Co. Mayo? *In:* A. Barclay, D., Field, and J. Leary, eds. *Houses of the dead?* Oxford: Oxbow, 145–157.

Smyth, J. and Evershed, R., 2015a. Milking the megafauna; Using organic residue analysis to understand early farming practice. *Environmental Archaeology*, 21, 214–229.

Smyth, J. and Evershed, R., 2015b. The molecules of meals: New insight into Neolithic foodways. *Proceedings of the Royal Irish Academy*, 115, 1–20.

Spielmann, K., 2014. The emergence of forager-farmer interaction in North America. *In:* V. Cummings, P. Jordan, and M. Zvelebil, eds. *The Oxford handbook of the archaeology and anthropology of hunter-gatherers*. Oxford: Oxford University Press, 881–900.

Spindler, K., 1995. *The man in the ice*. London: Harmony.

Stanton, D., Mulville, J., and Bruford, M., 2016. Colonization of the Scottish islands via long-distance Neolithic transport of red deer (Cervus elaphus). *Proceedings of the Royal Society B*, 283.

Stevens, C. and Fuller, D., 2012. Did Neolithic farming fail? *Antiquity*, 86, 707–722.

Stout, G. and Stout, M., 2008. *Newgrange*. Cork: Cork University Press.

Sturt, F., Garrow, D., and Bradley, S., 2013. New models of north-west European Holocene palaeogeography and inundation. *Journal of Archaeological Science*, 40.

Style, P., 2011. Mountains: Time out of mind? Contextualising the landscape. The significance and use of the Cumbrian Fells in the Neolithic and early Bronze Age. Unpublished Masters' Thesis. Preston.

Sweetman, D., 1976. An earthen enclosure at Monknewtown, Slane, Co. Meath. *Proceedings of the Royal Irish Academy*, 91C, 245–284.

Sweetman, D., 1985. A late Neolithic/early Bronze Age pit circle at Newgrange, Co. Meath. *Proceedings of the Royal Irish Academy*, 85, 195–221.

Teather, A., 2008. *Mining and materiality in the British Neolithic*. Unpublished PhD Thesis. University of Sheffield.

Teather, A., 2016. *Mining and materiality: Neolithic chalk artefacts and their depositional contexts in southern Britain*. Oxford: Archaeopress.

Thomas, A., 2020. Art in context: The decorated stone assemblage. *In:* N. Card, M., Edmonds, and A. Mitchell, eds. *The Ness of Brodgar: As it stands*. Kirkwall: The Orcadian, 132–149.

Thomas, J., 1988. Neolithic explanations revisited: The Mesolithic-Neolithic transition in Britain and south Scandinavia. *Proceedings of the Prehistoric Society*, 54, 59–66.

Thomas, J., 1996a. The cultural context of the first use of domesticates in continental central and northwest Europe. *In:* D. Harris, ed. *The origins and spread of agriculture and pastoralism in Eurasia*. London: UCL Press, 310–322.

Thomas, J., 1996b. *Time, culture and identity: An interpretive archaeology*. London: Routledge.

Thomas, J., 1999. *Understanding the Neolithic*. London: Routledge.

Thomas, J., 2004. *Archaeology and modernity*. London: Routledge.

Thomas, J., 2006. On the origins and development of cursus monuments in Britain and Ireland. *Proceedings of the Prehistoric Society*, 72, 229–241.

Thomas, J., 2007a. *Place and memory: Excavations at the Pict's Knowe, Holywood and Holm Farm, Dumfries and Galloway, 1994–8*. Oxford: Oxbow.

Thomas, J., 2007b. The internal features at Durrington Walls. *In:* M. Larsson and M. Parker Pearson, eds. *From Stonehenge to the Baltic*. Oxford: BAR, 145–158.

Thomas, J., 2010. The return of the Rinyo-Clachton folk? The cultural significance of the Grooved Ware complex in later Neolithic Britain. *Cambridge Archaeological Journal*, 20, 1–15.

Thomas, J., 2012. Introduction: Beyond the mundane. *In:* H. Anderson-Whymark and J. Thomas, eds. *Regional perspectives on Neolithic pit deposition*. Oxford: Oxbow, 1–12.

Thomas, J., 2013. *The birth of Neolithic Britain: An interpretive account*. Oxford: Oxford University Press.

Thomas, J., 2015a. *A Neolithic ceremonial complex in Galloway: Excavations at Dunragit and Droughduil 1999–2002*. Oxford: Oxbow.

Thomas, J., 2015b. What do we mean by 'Neolithic societies'? *In:* C. Fowler, D. Hoffman, and J. Harding, eds. *The Oxford handbook of Neolithic Europe*. Oxford: Oxford University Press, 1073–1092.

Thomas, J., 2022. Neolithization and population replacement in Britain: An alternative view. *Cambridge Archaeological Journal*, 32 (3), 507–525.

Thomas, J. and Tilley, C., 1993. The axe and the torso: Symbolic structures in the Neolithic of Brittany. *In:* C. Tilley, ed. *Interpretative archaeology*. Oxford: Berg, 225–324.

Thomas, J., Marshall, P., Parker Pearson, M., Pollard, J., Richards, C., Tilley, C., and Welham, K., 2009. The date of the Greater Stonehenge cursus. *Antiquity*, 83, 40–53.

Thomas, R. and McFadyen, L., 2010. Animals and Cotswold-severn long barrows: A re-examination. *Proceedings of the Prehistoric Society*, 76, 95–113.

Thompson, E., Cummings, V., and Peterson, R., 2015. The biography of early Neolithic pottery assemblages from chambered tombs in western Scotland and eastern Ireland. *In:* V. Cummings and G. Robinson, eds. *The southern Kintyre project: Exploring interactions across the Irish Sea from the Mesolithic to the Bronze Age*. Oxford: British Archaeological Reports, 113–137.

Thorpe, N., 2015. The Atlantic Mesolithic-Neolithic transition. *In:* C. Fowler, J. Harding, and D. Hofmann, eds. *The Oxford handbook of Neolithic Europe*. Oxford: Oxford University Press, 215–229.

Tilley, C., 1994. *A phenomenology of landscape*. Oxford: Berg.

Tilley, C., 1996. *An ethnography of the Neolithic*. Cambridge: Cambridge University Press.

Tilley, C., 2004. *The materiality of stone: Explorations in landscape phenomenology*. Oxford: Berg.

Tilley, C., 2007. The Neolithic sensory revolution. *In:* A. Whittle and V. Cummings, eds. *Going over*. London: British Academy, 329–345.

Tolan-Smith, C., 2008. Mesolithic Britain. *In:* G. Bailey and P. Spikins, eds. *Mesolithic Europe*. Cambridge: Cambridge University Press, 132–157.

Topping, P., 2011. Prehistoric extraction: Further suggestions from ethnography. *In:* A. Saville, ed. *Flint and stone in the Neolithic period*. Oxford: Oxbow, 271–286.

Topping, P., 2021. *Neolithic stone extraction in Britain and Europe*. Oxford: Oxbow.

Treasure, E., Gröcke, D., Caseldine, A., and Church, M., 2019. Neolithic farming and wild plant exploitation in western Britain. *Proceedings of the Prehistoric Society*, 85, 193–222.

Tresset, A. and Vigne, J.-D., 2007. Substitution of species, techniques and symbols at the Mesolithic-Neolithic transition in western Europe. *In:* A. Whittle and V. Cummings, eds. *Going over*. London: British Academy, 189–210.

Tringham, R., 2005. Weaving house life and death into places: A blueprint for a hypermedia narrative. *In:* D. Bailey, A. Whittle, and V. Cummings, eds. *(Un)settling the Neolithic*. Oxford: Oxbow, 98–111.

Ucko, P. and Layton, R., eds., 1998. *The archaeology and anthropology of landscape: Signing the land*. Oxford: Berg.

Vander Linden, M., 2013. A little bit of history repeating itself: Theories on the Bell Beaker phenomenon. *In:* A. Harding and H. Fokkens, eds. *The Oxford handbook of the European Bronze Age*. Oxford: Oxford University Press, 68–81.

Vanmortfort, B., 2001. The group of Spiere as a new stylistic entity in the middle Neolithic of the Middle Scheldt Basin. *Notae Praehistoricae*, 21, 139–143.

Viveiros de Castro, E., 1998. Cosmological deixis and Amerindian perspectivism. *Journal of the Royal Anthropological Institute*, 4 (3), 469–488.

Vyner, B., 1984. The excavation of a Neolithic cairn at Street House, Loftus, Cleveland. *Proceedings of the Prehistoric Society*, 50, 151–195.

Waddell, J., 1998. *The prehistoric archaeology of Ireland*. Galway: Galway University Press.

Wainwright, G., 1971. *Durrington Walls: Excavations 1966–1968*. London: Society of Antiquaries of London.

Walker, K., 2014. Breton axe-heads in Neolithic Britain. *Stonechat*, 2, 5–10.

Warren, G., 2005. *Mesolithic lives in Scotland*. Stroud: Tempus.

Warren, G., 2009. Belderrig: A new later Mesolithic and Neolithic landscape in northwest Ireland. *In:* N. Finlay, S. McCartan, N. Milner, and C. Wickham Jones, eds. *From Bann Flakes to Bushmills*. Oxford: Oxbow, 143–152.

Warren, G., 2022. *Hunter-gatherer Ireland*. Oxford: Oxbow.

Warren, G., Davis, S., McClatchie, M., and Sands, R., 2014. The potential role of humans in structuring the wooded landscapes of Mesolithic Ireland. *Vegetation History Archaeobotany Journal*, 23, 629–646.

Watkins, T., 1982. The excavation of an early Bronze Age cemetery at Barns Farm, Dalgety, Fife. *Proceedings of the Society of Antiquaries of Scotland*, 112, 48–141.

Watson, A. and Keating, D., 1999. Architecture and sound: An acoustic analysis of megalithic monuments in prehistoric Britain. *Antiquity*, 73, 325–336.

Weiner, A., 1992. *Inalienable possessions: The paradox of keeping while giving*. Berkeley, CA: University of California Press.

Welfare, A., 2011. *Great crowns of stone. The recumbent stone circles of Scotland*. Edinburgh: RCAHMS.

Whitehouse, N., Schulting, R., McClatchie, M., et al., 2014. Neolithic agriculture on the European western frontier: The boom and bust of early farming in Ireland. *Journal of Archaeological Science*, 51, 181–205.

Whitley, J., 2002. Too many ancestors. *Antiquity*, 76, 119–126.

Whittle, A., 1986. *Scord of Brouster: An early agricultural settlement on Shetland: Excavations 1977–1979*. Oxford: Oxford Committee for Archaeology Monograph, 9.

Whittle, A., 1995. Gifts from the earth: Symbolic dimensions of the use and production of Neolithic flint and stone axes. *Archaeologia Polona*, 33, 247–259.

Whittle, A., 1996. *Europe in the Neolithic*. Cambridge: Cambridge University Press.

Whittle, A., 1997. Moving on and moving around: Neolithic settlement mobility. *In:* P. Topping, ed. *Neolithic landscapes*. Oxford: Oxbow, 15–22.

Whittle, A., 2000. 'Very like a whale': Menhirs, motifs and myths in the Mesolithic-Neolithic transition of northwest Europe. *Cambridge Archaeological Journal*, 10, 243–259.

Whittle, A., 2004. Stones that float to the sky: Portal dolmens and their landscapes of memory and myth. *In:* V. Cummings and C. Fowler, eds. *The Neolithic of the Irish Sea: Materiality and traditions of practice*. Oxford: Oxbow, 81–90.

Whittle, A., 2017. *The times of their lives: Hunting history in the archaeology of Neolithic Europe*. Oxford: Oxbow.

Whittle, A. and Wysocki, M., 1998. Parc le Breos Cwm transepted long cairn, Gower, west Glamorgan: Date, contents and context. *Proceedings of the Prehistoric Society*, 64, 139–182.

Whittle, A., Atkinson, R. J. C., Chambers, R., Thomas, N., Harman, M., Northover, P., and Robinson, M., 1992. Excavations in the Neolithic and Bronze Age complex at Dorchester-on-Thames, Oxfordshire, 1947–1952 and 1981. *Proceedings of the Prehistoric Society*, 58, 143–201.

Whittle, A., Barclay, A., Bayliss, A., McFadyen, L., Schulting, R., and Wysocki, M., 2007. Building for the dead: Events, processes and changing worldviews from the thirty-eighth to the thirty-fourth centuries cal BC in southern Britain. *Cambridge Archaeological Journal*, 17 (1), 123–147.

Whittle, A., Bayliss, A., and Healy, F., 2022a. A decade on: Revised timings for causewayed enclosures in southern Britain. *In:* J. Last, ed. *Marking place: New perspectives on early Neolithic enclosures*. Oxford: Oxbow, 203–222.

Whittle, A., Bayliss, A., and Wysocki, M., 2007. Once in a lifetime: The date of the Wayland's Smithy long barrow. *Cambridge Archaeological Journal*, 17 (1), 103–121.

Whittle, A., Britnell, W., and Griffiths, S., 2022b. The first stones: Taking and keeping the land. *In:* W. Britnell and A. Whittle, eds. *The first stones: Penywyrlod, Gwernvale and the Black Mountains Neolithic long cairns of south-east Wales*. Oxford: Oxbow, 251–276.

Whittle, A., Healy, F., and Bayliss, A., 2011. *Gathering time: Dating the early Neolithic enclosures of southern Britain and Ireland*. Oxford: Oxbow.

Whittle, A., Pollard, J., and Greaney, S., eds., 2022. *Ancient DNA and the European Neolithic*. Oxford: Oxbow.

Whittle, A., Pollard, J., and Grigson, C., 1999. *The harmony of symbols*. Oxford: Oxbow.

Wickham Jones, C., 2009. Them bones: Midden sites as a defining characteristic of the Scottish Mesolithic. *In:* S. McCartan, R. Schulting, G. Warren, and P. Woodman, eds. *Mesolithic horizons*. Oxford: Oxbow, 478–484.

Wicks, K., Pirie, A., and Mithen, S., 2014. Settlement patterns in the late Mesolithic of western Scotland: The implications of Bayesian analysis of radiocarbon dates and inter-site technological comparisons. *Journal of Archaeological Science*, 41, 406–422.

Wilkin, N. and Vander Linden, M., 2015. What was and what would never be. *In:* H. Anderson-Whymark, D. Garrow, and F. Sturt, eds. *Continental connections*. Oxford: Oxbow, 99–121.

Williams, A., 1953. Clegyr Boia, St David's (Pembrokeshire): Excavation in 1943. *Archaeologia Cambrensis*, 102, 20–47.

Woodbridge, J., Fyfe, R., Roberts, N., Downey, S., Edinborough, K., and Shennan, S., 2014. The impact of the Neolithic agricultural transition in Britain: A comparison of pollen-based land-cover and archaeological c-14 date-inferred population change. *Journal of Archaeological Science*, 51, 216–224.

Woodman, P., 1977. Recent excavations at Newferry, Co. Antrim. *Proceedings of the Prehistoric Society*, 43, 155–199.

Woodman, P. and McCarthy, M., 2003. Contemplating some awful(ly interesting) vistas: Importing cattle and red deer into prehistoric Ireland. *In:* I. Armit, E. Murphy, E. Nelis, and D. Simpson, eds. *Neolithic settlement in Ireland and western Britain*. Oxford: Oxbow, 31–39.

Woodward, A., 2008. Bronze Age pottery and settlement in southern England. *Bronze Age Review*, 1, 79–96.

Woodward, A. and Hunter, J., 2015. *Ritual in early Bronze Age grave goods*. Oxford: Oxbow.

Woodward, A., Hunter, J., Ixer, R., *et al.*, 2006. Beaker age bracers in England: Sources, function and use. *Antiquity*, 80, 530–543.

Worley, F., Madgwick, R., Pelling, R., *et al.*, 2019. Understanding middle Neolithic food and farming in and around the Stonehenge world heritage site: An integrated approach. *Journal of Archaeological Science: Reports*, 26.

Wright, L., Viner-Daniels, S., Parker Pearson, M., and Albarella, U., 2014. Age and season of pig slaughter at late Neolithic Durrington Walls (Wiltshire, UK) as detected through a new system for recording tooth wear. *Journal of Archaeological Science*, 52, 497–514.

Wunderlich, M., Müller, J., and Hinz, M., 2019. Diversified monuments: A chronological framework of the creation of monumental landscapes in prehistoric Europe. *In:* J. Müller, M. Hinz, and M. Wunderlich, eds. *Megaliths, societies, landscapes*. Bonn: Verlag udolf Habelt, 25–31.

Wysocki, M., 2022. Neolithic people of the Black Mountains: Human remains from Penywyrlod, Pipton and Ty Isaf. *In:* W. Britnell and A. Whittle, eds. *The first stones: Penywyrlod, Gwernvale and the Black Mountains Neolithic long cairns of south-east Wales*. Oxford: Oxbow, 157–206.

Wysocki, M., Bayliss, A., and Whittle, A. 2007. Serious mortality: The date of the Fussell's lodge long barrow. *Cambridge Archaeological Journal*, 17 (1), 65–84.

Wysocki, M., Griffiths, S., Hedges, R., Bayliss, A., Higham, T., Fernandez-Jalvo, Y., and Whittle, A., 2013. Dates, diet and dismemberment: Evidence from the Coldrum megalithic monument, Kent. *Proceedings of the Prehistoric Society*, 79, 61–90.

Zeder, M., 2008. Domestication and early agriculture in the Mediterranean basin: Origins, diffusion and impact. *Proceedings of the National Academy of Sciences of the United States of America*, 105, 11597–11604.

Zheng, Z., Wang, X., Li, M., *et al.*, 2020. The origin of domestication genes in goats. *Science Advances*, 6. https://doi.org/10.1126/sciadv.aaz5216

Zvelebil, M., 1994. Plant use in the Mesolithic and its role in the transition to farming. *Proceedings of the Prehistoric Society*, 60, 35–74.

Zvelebil, M., 2000. The social context of the agricultural transition in Europe. *In:* C. Renfrew and K. Boyle, eds. *Archaeogenetics: DNA and the population*. Cambridge: McDonald Institute for Archaeological Research, 57–79.

Zvelebil, M. and Rowley Conwy, P., 1984. Transition to farming in northern Europe; A hunter-gatherer perspective. *Norwegian Archaeological Review*, 17, 102–128.

Zvelebil, M. and Rowley Conwy, P., 1986. Forager and farmers in Atlantic Europe. *In:* M. Zvelebil, ed. *Hunters in transition*. Cambridge: Cambridge University Press, 67–96.

Index

Note: page numbers in *italics* indicate a figure on the corresponding page.

Achnabreck rock art panel, Argyll *202*
Achnacree, Argyll and Bute *163*
Aghnaglack, Co. Fermanagh 113
agricultural revolution 15–16
Altar Stone, Stonehenge, Wiltshire 233
Amesbury Archer 254–256, *261*, 269, 270
Anatolian genetic signature 40, 41, 49
ancestral rites 124
An Corran, Skye 23, 159
animal hides 76
animal remains 66, 78–79, 137, 143, 190, 214, 245, 249, 268, 271
animals 29
Annagh Cave, Co. Limerick 103
antler 26, 76
antler maceheads 156
antler picks 66, 76, 194
Arbour Low, Derbyshire 277
archers 64, 254–256, *261*, 269, 279
archer's wristguard 261–262, *261*
Argyll, Northumberland 201, *202*
arrowheads 37, 64, 65, 119, *120*, 132, 153, 200, *201*, 214, 260–261, *261*, 262
Ascott-under-Wychwood, Oxfordshire 86, 113, 114, 119
Ashleypark, Co. Tipperary 137

Aubrey Holes, Stonehenge, Wiltshire *232*, 238
Aubrey, John *232*
Audleystown, Co. Down *111*, 113, 117, 118
Avebury, Wiltshire 206, 208–211, *209*, 220, *221*, *222*, 239, 243, 245, 248, 251, 282
axe extraction sites *58*, 59, *60*
axes 1, 8, 26, 40, 42, 46, 55, 56–63, *59*, 143, 153–154, 261, 264, 266, *267*

Balbirnie, Fife 159, 216, 238
Balbridie, Aberdeenshire 88, *89*
Balfarg, Fife 236, 278
Balfarg Riding School, Fife 192
Ballaharra, Isle of Man 238
Ballintaggart, Co. Armagh *71*
Ballygalley, Co. Antrim 91–92
Ballyglass, Co. Mayo 91, *91*
Ballymarlagh, Co. Antrim *111*, *112*, 119
Ballynahatty, Co. Down2 11, 236, 248
Balnuaran of Clava 278, *278*
Bandkeramik 41, 44, 46
banks 131, 139–141, 145, 147, 149, 174, 176–177, 188, 189, 208, 210, 211, 212, 213, 214, 216, 218–221, 222, 223, 232, 233–236, 243, 244, 245, 247–248, 249, 250, 268, 276

Bann flake 26, 29
barbed and tanged arrowhead 260–261, *261*
bark 74
barley 37, 38, 81, 85
Barnenez *43*
Barnhouse, Orkney 8, 157, 184–185, *184*, 187, 191, 224–226
Barnhouse Structure 2, Orkney *184*, 187, 224, 247
Barnhouse Structure 8, Orkney *184*, 185, 224–225, *225*
Barnhouse Structure 10, Orkney 225, 226
Barnhouse Structure 27, Orkney 225–226
Barntick Cave, Co. Clare 159
Barrett, John 243
Barrow Hills, Radley, Oxfordshire 102, *102*, 175, *176*, 262
basketry 23, *24*, 27, 31, 56, 65, 74–75, *75*, 134, 171, 194, 220, 254, 255, 256, 260, 270
Bayesian modelling 49, 121–122, 142, 288
Beacharra, Argyll and Bute *73*
Beacharra Ware 69, *73*
Beckhampton Road, Wiltshire 134
Beg-er-Vil, Brittany 41
belief systems 8, 17, 33, 62, 105–106, 125, 126, 147–148, 150, 159, 172, 179, 190, 206, 242, 248–249, 250, 251, 280
Bell, Martin 96
Belmarsh, London 96
Benbulbin, Co. Sligo *11*
Bexhill Points 26
Bharpa Langass, North Uist, Outer Hebrides *167*
Biggar Common, South Lanarkshire 135
biological relationships 2–4, *4*
birds 23, 34
Blackhammer, Rousay *110*
Blackhouse Burn, South Lanarkshire 244
Blackpatch 66
Blasthill chambered tomb, Kintyre *110*
Blasthill, Kintyre *72*, 116, 122–123
Bluestonehenge, Wiltshire 233–234, 242

bluestones *232*, 233, 242, 245
body disposal, rivers/waterways 179
bone objects 6, 18, 26, 56, 76, 185, 194, 262
Boscombe Bowmen 270–271
Bowl burials 262, 279
bowl pottery *70*
Bradly, Richard 186, 248, 276
Bremore/Gormanstown, Co. Dublin 165
Broadsands, Devon 117
Brodgar-Stenness complex, Orkney 222–227, *223*, 242, 246; see also Ness of Brodgar, Orkney; Stones of Stenness, Orkney
Broken Cavern, Devon 104
bronze 265–266
bronze axes 261
Broome Heath, East Anglia 87
Broomend of Crichie, Aberdeenshire 276, *276*
brown bear 33
Browndod, Co. Antrim *111*
Brownshill, Co. Carlow *128*, 202
Brú na Bóinne, Co. Meath 7, 160, 164–165, 171, 230–231, *230*, 240, 285
brushwood platform 29
Buckan, Orkney 8
burial practices see cremation; disarticulation; excarnation; inhumations; mortuary practices; predation; water burial
Burn Ground, Gloucestershire 117
Burton Agnes, Yorkshire 199

Caerau, Cardiff 138
Cairnholy I, Dumfries and Galloway 59, *71*, *114*
Cairnpapple, West Lothian 212, 277
Caisteal nan Gillean II, Oronsay 20
Calanais, Isle of Lewis 228–230, *228*, *229*
capstones 127–128
Cardial group 41
Carding Mill Bay, Oban, Western Scotland 23, 87, 104
carinated bowls 49, 100
Carnac mounds 43
Carn Brea, Cornwall 93, 140

Carreg Coetan, Pembrokeshire 238
Carrigmurrish Cave, Co. Waterford 159
Carrowkeel/Keshcorran, Co. Sligo 160, 165, 167, 170, 172, *173*, 283
Carrowkeel Ware 155
Carrowmore, Co. Sligo 238
carved stone balls 1, 198, *199*
Castlerigg, Cumbria 214, *215*, 242
cattle (*Bos taurus*) 1, 31, 38, 48, 78, 79, 85, 97, 98, 143, 153, 156, 171, 190, 191, 267–268, 271
causewayed enclosures: abandonment 152, 158–159; animal remains 79; antler picks 76; cereals 81; cordage 75; dates 141–142; distribution *139*, 150; domesticated animals 80; incised chalk blocks 66; interpretation 146–148; monumental form 37, 100, 139–141; mortuary practices 102, 137–138, 144–145, 150, 177; plans *140*; polissoirs 63; pottery 69; social negotiations 8, 68–69, 135; stone axes 58; use 142–144, 179
Cave Ha 3, North Yorkshire 103
caves 32, 87, 103–104, 105, 106, *119*, 121, 148, 149, 159, 179, 273
Céide Fields, Co. Mayo 82, *82*
celestial alignments 166, *168*, 178, 234, 242
celestial bodies 159
cemeteries 32
cereals 1, 25, 37, 39, 55, 65, 81–83, 85, 88–89, 94, 97, 100, 152, 191, 204, 268
cetaceans 18
chaff 81–82
chalk objects 199, 214
chambered tombs: abandonment 152, 159; animal remains 79; Avebury, Wiltshire 210, 239; burial deposits 2; Calanais, Isle of Lewis 230; containment of bad deaths 119, 120–121, 124, 174; dates 121–124; distribution *106*, 108, 150; early Neolithic 100, 106–126; Hazleton North, Gloucestershire 1–4, *2*, *3*, *4*, 8, 67, 115, 118, *118*, 120, 129, 150, 283; interpretation 120–121, 124–126; monumental form 37, 100, 112–114, 125, 126, 150; mortuary practices 104, 117–121, 149–150, 158, 179; sequences of construction 114–117
Charnwood Forest, Leicestershire 143
chert 25, 64, 200
Chilbolton, Hampshire 270
Childe, V. G. 48, 183
Church Hill 66
circularity 210–211
Cissbury 66, *67*, 68
cists 137, 159, 265
Clachaig, Arran 117
Cladh Aindreis, Highlands 123
Claish *88*
Clava cairns 280
Cleaven Dyke, Perthshire 177
Clegyr Boia, Pembrokeshire 93
Clonava Island, Lough Derravaragh, Co. Westmeath 28
Clowanstown, Co. Meath 23, 27
Clyde cairns *109*, 113, 115, 116, 117, 122–124, 158
Cnoc Coig, Oronsay *19*, 20, 25
coastal occupation 28–29, 32–33, 34
Coldrum, Kent 117, 122
community projects 68
Companion 256, 270
Coneybury Anomaly, Wiltshire 77–78, *77*, 85, 87
Conneller, Chantal 15, 29
contact networks 29–32, 34
cooking pits 28
cooking vessels 71–72, 156; *see also* food vessels
Cooney, Gabriel 61–62
copper 262–264, 271, 279
copper axes 261, *267*
copper dagger *266*
copper knife *263*
copper mines 264–265

cordage 75–76
Corlea 9, Co. Longford 96
corporate negotiations 8
Cotswold–Severn monuments 3, *107*, 108, 112–117, 121–124, *123*, 125, 129, 130, 135, 158
court cairns 100, 108, *111*, 112, *112*, 116, 124, 130, 158
Cowie Road, Bannockburn, Stirling 148, *148*, 149
Cowie, Stirling 93
Craig Rhos-y-felin, Pembrokeshire 245
Creag na Caillich, Killin, Perthshire. 62, 195–196
Creevykeel, Co. Sligo 116
Creggandevesky, Co. Tyrone 119
cremation 2, 6, 72, 74, 105, 115, 119, 123, 132, 136, 159, 167, 170, 172, 179, 230, 232, 237–238, 270, 273, 274, 277
Crickley Hill, Gloucestershire 142
Cumbrian Fells 59
cursus monuments: early Neolithic 140, 148–149, 152, 158; middle Neolithic 176–178, 179, 249; monumental complexes 37, 221–222, 239, *240*; plans *148*

dairy products 71, 72, 85, 97, 156, 190, 193, 268
dating *see* Bayesian modelling; radiocarbon dating
debitage 26, 64, 65, 104, 270
decoration 162, 165, *165*, 166–167, 173, 181
deer 19, 20, 22, 23, 33
Deerpark, Co. Sligo *111*, 113
defleshing *see* excarnation
Den of Boddam, Aberdeenshire 195
diet: domesticated animals 1, 22, 37, 38, 39, *39*, 40, 45, 55, 64, 77–81, 97; domesticated plants 22, 38, 40, 81–83, 85, 97; early Neolithic 71–72, 76–85; foodways 84–85; late Neolithic 190–191; Mesolithic 18, 20, 22–25, 33–34

disarticulation 2, 20, *103*, 104, 117–118, 132, 134, 136, 137, 143, 144–145, 146, 149–150, 159, 270–271, 273
ditches 45, 66, 68, 74, 80, 137, 139, 139–144, 145, 146, 147, 149, 159, 174, 176–178, 189, 208, 210, 211, 212, 213, 214, 216, 218–221, 222, 223, 232, 233–236, 241, 244, 245, 247–248, 249, 250, 268, 276
Doggerland 17, 34, 46
dogwhelk 23
dolmens 37, *106*, 126–130
domesticated animals 1, 16, 22, 31, 37, 38, 39, *39*, 40, 45, 48, 53, 55, 64, 77–81, 97, 171
domesticated dogs 16, 22, 38, 78, 80, 143
domesticated plants 22, 25, 38, 40, 81–83, 86
Donegore Hill, Co. Antrim *140*, 143, 144
Dooey's Cairn, Co. Antrim 132, 133
Dorchester-on-Thames, Oxfordshire 236, 238
Dorset cursus 177, *178*
Dorstone Hill, Herefordshire 138
Douglasmuir, Angus *148*, 149
Dowd, M. 103
Dowth South, Co. Meath 7, *162*, 165
drinking vessels 271
Duggleby Howe, Yorkshire 175–176, 238
Dunragit, Dumfries and Galloway 148, 213, 236, 238, 239, 242
Dun Ruadh, Co. Tyrone 277
Durrington Walls, Wiltshire 188–189, *188*, 190, 206, 212, 216, 220–221, 232, 234–236, *235*, 240, 245, 246, 247, 249
Dyffryn Ardudwy, Wales 128

East Bennan, Arran *109*
Easter Aquhorthies, Aberdeenshire 277
Edmonds, Mark 63
eels 23
Ehenside Tarn, Cumbria 63
Eilean Dhomnuill, North Uist 93–94, *94*
enclosures 218–221
Epicardial group 41

Ertebølle groups 46
Eton rowing course, Buckinghamshire 87
Etton, Cambridgeshire 63, 74, 75, 143, 145, *145*
Evans, Estyn 10
excarnation 20, 32–33, 104, 105, 120, 144, 145, 146, 159, 179, 239, 273
exchange networks 13
exotic stones 245
exposure 32, 150

fabric 76
Falkner's Stone Circle, Avebury, Wiltshire 208
Fanore, Co. Clare 28
Fanore More, Co. Clare 23
Fargo Plantation, Wiltshire 277
feasting 72, 89, 97, 124, 137, 143, 190, 203, 249, 251, 271
felsite 64
Ferriter's Cove, Co. Kerry 25, 28, 32
Fertile Crescent 38
fields 12
fire pits 26
Firths Voe, Shetland 157–158
fish 18, 23, 44, 46, 79, 96
fishing 16, 18, 23, 25, 26, 31, 33–34, 44, 46, 153
Flagstones, Dorset 178
flat graves 102, *102*, 159
flax 37, 75–76, 81
flint 25, 64, 114, 196
flint axes 58, 100
'flint knapper' 117, 118, *118*
flint mines 37, 40, 65–69, *67*, *68*, 154, 194, *196*
Folkton Drums *200*
Folkton, Yorkshire 199
food vessels 71–72, 155, 259–260, *260*
forecourt 113–114, 158
Forteviot, Perth and Kinross 159, 237, 242
founder families 120, 124, 150
Fourknocks I, Co. Meath *169*
Fowler, Chris 121

Fox, Cyril 10
Freston, Suffolk *140*
fur 25, 76
Fussell's Lodge, Wiltshire 131, 133

Gamelands, Cumbria 246
Garn Turne, Pembrokeshire *12*, 126, 127, *127*, 130
George Rock Shelter 103, *103*
Giant's Hill I, Skendleby, Lincolnshire 134–135, *134*
Giant's Leap wedge tomb, Co. Cavan *274*
Giant's Ring, Belfast 241
glacial debris 12
goats (*Capra hircus*) 38, 55, 78, 79, 143, 267–268
Göbekli Tepe, Türkiye 39
gold 265, 271
Goldcliff, Gwent 22, 25, 27, 28
gold lunula *266*
Goldsland Caves 103, 104
Goodland Ware 155
Gorhambury, Hertfordshire 93
Gort na h'Ulaidhe, Kintyre *109*, 113
Graig Lwyd, North Wales 59
granite 171
granodiorite 171
grave furniture 271
grave goods 32, 44, 159, 167, 170, 172, 175, *256*, 262, 270–271, *272*, 276
graves 159
Greater Stonehenge cursus monument 149
Green, Eday, Orkney 157
Greyabbey Bay, Co. Down 153
greywacke 171
Grime's Graves, Norfolk 194–196, *196*, 199, 204
Gristhorpe log-coffin burial, Yorkshire 265–266
Grooved Ware 155, 181, 185–186, 187, 188, 191–194, *192*, *195*, 197, 199, 200, 202, 203, 229, 248
Gwernvale, Powys 115

Ha'Breck, Wyre, Orkney 94, *95*, 157
Haddenham, Cambridgeshire 131, 132, *140*, 142
hafted functional tools 58–59
Hambledon Hill, Dorset 81, 82, 137–138, *138*, 142–145
Harrow Hill 66
Hayscastle, Pembrokeshire *59*
hazelnut 23, 28, 83, *84*, 153, 191
Hazleton North, Gloucestershire 1–4, *2*, *3*, *4*, 8, 87, 115, 118, *118*, 120, 129, 150, 283
Heapstown, Co. Sligo 163
hearths 18–19, 28, 156, 187, 248, 267
Hebridean Ware 69, 155
Helman Tor, Cornwall 140, 141
Helmholtz resonance1 73
Hemp Knoll Beaker burial *269*
henges 188, 190, 208, *209*, 212, 218–221, *221*, *222*, 239, 246, 248, 268
hengiforms 276–277, 280
Hensey, Robert 172
Hill of Finglenny, Aberdeenshire 266
hilltop enclosures 93
Hindwell palisade enclosure, Walton Basin, Powys 212–213, *214*
Hindwell, Walton Basin, Powys 213, *214*
Hoëdic Island, Brittany 32, 41, *42*
Holm, Dumfries and Galloway 148
Holme-next-the-Sea, Norfolk 212
Holm of Papa Westray North, Orkney 116
Holywood North, Dumfries and Galloway 148, *148*, 149
Horton, Berkshire 74, 93
house horizons 91–93, *92*, 98, 156
houses 8, *90*, *91*, *92*, *95*, 183–189, 235, 267; *see also* stone houses; timber houses
human remains 18, 20, 32–33, 42, 66, 79, 100, 129; *see also* mortuary practices
hunter-gatherers 16–17, 22, 25, 29, 33, 38–40, 41, 44–45
hunting camps 28
Hurlers, Cornwall 215
Hurst Fen, East Anglia 87
hut-like structures 18–19

identity 27, 29, 33–34, 85, 156, 171, 179, 204–205, 280, 284–285; *see also* social identity
Impressed Wares 154–156, *155*
incised lines 66
inhumations 2, 6, 102, 134, 137, 145, 159, 170, 175, *176*, 179, 238, 253, 265, 270, 273, 275, 279
Irish house horizon *92*
Irish mythology 10
island living 17–21, 22, 23, 25, 26, 28–29, 32, 33, 34
Island wedge tomb, Co. Cork *275*
Isle of Lewis 74
Isle of Man 29

jade 41
jadeitite axes 40, 43, 59–62, *61*
jet belt sliders 156, 175
Jones, R. 185

kerbs 163–164
Kerry Points 26
Kierfea Hill, Rousay *110*
Kilgreany Cave, Co. Waterford 103
Killuragh Cave, Co. Limerick 32
Kilmartin, Argyll 236
Kilmonaster, Co. Donegal 165
Kilverstone, East Anglia 87
King Arthur's Round Table, Cumbria 241
Kinsey Cave, North Yorkshire 103
kinship 2–4, 13, 27, 72–73, 89, 98, 120, 129, 135, 146–147, 285
Knap of Howar, Papa Westray, Orkney 87, 157
knapping 65, 66, 87
Knocknarea/Carrowmore, Co. Sligo 130, 160, 165, 167, 170, 238
Knowe of Yarso, Rousay, Orkney *110*, 118, *119*
Knowes of Trotty, Orkney 157
Knowth, Co. Meath 5–8, *5*, *6*, *161*, 163, *164*, 165, 168, 170, 174, 197, *231*, 248, 282

Labbacallee, Co. Cork 274–275
landscapes 7, 10–13, 21, 34, 87, 97, 124–125, 147, 150, 165–166, 171–172, 204–205, 210–211, 248–249, 280
Langdale axe 245
Langdale Pikes, Cumbria 56, *58*, 59, 61, 62, 196, 264
Lavant, Sussex 199
LBK culture 135, 136
leaf-shaped arrowheads 37, 64, *120*
leather 18, 26, 56, 64, 76, 261
Le Grand Menhir Brisé 43, *43*, 129
Le Haut Mée 41, *42*
Levallois-like reduction method 200
Liff's Low, Derbyshire 175
limpet 23
lineages 3, 89, 97, 120, 124, 147, 150, 171, 179, 185, 197, 204, 205, 238, 248, 272, 280, 282, 284, 287
Linkardstown cists 137
Lismore Fields, Derbyshire 82
lithic scatters 23, 27, 28, 86, 189
Little Hoyle Cave, Pembrokeshire 103
Llandegai henge, Gwynedd 196
Llanfaethlu, Anglesey 93
Loch a'Bharp, South Uist *163*
Lochhill, Dumfries and Galloway 132
long barrows 37, 46, 68–69, 79, 82, 108, 122, 135, 136, 137, 142, 145, 149, 150, 177, 238, 239, 273, 282
Long Down 66
long houses 41, 43–44, 135, 136–137
Long Meg and Her Daughters, Cumbria 242
long mounds 43, 44, 76, 132, 133–137, 142, 147
Longstones Enclosure, Avebury, Wiltshire 208
Loughcrew, Co. Meath 160, *162*, 164, 165–166, *169*, 174
Lough Derravaragh, Co. Westmeath 28
Lough Gara, Co. Sligo 27
Lough Kinale, Co. Longford 29
Low Countries (modern-day Belgium and the Netherlands) 44–45
Low Hauxley, Northumberland 25
Lullymore Bog, Co. Kildare2 7
lunulae 265
Lydstep, Pembrokeshire 22–23
Lyles Hill, Co. Antrim 144

maceheads 1, 6, *7*, 8, 156, 170, 175, 185, 194, 197–198, *197*, *198*
Machrie Moor, Arran 215, 216, 236, *237*, 278
Maeshowe, Orkney 8, *163*, 166, 225, 227
Magheraboy, Co. Sligo 49, 141
Maiden Castle, Dorset 143
Mané er Hroëck 43
Manor Farm, Milton Keynes 178
Manston, Kent 270
marine foods 18, 20, 23–25, 33–34; *see also* fishing
maritime networks 11, 33–34, 285–286
Maumbury Rings, Dorset *215*
Mayburgh, Cumbria 241
Medway group 117, 129
mega-henge 218–220
metals 262–266, 280
microliths 26, 27
micro-tranchets 26
middens 8, 17–21, *17*, 22, 23, 26, 28, 32, 33, 41, 47, 79, 86–87, *90*, 97, 98, 104, 114–115, 134, 156, 159, 183, 188, 226, 245, 267
Mid Gleniron I, Dumfries and Galloway 115, *115*
Mid Gleniron II, Dumfries and Galloway 116
Midhowe, Rousay, Orkney *111*, 118, 282
midsummer solstice 166, 234
midwinter sunset alignment 178, 234, 242
Migdale, Sutherland 266
Milfield Basin, Northumberland 236
Misbourne Viaduct, Buckinghamshire 22
Monamore, Arran *109*
monumental complexes: Avebury, Wiltshire 206, 208–211, *209*, 220, *221*, *222*, 239, 243, 245, 246, 248, 251, 282; Brodgar-Stenness complex, Orkney

8–10, *9*, 186–187, *187*, 198, 202, 206, 216, 222–227, *225*, *226*, *227*, 229, 242, 246; Brú na Bóinne, Co. Meath 7, 160, 164–165, 171, 230–231, *230*, 240; Calanais, Isle of Lewis 228–230; cursus monuments 37, 221–222, 239, *240*; Durrington Walls, Wiltshire *186*, 188–189, 190, 206, 212, 216, 220–221, 232, 234–236, 240, 242, 245, 246, 247, 249–250; other complexes 236–237; Stonehenge, Wiltshire 159, 181, 206, 216, 220, 232–234, *232*, *233*, 238, 239, 240, 242, 243, 245, 246, 251, 256, 282

monumental form: causewayed enclosures 37, 139–141; chambered tombs 37, 112–114; houses 247–249; origination 39–40; passage graves/tombs 161–167, 186

monuments: Beaker period 274–279, 280; belief systems 250; Clava cairns 278–279, 280; enclosures 218–221; henges 218–221, 239, 246, 268; hengiforms 276–277, 280; as houses 247–249; late Neolithic 250; monument construction 43–44; mortuary practices 237–239; palisade enclosures 208, 210, 212–213; pit circles 213–214, 239; recumbent stone circles 216, 277–278, *277*, 280; round mounds/cairns 136–137, 158, 162–163, 175–176, 179, 275–276; stone circles 191, 206, 208, 211, 212, 214–218, *215*, 220, 226, 228–230, 231, 233, *237*, 238, 242, *243*, 245, 246, 247, *247*, 248, 250, 268, 277–278, 280; timber circles 211–212, 220, 239, 245, 268; types 211–221; wedge tombs 274–275

Morton, Fife 28

mortuary practices: Beaker period 254–256, 260, 268–273, 279–280; causewayed enclosures 102, 137–138, 144–145, 149, 150; chambered tombs 106–126, 149–150, 179; cists 137; dolmens 126–130; early Neolithic 100, 102–106; Mesolithic 19–21, 32–33; middle Neolithic 158–159, 179; passage graves/tombs 158–159; rituals 105–106; round mounds/cairns 136–137, 179; timber mortuary structures 131–133; unchambered long mounds/cairns 133–137; *see also* cremation; disarticulation; excarnation; inhumations; predation; water burial

Mound of the Hostages, Tara, Co. Meath 170, 230, 238

Mount Pleasant, Dorset 218–220, *219*, 236, 241, 245

Moynagh Lough, Co. Meath 29

Moynagh Points 26

Mull Hill, Isle of Man 117

Must Farm 76

Nant Hall, Prestatyn 23

Needham, S. 254

Neolithic package 37–40, 48–49, 50–51, *51*, *52*

Neolithic revolution 15–16

Neolithic transition: arrival in Britain and Ireland 48–49; first appearance 49–51; key elements 37–38; knowledge gaps 51–53; Low Countries 44–45; northern Europe 40–48; northern France 41–44; northern Germany 46–48; origination 38–40; southern Scandinavia 46–48

Ness of Brodgar, Orkney 8–10, *9*, 186–187, *187*, 198, 202, 206, *223*, 224–226, *226*, *227*, *227*, 247

Ness of Brodgar, Structure Eight, Orkney 8, *9*

Newferry, Co. Antrim 26

Newgrange, Co. Meath 7, 161, *162*, *164*, 165, *165*, 166, *166*, 168, *168*, 214, 249, 282, 283

Northborough, Cambridgeshire 143

Northern Chasséen groups 44

Northern Circle, Avebury, Wiltshire 243, 246

Northern Circle, Durrington Walls, Wiltshire 234

Northern France 41–44

Northern Germany 46–48

North Mains, Perth and Kinross 212, *213*, 243

North Park Farm, Bletchingley, Surrey 26

Norton Bevant, Wiltshire 134

Notgrove, Gloucestershire 116
Nutbane, Hampshire 132

Oddendale, Cumbria 278
Orcadian stone houses 8
organic materials 16, 27, 29, 56, 65, 74–76, 81, 86, 194, 260, 267
Oronsay 17–21, 22, 23, 25, 26, 28, 32, 33
otters 18
ox scapulae (shoulder blades) 66
oyster 23

palisade enclosures 208, 210, 212–213
Parc Bryn Cegin, Llandygai 93
Parc le Breos Cwm, Glamorgan 107, 113
Parker Pearson, Mike 189, 245
Parks of Garden trackway, Stirlingshire 153
passage graves/tombs: burial deposits 6; Calanais, Isle of Lewis 230; celestial alignments 166, 166; Co. Meath 11; conversion 117, 130, 170; dating 167; for the dead 173–175; decoration 162, 165, 166–167, 173; distribution 160, 160; interpretation 170–175; Knowth, Co. Meath 5–8, 5, 6, 161; landscapes 125; for the living 172–173; Maeshowe, Orkney 225; monumental form 161–167; mortuary practices 158–159; plans 162, 163, 168; scratch marks 66; sequences of construction 168–170; use 170–171, 179; wrapping 174–175
Passy type mounds/enclosures 44
Penmaenmawr 12
Penmaenmawr, north Wales 62
Pentre Ifan, Pembrokeshire 130
Penywyrlod, Powys 107, 107, 112, 113, 115, 119
periwinkle 23
persistent places 21, 34, 87, 97
Personality of Britain, The (Fox) 10
personal ornamentation 262, 264, 265, 279
Peterborough Ware 155
Piggott, S. 48
pigment 202

pigs 1, 33, 55, 78, 79, 143, 153, 190, 191, 193, 249; see also wild boar (pig)
pit and post-defined cursus monuments 148
pitchstone 64, 200
pit circles 213–214, 239
Pitnacree, Perth and Kinross 132
pit sites 87, 90, 98, 145, 149, 156, 159, 189, 267
plague 153, 179, 238, 249, 283
plaques 199
Point of Cott, Westray, Orkney 117
polished flint axes 46
polished flint knife 175
polished stone axes 1, 8, 26, 40, 42, 55, 56–63, 59, 143, 196, 264
polished stone rings 41
polissoirs 63, 143
portal dolmens 108, 126
portal tombs 108, 126
Portland, Culverwell 23
Port Lobh, Colonsay 23
post-Bandkeramik culture 135
postholes 93, 115, 115, 131, 131, 132, 144, 212, 235, 238
Post Track, Somerset 95
pottery: Beacharra Ware 69, 73; Beaker period 258–260, 273; bowl pottery 37, 70, 73, 74; carinated bowls 71, 100; Carrowkeel Ware 155; causewayed enclosures 143; early Neolithic 1, 38–39, 55, 56, 69–73, 97; Ertebølle groups 46; food vessels 71–72, 155, 259–260, 273; Goodland Ware 155; Grooved Ware 155, 181, 185–186, 187, 188, 191–194, 192, 195, 197, 199, 200, 202, 203, 248; Hebridean Ware 69, 155; hunter-gatherer pottery 45; Impressed Wares 154–156, 155; late Neolithic 191–194; Low Countries (modern-day Belgium and the Netherlands) 44, 45; Mesolithic 38–39; Peterborough Ware 155; Sweet Track, Somerset 84; Unstan Ware 69, 155
Poulawack, Co. Clare 137
Poulnabrone, Burren, Co. Clare 129, 130

Poulnabrone, Co. Clare 119
pre-cairn occupation 113–114
predation 20, 32, 105, 120, 150, 159, 239, 273
Preseli mountains, south Wales 62
Prestatyn, Denbighshire 28
Prestatyn, north Wales 102
Preston, Lancashire 104
Priddy Circles, Somerset 236
Priory midden 20

Quanterness, Orkney 170
quarries 12, 62, 154, 195
quartz 25, 64, 171, 174, 200, 202
quoits 126
Quoyness, Orkney *163*

radiocarbon dating 2, 16, 20, 49, 121, 122, 132, 187, 192; *see also* Bayesian modelling
Radley, Oxfordshire 238
Rameldry, Fife 265
Raschoille Cave, Argyll and Bute 87
Raschoille Cave, Oban 104
Rathlackan, Co. Mayo 115
Rathlin Island 59
Raunds, Northamptonshire 149
recumbent stone circles 216, 277–278, *277*, 280
red deer 20, 22, 23, 26, 66, 78, 156
regional practices 8–9
religious practice 8, 10, 206, 226, 242, 250, 251; *see also* belief systems
Renfrew, Colin 120
resource specialisation 85
Rhendhoo 29
rhyolite 245
Richards, Colin 185
Ring of Bookan, Orkney 223, 227
Ring of Brodgar, Orkney *218*, 244, *244*, 282
Rinyo, Orkney 192
Risga, Argyll and Bute 26
ritual training 172–173, 243
River Avon 233, 234, 240, 242

River Boyne 7, 11, 231
River Earn 237, 242
River Frome 218
River Greta 242
River Kennet 241
River Lagan 211, 241
River Medway 37
rivers 33, 104–105, 147, 149, 177, 180, 240–242; *see also* waterways
River Thames 100, 104, 156
River Ure 220, 240, *240*
Robin Hood's Cave, Derbyshire 104
rock art 201–202, *202*, *203*
Rockmarshall, Co. Louth 23, 32
roe deer 22, 85
Rollright Stones, Oxfordshire *219*
Ronaldsway, Isle of Man 187–188, 202
Ross Island copper mine 264
Rotten Bottom, Dumfries and Galloway 74
round barrows 136, *232*, 275
round mounds/cairns 136–137, 158, 162–163, 175–176, 179, 275–276
routeways 147, 166, 177, 179, 202, 229, 239, 242–243, 271
Rudston, Yorkshire 178, 190
Runnymede Bridge 28
Rydal Park, Cumbria *203*

saithe 18
Sale's Lot, Gloucestershire 116
salmon 23
Sanctuary, The, Overton Hill, Wiltshire 208, 216, *217*, 243, 246
sarsen stones 233, 242
Scafell Pike 61
scrapers 26, 64, 200, 261
sea birds 18
sea levels 13, 17
seals 18, 20, 23, 33, 34
Seefin, Co. Wicklow *162*
settlement: Beaker period 267–268; Durrington Walls, Wiltshire 188–189, 234–235; early Neolithic 8–9, 51, 55, 58, 64–65, 85–97; flint mines 37, 40, 65–69,

67, *68*; henges 220; house horizons 91–93, *92*, 98; late Neolithic 157, 183–190, 203–205; Mesolithic 19, 27–29; middle Neolithic 153–158; Orcadian evidence 94; other knwn houses 93–94; seasonal 19; Shetland evidence 94–95; stone axes 1, 8, 26, 40, 42, 55, 56–63, *59*, *64*; stone houses 8–9; stone tools 16, *22*, 25–26, *27*, 29, *30*, 37, 64–65, *65*, 77; timber halls 87–90, 97, 98; timber houses 37, 94–95, *95*, 97, 98; timber trackways 58, 95–97; *see also* pottery
Sewell's Cave, North Yorkshire 104
shafthole adzes 46
sheep (*Ovis aries*) 1, 38, 55, 78, 79, 143, 156, 190, 267–268
shellfish 23
shell middens 17–18, *18*, 23, 32–33, 41, 47, 115; *see also* middens
Sheridan, A. 49
Shewalton, North Ayrshire 26
Shulishader axe *64*, 74
Silbury Hill, Wiltshire 208–210, *210*, 239, 241, 268
Silvertown trackway, London 153
'simple passage tombs' 126
Skara Brae, Orkney 94, 183, *183*, 185, *186*, 187, 191, 198
Skateholm, Sweden 32
Skendleby 2, Lincolnshire 158
Slewcairn, Dumfries and Galloway 132
Slieve Donard, Co. Down 172
small island settlements 93–94
Smerquoy, Orkney 157
social identity 27, 56, 73, 76, 85, 171, 179, 185, 198, 204–205, 248–251, 262, 279
social networks 68, 97, 124, 125, 135, 146–147, 150, 178, 185, 210, 243–244, 248–251, 284–285
Somerset Levels 95
Southern Circle, Avebury, Wiltshire 243, 246, 248
Southern Circle, Durrington Walls, Wiltshire 212, 234–235, 242

Southern Scandinavia 46–48
South Street long barrow 82
South Street long mound, Wiltshire 135
Spong Hill, East Anglia 87
Sramore, Co. Leitrim 32
Stainton West, Cumbria 26, 30
stakeholes 28, 267
stalled cairns *111*, 112, 113, 114, 116, 117, 124, 158
stalled chambered tombs 110
Stanton Drew, Somerset 216, 248
Stanwell C1, Heathrow Airport 177
Steppe ancestry 253–254
Stoke Down 66
stone axe extraction sites 37, 40, 195–197
stone axes 1, 8, 26, 37, 40, 42, 43, 55, 56–63, *59*, *64*, 100, 143, 153–154, 196–197, 261
stone basins *166*, 170–171
stone-built chambered tombs 117
stone circles 8, 191, 206, 208, 211, 212, 214–218, *215*, 220, 226, 228–230, *228*, *229*, 233, *237*, 238, 239, 242, *243*, 245, 246, 247, *247*, 248, 250, 268, 277–278
Stonehall, Orkney 157
Stonehenge Riverside Project 233–234
Stonehenge, Wiltshire 159, 181, 206, 216, 220, 232–234, *232*, *233*, 235, 238, 239, 240, 242, 243, 245, 246, 251, 256, 282
stone houses 8–9, 157–158, *157*, 183–190, 267
stone passage graves 43
Stones of Stenness, Orkney 216, 223–224, *223*, *224*, *226*, 247
stone tools 16, *22*, 25–26, *27*, 29, *30*, 37, 64–65, *65*, 77, 100, 143, 194–201, 203–204, 267
Stoney Island, Co. Galway 32
Storrs Moss, Yealand Redmayne, Lancashire 96
Street House, North Yorkshire 131, *131*, 132, 134
Structure Eight *9*

subsistence: Beaker period 267–268; early Neolithic 48, 76–85, 94, 97; late Mesolithic 18, 34; late Neolithic 181, 182, 190–191; middle Neolithic 153–158
Sweet Track, Somerset 58, 74, 83, *84*, 95–96, *96*
Swifterbant groups 45–46
Swinside, Cumbria *243*

Tanrego West, Co. Sligo 130
Tarradale, Highland 23
T-axes (antler mattocks) 26, *27*
Tayside, Dumfries and Galloway 201
Templewood, Argyll and Bute 216
Téviec, Brittany 41
Thame, Oxfordshire 138
Thaw Head Cave, both, North Yorkshire 103
Thickthorn Down, Dorset 134, 273
Thomas, Julian 135, 149
Thornborough, Yorkshire 236, 240, *240*
three-tier cosmology 172
Tievebulliagh, Co. Antrim 59, 62, *62*, 264
timber 74
timber circles 208, 211–212, 216, 220, *231*, 236, 239, 245, 268
timber halls *88*, *89*, 92, 93, 97, 98, 156, 190
timber houses 37, 94–95, *95*, 97, 98, 157
timber mortuary structures 131–133
timber structures 23–25, 27, 28–29, 34, 114, 115
timber trackways 58, 95–97, 153
Tinkinswood, Cardiff 104, 130
tor enclosures 140–141
Totty Pot, Somerset 159
Townleyhall, Co. Meath 166
transverse arrowheads 200, 260
trapezoidal houses 41
TRB (*Trichterbecherkultur*) 46, 135
Trelystan, Powys 187
trilithon horseshoe 233
Tullahedy, Co. Tipperary 93
Tulloch of Assery B, Caithness 119
Twyford, Co. Westmeath 74, *75*
Ty Isaf, Powys *107*, 116

Ulva Cave, Western Scotland 87
unchambered long mounds/cairns 113, 132, 133–137
Unstan Ware 69, 155

'Villeneuve-Saint-Germain' 41, 43–44

Walton Basin, Powys 239
Warehouse North, Caithness *110*
Warren Field, Aberdeenshire 88, *89*
Warren, Graeme 15
water burial 104–105, 149, 159, 177, 273
waterways 11, 33, 125, 180, *229*, 239, 240–242, 273, 285–286
Wayland's Smithy II, Oxfordshire 122
Wayland's Smithy I, Oxfordshire 131–132, 133
wedge tombs 273, 274–275
West Kennet, Wiltshire 63, *107*, *108*, *109*, 112, 117, 118–119, 122, 132, 282
Westward Ho! 23
whale 18
wheat 37, 38, 81, 85
Whitehawk causewayed enclosure *146*
Whitewell, Lancashire 138
Wideford Hill, Orkney 94, 157
wild animals 78, 85
wild boar (pig) 19, 20, 22–23, *22*, 38, 78
wild cattle (aurochs) 22, 23, 33, 38, 78
wild plant foods 23, 191
windbreaks 28
Windmill Hill, Wiltshire *70*, 81, 138, 142, 143, 145, 159
winter solstice solar alignment *168*
wooden coffins 265, 271
wooden objects 31, 56, 74, 194
wooden platforms 23–25, 27, 28–29, 34
Woodhenge, Wiltshire 199, 212, 236, *236*, 243, 245
woodland 12, 16–17, 74, 82–83, 107, 191
woodworking 58–59, 63
Wootton-Quarr, Isle of Wight 96
wrapping 174–175, 194
Wyke Down, Dorset 194, 214, 246, 248

Yabsley Street, London 100, 102